D1554166

Democratic Deficit
Critical Citizens Revisited

Many fear that democracies are suffering from a legitimacy crisis. This book focuses on 'democratic deficits,' reflecting how far the perceived democratic performance of any state diverges from public expectations. Pippa Norris examines the symptoms by comparing system support in more than fifty societies worldwide, challenging the pervasive claim that most established democracies have experienced a steadily rising tide of political disaffection during the third wave era of democratization since the early 1970s. The book diagnoses the reasons behind the democratic deficit, including *demand* (rising public aspirations for democracy), *information* (negative news about government), and *supply* (the performance and structure of democratic regimes). Finally, Norris examines the consequences for active citizenship, for governance, and ultimately, for democratization.

This book provides fresh insights into major issues at the heart of comparative politics, public opinion, political culture, political behavior, democratic governance, political psychology, political communications, public policymaking, comparative sociology, cross-national survey analysis, and the dynamics of the democratization process.

Pippa Norris is the McGuire Lecturer in Comparative Politics at the John F. Kennedy School of Government, Harvard University. Her work analyzes comparative democratization, elections and public opinion, gender politics, and political communications. Recent companion volumes by this award-winning author, also published by Cambridge University Press, include *Sacred and Secular* (2004, with Ronald Inglehart), *Driving Democracy* (2008), and *Cosmopolitan Communications* (2009, with Ronald Inglehart).

Also from Cambridge University Press by the Author

Political Recruitment: Gender, Race and Class in the British Parliament. Pippa Norris and Joni Lovenduski (1995)

Passages to Power: Legislative Recruitment in Advanced Democracies. Pippa Norris, editor (1997)

A Virtuous Circle: Political Communications in Post-Industrial Societies. Pippa Norris (2000) (Awarded the 2006 Doris Graber award by APSA's political communications section)

Digital Divide: Civic Engagement, Information Poverty, and the Internet Worldwide. Pippa Norris (2001)

Democratic Phoenix: Reinventing Political Activism. Pippa Norris (2002)

Rising Tide: Gender Equality and Cultural Change around the World. Ronald Inglehart and Pippa Norris (2003)

Sacred and Secular: Politics and Religion Worldwide. Pippa Norris and Ronald Inglehart (2004) (Awarded the 2005 Virginia A. Hodgkinson prize by the Independent Sector)

Electoral Engineering: Voting Rules and Political Behavior. Pippa Norris (2004)

Radical Right: Voters and Parties in the Electoral Market. Pippa Norris (2005)

Driving Democracy: Do Power-Sharing Institutions Work? Pippa Norris (2008)

Cosmopolitan Communications: Cultural Diversity in a Globalized World. Pippa Norris and Ronald Inglehart (2009)

Democratic Deficit

Critical Citizens Revisited

PIPPA NORRIS

Harvard University

CAMBRIDGE UNIVERSITY PRESS
Cambridge, New York, Melbourne, Madrid, Cape Town,
Singapore, São Paulo, Delhi, Tokyo, Mexico City

Cambridge University Press
32 Avenue of the Americas, New York, NY 10013-2473, USA

www.cambridge.org
Information on this title: www.cambridge.org/9780521127448

First published 2011

Printed in the United States of America

A catalog record for this publication is available from the British Library.

Library of Congress Cataloging in Publication data

Norris, Pippa.
Democratic deficit : *Critical Citizens* revisited / Pippa Norris.
    p.   cm.
Includes bibliographical references and index.
ISBN 978-0-521-19751-9 (hardback) – ISBN 978-0-521-12744-8 (pbk.)
1. Democratization.   2. Democracy.   3. Public administration – Evaluation.   4. Political
indicators.   5. Comparative government.   I. Title.
JC423.N66   2010
321.8 – dc22   2010021403

ISBN 978-0-521-19751-9 Hardback
ISBN 978-0-521-12744-8 Paperback

Contents

List of Tables

List of Figures

Preface and Acknowledgments

As always, this book owes multiple debts to many friends and colleagues. The analysis draws upon a unique database, the World Values Survey (WVS) and the European Values Surveys (EVS); these surveys were conducted from 1981 to 2007. Enormous gratitude is owed to all the WVS and EVS participants for creating and sharing this invaluable dataset, not least to Ronald Inglehart, as well as to all the executive committee and the survey contributors. More information about the World Values Survey is available at the WVS Web site, http://www.worldvaluessurvey.org. The European surveys were gathered by the European Values Study group. For more information, see the EVS Web site, http://www.europeanvalues.nl/.

This study builds on a previous edited book, *Critical Citizens: Global Support for Democratic Governance*, published by Oxford University Press in 1999. Many of the core ideas that are developed, updated, and expanded in this book first arose a decade ago with the earlier volume, and I remain indebted to all the original contributors, not least to Joseph Nye and the Visions of Governance project. Some preliminary ideas from this study were also first presented as conference papers, generating useful feedback from discussants and colleagues at various professional meetings, including the IPSA general conference in Santiago, Chile, in June 2009; the research seminar at the Wissenschaftszentrum Berlin fur Sozialforschung, Berlin, in September 2009; the ECPR General Conference plenary roundtable in Potsdam, September 2009; the American Political Science Association (APSA) Taskforce on Democratic Indicators at the University of California, Berkeley, in October 2009; a visiting talk at the University of Sydney in January 2010; the University of Connecticut Democracy and Democratization conference in February 2010; and the APSA annual meeting in Washington, DC, in August 2010, as well as the faculty seminar at Harvard's Kennedy School of Government.

The theme of the book developed in conversations over the years with many colleagues. I am also most grateful to all those who went out of their way to provide thoughts on initial ideas or to read through draft chapters and provide chapter-and-verse comments, including Henry Brady, Michael Bratton, Ivor Crewe, Mark Franklin, Ronald Inglehart, Jane Mansbridge, Wolfgang Merkel, Mitch Seligson, Matthew Singer, and Christian Welzel, among others. Roland Schatz and Christian Kolmer at Media Tenor International deserve a special vote of thanks for generously contributing the content analysis data used in Chapter 9. Camiliakumari Wankaner has provided excellent administrative help and assistance at Harvard. The support of Cambridge University Press has also always proved invaluable, particularly the continuous encouragement and assistance of Lew Bateman, as well as the comments of the reviewers. Lastly, this book would not have been possible without the support and stimulation provided by many colleagues and students at Harvard University's Kennedy School of Government.

Cambridge, Massachusetts

PART I

INTRODUCTION

I

Democratic Hopes and Fears

Are contemporary democratic states experiencing a major legitimacy crisis? Does the public lack trust in government and confidence in the political process? Has public skepticism spread upward to corrode citizens' evaluations about the performance of democracy? Many think so. Since the early 1990s, several scholars of American public opinion have detected signs of a rising tide of popular discontent and voter anger (Dionne, Craig, Tolchin, Wood) as well as deep mistrust of government (Nye, Zelikow and King, Hetherington), with the U.S. Congress held in especially low regard (Hibbing and Theiss-Morse).[1] These observations are commonly coupled with behavioral indicators of civic engagement, notably low or falling voter turnout (Teixiera, Wattenberg), eroding social capital (Putnam), and declining party loyalties (Aldrich), weakening connections between citizens and the state.[2] Commentators point to multiple signs which are thought to indicate contemporary discontent with American democracy, from voter anger against incumbents of both major parties and the outbreak of the Tea Party populist rebellion to public frustration with gridlock and divisive partisanship in Washington, DC.

During the last decade, similar anxieties have infected other post-industrial societies.[3] In Western Europe, it is claimed that people hate politics (Hay), political parties have lost loyal voters (Franklin et al., Dalton and Wattenberg) as well as grassroots members (Mair and Biezen), while electoral turnout has fallen (Franklin) and public disaffection has spread (Torcal and Montero, Dogan, Andrain, and Smith).[4] Support for populist and radical right parties is seen as another symptom of the rejection of mainstream European politics.[5] Reflecting upon the broader meaning of these entrails, haruspices have even speculated gloomily about the 'winter of democracy' (Hermet), the era of 'post-democracy' (Crouch), and the 'death of democracy' (Keane).[6] The most comprehensive and thorough diagnosis of the cross-national survey evidence, by Russell Dalton, concludes, more cautiously, that citizens in advanced industrial societies remain staunchly committed to democratic principles although they have gradually become more distrustful of politicians, detached from parties, and doubtful about public sector institutions.[7] Signs of parallel developments elsewhere in the world remain more mixed.[8] If long-established democracies are in trouble, however, and if these problems spread, this may contribute toward what some observers have identified as a global democratic recession.[9]

To be sure, the picture should not be exaggerated or overblown, as anxiety about public trust in government usually ebbs and flows over the years. Not all commentators share a common interpretation of the available indicators, by any means; indeed a long-standing debate about their meaning remains unresolved after more than four decades.[10] Nevertheless the prevailing view suggests that, for reasons which continue to remain unclear, political disaffection has worsened in recent decades, with significant consequences for democratic governance.

THE CENTRAL ARGUMENT

Why another book about these issues? Is there anything new to say? Perhaps surprisingly, a lot. This book lays out a series of reasons, backed by systematic survey evidence drawn from more than fifty countries worldwide, which challenge the conventional diagnosis, reframe the debate, and recalibrate the evidence about citizens' attitudes toward democratic governance. There is no question that the conventional 'crisis of democratic legitimacy' thesis needs revising. Several core claims lie at the heart of this book.

(i) Trendless fluctuations in system support

First, the evidence demonstrates that, contrary to the prevalent view, *public support for the political system has not eroded consistently across a wide range of countries around the world* – including in established democracies. Nationalism maintains identification with the nation-state, confidence in government does not decline uniformly, and popular support for authorities fluctuates among states. Despite widespread concern about a legitimacy crisis, in the United States and Western Europe, the evidence available to monitor long-term trends in public opinion demonstrates no systematic and consistent loss of support for the political system and its components. Instead, trust and confidence in political institutions usually waxes and wanes over the years in these societies, as well as varying among the different branches of government. Indicators of political behavior – such as any erosion of voter turnout, associational membership and party activism which has occurred – can be attributed to multiple factors which are not necessarily related to feelings of political legitimacy.

(ii) The importance of the democratic deficit

Nevertheless this does not imply that widespread concern about the health of democratic cultures is groundless, all smoke and no fire, by any means. Closer scrutiny of the evidence highlights the second argument presented in this study: *in many countries today, satisfaction with the performance of democracy diverges from public aspirations.* It has long been thought that regimes are more likely to endure and flourish where a balanced equilibrium exists between citizens' aspirations for democracy (measured by how much people value democratic ideals and reject autocratic alternatives) and its perceived supply (monitored by public satisfaction with the democratic performance of their own country).[11]

The gap between aspirations and satisfaction is captured here by the concept of *democratic deficits*. The notion first arose in debates about the legitimacy of the European Union (EU). The core decision-making institutions in the EU have been regarded by some commentators as falling well short of the standards of democratic accountability and transparency that exist at the national level within each of the member states.[12] The original idea of deficits judged the legitimacy of decision-making processes within the European Union against the democratic standards of European nation-states. But this useful concept is not confined to this context; it can be applied more widely to any object where the perceived democratic performance fails to meet public expectations, whether concerning a specific public sector agency or institution, the collective regime or constitutional arrangements governing the nation-state, or the agencies of global governance and multilateral organizations, including the United Nations.[13] The idea of a democratic deficit also builds upon work developed more than a decade ago which first identified the phenomenon of 'critical citizens.'[14] This group aspires to democracy as their ideal form of government, yet at the same time they remain deeply skeptical when evaluating how democracy works in their own country. This book can be seen as the direct descendent of the earlier study, although it seeks to update and expand the evidence, reframe the analysis, and refine the diagnosis.

(iii) Explaining the deficit

What explains the size and distribution of democratic deficits in different states worldwide, and thus why satisfaction with the way that democracy works fails to match citizens' aspirations for democracy? This question leads to the third core claim which is central to this book: *The most plausible potential explanations for the democratic deficit suggest that this phenomenon arises from some combination of growing public expectations, negative news, and/or failing government performance.* The extensive research literature focused on explaining satisfaction with democracy and trust in government has proposed a long shopping list of potential causes, whether ad hoc explanations (including the impact of particular historical events) or more systematic generalizations. The number of rival hypotheses can prove daunting; a recent study in the Netherlands, for example, identified ten distinct propositions that were thought to account for falling public confidence and trust in the Dutch government.[15] In the United States, the events during the late 1960s and 1970s are commonly cited, from the aftermath of Vietnam and Watergate, to stagflation, malaise, the energy crisis, and urban riots.[16] The long list of potential causes can be whittled down and integrated into the more comprehensive, parsimonious, and coherent general theory to explain why satisfaction with the perceived democratic performance of any regime diverges from public aspirations, as illustrated schematically in Figure 1.1.

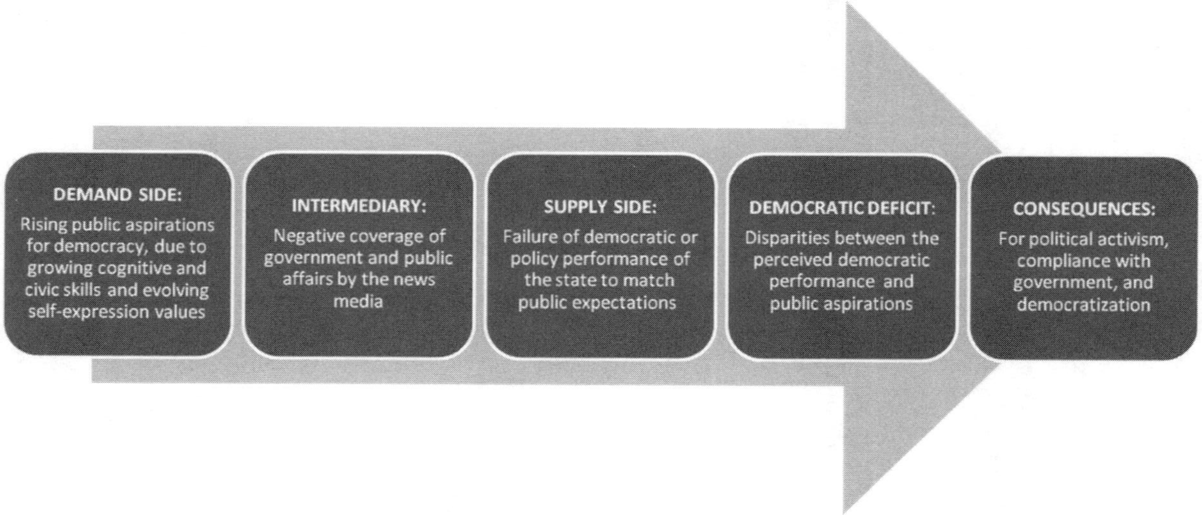

DEMAND SIDE: Rising public aspirations for democracy, due to growing cognitive and civic skills and evolving self-expression values

INTERMEDIARY: Negative coverage of government and public affairs by the news media

SUPPLY SIDE: Failure of democratic or policy performance of the state to match public expectations

DEMOCRATIC DEFICIT: Disparities between the perceived democratic performance and public aspirations

CONSEQUENCES: For political activism, compliance with government, and democratization

FIGURE 1.1. General model of democratic deficits.

Each of the interrelated components featuring in Figure 1.1 generates certain logical general propositions that can be tested against the empirical evidence.

- *Demand-side theories* focus upon enduring cultural shifts among the mass citizenry.

  - Societal modernization theories attribute rising democratic aspirations to long-term processes of human development, especially growing levels of literacy, education, and cognitive skills, leading to emancipative values. If correct, then the public living in affluent, post-industrial societies, especially the younger generation and better educated sectors, should display the strongest endorsement for democratic values.
  - Alternative theories of social capital predict that a long-term erosion of social trust and community networks has undermined faith in democratic governance. If true, then attitudes toward democracy should reflect indices of social capital.

- *Intermediary accounts* emphasize the role of political communications in how people learn about democracy and regime performance.

  - Cognitive theories regard the mass media as one of the primary agencies for learning about democracy, alongside education and the legacy of historical political traditions.
  - Theories of priming and framing suggest that the news media shape public perceptions of government performance. If true, stronger disenchantment with the way democratic governance works should be linked with negative news and scandal coverage about politics, government, and public affairs.

- *Supply-side theories,* by contrast, lay the blame for public dissatisfaction with either the process or the policy performance of democratic governments, as well as with the institutional arrangements.

  - *Process* accounts emphasize that rational citizens have the capacity to judge how democracy works in their own country; it follows that public satisfaction should reflect the quality of democratic governance existing in different countries.
  - *Policy* performance explanations emphasize public dissatisfaction with the capacity of governments to manage the delivery of public goods and services. If true, democratic deficits should relate to perceptual and/or aggregate indicators of policy outputs and outcomes.
  - Last, *structural* accounts emphasize that democratic deficits are conditioned by the constitutional arrangements in any state, especially by power-sharing arrangements. If correct, satisfaction with democracy should prove greater among electoral winners than losers, as well as being minimized in countries with power-concentrating regimes.

These components have often been treated separately by sub-disciplines in the fragmented and scattered research literature. A more satisfactory and integrated understanding arises where these are understood as building blocks in a sequential process. In a loose market model, mass culture reflects the demand side, communications is the connective information environment, and government performance represents the supply side of the equation. In short, deficits may arise from complex interactions involving rising democratic hopes, negative political news, and perceptions of failing performance. The logical arguments, and the empirical evidence supporting each of these explanations, and how they fit together like pieces of a complex jigsaw puzzle, deserve careful scrutiny and systematic examination.

(iv) Why does the deficit matter?

Last, why does this phenomenon matter? Debate continues about all these issues. The most sanguine and positive interpretation suggests that any symptoms of disaffection reflect the run-of-the-mill midterm blues and public disgruntlement directed against specific politicians and parties, resolved periodically in democracies through the ballot box. On the positive side of the equation, citizen dissatisfaction may also spark progressive reform movements, catalyze citizen activism, and thus serve ultimately to strengthen processes of democratization in all societies.[17] Some emphasize that any loss of public confidence and trust in government has not contributed toward regime instability.[18]

More commonly, however, commentators regard opinion polls as the canary in the coal mine where signs point toward pervasive doubts about the role and powers of government, sentiments which, it is feared, can slide into deep-rooted popular aversion and hostility toward all things political. A leaking reservoir of political trust is seen as tying policy makers' hands and limiting voluntary compliance with government authority.[19] Dissatisfaction with democratic performance is also usually regarded, at least implicitly, as an important cause of civic disengagement, encouraging an erosion of conventional participation among citizens. At worst, fragile regimes lacking a broad and deep foundation of legitimacy among the mass public are widely believed to face serious risk of instability and even breakdown.[20]

Rather than supporting blasé assumptions that no serious implications follow, or alternatively presenting exaggerated claims that the sky is falling, the fourth and final argument presented in the book suggests that *the democratic deficit has important consequences – including for political activism, for allegiant forms of political behavior and rule of law, and ultimately for processes of democratization.*

Accordingly, this book seeks to understand the causes and consequences of the democratic deficit, integrating prior knowledge into a theoretical framework which challenges conventional assumptions and provides a more complete and accurate diagnosis and prognosis. The remainder of this chapter clarifies the core argument and provides a roadmap to guide readers through the rest of the book.

ROAD MAP OF THE BOOK

Part I: Theoretical Framework

The first section of the book clarifies the core concepts, the central theoretical argument, and the primary sources of evidence and multilevel methods of analysis. Scholars have long debated how best to understand public attitudes toward government. For example, do the available indicators concerning trust and confidence in political institutions reflect a relatively superficial and healthy skepticism about the performance of politicians and the normal ups and downs in popular fortunes expected of any party in government? Or alternatively, do signs suggest more deep-rooted loss of citizens' trust in all public officials, lack of faith in core institutions of representative democracy, and ambivalence about fundamental democratic principles? Another important issue that remains unresolved concerns the relationship between support for democratic ideals and practices. In particular, will public faith in democratic values gradually spread downward to encourage trust and confidence in the core institutions of representative democracy? Or instead, will skepticism about the way that democratic states work eventually diffuse upward to corrode and undermine approval of democratic principles? Or, alternatively, it may be that these ambivalent tensions between ideals and practices will persist in parallel. There is nothing particularly novel about these concerns; after all, the post–World War II era is commonly assumed to be the halcyon era of trust in the federal government in Washington, DC; yet one of the first studies of U.S. public opinion documented ambivalent attitudes during the late 1950s, concluding that American citizens "tend to expect the worst in politics but hope for the best."[21] Following the turbulent street protests, urban riots, and rise of new social movements during the 1960s and early 1970s, a major report for the Trilateral Commission warned that a legitimacy crisis was undermining Western democracies.[22] The latest angst is thus only the most recent of a long series of similar waves of concern which have moved in and out of intellectual fashion over the years.

To explore these issues, Chapter 2 unpacks the core concepts. The traditional foundation for understanding how citizens orient themselves toward the nation-state, its agencies, and actors rests on the idea of 'system support,' originally developed by David Easton in the 1960s. In an earlier book, *Critical Citizens* expanded the Eastonian conceptual framework to distinguish five dimensions of system support, and the updated survey evidence presented in this chapter demonstrates that these distinctions continue to prove robust. Building upon these ideas, the chapter clarifies and operationalizes the concept of democratic deficits. This chapter also outlines the reasons that certain behavioral indicators adopted by other studies to monitor political support are rejected as inappropriate here, including evidence concerning partisan dealignment and declining party membership, behavioral indicators of civic engagement such as voting turnout or campaign activism, and measures of social capital, including associational membership and interpersonal trust. Behavioral factors are a vital part of any comprehensive understanding of democratic citizenship and civic engagement. But social psychological attitudes and values are treated here as analytically distinct from any acts flowing from these orientations.

To examine the comparative evidence, more than a decade ago, I edited a volume, *Critical Citizens*,[23] that brought together a network of international scholars to consider the global state of public support for democratic governance in the late twentieth century. David Easton's seminal insights into the conceptual framework of political support provided the classic starting point for the study.[24] Drawing upon these ideas, the earlier book framed the idea of 'political support' broadly as a multidimensional phenomenon ranging from the most diffuse to the most specific levels. Hence this notion was conceived to include five components:

1. The most general and fundamental feelings of citizens toward **belonging to the national community**, exemplified by feelings of national pride and identity.
2. **Support for general regime principles**, including approval of democratic and autocratic values.
3. **Evaluations of the overall performance of the regime**, exemplified by satisfaction with the workings of democracy.
4. **Confidence in state institutions**, notably governments, parliaments, parties, the civil service, the courts, and the security forces.
5. Trust in elected and appointed **officeholders**, including politicians and leaders.

Critical Citizens scrutinized a wide range of survey indicators for evidence concerning each of these dimensions, including global, regional, and national comparisons of public opinion from the 1960s until the mid-1990s. The volume brought together experts on diverse countries and regions, utilizing different datasets and surveys, as well as assembling scholars drawn from multiple theoretical perspectives and disciplines. Despite the multiplicity of viewpoints, based on the survey evidence, a common understanding quickly emerged about the most appropriate interpretation of trends. The collaborative volume concluded that citizens in many countries had proved increasingly skeptical about the actual workings of the core institutions of representative democracy, notably political parties, parliaments, and governments. At the same time, however, public aspirations toward democratic ideals, values, and principles, or the demand for democracy, proved almost universal around the globe. The tension between unwavering support for democratic principles but skeptical evaluations about democratic practices was interpreted in the book as the rise of 'critical citizens.' Subsequent studies have understood this phenomenon, with perhaps an excess of alliteration, as 'disaffected,' 'dissatisfied,' or 'disenchanted' democrats.[25] Each of these accounts, however, framed the central issue in terms of individual citizens. Reframing the phenomenon to understand how social-psychological orientations relate to the broader environmental context set by the news media and regime performance provides a more comprehensive account.

Building upon this foundation, this book updates the evidence by analyzing trends in citizens' attitudes and orientations toward the nation-state, regime, and authorities within established democracies, comparing the United States and Western Europe. Support for the political system continues to be understood as a multidimensional phenomenon ranging from the most generalized feelings of attachment and belonging to a nation-state, through confidence and trust in the regime and its institutions, down to specific approval of particular authorities and leaders. Trends over time are established using survey indicators to relate this study to the broader research literature and to clear away some of the most pervasive myths. After providing a general overview of a wide range of indicators of system support, the book then focuses upon comparing disparities worldwide in the democratic deficit, understood to combine the components of values and judgments.

Chapter 3 outlines the technical detail of this study, including the sources of evidence, the comparative framework, the methods of multilevel analysis, and the classification of regimes used throughout the study. The empirical foundation for the body of work comparing attitudes toward democracy was established by Gabriel Almond and Sidney Verba's *The Civic Culture*.[26] Previously only a few other cross-national attitudinal surveys had ever been deployed, notably William Buchanan and Hadley Cantril's nine-country *How Nations See Each Other* (1953), sponsored by UNESCO; sociological surveys of social stratification; and USIA (United States Information Agency) surveys of attitudes toward international affairs.[27] The pathbreaking civic culture survey, conducted in 1959–1960, laid the groundwork for a long series of cross-national public opinion surveys. The series of American National Election Surveys are commonly regarded as canonical, not least because they now facilitate analysis of more than a half-century of public opinion trends in the United States. The geographic scope of cross-national surveys grew considerably in the early 1980s and 1990s to facilitate comparison of citizens' political and social attitudes in a wide range of states worldwide.[28] This includes the Eurobarometer and related European Union (EU) surveys (which started in 1970), the European Election Study (1979), the European Values Survey and the World Values Survey (1981), the International Social Survey Programme (1985), the Global Barometers (including regional surveys conducted in Latin America, sub-Saharan Africa, Arab states, and Asia (1990 and various), the Comparative National Elections Project (1990), the European Voter and the Comparative Study of Electoral Systems (1995), the European Social Survey (2002), the Transatlantic Trends survey (2002), the Pew Global Attitudes project (2002), World Public Opinion, and the Gallup World Poll (2005). Numerous survey datasets are also available for detailed case studies of trends in public opinion within particular countries, including the extensive range of academic national election studies, general social surveys, and commercial public opinion polls.

Unfortunately, despite the wealth of cross-national and time-series survey evidence now available, much popular discourse continues to be based upon flimsy claims and piecemeal anecdotes. Many arguments rest upon real changes in citizen behavior, which have indeed occurred, where commentators immediately speculate about the motivations that lie behind these developments rather than looking directly at public opinion. Some academic research, as well, exaggerates any selective evidence of 'crisis,' in the fashionable attempt to be 'policy-relevant,' while neglecting contrary indicators. Empirical analysis often rests unreflectively upon outdated normative foundations. Scholars are often imprisoned by theoretical roots that can be traced back to the textbook conventions established during the 1950s, when Anglo-American democracies were once regarded as the paradigm for the world. This study draws upon the rich resources of the World Values Survey, especially the fifth wave conducted in 2005–7 and covering more than fifty societies. Until recently, more systematic research usually relied upon standard regression models that combine individual and macro-level variables, but it is now widely recognized that these can produce misleading results, particularly by exaggerating the statistical significance of any contextual effects.[29] Hence multilevel regression models are utilized for this study, as the most appropriate technique for analyzing both individual (survey) and aggregate (national) data. At the same time, the analysis has the advantage that the interpretation of the results remains similar to any standard ordinary least squares (OLS) regression models, depending upon the strength and significance of the coefficients.

Part II: Symptoms

To establish the general symptoms and to clear away some pervasive myths and accumulated brushwood, Part II analyzes longitudinal trends and cross-national patterns in multiple indicators of system support. Using the expanded version of the conventional Eastonian conceptual framework, the study examines generalized support for the national community, approval of democratic regimes and rejection of autocratic principles, evaluations of democratic performance, confidence in public sector institutions, and approval of incumbent authorities.

Chapter 4 focuses on comparing system support in a range of established democracies. The U.S. analysis draws upon survey evidence from the American National Election Study (ANES), which has measured trust in politicians and government since 1958, and from the American General Social Survey (GSS), which has monitored confidence in the leaders of public and private sector institutions since the early 1970s. The Eurobarometer provides comparable time-series indicators for EU member states. The results challenge the claim that established democracies have experienced a rising tidal wave of political disillusionment or growing disaffection with government during the third wave era; instead confidence in public sector institutions ebbs and flows during these decades. Neighboring European Union member states, sharing relatively similar post-industrial economies, modern societies, and democratic institutions, display persistent and enduring contrasts in their political cultures rather than any convergence. Even in the United States – where perhaps most concern has been expressed recently about the breakdown of civil discourse blamed on growing political cynicism, extreme ideological polarization, and 'tea-party' confrontations with elected representatives – in fact support for government institutions and leaders has both risen and fallen over time in recent decades. Far from confidence in political institutions being all of one piece, Americans differentiate among the major branches of the federal government. The standard interpretation of ever-growing public disenchantment with politics and government in established democracies is over-simple and misleading, requiring significant revision.

Chapter 5 broadens the comparison by analyzing cross-national patterns of system support in more than fifty countries around the world. Most comparative survey analysis of trends in public opinion has focused upon the United States and Western Europe, in part because some of the longest time-series evidence is available in these societies. Today, however, it is possible to analyze survey evidence of contemporary attitudes toward politics and government in many global regions, including around fifty societies covering a wide range of developing societies and third-wave democracies. The evidence presented in this chapter, derived from the World Values Survey, compares indicators of system support ranging from the specific to the most diffuse, including confidence in public sector institutions, evaluations of democratic performance, support for democracy and rejection of autocratic forms of government, the saliency of democratic values, and feelings of nationalism.

Chapter 6 expands upon this foundation by documenting the time-series evidence available in eleven nations contained in the five successive waves of the World Values Survey conducted since the early 1980s. These cases include several countries that have experienced regime change during this period – including South Africa, South Korea, and Argentina – providing 'before' and 'after' natural experiments to monitor the impact of regime change and democratization on system support. This chapter also operationalizes the notion of the democratic deficit – and thus highlights the disparities that exist between democratic aspirations and democratic satisfaction – a process that allows us to document the size and distribution of this phenomenon across and within countries around the world.

Part III: Diagnosis

Building upon this foundation, the third part of the book diagnoses the causes of the democratic deficit. Chapter 7 examines the role of culture as the main *demand-side* explanation of this phenomenon. Modernization theories suggest that citizens' orientations toward democratic governance have evolved over time, with rising aspirations fueled by social structural changes in the spread of education in post-industrial societies, and thus citizens' cognitive and civic skills, as well as in terms of their cultural values and orientations toward authority.[30] These developments are believed to have occurred in response to long-term processes of societal modernization, human development, and generational change. Even if the state does not alter, in this perspective, cultural accounts contend that citizens have evolved in their social psychological orientations, becoming more informed, less deferential, and more demanding in their expectations about the democratic performance of government. If correct, then strong links should be evident at the individual level between democratic orientations and the distribution of educational skills, as well as with the endorsement of post-material and self-expression values. Moreover at the macro-level, democratic aspirations and satisfaction should be predictable by levels of societal modernization, using aggregate indicators of economic and human development. Alternative theories of social capital, associated with the seminal work of Robert Putnam, emphasize the importance of generalized interpersonal trust and associational networks on trust in government.[31] If social capital accounts are right, then patterns of social trust and associational activism should help to account for the democratic deficit.

Chapter 8 focuses on understanding knowledge about democracy. The general public's judgment can be based on a rational understanding of democracy, compared against standard ideas of liberal democracy. Alternatively, as with many other complex issues, such as rates of crime, the degree of global warming, or the size of the federal deficit, awareness about democracy may be incoherent, partial, biased, inflated, shallow, or factually erroneous. The book seeks to establish citizens' knowledge and beliefs about democracy, as well as understanding their values and judgments. Awareness about how liberal democracy works is expected to be influenced by the historical political traditions within each state, as well as by access to the independent news media and by levels of literacy and formal education. A battery of survey items concerning the essential characteristics of democracy are analyzed to see whether a common meaning of this concept is shared in different cultural regions. Evidence is derived from the fifth wave of the World Values Survey (2005–7) in more than fifty societies worldwide. Enlightened knowledge about democracy is defined in this book by the capacity to identify accurately a few of the basic procedures and principles, or rules of the game, which characterize liberal democracies. Democracy is an abstract and complex idea, and the meaning continues to be contested among experts. Even ill-informed public perceptions are meaningful for those holding these beliefs, providing the social construction of reality. But citizens need to demonstrate at least some minimal cognitive awareness about the basic procedural characteristics and core institutions of liberal democracy if they are to make rational and enlightened judgments about both the quality of democratic performance and the importance of democracy as the ideal regime for governing their own country. The evidence confirms that knowledge about the essential characteristics of liberal democracy is greatest in states with the longest historical experience of this form of governance, as well as being strengthened by education and access to the independent media. In younger democracies, however, contemporary public opinion lags behind processes of regime change.

Chapter 9 examines the influence of the coverage provided by the news media in shaping public perceptions of politics and government.[32] Theories of media framing suggest that public evaluations of democratic performance are often influenced by journalism. Excessively negative news, and in particular extensive coverage of sexual scandals and financial corruption, are both widely believed to tarnish the reputation of the legislative, executive, or judicial branches of government, leading to broader disillusionment with how democracy works.[33] Despite the popular appeal of this account, little cross-national evidence has demonstrated a systematic connection between news media coverage of scandals and corruption and subsequent levels of trust and confidence in government or satisfaction with democracy.[34] Evidence is unavailable to examine media coverage in all the countries under comparison, but detailed case studies can be analyzed in two established democracies with similar cultural roots but with different types of media environments and political systems – namely Britain and the United States. This chapter therefore uses longitudinal evidence, derived from annual content analysis of the media coverage of political scandals in recent decades, compared against public opinion trends in institutional confidence and satisfaction with democratic performance in these countries.

Chapter 10 turns to supply-side explanations emphasizing how satisfaction with democracy responds to the process and policy performance of governments, and to the institutional structure of regimes. Process accounts assume that citizens are capable of making informed and rational assessments about whether regimes meet standards of transparency, accountability, effectiveness, social justice, and participation. Alternative theories suggest that democratic satisfaction is a product of the government's record and public policy performance, especially the government's management of bread-and-butter economic issues, including growth, jobs, and prices.[35] Output performance is not confined to the economy, however, since the government's foreign policy record is also thought to be important, including how leaders handle an international crisis or the outbreak of armed conflict. Rally-round-the-flag effects, with a temporary burst of government popularity, are commonly registered in opinion polls following the outbreak of crisis or major wars.[36] The shock of 9/11, for example, generated a sharp but short-lived spike in American confidence in the Executive and Congress.[37] Moreover beyond policy output and outcomes, process accounts suggest that perceptions of procedural fairness in how the decision-making process works also shape how much people are willing to trust the authorities, including the importance of issues of social justice and welfare.[38] Theorists emphasize that the traditional scope and autonomy of the modern states has diminished due to processes of globalization, privatization, and deregulation.[39] Moreover policy problems are thought to have become increasingly complex, while issue publics have simultaneously become more fragmented.[40] For these reasons, policy performance may have gradually fallen over time.

In addition, another related strand of the research literature is provided by institutional theories that emphasize how power-sharing democratic regimes influence democratic satisfaction.[41] This thesis suggests that the pattern of winners and losers from the political system is structured by the constitutional arrangements, meaning the core institutions of state and the rules of the game, both written and unwritten. Some citizens win, others lose. Some parties and groups are mobilized into power, others are mobilized out. Over a long period of time, this accumulated experience can be expected to shape general orientations toward the political regime. At the simplest level, if citizens feel that the rules of the game allow the party they endorse to be elected to power, they are more likely to feel that representative institutions are responsive to their needs, so that they can trust the political system. On the other hand, if they feel that the party they prefer persistently loses, over successive elections, they are more likely to feel that their voice is excluded from the decision-making process, producing generalized dissatisfaction with political institutions. Over time, where constitutional arrangements succeed in channeling popular demands into government outcomes, then we would expect this to be reflected in diffuse support for the political process. The structure of power-sharing and power-concentrating democratic institutions can be compared – along with levels of institutional confidence among partisan winners and losers within each context.

Part IV: Prognosis

Chapter 11 identifies the consequences of this phenomenon. What is the impact of any democratic deficit – and why does this matter – including for political activism, for the capacity of governments to ensure compliant behavior and rule of law, and for processes of democratization?

The broadest consensus among scholars concerns the implications for citizen activism at the micro-level. It is widely assumed that more critical evaluations of democratic governance will deter conventional forms of political participation and civic engagement. Ever since Almond and Verba, an extensive body of evidence has examined how social psychological attitudes influence why and how citizens choose to engage in public affairs.[42] Hence, positive feelings of political trust, internal efficacy, and institutional confidence in parties, legislatures, and the government are widely assumed to strengthen conventional activism such as voting participation, party membership, and belonging to voluntary associations. Conversely, indicators such as falling voter turnout and declining party membership in established democracies are commonly regarded as signs of citizen disenchantment or cynicism about politics.[43] Moreover political disaffection is commonly expected to encourage protest politics, if lack of trust in the democratic process fosters unconventional activism, support for anti-state radical movements, and even occasional outbreaks of radical violence seeking to challenge state authorities.[44]

Yet in fact, the actual evidence linking democratic orientations with patterns of political activism is far from straightforward; disenchantment with the performance of democracy may depress conventional forms of participation, but alternatively it may also mobilize people, for example, to support reform movements.[45] In Latin America, for example, Booth and Seligson report that citizens who are unhappy with their government's performance do not drop out of politics or resort to protest politics. Rather, disaffected citizens in Latin America participate at high rates in conventional and alternative political arenas.[46] There may also be implications for compliant behavior, including whether citizens voluntarily obey the law and respect government decisions – for example, political trust has been found to encourage the willingness of citizens to pay taxes.[47] Where they do, this should strengthen the capacity of the state and thus processes of rule of law.

Last, this chapter also examines the significant consequences arising from this phenomenon for the broader processes of democratization and legitimacy. The concept of 'regime legitimacy' can be best understood, in Seymour Martin Lipset's words, as "the capacity of a political system to engender and maintain the belief that existing political institutions are the most appropriate and proper ones for the society."[48] In countries that have recently transitioned from autocracy, in particular, any deep and enduring democratic deficit is often thought to undermine processes of regime consolidation; the new rulers cannot count on institutional inertia or the bonds of habitual support to maintain a deep reservoir of popular legitimacy and to deter elite challenges. The third wave of democratization represents a remarkable historical era. During the late twentieth century, human rights strengthened in all parts of the globe. Freedom House estimates that the number of liberal democracies doubled from the early 1970s to 2000.[49] In the last decade, however, progress slowed to a sluggish and uncertain pace.[50] Electoral democracies where progress once appeared promising – such as Kenya, Honduras, Afghanistan, Thailand, and Fiji – have been undermined and destabilized by diverse events, whether inconclusive or disputed election results, partisan strife, recurrent corruption scandals, internal conflicts, over-powerful executives, or coups d'états.[51] Freedom House's 2009 survey of democracy around the world noted further erosion:

According to the survey's findings, 2009 marked the fourth consecutive year in which global freedom suffered a decline – the longest consecutive period of setbacks for freedom in the nearly 40-year history of the report. These declines were most pronounced in Sub-Saharan Africa, although they also occurred in most other regions of the world. Furthermore, the erosion in freedom took place during a year marked by intensified repression against human rights defenders and democracy activists by many of the world's most powerful authoritarian regimes, including Russia and China.[52]

The muscular democracy promotion initiatives advocated by the Bush administration, notably attempts at state-building in Iraq and Afghanistan, encouraged an active push-back among oil-rich emerging economies, including

Russia, Venezuela, and China.[53] Some observers suggest that a major 'reverse' wave or 'democratic recession' is under way.[54] Moreover, Huntington emphasized a cyclical historical pattern, noting that two previous long waves of democratization were followed by regressive eras.[55] In marked contrast to the heady revolutions that occurred with one autocracy after another rapidly toppling around the time of the fall of the Berlin Wall in 1989, multiple challenges continue to limit further dramatic global advances in democratization. Accordingly, this chapter evaluates how far cultural orientations provide insights into the underlying processes leading toward the advance and breakdown of democratic governance.

Finally the conclusion in Chapter 12 summarizes the major findings and considers their implications for revising theories about the legitimacy and stability of democratic regimes, and for the broader public policy agenda.

2

The Conceptual Framework

Ideas such as 'political trust,' 'democratic values,' 'political disaffection,' and 'systems support' are far from simple. Their measurement is not straight-forward. And the thoughtful interpretation of the underlying meaning of the evidence is even more complicated. This chapter seeks to establish and clarify the conceptual framework, an important first step before examining both longitudinal trends and cross-national evidence. This chapter first identifies the idea of levels and components of systems support, drawing upon the seminal work of David Easton. It then builds and extends these concepts further by outlining the core idea of democratic deficits, reflecting the ambivalent tensions between aspirations for democracy and judgments about its performance. The deficit arises, in essence, because many citizens today believe that it is important to live in a democratic state, yet they remain dissatisfied when evaluating how democracy works. If this attitudinal syndrome translates into actions and behavior – an issue explored in the final section of this book – then any deficit is potentially an important resource for mobilizing social movements seeking to deepen participation, accountability, and transparency within liberal democracies, as well as encouraging popular demands for reform in autocratic states.

THE CONCEPTUAL FRAMEWORK OF SYSTEMS SUPPORT

Ideas about support for the political system are too often muddied in the literature; for example, when distinguishing citizens' orientations toward government and parliaments, common language often skims over, or fails to acknowledge, important distinctions such as those concerning ideas of institutional *confidence* (which can be understood to represent belief in the capacity of an agency to perform effectively), *trust* (reflecting a rational or affective belief in the benevolent motivation and performance capacity of another party), *skepticism* (or suspended judgment), and *cynicism* (meaning jaded negativity). Moreover, media commentary often exaggerates any signs, for example, describing American dissatisfaction with the process of health care reform or with partisan squabbling in Congress as voter 'anger' or 'disgust,' without any direct evidence for affective orientations.

Additionally, the normative implications of each of these concepts remain ambiguous. For example, commentators often assumed, at least implicitly, that trust by citizens is a desirable quality, irrespective of the trustworthiness of the object.[1] If the reservoir of public trust in bodies such as the Norwegian Stortinget or the Swedish Riksdag has drained over time, then this should indeed be a matter of genuine concern. Yet if government ministers or legislators repeatedly prove venal, self-serving, and corrupt, then trust would be foolish and naïve. Similarly, skepticism is usually regarded negatively; yet this could be the most appropriate stance, for example, if policymaking processes are so complex in divided governments that citizens lack accurate information to evaluate institutional performance and to attribute praise and blame. In the first founding elections held after any transition from autocracy, many citizens may well know little about their elected representatives and may lack information about how government decision-making processes work; in this context, agnostic skepticism may well be the most rational and suitable response.

Given the complexity of the ideas at the heart of this study, we need to establish clarity about the core concepts. The traditional theoretical framework of systems support was established during the mid-1960s by David Easton.[2] The concept of 'system support' is understood in this study to reflect orientations toward the nation-state, its agencies, and actors. Where orientations are positive, citizens accept the legitimacy of their state to govern within its territorial boundaries. They do not challenge the basic constitutional structure and rules of the game or the authority of officeholders.[3] Systems support is therefore understood as a psychological orientation.

Attitudes are commonly inferred from tacit actions, such as the voluntary acts of paying taxes, obeying the law, and casting a ballot. Hence numerous popular studies often regard eroding voting turnout or falling party membership as an expression of cynicism or disenchantment among the electorate.[4] But it is often deeply problematic, indeed foolhardy, to infer psychological orientations from behavior; citizens may be acting from many complex motives, such as voting out of fear of reprisal or legal sanctions, habit, or a sense of duty, without necessarily supporting the regime. For example, when nine out of ten registered voters (93%) cast a ballot in the 2006 presidential elections in Belarus, few commentators would regard this as a legitimate and reliable sign of public affection for the repressive Lukashenko regime. It is similarly misleading to infer that the fall in voter turnout in European parliamentary elections – down overall from 62% in 1979 to 43% three decades later – necessarily or automatically represents public disenchantment with the European Union; this decline could simply reflect growing indifference or even satisfaction with the status quo, as well as the changing composition and membership of the European Union.[5] More reliable indicators of citizens' psychological orientations toward government are derived from public opinion surveys conducted according to rigorous scientific standards. Common indicators are exemplified by a sense of belonging to, and identification with, the national community; positive attitudes toward the state and the core institutions governing the territorial unit; and approval of the incumbent officeholders within the state.

Citizens' orientations toward the nation-state, its agencies, and actors (systems support) thus need disentangling. It is worth underlining that the idea of systems support is not strictly equivalent to the related idea of political trust or institutional confidence, although these concepts are frequently conflated in the popular literature.[6] The independence of these ideas is easily illustrated by a few simple examples; people can trust a particular party leader, for instance, without necessarily casting a ballot to actively support the person (if they disagree with the leader's ideology or policy positions). Conversely, people can support a leader (because they like his or her character and personality) without necessarily trusting the person or having any confidence in the leader's performance (for example, if skeptical about the ability of all politicians to deliver on their promises). Political support can be regarded as a dichotomy (citizens either do or do not reject the authority of the nation-state) or more commonly as a continuum (with varied degrees and levels). Support for the nation-state is also rarely unconditional; instead it is usually directed toward particular components. For instance, Russians may approve of Vladimir Putin but simultaneously disapprove of the actions and decisions of the Duma. Or Americans may be cynical and wary about the workings of Congress as an institution but still give high marks to their local senator. Or Mexicans may value the abstract principles of democracy, such as the importance of freedom of speech, tolerance, and respect for human rights, but still wish to ban certain specific publications or parties. Systems support has both affective and evaluative aspects. Citizens may accept the authority of the nation-state, its agencies, and actors out of a deep sense of blind loyalty and strong feeling of patriotism ('my country, right or wrong'). Or support may be more conditional, depending upon a more rational calculation of state performance.

LEVELS OF SYSTEM SUPPORT

The Eastonian classification built upon the idea that the independent nation-state can be regarded as a political system.[7] In this account, David Easton drew an important conceptual distinction between specific and diffuse levels of citizens' support.

Specific political support focuses upon elected and appointed officeholders responsible for making and implementing political decisions within the nation-state. Indicators of such support include the popularity of incumbent presidents, prime ministers, cabinet ministers, party leaders, and local representatives, as well as support for particular political parties (in government and opposition). It also covers attitudes toward leadership elites and authorities in other public sector agencies, such as confidence in high-ranked civil servants, judges, the military, and the police. Specific support for incumbent officeholders is expected to fluctuate over time in response to short-term contextual factors, such as the performance of particular administrations, major shifts in public policy, or changes in party leadership. For elected officials, evaluations are also expected to be strongly filtered by partisan forces; the perception of government performance, for instance, is expected to vary sharply among citizens who are winners and losers, defined by their party identification. Specific support is typically measured by regular opinion polls where approval of incumbents fluctuates over time as part of normal politics in democratic states. This suggests that specific support for officeholders should be explicable by short- and medium-term factors, such as the government's management of economic, social, and foreign policy; fluctuations in financial markets; the impact of global events and international affairs; and regular shifts in party fortunes during the normal electoral cycle. A persistent lack of specific support is widely believed to have consequences for governance in all countries, but it does not thereby undermine the legitimacy of the nation-state or erode the fundamental authority of its agencies and actors.

By contrast, for Easton, *diffuse* or *generalized* political support represents more abstract feelings toward the nation-state and its agencies. Political institutions persist even though incumbent leaders are removed from office. Generalized support toward the community and regime helps citizens accept the legitimacy of the state, its agencies, and officeholders, even when people are highly critical about particular political processes, incumbent party leaders, or specific public policies and outcomes. In this regard, evaluations about the performance of the government are predicted to fluctuate over time, but generalized attachments to the nation-state are expected to prove more stable and enduring, providing officeholders with the authority to act based on a long-term reservoir of favorable attitudes or affective goodwill.[8] Diffuse support represents more lasting bonds to the nation-state, as exemplified by feelings of national pride and identity, as well as by adherence to core regime values and principles. Diffuse support is expected to be particularly important for stability in fragile states emerging from deep-rooted internal conflict, as well as for processes of regime transition, by strengthening popular acceptance of the legitimacy of new constitutional arrangements and the authority of officeholders.

The conceptual distinction between specific and generalized support seems plausible theoretically and worth maintaining, especially if this is understood as a continuum rather than as a dichotomous typology. It implies, for instance, that particular scandals or a dramatic failure of public policy can bring down a president or prime minister without damaging citizens' belief in the legitimacy of their basic constitutional arrangements or, indeed, weakening deep feelings of patriotism about their country. In more fragile states, however, with shallower reservoirs of legitimacy, similar events could destabilize the government and trigger a regime crisis. In practice, however, it often remains difficult to match these concepts precisely to the available survey measures – for example, satisfaction with democracy may reflect both approval of democracy as an abstract principle as well as positive evaluations of how democratic states perform in practice.[9] Empirical research finds that support for elected officials can carry over to shape support for state institutions.[10] Subsequent chapters focus upon the relationship among middle levels, including positive approval of democratic values and negative evaluations of the democratic performance of regimes.

COMPONENTS OF POLITICAL SUPPORT

Equally important, the traditional conceptual framework developed by Easton further distinguished among three distinct components of the political system, namely the nation, the state, and the incumbent authorities.[11] In this conception, the *nation-state* represents the community to which people belong. The *regime* constitutes the basic framework for governing the nation-state within its territorial boundaries. This includes the overarching constitutional arrangements and the core government institutions at national, regional, and local levels, reflecting the accepted formal and informal rules of the game. Regimes fall into distinct eras, for example, with the breakdown of Communist rule in the Soviet Union and the transition toward democracy. In some cases, such as Czechoslovakia and Yugoslavia, the nation-state also dissolved, but in most countries the shift involved the adoption and revision of a new constitutional settlement within established territorial boundaries. Last, the *authorities* represents the elected and appointed actors holding state office and the key decision makers in the public sector. Of all these elements, the authorities change most frequently, in democratic states with the rotation of parties from government into opposition following electoral defeat. These elements can be understood to be related to each other, like Russian dolls, in an embedded model.

According to this conceptualization, people could not pick and choose between different state agencies, approving of some parts, while rejecting others. Yet in practice citizens do seem capable of making these distinctions. During the final years of the Bush administration, for example, Pew surveys report that Americans expressed deep dissatisfaction with the performance of the incumbent president, while views about the federal government and Congress deteriorated badly, and identification with the Republican Party ebbed away.[12] Nonetheless loss of faith in the Bush administration and the legislature did not spread to the judicial branch; the Supreme Court continued to be held in high regard. Discontent with the federal government also did not erode pride and patriotism in America, nor trigger any deep disaffection with the basic constitutional arrangements in American government, nor raise any serious doubts about basic democratic principles and ideals.[13] Discontent was highly partisan, centered upon polarizing the leadership of President Bush and the Republican Party, and attitudes shifted with the election of President Barack Obama. The Eastonian framework for understanding components of political support in a political system provides the standard conceptual foundation for analysis. Updating the language to reflect contemporary usage, and greater refinement of these categories, are both important, however, to make these ideas relevant to modern concerns.

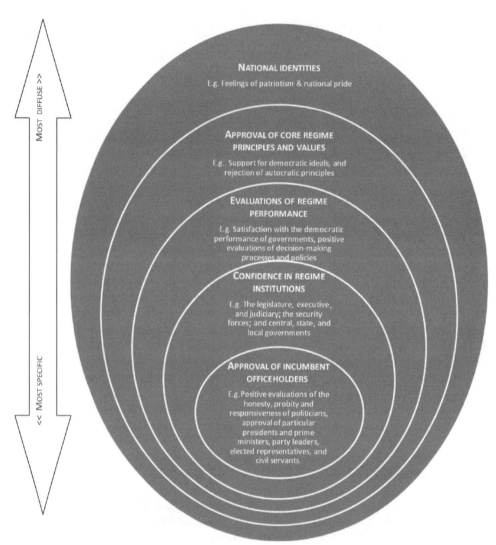

FIGURE 2.1. Indicators of systems support.

Drawing upon these notions, the concept of 'political support' is understood in this book as a multidimensional phenomenon ranging on a continuum from the most diffuse to the most specific levels. Moreover, the middle category in the original framework is expanded conceptually to recognize five distinct components of support in a nested model, each with a series of operational empirical measures (see Figure 2.1):

1. The most general and fundamental attitudes of citizens toward **belonging to the nation-state,** exemplified by feelings of national pride, patriotism, and identity

2. **Agreement with core principles and normative values** upon which the regime is based, including approval of democratic values and ideals
3. **Evaluations of the overall performance of the regime,** exemplified by satisfaction with democratic governance and also general assessments about the workings of democratic processes and practices
4. **Confidence in regime institutions,** notably the legislative, executive, and judicial branches of government, the security forces, as well as central, state, and local governments
5. **Approval of incumbent officeholders,** including attitudes toward specific party leaders, legislators, and public officials, as well as support for particular parties and for leadership elites and authorities in public sector agencies

These components are regarded as ranging in a continuum from the most generalized support for the nation down through successive levels to the most concrete and specific support for individual actors.

1. National Identities

From this perspective, at the most diffuse level, support for the community represents general orientations toward belonging to a common nation, including enduring bonds typically expressed through feelings of patriotism, national pride, and a sense of national identity, as well as feelings toward people of other nations and toward multilateral institutions, such as the United Nations and European Union. The idea of 'national identity' is understood to mean the existence of communities with bonds of 'blood and belonging' arising from sharing a common homeland, cultural myths, symbols and historical memories, economic resources, and legal-political rights and duties.[14] Nationalism can take *civic* forms, meaning ties of soil based on citizenship within a shared territory and boundaries delineated by the nation-state, or it may take *ethnic* forms, drawing on more diffuse ties based on religious, linguistic, or ethnic communities.[15] In many countries, national identities are taken for granted, but they have particularly important consequences for social cohesion and state legitimacy in multicultural communities containing several distinct nationalities, especially in fragile states recently emerging from deep-rooted conflict.[16] In the modern world, national identities underpin the nation-state and its institutions exercising legitimate political authority within a given territory, although there are many multinational states such as the United Kingdom, Belgium, and Canada, as well as stateless national communities, exemplified by the Kurds and the Roma.

Although often assumed to reflect long-term, deep-rooted, and stable orientations, in fact national orientations vary systematically in predictable ways, for example, sudden spikes in national pride are often documented around the outbreak of war or external threat, in a commonly observed 'rally-around-the-flag' effect.[17] National identities may also be gradually weakening as a result of processes of globalization, expanding networks of interdependence that span national boundaries and follow the increasingly swift movement of ideas, money, goods, services, ecology, and people across territorial borders. By contrast to national identities, globalization is expected to strengthen cosmopolitan identities, understood as those outlooks, behaviors, and feelings that transcend local and national boundaries.[18] Typically, cosmopolitans are tolerant of diverse cultural outlooks and practices, valuing human differences rather than similarities, cultural pluralism rather than convergence, and deemphasizing territorial ties and attachments.[19] Nationalism and cosmopolitanism are usually regarded theoretically as oppositional, although it remains to be seen empirically whether these feelings could potentially coexist without contradiction, for example, if people have strong feelings of national pride but also favor multilateral solutions to world problems. Using the World Values Survey, nationalism and cosmopolitanism can be analyzed through examining attitudes toward the state and institutions of multilateral governance, feelings of belonging and attachment to different communities, as well as support for policies that facilitate protectionism or globalization, such as attitudes toward free trade or open labor markets.[20]

2. Approval of Regime Principles and Values

The second level represents adherence to the principles and normative values upon which the regime is founded, reflecting beliefs about the legitimacy of the constitutional arrangements and the formal and informal rules of the game. Democracy remains an essentially contested concept, open to multiple meanings for alternative deliberative, representative, and pluralist conceptions, so there is no universal consensus about which values, procedures, and principles are most important. Schumpeterian notions emphasize a minimalist or 'thin' definition of representative democracy as an institutional arrangement for governing the state where all adults have opportunities to vote through free and fair competitive elections for their national legislature.[21] From this viewpoint, representative democracies hold multiparty electoral contests at regular intervals which meet the essential conditions of an inclusive suffrage giving voting rights to all adult citizens, unrestricted rights by all citizens and parties to compete for elected offices, and transparent and honest processes for translating votes into seats. This parsimonious approach to defining democracy remains popular in the research literature. For empiricists, it has the considerable advantage of reducing the number of elements required for the accurate measurement and classification of electoral democracies.[22] The most commonly acknowledged danger of this conceptualization, however, is leaving out certain important dimensions of the richer concept of liberal democracy which are emphasized in more comprehensive measures. For example, minimalist definitions do not consider the quality of democratic performance, such as how far states achieve socially inclusive representation, accountable leaders, freedom of expression, and equality of participation, in part because these factors are often difficult to gauge systematically with any degree of reliability and consistency.

By contrast, thicker or more maximalist understandings of the key structural framework of representative or liberal democracy have been strongly influenced by Robert Dahl's body of work, including *Politics, Economics, and Welfare* (1953), *A Preface to Democratic Theory* (1956), and *Polyarchy* (1971).[23] Dahl argued that liberal democracies are characterized procedurally by two main attributes – contestation and participation. In practice, Dahl suggested that democratic regimes or 'polyarchies' can be identified by the presence of certain key political institutions: (1) elected officials, (2) free and fair elections, (3) inclusive suffrage, (4) the right to run for office, (5) freedom of expression, (6) alternative information, and (7) associational autonomy.[24] Dahl also emphasized that competitive multiparty elections are used to fill offices for the national legislature and the chief executive. For electoral competition to be meaningful, however, he added a broader set of essential conditions, as polyarchies need to allow freedom of expression, the availability of alternative sources of information (freedom of the media), and associational autonomy (freedom to organize parties, interest groups, and social movements). In short, in democratic states citizens must consent to their rulers, and public officials are accountable to those they govern. Democratic principles also involve support for the underlying values of freedom, opportunities for participation in decision making, equality of rights and tolerance of minorities, respect for human rights, and the rule of law.

The Global Barometer surveys provide some of the most comprehensive evidence of attitudes toward each of these general democratic principles and values.[25] An extensive literature has analyzed the distribution of democratic values, especially in post-Communist Europe, Latin America, Africa, and Asia, as well as the Middle East.[26] Most commonly, surveys have tapped agreement with the idea of democracy as the most appropriate or ideal form of government for particular nations compared with alternative types of regime. Hence the Global Barometer surveys have asked respondents to choose among three alternative statements: *"Democracy is always preferable to any other kind of government," "Under some circumstances, an authoritarian government can be preferable to a democratic one,"* and *"For people like me, it does not matter whether we have a democratic or a non-democratic regime."*[27] It is more difficult to find alternative items seeking to gauge support for autocratic principles, since these regimes are founded upon different forms of rule, such as the monarchies governing the emirates in Arab states, the military juntas controlling Thailand and Burma, the dynastic dictatorship in North Korea, one-party Communist states such as China and Cuba, and strongman populism in Venezuela and Zimbabwe. The World Values Survey measures whether the public approves of regimes based on having military rule, non-elected strongman rule, or government by experts, as well as having a democratic political system. These items have been combined, with pro-democratic responses represented by disagreement with the first three types of regimes and agreement with the last, and used as a Democratic Regime Index.[28] Most important, the fifth wave of the World Values Survey (WVS) also monitors which characteristics are regarded as essential to democracy, which allows us to examine whether there is a universal understanding to the meaning of this form of government in different parts of the world, or whether meanings are culturally specific.

3. Evaluations of Regime Performance

The third level concerns generalized support for the state, meaning support for how democratic or autocratic regimes function in practice. This taps a 'middle level' of support which is often difficult to gauge. Many surveys, including the Eurobarometer and the Comparative Study of Electoral Systems, have regularly measured 'satisfaction with the performance of democracy' or 'satisfaction with the way democracy works.' The standard question in the Eurobarometer and many other surveys seeks to tap these attitudes by asking: "*On the whole, are you very satisfied, fairly satisfied, not very satisfied, or not at all satisfied with the way democracy works in your country?*" This item has been extensively analyzed in the research literature; nevertheless, responses are open to alternative interpretations.[29] On the one hand, the item can be seen to tap approval of 'democracy' as a value or principle. In this study, however, we agree with Linde and Ekman that the phrasing of the question (by emphasizing how democracy is *performing*) makes it most suitable to test public evaluations of the workings of democratic regimes and assessments of democratic practices, not principles.[30] Another related strategy compares evaluations of the performance of the current regime against that of the past regime, a particularly effective approach when used to analyze public opinion in countries with recent memories of regime transition, such as in Central and Eastern Europe. This process is believed to provide a common standard rooted in people's concrete experience, rather than comparing the current regime against an idealized and therefore more abstract notion of representative democracy.[31]

In measuring how democratic regimes perform in practice, the third and fourth waves of the World Values Survey asked the following questions:

I'm going to read off some things that people sometimes say about a democratic political system. Could you please tell me if you agree strongly, agree, disagree or disagree strongly, after I read each one of them? In democracy, the economic system runs badly; Democracies are indecisive and have too much quibbling; Democracies aren't good at maintaining order; Democracy may have problems but it's better than any other form of government.

This battery of items allows respondents to express doubts about the broad way that democratic states work in practice, without simultaneously rejecting democratic principles. Analysts have recoded these responses in a consistent direction and then combined them to create a Democratic Process index.[32] Using an alternative phrasing, the fifth wave WVS asks the following question:

And how democratically is this country being governed today? Again using a scale from 1 to 10, where 1 means that it is "not at all democratic" and 10 means that it is "completely democratic," what position would you choose?

The way that this question emphasizes evaluations of how democratically each country is being *governed* makes the scale even more suitable to test public satisfaction with the perceived performance of democratic governance in each nation.[33]

4. Confidence in Regime Institutions

The fourth level concerns trust and confidence in the core institutions of state, including the legislature, executive, and judicial branches of government, as well as other public sector agencies, such as the police, military, and civil service. Studies seek to measure generalized support for the institution – that is, approval of the powers of the presidency as chief executive rather than support for President Barack Obama – although in practice the precise dividing line between the office and the incumbent is often fuzzy. A conventional distinction is often made between 'public' and 'private' institutions, although this line varies depending upon the degree of state control in each country, for example, whether a country has public service or commercial television broadcasters, and whether religious institutions are disestablished.[34] Since 1973, for example, the U.S. General Social Survey conducted by National Opinion Research Center (NORC) has monitored confidence in 'the people running' the executive branch of government, the U.S. Supreme Court and Congress, and the military, as well as private sector agencies, such as major companies, medicine, banks and financial institutions, the press, television, and labor unions.[35] Much can be learned by examining the dynamics of support for particular agencies because evidence suggests that the public distinguishes among them; hence, Americans consistently express considerable confidence in the Supreme Court, for example, while simultaneously increasingly disapproving of Congress and the executive branch.[36] Institutions are large, impersonal, and broadly based, and the public's estimation of them is less immediately affected by particular news items or specific events than support for specific actors. Thus, loss of confidence in institutions may well be a better indicator of public disaffection with the modern world because they are the basic pillars of society. If they begin to crumble, then there is, indeed, cause for concern.[37]

Public approval of the general performance of the governing party, as well as evaluations of the government's handling of major policy areas such as the economy, foreign policy, and social policy, are regularly monitored within particular nations in numerous election surveys and commercial public opinion polls. This facilitates longitudinal analysis within each country. Moreover the International Social Survey Program (ISSP) Role of Government cross-national survey module (conducted in 1985, 1990, 1996, and 2006) allows analysts to compare more detailed judgments about the government's past policy record, expectations about the appropriate scope of the government's role and responsibility, and approval of levels of public spending on a range of major public policy issues, such as the economy, employment, education, the environment, housing, and health care.

5. Approval of Incumbent Officeholders

Last, at the most specific level, orientations toward incumbent officeholders represent attitudes toward particular leaders in positions of authority. This is typified by levels of satisfaction with the performance of specific presidents or prime ministers, as well as support for particular parties, and confidence in leaders in other public sector agencies, such as the military or government bureaucracy. Loss of support for incumbent officeholders may have consequences, but no matter how grave or sudden any drop (such as the Watergate crisis), in most long-established regimes it is unlikely to pose a threat to the functioning or stability of the nation-state. In more fragile states, however, a leadership crisis, such as the death or overthrow of a president, may trigger broader processes of regime change. As Easton notes: "Typically, members of a political system may find themselves opposed to the political authorities, disquieted by their policies, dissatisfied with their conditions of life and, where they have the opportunity, prepared to throw the incumbents out of office. At times, such conditions can lead to fundamental political and social change. Yet at other times, in spite of widespread discontent, there appears to be little loss of confidence in the regime – the underlying order of political life – or of identification with the political community. Political discontent is not always, or even usually, the signal for basic political change."[38]

To analyze support for incumbent officeholders, studies are heavily dependent upon national polls rather than cross-national surveys. We can examine longitudinal trends in popular approval of presidents or prime ministers in particular countries, using monthly polls to analyze whether satisfaction with leadership has declined since the postwar period.[39] More often, analysis has focused on trust in incumbent politicians, using the items developed by the American National Election Study (ANES) in 1958, and subsequently replicated in some other national election studies.[40] The standard ANES items monitor how the public feels about the performance of public officials in terms of their ethical standards, efficiency, and integrity. The ANES asks Americans to assess whether the 'government in Washington' can be trusted to do what is right, an item which is understood here to tap the broader level of general confidence in the state, since the item refers to the federal agency collectively rather than the incumbent officeholders. In addition, the ANES survey asks whether 'people running the government' waste taxes, whether government is run for the benefit of a few big interests, or whether public officials are 'crooked.'[41] Separate items monitor a sense of how far people believe the public sector is responsive to public opinion, representing the notion of 'external efficacy.'

There are some important issues about interpreting all these measures, however, which need to be considered. Most important, they are not designed to tap into more generalized levels of support toward the community and regime. Thus the ANES does not regularly monitor public approval of the basic U.S. constitutional principles, adherence to democratic values and principles, or indicators of American pride and patriotism. The NORC US General

Social Survey has also only asked sporadically about these matters, making it difficult to analyze long-term trends. The ANES standard 'trust in government' items are regarded as the canonical measures for analyzing trends in American public opinion, and although there is some ambiguity about the specific branch of government, the referents of these items are clearly worded to be incumbent-oriented ('the people in the government,' 'the government in Washington,' 'the people running the government').[42] Moreover as Levi and Stoker point out, although commonly assumed to reflect *trust* in government, in fact the measures tap other related dimensions, such as the ability and efficiency of public officials (to do 'what is right'), as well as their ethical qualities (to be honest or crooked), and the responsiveness of government (toward special interests or the general good), all of which generate favorable or unfavorable evaluations.[43] The concept of trust, Levi and Stoker note, never featured in the original design of these survey items by Donald Stokes. In addition, in the ANES questions it is unclear what American respondents understand when they are asked to evaluate the performance of 'the government' or 'the people running the government,' since U.S. decision making is divided horizontally among the executive, legislative, and judicial branches, as well as vertically among districts, states, and the federal levels.

THE IDEA OF DEMOCRATIC DEFICITS

All these elements of system support are important but not all are central to the idea of democratic deficits. The second and third elements derived from the general conceptual framework are useful to understand the links between the demand and supply of democracy, in the theory developed in this volume. The size of any democratic deficit derives from the overwhelming approval of democratic values and principles, which are widely expressed in most societies today, and yet the more skeptical evaluations of the democratic performance of governments, which are also relatively common. The informational basis of any evaluations is also important for the accuracy of any judgments about the performance of democracy. In emphasizing these dimensions, this study returns to the classic framework at the heart of Almond and Verba's original *Civic Culture* study. This focused upon "(1) *'cognitive orientations,'* that is, knowledge and beliefs about the political system ... (2) *'affective orientations'* or feelings about the political system ... and (3) *'evaluational orientations,'* the judgments and opinions ... that typically involve the combination of value standards and criteria with information and feelings."[44]

Democratic Aspirations

The first aspect concerns democratic aspirations and values, which can be understood to reflect the demand for democracy. Aspirations and values reflect desirable goals – whether for the individual, household, community, nation-state, and indeed the world. Aspirations concern what people want out of life or what they regard as most important. People typically juggle a variety of competing aspirations – such as the desire for physical security, social status and material affluence, autonomy and freedom, or self-expression and creativity. The relative ranking of these goals determines priorities. As such, aspirations are understood to tap into relatively durable aspects of social psychology that orient people toward specific attitudes and cognitive beliefs. Aspirations may concern personal goals, such as the importance of family, self-fulfillment through work, or the acquisition of material goods. Or they may concern the goals for society as a whole. People living within Scandinavian cultures, for example, which typically display socially egalitarian values, are expected to express strong support for public policies strengthening the role of government, a comprehensive and universal welfare state, and redistributive taxation designed to reduce income differentials. On the other hand, Americans, who usually give greater importance to the values of rugged individualism and the free market, can be expected to oppose these types of policies. Political values reflect the desires that citizens express toward the ideal type of principles for governing their own state, irrespective of the type of regime actually in power. Unlike political attitudes, values and aspirations can be understood to transcend specific cultural contexts, institutional arrangements, and particular situations. Hence general preferences for competition or cooperation, social equality or individual success, for example, can be applied to the different spheres of work, school, business, and politics.[45] The diffuse nature of values also facilitates wide-ranging comparisons across diverse countries and cultures.

One counter-argument, suggested by Schedler and Sarsfield, is that instead of asking about values, surveys should monitor more concrete attitudes toward specific democratic procedures, for example, whether respondents support the use of referenda and plebicites, the adoption of proportional representation or majoritarian electoral systems, freedom of speech and equal rights for political minorities, or the decentralization of decision making through federalism. Yet it makes little sense to ask people about technical issues where citizens lack experience or awareness, as Converse argued. Even in established democracies where political elites have long debated the pros and cons of alternative electoral reforms, such as the United Kingdom and New Zealand, citizens' preferences for proportional or majoritarian types of electoral systems have been found to be strongly conditioned by the precise wording, order, and framing of survey questions, with successive polls generating unstable and unreliable insights into public opinion, rather than reflecting deep-seated prior attitudes.[46] In these circumstances, a more effective strategy for tapping public opinion is to monitor more general values that are applicable to multiple institutional contexts and life experiences. Political values can be regarded as a trade-off. When considering the risks and benefits of becoming actively engaged in democratic reform movements, for example, citizens living under long-standing autocracies, such as Saudi Arabia, China, and Iran, need to weigh the importance of maintaining traditional sources of political authority, social stability, and security against the dangers and uncertainties that flow from regime transitions. When measuring values, citizens who endorse the importance of living in a democracy, and who also reject authoritarian principles, are regarded in this study as holding democratic values.

Evaluations of Democratic Performance

The second dimension concerns the supply of democratic governance, representing citizens' evaluations or satisfaction with the performance of democratic governance in their own country. Where there is congruence between supply and demand, this implies a close fit between the public's aspirations for democratic governance and their satisfaction with how far this is being met in each country. Eckstein's congruence theory suggests that where demand matches supply, this should reinforce regime stability and the political status quo.[47] The public will be content with how far government reflects their expectations. Where demand and supply fail to balance, however, then Eckstein predicts that regimes will prove more fragile and open to challenge. Where the public demand for democracy outruns its perceived supply by the regime, this has important implications for the potential mobilization of reform movements. In contrast, where the perceived supply of democracy runs ahead of public demand for this form of governance – for example, if the international community insists on holding multiparty competitive elections in deeply traditional societies such as Afghanistan which lack any democratic traditions – then electoral democracies are also expected prove fragile, as they lack mass legitimacy. To measure these ideas, citizens' aspirations can be compared against satisfaction with democratic performance in each country.

Cognitive Awareness of Democratic Procedures

Last, citizens may be well or ill informed about the core characteristics of liberal democratic procedures and principles. When seeking to understand whether people support democracy or whether they believe that their own government follows democratic principles or respects human rights, surveys often ask direct or overt questions that fail to monitor what people actually understand by the complex concept of democracy. In response to the interviewer's questions, 'manufactured,' 'top of the head,' 'non-attitudes' can always be offered by survey respondents. But such responses are unlikely to prove stable, deep-rooted, well-structured, or reliable indicators of public opinion.[48] Converse first noted that people often try to give some response to survey questions, when asked to do so, despite having no prior attitudes toward the issue.[49] Zaller also emphasizes that people often try to generate opinions from the cues provided by the questions asked during the interview, especially when they lack information or prior experience concerning the issue. However, these responses should not be regarded as recording attitudes or preferences that existed prior to the start of the survey.[50] For example, if respondents are asked about whether their country should adopt proportional representation, people may offer an opinion even when they lack any detailed experience, knowledge, or information about how this type of electoral system works.[51] This issue is least problematic in survey questions where most people can draw upon direct personal experience, for example, when respondents are asked about the priority they give to their family, work, or religion. Relatively technical and abstract issues about which the public has little cognitive knowledge or direct experience, however, are particularly vulnerable to these problems, such as the issue of climate change, concern about the size of the federal deficit, or questions about constitutional reform. Opinions about these matters can always be offered by respondents, but in the absence of full information, these are not necessarily well grounded or stable. For these reasons, cognitive awareness of at least some of the basic procedures associated with liberal democracy is therefore essential as a filtering condition for the meaningful expression of democratic values and for informed evaluations of the quality of democratic governance by citizens. The most informed critical citizens, using these concepts, are those who grasp some of the basic procedures of liberal democracy, who hold democratic values as important to their lives, and who are simultaneously dissatisfied by the performance of democracy in their own country.

WHAT IS EXCLUDED FROM THIS FRAMEWORK?

The fivefold classification of system support, expanding upon Easton, provides a coherent way to understand citizens' orientations toward the nation-state, its agencies, and actors. The selective focus on discrepancies between widespread adherence to democratic values and endemic doubts about democratic practices is in accordance with others who have emphasized these tensions. Nevertheless, it is worth emphasizing what this conceptual framework excludes and the reasons why.

Partisan Identification and Membership

One issue concerns indicators of public support for political parties. A wealth of evidence derived from successive national election studies since the 1960s and 1970s demonstrates the long-term erosion of party loyalties which has occurred in many established democracies.[52] Dealignment has progressively weakened the social psychological attachments binding loyalists to the same party over successive elections, contributing to aggregate electoral volatility and more individual vote switching, facilitating the sudden breakthrough of new parties and restructuring party competition, as well as more generally weakening linkages between citizens and the state.[53] In a related but distinct development, there is also solid evidence that official party membership rolls have dropped markedly in West European societies, eroding the basis for grassroots voluntary party work and financial contributions.[54] Parties in the electorate, as organizations, and in parliament play an essential role in representative democracy. Parties serve multiple functions: simplifying and structuring electoral choices; organizing and mobilizing campaigns; articulating and aggregating disparate interests; channeling communication, consultation, and debate; training, recruiting, and selecting candidates; structuring parliamentary divisions; acting as policy think tanks; and organizing government. Not only are parties one of the main conduits of political participation but they also strengthen electoral turnout. If mass membership is under threat, as many suspect, and if party loyalties are eroding, this could have serious implications for representative democracy. Many European commentators have seen these changes as posing severe legitimacy problems for party government; Peter Mair, for example, regards these developments as reflecting "a massive withdrawal of public support and affection."[55]

Nevertheless, it still remains unclear whether either of these trends should be interpreted as a sign of psychological disengagement from regime institutions or from political authorities. The idea of institutional confidence concerns generalized orientations toward the party system rather than attitudes such as identification with particular parties. Moreover, as noted earlier, it is always dangerous to attribute psychological motivations to particular actions; citizens may not see themselves as party loyalists over successive elections because they want to exercise greater choice over candidates or party programs at the ballot box – for example, splitting their ticket in local, national, and European elections, or voting for strategic reasons – without necessarily disengaging from electoral politics or expressing disaffection with the party system as a whole. Similarly, party membership rolls may be dwindling for multiple reasons, such as the availability of alternative channels of mediated political communication, the professionalization of campaigning, and public sources of party funding, so that party leaders are no longer so keen to recruit members for these functions.[56] Overall measures of confidence and trust in political parties are more direct indicators of how far the public sees these institutions – as well as facilitating clear comparisons with support for similar mediating political organizations linking citizens and the state, including the news media, interest groups, and new social movements.

Social Capital

In recent years, the research community has commonly related issues of how people feel about their government to theories of social capital. Theorists from de Tocquevill and John Stuart Mill to Durkheim, Simmel, and Kornhauser have long emphasized the importance of civic society and voluntary associations as vital to the lifeblood of democracy. Modern theories of social capital, originating in the seminal ideas of Pierre Bourdieu, James Coleman, and Robert Putnam, build upon this tradition.[57] In particular, in *Making Democracies Work* (1993) and in *Bowling Alone* (2000), Putnam emphasized the importance of civic associations and voluntary organizations for political participation and effective democratic governance.[58] The theory claims that typical face-to-face deliberative activities and horizontal collaboration within voluntary

associations far removed from the political sphere, such as sports clubs, agricultural cooperatives, or philanthropic groups, promote interpersonal trust,
fostering the capacity to work together in the future, creating the bonds of
social life that are the basis for civil society and democracy. Organized groups
not only achieve certain instrumental goals but, it is claimed, in the process
of doing so they also create the conditions for further collaboration, or social
capital.

While attracting a substantial body of literature, the analysis of citizens'
psychological orientations toward the nation-state, its agencies, and actors
should be separated from the potential causes of these orientations. It may
be that a deeper reservoir of interpersonal trust in the community serves to
strengthen confidence in democratic government and regime institutions, but
debate continues to surround both the logic of the theoretical linkages and
the interpretation of the empirical evidence about this relationship.[59] As one
recent review by Zmerli and Newton summarized the evidence: "The claim that
the socially trusting individuals are also politically trusting has poor empirical
support. A good deal of individual-level survey research suggests that social and
political trust are rather weakly correlated, if at all."[60] In this study, therefore,
theories of social capital are treated as furnishing potential explanations that
could help to account for the phenomenon of critical citizens, but psychological
orientations toward the political system are treated as distinct from indicators
of generalized social trust and associational activism.

The Consequences of Citizen Orientations for Political Behavior

In this framework, it is also worth emphasizing that the concept of systems support and the core ideas of critical citizens remains separate analytically from
its consequences. Many popular commentators mix together a wide rag-bag of
attitudinal and behavioral indicators, such as weakening partisan identification
and political activism, which are regarded as signs of public disenchantment
or discontent with democracy.[61] Lack of confidence in democratic government
may be expressed through eroding voter turnout, falling party membership,
or declining engagement in voluntary associations, but it is equally plausible
that attitudes and behavior are wholly separate phenomena. For example, a
wealth of evidence indicates that voter participation may rise and fall for many
reasons – such as the frequency of elections, the popularity of the governing
party, and the closeness of the race – all of which are unrelated to trust and
confidence in government.[62] Moreover, the relationship between cultural attitudes and behaviors is complex; voter anger at incumbents, for example, may
spur greater participation at the ballot box, not less. By contrast, public satisfaction with the status quo can encourage people to stay home on polling day.
It is foolhardy to assume prior psychological motivations directly from actions
unless the linkage is corroborated by independent evidence. Equally, at the
individual level, multivariate models commonly report that trust or cynicism
in government is a poor predictor of political participation, although some

significant bivariate relationships have been detected.[63] The exact relationship between systems support and its behavioral and systemic consequences can only be determined by careful analysis of the empirical evidence, as considered in the final section of this book. It is conceptually confusing if all the factors that scholars regard as different indicators of a decline in civic engagement and political participation are bundled together willy-nilly, and such an approach restricts our capacity to separate attitudes toward the regime from the behavioral impact of these orientations.

As discussed in the final section of the book, public support for the nation-state, its agencies, and actors is regarded as important for governance in all countries, including the willingness of citizens to obey the law voluntarily, to pay taxes that contribute toward public revenues, and to participate in civic affairs. Lack of system support, on the other hand, is widely assumed to strengthen reform movements, to encourage protest politics through peaceful or radical means, and, ultimately, to foster regime instability. Regime legitimacy is widely seen as most vital in multicultural communities, especially in countries where secessionist movements and breakaway nationalist minorities seeking independence are challenging the fundamental foundations and authority of the state. In extreme cases, such as Somalia, Colombia, and Sudan, states suffer from a severe legitimacy deficit, where the authorities lack the capacity to deal effectively with long-standing regional rebellions or enduring problems of ethnic conflict.[64] One of the most complex challenges facing the international community engaged in peace-building initiatives is to strengthen state legitimacy and good governance, arguably as important as the priorities of restoring security and expanding the delivery of public goods and services.[65] But the impact of citizens' psychological orientations on all these aspects of behavior needs to be carefully examined with close attention to the evidence rather than bundling them all together. For these reasons, the idea of democratic deficits that is developed here provides a clear and comprehensive way of understanding public opinion toward democracy, while not throwing in so many components that the core idea becomes muddied and confused. The task of the next chapter is to build upon this framework by operationalizing these concepts and describing the sources of evidence and survey data.

3

Evidence and Methods

What benchmarks and indicators are appropriate to monitor and compare the health of democratic governance? If the majority of Americans express dissatisfaction with the performance of the federal government, for example, does this signal deep anger and disaffection among the public or just routine mistrust? If only one in five British citizens expresses confidence in Westminster politicians, in the wake of the 2009 MP expenses scandal, is this a signal that something is seriously wrong with parliament – or does this just reflect healthy skepticism toward authority figures?[1] If two-thirds of Italians persistently lack confidence in the courts and judiciary, this may appear problematic compared with typical attitudes in Scandinavia, but what is the appropriate yardstick? Are Italians too cynical? Are Scandinavians perhaps too trusting?[2] We should recognize that legitimate interpretations can and do differ, on both normative and empirical grounds. Democratic theories offer alternative visions about these matters, without any yardsticks etched in stone.

To understand these issues, the technical detail and research design used for this book need clarification, including how the fivefold conceptual schema delineated in the previous chapter is operationalized and measured, before the evidence can be interpreted. This chapter therefore describes the primary data sources for analyzing public opinion, including the comparative framework and the classification of regimes for the societies included in the pooled World Values Survey 1981–2005, used as the main dataset for global cross-national comparisons, as well as the Eurobarometer, employed for the annual time-series analysis from 1972 to 2008. The chapter then describes the indicators monitoring government performance and the content analysis of the news media, as well as explaining the selection of multilevel methods for analysis.

EVIDENCE FROM THE WORLD VALUES SURVEY

Individual-level evidence about cultural values in many different societies is derived from analysis of many cross-national social surveys. The broadest cross-national coverage is available from the pooled World Values Survey/ European Values Survey (WVS), a global investigation of sociocultural and political change conducted in five waves from 1981 to 2007. This project has carried out representative national surveys of the basic values and beliefs of the publics in more than ninety independent countries, containing over 88% of the world's population and covering all six inhabited continents. It builds on the European Values Survey, first carried out in twenty-two countries in 1981. A second wave of surveys was completed in forty-three countries in 1990–1991. A third wave was carried out in fifty-five nations in 1995–1996, and a fourth wave, in fifty-nine countries, took place in 1999–2001. The fifth wave covering fifty-five countries was conducted in 2005–2007.[3] This dataset is best designed for a global cross-national comparison although the subset of the eleven nations included in all five waves facilitates some consistent time-series analysis over a twenty-five-year period.

As Table 3.1 illustrates, the WVS survey includes some of the most affluent market economies in the world, such as the U.S., Japan, and Switzerland, with per capita annual incomes over $40,000, together with middle-level countries including Mexico, Slovakia, and Turkey, as well as poorer agrarian societies, such as Ethiopia, Mali and Burkina Faso, with per capita annual incomes of $200 or less. There are also significant variations in levels of human development in the countries under comparison, as monitored by the UNDP Human Development Index combining per capita income with levels of education, literacy and longevity. Some smaller nations also have populations below one million, such as Malta, Luxembourg and Iceland, while at the other extreme both India and China have populations of well over one billion people. The survey contains older democracies such as Australia, India and the Netherlands, newer democracies including El Salvador, Estonia and Taiwan, and autocracies such as China, Zimbabwe, Pakistan, and Egypt. The transition process also varies markedly: some nations have experienced rapid process of democratization during the 1990s; today the Czech Republic, Latvia, and Argentina currently rank as high on political rights and civil liberties as Belgium, the United States, and the Netherlands, all of which have a long tradition of democratic governance.[4] The survey also includes some of the first systematic data on public opinion in several Muslim states, including Arab countries such as Jordan, Iran, Egypt, and Morocco, as well as in Indonesia, Iran, Turkey, Bangladesh and Pakistan. The most comprehensive coverage comes from Western Europe, North America and Scandinavia, where public opinion surveys have the longest tradition, but countries are included from all world regions, including sub-Saharan Africa.

For longitudinal data, we can compare the eleven countries included in all waves of the World Values Survey since the early 1980s, as discussed in Chapter 6. Other sources provide a regular series of annual observations, suitable to monitor the responsiveness and sensitivity of public opinion to specific events, variations in government performance, or major changes in regime. Accordingly to understand longitudinal trends this book draws upon

TABLE 3.1. *Countries in the World Values Survey by Levels of Development*

	High income societies ($15,000+)	GDP per capita ppp[a] 2006 (World Bank 2007)	Human Development Index 2005 (UNDP 2007)	Medium income societies ($2,000–14,999)	GDP per capita ppp 2006 (World Bank 2007)	Human Development Index 2005 (UNDP 2007)	Low income societies ($1,999 and below)	GDP per capita ppp 2006 (World Bank 2007)	Human Development Index 2005 (UNDP 2007)
1	Luxembourg	$54,779	0.944	Korea, Republic	$13,865	0.921	Macedonia	$1,940	0.801
2	Norway	$40,947	0.968	Greece	$13,339	0.926	Guatemala	$1,771	0.689
3	Japan	$40,000	0.953	Slovenia	$12,047	0.917	Bosnia and Herzegovina	$1,741	0.803
4	Andorra	$38,800	.	Portugal	$11,124	0.897	Egypt, Arab Republic	$1,696	0.708
5	United States	$38,165	0.951	Trinidad and Tobago	$10,268	0.814	Albania	$1,604	0.801
6	Iceland	$35,782	0.968	Saudi Arabia	$9,910	0.812	China	$1,595	0.777
7	Switzerland	$35,696	0.955	Malta	$9,618	0.878	Azerbaijan	$1,576	0.746
8	Denmark	$32,548	0.949	Argentina	$8,695	0.869	Serbia and Montenegro	$1,455	.
9	Ireland	$31,410	0.959	Czech Republic	$7,040	0.891	Morocco	$1,439	0.646
10	Sweden	$31,197	0.956	Uruguay	$6,987	0.852	Armenia	$1,284	0.775
11	Taiwan	$29,500	.	Estonia	$6,945	0.860	Philippines	$1,175	0.771
12	Singapore	$27,685	0.922	Mexico	$6,387	0.829	Georgia	$1,071	0.754
13	United Kingdom	$27,582	0.946	Hungary	$6,126	0.874	Ukraine	$1,040	0.788
14	Finland	$27,081	0.952	Chile	$5,846	0.867	Indonesia	$983	0.728
15	Austria	$26,110	0.948	Latvia	$5,683	0.855	India	$634	0.619
16	Canada	$25,562	0.961	Poland	$5,521	0.870	Pakistan	$623	0.551
17	Netherlands	$25,333	0.953	Croatia	$5,461	0.850	Vietnam	$576	0.733
18	Germany	$24,592	0.935	Venezuela	$5,447	0.792	Moldova	$492	0.708

No.	Country	GDP (ppp)	Index	Country	GDP (ppp)	Index	Country	GDP (ppp)	Index
19	Belgium	$24,541	0.946	Lithuania	$5,247	0.862	Bangladesh	$454	0.547
20	France	$23,899	0.952	Slovak Republic	$5,126	0.863	Nigeria	$439	0.47
21	Australia	$23,372	0.962	Malaysia	$4,623	0.811	Zimbabwe	$409	0.513
22	Cyprus	$22,699	0.903	Brazil	$4,055	0.800	Zambia	$365	0.434
23	Italy	$19,709	0.941	Iraq	$3,600	.	Tanzania	$335	0.467
24	Israel	$18,367	0.932	Turkey	$3,582	0.775	Kyrgyz Republic	$326	0.696
25	Spain	$16,177	0.949	South Africa	$3,562	0.674	Ghana	$300	0.553
26	New Zealand	$15,458	0.943	Dominican Republic	$2,694	0.779	Uganda	$274	0.505
27				Russian Federation	$2,621	0.802	Rwanda	$268	0.452
28				Thailand	$2,549	0.781	Burkina Faso	$267	0.37
29				Peru	$2,489	0.773	Mali	$250	0.38
30				Romania	$2,443	0.813	Ethiopia	$155	0.406
31				Colombia	$2,317	0.791			
32				Bulgaria	$2,256	0.824			
33				Jordan	$2,193	0.773			
34				El Salvador	$2,173	0.735			
35				Algeria	$2,153	0.733			
36				Belarus	$2,070	0.804			
37				Iran, Islamic Republic	$2,029	0.759			

Note: The 93 countries in the World Values Survey, 1981–2007, are classified and ranked by GDP per capita in purchasing power parity, 2006.

[a] ppp = purchasing power parity

Source: World Bank Development Indicators, 2007.

the Eurobarometer surveys, with national coverage expanding from the original states to reflect the larger membership of the European Union. This survey has monitored satisfaction with democracy since 1973 and confidence in a range of national institutions since the mid-1980s. In addition, since 2002 the European Social Survey had provided added data on twenty-five countries in this region. For the United States, the American National Election Survey conducted almost every election year since 1958 (monitoring trust in incumbent government officials) and the NORC General Social Survey since 1972 (monitoring institutional confidence) provide further resources for longitudinal analysis. Other more occasional surveys, such as those for World Public Opinion and Gallup International, allow the analysis to be expanded further.

THE SELECTION OF INDICATORS

The evidence for any decline in political support is commonly treated as straightforward and unproblematic by most popular commentary, based on one or two simple questions reported in public opinion polls. The conventional interpretation suggests that trust in parties, parliaments, and politicians has eroded in established democracies and, by assumption, elsewhere as well. On this basis, recent British studies have tried to explain why 'we hate politics' or why Europeans are 'disenchanted' with democracy or 'alienated' from politics.[5] Scholars in the United States as well have sought to understand 'angry Americans,' or why Americans 'hate' politics.[6] Comparative work has also seen public doubts about politicians, parties, and political institutions spreading across almost all advanced industrialized democracies.[7] Yet the orientation of citizens toward the nation-state, its agencies, and actors is complex, multidimensional, and more challenging to interpret than these headline stories suggest. Evidence of public opinion toward government should ideally meet rigorous standards of reliability and validity that characterize scientific research.[8]

Reliable empirical measures prove consistent across time and place, using standardized measures and data sources that can be easily replicated, allowing scholars to build a cumulative body of research. Indicators such as satisfaction with the performance of democracy and confidence in public sector agencies have been carried in multiple surveys and employed in numerous comparative studies over recent decades.[9] The ANES series on trust in incumbent government officials, where trends can be analyzed over half a century, has become the standard indicator used in studies of American politics.[10] The accumulation of research from multiple independent studies, where a community of scholars shares similar indicators, builds a growing body of findings. This process generates the conventional textbook wisdom in social science – and the authority established by this view within the discipline often makes it difficult to recognize alternative perspectives.

Empirical measures do not just need to prove reliable; they should also be *valid*, meaning that they accurately reflect the underlying analytical concepts to which they relate. The empirical analysis of critical citizens requires careful attention to normative ideas, including complex notions of trust, legitimacy, and representative democracy, prior to the construction of appropriate operational empirical indicators. Measurement validity is weakened by minimalist indicators that focus too narrowly upon only one partial aspect of a broader phenomenon, limiting the inferences that can be drawn from the evidence. The U.S. literature that relies solely upon the ANES series on trust in incumbent government officials, for instance, can arrive at misleading conclusions if studies fail also to examine confidence in the basic constitutional arrangements and deep reservoirs of national pride and patriotism characteristic of the American political culture.[11] Maximalist or 'thicker' concepts and indicators commonly prove more satisfactory in terms of their measurement validity, by capturing all relevant dimensions and components of the underlying notion of political legitimacy. But they also have certain dangers; more comprehensive measures raise complex questions about how best to measure each aspect and how to weigh the separate components in constructing any composite scales. In practice, multidimensional measures also become more complex to analyze; it often proves necessary to compare similar but not identical items contained in different surveys and time-periods, since few datasets monitor all components of political support.

When selecting appropriate indicators, unfortunately there is often a trade-off between their reliability and validity. The fivefold schema originally developed in *Critical Citizens* attempts to strike a reasonable balance between these demands. One advantage is that this framework provides a comprehensive way to map the separate elements involved in citizens' orientations toward the nation-state, its agencies, and actors, meeting the criteria of measurement validity. It has also now become more standardized, through being widely adopted in the research literature, increasing the reliability of the body of research and its cumulative findings. Figure 3.1 shows how the fivefold schema has been operationalized in the research literature, and the variety of typical indicators used in many social surveys.

The fivefold conceptualization proposed for this study expands upon the Eastonian notions but it still provides clear and useful theoretical distinctions among different major components. But does the public actually make these distinctions in practice? Principle component factor analysis is the most appropriate technique to test how tightly and consistently attitudes cluster together.[12] A coherent viewpoint would suggest that confidence in parliaments, for instance, would be closely related in the public's mind to similar attitudes toward parties, the civil service, and the government. Alternatively, if the public is largely unaware of the overarching principles that connect these institutions, these components would be seen as separate by the public. A series of items from the pooled World Values Survey 1981–2005 was selected to test orientations toward the nation-state, its agencies, and actors. The WVS cannot be used to monitor attitudes toward incumbent officeholders, such as presidents and party leaders in particular countries, and subsequent chapters analyze other surveys, such as World Public Opinion, which are suitable for this purpose.

	Levels of support	Survey measures and operational indicators
MOST DIFFUSE >>	Support for the nation-state	**Feelings of national pride**, such as in national achievements in the arts, sports, or the economy, feelings of national identity, and willingness to fight for country.
	Support for regime principles	**Adherence to democratic values and principles,** such as the importance of democracy, respect for human rights, separation of religious and state authorities, and rejection of autocratic principles.
	Evaluations of regime performance	**Judgments about the workings of the regime,** including satisfaction with the democratic performance of governments, and approval of decision-making processes, public policies, and policy outcomes within each nation-state.
	Confidence in regime institutions	**Confidence and trust in public sector institutions** at national, regional, and local levels within each nation-state, including the legislature, executive, and civil service, the judiciary and courts, the security forces, and political parties.
<<MOST SPECIFIC	Approval of incumbent office-holders	**Approval of specific incumbents** including popular support of individual presidents and prime ministers, ministers, opposition party leaders, and elected representatives.

FIGURE 3.1. Operationalizing indicators of system support.

Details about the specific questions and coding of all variables are provided in the book's Technical Appendix A.

The result of the factor analysis of the WVS pooled data, presented in Table 3.2, confirms that the theoretical distinctions are indeed reflected in the main dimensions of public opinion. The first set of items corresponds to generalized *support for the nation*, including feelings of national pride, the strength of national identity, and willingness to fight for one's country. The second dimension reflects *approval of democratic regimes*, including attitudes toward democracy as the best system for governing the respondent's country, and the importance of living in a country that is governed democratically. The third dimension reflects a *rejection of autocratic regimes*, including the alternative of rule by the military, dictatorships, and bureaucratic elites unconstrained by electoral accountability. This distinct dimension suggests that the public may reject autocracy in some cultures, but this does not necessarily mean that they wholeheartedly embrace democratic regimes. The fourth dimension concerns

TABLE 3.2. *Components of Systems Support*

Var	Period of measurement	Survey items	Nationalism (i)	Approval of democratic values (ii)	Rejection of autocratic values (ii)	Evaluations of regime performance (iii)	Confidence in regime institutions (iv)
V209	1981–2005	Strength of feelings of national pride	.739				
V212	2005	Strength of identification with nation	.694				
V75	1981–2005	Willing to fight for country in a war	.593				
V151	1995–2005	Approve of having a democratic system as 'very/fairly good'		.804			
V162	2005	Importance of living in a country governed democratically		.734			
V149	1995–2005	Anti-bureaucratic elite rule (experts take decisions)			.803		
V148	1995–2005	Anti-dictatorship (strong leader rules without elections)			.765		
V150	1995–2005	Anti-military rule			.619		
V163	2005	Evaluation of performance of democracy in own country				.803	
V164	1995–2005	Evaluation of respect for human rights in own country				.787	
V140	1981–2005	Confidence in parliament					.809
V139	1990–2005	Confidence in parties					.749
V138	1990–2005	Confidence in government (in nation's capital)					.787
V137	1981–2005	Confidence in courts					.760
V141	1981–2005	Confidence in civil service					.744
V136	1981–2005	Confidence in police					.723
V132	1981–2005	Confidence in armed forces					.577
		Percentage of variance explained	*9%*	*9%*	*10%*	*9%*	*24%*

Note: The coefficients represent the loadings of Principal Component Factor Analysis with varimax rotation and Kaiser normalization. Coefficients under .45 were excluded. The factor analysis was run with individual-level data.

Source: World Values Survey pooled 1981–2005.

evaluations of regime performance by citizens in each country, including judgments about respect for human rights and satisfaction with the performance of democracy in their own country. Both these items ask for evaluations about practices in each state rather than broader aspirations or values. The fifth cluster of attitudes reflects *confidence in regime institutions*, including the legislative, executive, and judicial branches, as well as political parties, the security forces, and the government as a whole. The results of the factor analysis from the pooled WVS therefore demonstrate that citizens do indeed distinguish among these aspects of systems support, as theorized, and a comprehensive analysis needs to take account of each of these components. Most important, the analysis confirms the robustness of the framework originally developed in *Critical Citizens*, even with a broader range of countries under comparison and with the inclusion of additional survey questions drawn from the fifth wave of the WVS. The survey items identified in each dimension were summed and standardized to 100-point continuous scales, for ease of interpretation, where a higher rating represents a more positive response.

COMPARING REGIMES

To understand global cultural attitudes, public opinion needs to be compared in a wide range of social and political contexts, including those citizens living under different types of regimes, as well as in many diverse regions worldwide. When classifying countries, the colloquial use of terms such as 'transitional states,' 'consolidating democracies,' and even the classification of 'newer' or 'younger' democracies often turns out to be remarkably slippery and complicated in practice.[13] Moreover public opinion is expected to reflect both the current regime in power as well the cumulative experience of living under different types of regimes. People are expected to learn about democracy from their experience of directly observing and participating in this political system, as well as from broader images about how democracies work as learned in formal civics education and conveyed in the mass media. To develop a consistent typology of regimes and to monitor historical experience of democratization, this study draws upon the Gastil index of civil liberties and political rights produced annually by Freedom House. The index has the advantage of providing comprehensive coverage of all nation-states and independent territories worldwide, as well as establishing a long historical time-series of observations conducted annually since 1972. The measure has also been widely employed by many comparative scholars.[14]

Freedom House, an independent think tank based in the United States, first began to assess political trends in the 1950s with the results published as the Balance Sheet of Freedom. In 1972, Freedom House launched a new, more comprehensive annual study called *Freedom in the World*. Raymond Gastil developed the survey's methodology, which assigned ratings of their political rights and civil liberties for each independent nation-state (as well as for dependent territories) and then categorized them as 'free,' 'partly free,' or 'not free.' Subsequent editions of the survey have followed essentially the same format. The index monitors the existence of political rights in terms of electoral processes, political pluralism, and the functioning of government. Civil liberties are defined by the existence of freedom of speech and association, rule of law, and personal rights. The research team draws upon multiple sources of information to develop the classifications based on a checklist of questions, including ten separate items monitoring the existence of political rights and fifteen on civil liberties.[15] Each item is allocated a score from 0 to 4 and each is given equal weight when aggregated. The raw scores for each country are then converted into a 7-point scale of political rights and a 7-point scale for civil liberties, and in turn these are collapsed by Freedom House to categorize each regime worldwide as either 'free,' 'partly free,' or 'not free.' The 14-point scales provided annually by Freedom House are matched to the year of the WVS survey and standardized into a 100-point democratization scale in this study, to facilitate ease of interpretation.

Historical Index of Democratization

As well as looking at contemporary patterns, it is clearly important to consider the accumulated years citizens have lived under different types of regimes. People can be expected to learn more about the practice of democracy by living under conditions of freedom and human rights, where they have opportunities to participate in civic life, as well as through political images and awareness conveyed by schooling and the mass media. When people have extended experience, their attitudes toward democracy can be expected to become more coherent, consistent, and stable, whereas those who have little experience of living under this type of regime may have less structured attitudes. Popular and scholarly usage often loosely refers to 'newer' or 'younger' democracies, but in practice there are several alternative ways to operationalize these concepts. To measure the historical experience of living under democratic regimes during the third wave era, several studies have used somewhat different rules. For example, in his classic study, Lijphart compared three dozen countries which had been continuous uninterrupted democracies for a twenty-year period.[16] Nevertheless the adoption of any particular time-period generates some arbitrary cutoff dates; why twenty years, for example, rather than ten or thirty? Moreover although these sorts of decisions appear technical, in fact they can have a critical impact upon the results of the analysis. For example, the rule used by Lijphart automatically excluded countries that experienced democratic breakdown during these two decades. By limiting the comparison to stable political systems, Lijphart's research design was unable to test the institutional conditions leading toward consolidation, one of the key issues the study sought to analyze. Historical events can also be used as alternative benchmarks, but these too involve some arbitrary judgments; for example, while the fall of the Berlin Wall is adopted as a commonsense watershed event for comparing pre- and post-communist societies, this does not work for the key date of transitions in Mediterranean Europe, Latin America, or Asia.

As an alternative, this study uses the cumulative Freedom House ratings of political rights and civil liberties during the third wave era, 1972–2006, to measure the historical experience of democratic states. If citizens learn about democracy and acquire their political attitudes and values from living within this form of regime, as socialization theories suggest, then historical patterns should leave a clear imprint upon contemporary public opinion. One advantage of using the cumulative annual score in the historical index is that this is sensitive to short-term fluctuations over time, including back-tracking by regimes such as Venezuela, Thailand, and Colombia, fluctuations in Nigeria and Russia, as well as substantial and sustained advances that have occurred elsewhere, such as in Spain, Uruguay, and South Korea. The historical democratization index is also standardized for ease of interpretation; hence, countries with a 100% score have been governed continuously by democratic regimes throughout the third wave era (since 1972). The classification of regimes uses this measure by subdividing liberal democracies into older and younger categories, where the standardized 100-point historical democratization index is divided; scores of 69 or less represent younger democracies, whereas scores from 70 and above represent older democracies with the most extensive cumulative experience of democracy.

Classifying Contemporary Types of Regimes

Based on this source, *liberal democracies* are defined in this study as independent nation-states with regimes that the Freedom House survey *Freedom around the World* 2006 classifies as 'free' in terms of a wide range of political rights and civil liberties. The concept of liberal democracy has been most clearly articulated by Robert Dahl, who argued that this type of regime is characterized by two main attributes – contestation and participation.[17] In practice, multiparty competition for elected office and suffrage for all adult citizens represent the essential conditions, and, to ensure that electoral competition is meaningful, liberal democracies also respect freedom of expression, the availability of alternative sources of information (freedom of the media), and associational autonomy (freedom to organize political parties, interest groups, and social movements). Based on their assessments of these characteristics, Freedom House suggests that today almost half (46%) of all independent nation-states worldwide (89) fall into this category, with institutions meeting the full panoply of civil liberties and political rights. The expansion in the number of liberal democracies during the third wave era has been dramatic; in 1978, only forty-seven states fell into this category (30%). As shown in Table 3.3, a wide range of liberal democracies are included in the pooled WVS. This includes twenty-eight older democracies that expanded the franchise to all citizens during the late nineteenth and early twentieth centuries, with a high historical democratization index throughout the third wave era, such as Australia,

TABLE 3.3. *Regimes in the World Values Survey*

	Older liberal democracies	1975	2006	Historical index	Younger liberal democracies	1975	2006	Historical index	Electoral democracies	1975	2006	Historical index	Autocracies	1975	2006	Historical index
1	Australia	100	100	86	Andorra	57	100	75	Venezuela	86	57	66	Pakistan	43	36	30
2	Austria	100	100	86	Dominican Republic	71	86	66	Colombia	79	71	57	Zimbabwe	36	21	25
3	Canada	100	100	86	India	64	79	61	Philippines	43	71	49	Egypt	43	36	25
4	Denmark	100	100	86	Uruguay	43	100	59	Russia	79	36	49	Russia	21	36	23
5	Iceland	100	100	86	Argentina	71	88	57	Turkey	79	71	48	Kyrgyzstan	21	50	21
6	Netherlands	100	100	86	Antigua Barbuda	71	86	57	Bangladesh	29	57	43	Algeria	21	36	17
7	New Zealand	100	100	86	El Salvador	79	79	55	Guatemala	64	64	43	Ethiopia	21	43	17
8	Norway	100	100	86	Brazil	50	86	54	Malaysia	64	57	42	Iran	29	29	16
9	Switzerland	100	100	86	Mexico	64	79	51	Zambia	43	64	35	Azerbaijan	21	36	16
10	United States	100	100	86	Korea, Republic	43	93	51	Morocco	43	50	34	Belarus	21	21	15
11	Sweden	93	100	86	Hungary	29	100	50	Singapore	43	50	33	Rwanda	29	36	13
12	Luxembourg	93	100	85	Poland	29	100	50	Burkina Faso	43	57	32	China	14	21	7
13	Germany	100	96	85	Chile	29	100	49	Nigeria	36	57	30	S. Arabia	29	21	7
14	Belgium	100	100	84	Czech Republic	100	100	49	Jordan	29	50	28	Viet Nam	14	29	3
15	Ireland	93	100	84	Slovak Republic	93	100	49	Bosnia-Herzegovina	21	71	28	Iraq	14	29	3
16	UK	100	100	83	Taiwan	36	93	47	Macedonia	21	71	28				
17	Italy	93	100	80	South Africa	50	86	47	Moldova	21	64	27				
18	Japan	93	93	80	Peru	43	79	47	Georgia	21	71	25				
19	France	93	100	80	Slovenia	21	100	42	Tanzania	29	64	25				
20	Finland	86	100	79	Lithuania	21	100	41	Armenia	21	50	24				
21	Malta	100	100	78	Estonia	21	100	41	Uganda	14	50	24				
22	Cyprus	57	100	75	Latvia	21	100	40	Albania	14	71	23				
23	Portugal	57	100	75	Ghana	29	93	37								
24	Trinidad Tobago	86	86	74	Bulgaria	14	93	35								
25	Spain	43	100	71	Mali	14	79	33								
26	Israel	79	93	71	Romania	21	86	32								
27	Greece	86	93	71	Indonesia	43	79	30								
28					Croatia	29	86	29								
29					Ukraine	21	79	29								
30					Serbia	29	79	28								
	TOTAL	89	99	81	TOTAL	40	91	48	TOTAL	39	60	35	TOTAL	30	30	19

Notes: Nations in the WVS pooled survey are classified by the type of regime in 2006 (the year closest to fieldwork of the fifth wave of the WVS) and liberal democracies are further sub-divided by their historical experience of democracy. The 1975 and 2006 democracy scales are the annual Gastil 14-point index of civil liberties and political rights, estimated by Freedom House, standardized to 100 points. The historical democratization index represents the sum of the annual Gastil index of civil liberties and political rights, by Freedom House, from 1972 to 2006, standardized to 100 points.

Source: The Mannheim Eurobarometer Trend File 1970–2002.

Canada, Norway, the Netherlands, and New Zealand. The comparison also includes twenty-nine younger liberal democracies that made the transition after the early 1970s, exemplified by Mali, South Africa, Mexico, and Indonesia, all with a lower historical democratization index.

The broader category of *electoral democracies* used in this research is defined as those contemporary independent nation-states that Freedom House defines as 'partly free.' Out of 193 independent nation-states worldwide, one-third (62) fell into this category in 2006.[18] This middle group of regimes represents a gray area that proves more difficult to classify; they are neither absolute autocracies, such as military juntas, personal dictatorships, and monarchies that lack even the fig leaf of an elected legislature, nor do they meet the full conditions of political rights and civil liberties to qualify as liberal democracies. Commentators have termed this intermediate category, alternatively, 'illiberal democracies,' 'semi-free,' and 'hybrid regimes' as well as 'electoral autocracies.'[19] In this study, electoral democracies represent contemporary states that have adopted contests for the national legislature, and where there is a universal franchise for all citizens, but where there remain serious restrictions on civil liberties and political rights. There are almost two dozen contemporary electoral democracies contained in the pooled World Values Survey, including Venezuela, Colombia, and Thailand, which have regressed sharply in human rights during the third wave era, as well as others like Albania, Tanzania, and Georgia, which have made considerable progress in democratization during these decades. In states such as Singapore and Uganda there are major restrictions on party competition; others such Pakistan, Nigeria, Thailand, and Bangladesh have experienced interrupted periods of military rule temporarily suspending democratic politics.

Last, greater agreement surrounds the concept of *autocracies*, representing the contemporary states that have proven most repressive, using multiple techniques to suppress human rights and fundamental freedoms, without elections for either the executive or legislative office. In this study, autocracies are defined as the countries which are classified as 'not free' by Freedom House. If we compare all countries around the globe in 2006, Freedom House estimates that roughly one-fifth of all states (42) fall into this category, of which only six continue to lack an elected parliament because they are ruled by military juntas, dictators, or absolute monarchs with appointed consultative assemblies. Other autocracies hold legislative elections but with conditions so restricted, and with results so flawed and manipulated, that they fail to meet international standards, especially the need for multiparty competition, universal adult franchise, regular free and fair contests, and open political campaigning. The pooled World Values Survey allows comparison of public opinion in diverse contemporary autocracies, including Zimbabwe, Egypt, Russia, China, and Saudi Arabia.

Table 3.3 shows all the states contained in at least one wave of the pooled World Values Survey, categorized into the contemporary type of regime (in 2006) as older liberal democracies, younger liberal democracies, electoral democracies, and autocracies. For comparison, the table lists the level of democracy for each state as measured by the Freedom House Gastil index in the mid-1970s (the conventional start of the third wave era), the contemporary level of this index (in 2006), and the historical democratization index during the third wave era. The results highlight the diversity of the regime types and pathways of change, which are included in societies under comparison. It is important to monitor public opinion within this broader context, especially if we hope to analyze how far orientations toward the political system relate systematically to historical experiences.

Polity IV

Despite the advantages of the Freedom House index in terms of continuity over time and replicability in the research literature, the measure has been criticized on a number of methodological grounds.[20] To have confidence that the results of the analysis are reliable and robust, therefore, this research replicates the core models where the Polity IV scale of democracy-autocracy is substituted for the Freedom House index. The Polity project was initiated by Ted Robert Gurr in the 1970s. The latest version, Polity IV, provides annual time-series data in country-year format covering 161 countries from 1800 to 2006.[21] Coders working on the Polity IV project classify democracy and autocracy in each nation-year as a composite score of different characteristics relating to authority structures. Democracy is conceived of conceptually as reflecting three essential elements: the presence of institutions and procedures through which citizens can express preferences about alternative policies and leaders; the existence of institutionalized constraints on the power of the executive; and the guarantee of civil liberties to all citizens (although not actually measured). The classification emphasizes the existence or absence of institutional features of the nation-state. The dataset constructs a 10-point democracy scale by coding the competitiveness of political participation (1–3), the competitiveness of executive recruitment (1–2), the openness of executive recruitment (1), and the constraints on the chief executive (1–4). Autocracy is measured by negative versions of the same indices. The two scales are combined into a single democracy-autocracy score varying from −10 to +10. Polity has also been used to monitor and identify processes of major regime change and democratic transitions, classified as a positive change in the democracy-autocracy score of more than 3 points. Replicating models using alternative Freedom House and Polity IV indices lends greater confidence to the major findings but, given limited space, the full results of the latter are not presented in tables, unless they differ significantly in certain important regards.

INDICATORS OF REGIME PERFORMANCE

Recent decades have witnessed a burgeoning array of approaches and indicators designed to evaluate the performance of the state and its core institutions.

Indicators are particularly valuable to analyze whether public opinion reflects the actual performance of the regime. Trends over time, and also cross-national average benchmarks and rankings, provide readings on the health of democratic governance in any state. The era since the early 1970s has seen important gains in the level of conceptual sophistication, methodological transparency, scope, and geographic coverage of these measures. Literally dozens of indicators, of varying quality and coverage, are now widely available to gauge the quality of democracy in general, as well as multiple measures of 'good governance,' human rights, corruption, women's empowerment, civic engagement, legislative power, and many other related issues.[22]

Many of these measures are constructed from surveys of national and international 'experts,' exemplified by Transparency International's Corruption Perception Index, as well as various assessments of political risk, such as the team of editors who generate the International Country Risk Guide index.[23] Various composite measures have drawn heavily upon a variety of expert survey resources, as exemplified by the World Bank Institute's six indicators of good governance, developed by Daniel Kaufmann, Aart Kraay, and colleagues.[24] Other indicators have relied solely upon aggregate national data, exemplified by the Inter-Parliamentary union's database on the proportion of women in national parliaments, used to evaluate gender equality in elected office; the International Institute for Democracy and Electoral Assistance (International IDEA)'s dataset on electoral turnout worldwide since 1945, to document trends in voter participation; and the Cingranelli-Richards (CIRI) human rights index, monitoring national ratification and implementation of major international conventions and treaties.[25] Other aggregate measures standardized by multilateral agencies such as the World Bank and UNDP provide insights into particular dimensions of policy performance, including per capita growth of GDP to monitor economic performance, rates of schooling, and levels of child and maternal mortality as proxy measures of health care. Where reliable official statistics are collected and standardized, these indices facilitate global comparisons across states and over time.[26] To assess performance-based explanations of political support, this book draws on a wide range of indicators, notably those collected in the Quality of Governance datasets by the University of Gothenburg.[27]

News Media Content Analysis

The last source of data concerns the news media. Systemic evidence for news coverage of government and public affairs requires content analysis that is standardized over time as well as among different countries and types of media. Such cross-national evidence is scarce but this study draws upon the resources of Media Tenor Institute.[28] This study uses their content analysis of the news media coverage of public affairs in newspapers and television in two comparable cases, the United States and Britain. These Anglo-American democracies share many cultural characteristics and historical traditions although they differ significantly in their political and media systems. The time-series evidence allows us to see whether the positive and negative news coverage of government and public affairs in these countries is systematically linked with subsequent changes in public opinion, such as satisfaction with government and confidence in the legislature.

MIXED METHODS

Any single approach, taken in isolation, has limits. Consequently this study opts for a mixed research design, combining the virtues of pooled survey data in more than ninety nations with rich and detailed narrative studies of contrasting paired cases.[29] A large-N pooled dataset is used to establish the overall picture. All variables are described in Technical Appendix A, including the key dependent variables used to construct the democratic deficit scale. The list of countries and surveys included in the study is described in Technical Appendix B. The use of hierarchical linear models, in particular multilevel regression analysis, is described in detail in Technical Appendix C.

The key models in the book involve measurement at two distinct levels. A representative sample of individual respondents (level 1) is nested within national-level contexts (level 2). The World Values Survey was conducted among a representative random sample of the adult population within each nation-state. Given the use of multilevel data, hierarchical linear models (HLM) are most appropriate for analysis, including multilevel regression analysis.[30] Those who are interested in the multilevel regression methods employed should look at Technical Appendix C for a more detailed description. The study draws upon cross-sectional time-series (CS-TS) panel data, consisting of repeated observations (each wave of the survey) on a series of random units (the countries included in the WVS). The analysis of panel datasets through regression faces certain important challenges and the interpretation of the results is quite sensitive to the choice of specification issues, alternative models, and diagnostic tests.[31] Ordinary least squares (OLS) regression estimates assume that errors are independent, normally distributed, and with constant variance. Panel data violate these assumptions and raise potential problems of heteroscedasticity, autocorrelation, robustness, and missing data. In particular, autocorrelations are generated because, with time-series data, the same countries are being counted repeatedly and the additional observations do not provide substantially new information. The danger of OLS analysis is that the beta coefficients will remain unbiased but the disturbance terms from the errors (i.e., omitted variables) are likely to be correlated. In other words, if OLS regression models are used, the significance of any coefficients may be inflated, generating Type II errors, suggesting that significant relationships exist when in fact they do not. Various techniques have been designed to handle panel datasets, including ordinary least squares linear regression with panel corrected standard errors (PCSE), and the use of robust regression.[32] In this study, we extend the use of generalized hierarchical linear models (HLM). Our multilevel regression models include both subjects (countries) and repeated variables (waves) with correlated residuals within the random effects.

Last, we also use selected narrative paired case studies to illustrate the underlying causal mechanisms at work, taking account of historical developments and processes of cultural change within particular nations.[33] Cases allow researchers to develop theories, to derive hypotheses, and to explore causal mechanisms. This approach is particularly useful with outliers that deviate from the generally observed pattern. The case comparison examines societies that are similar in certain important regards, such as sharing a cultural tradition and level of socioeconomic development, while differing in their levels of system support. Case studies must always be sensitive to problems of selection bias, and it remains difficult to determine how far broader generalizations can be drawn from the particular countries.[34] Nevertheless the combination of cross-national large-N comparisons with selected cases is a strong design that maximizes the potential benefits of each approach. If the two contrasting approaches point to similar conclusions, it increases confidence in the robustness of the findings.

To go further, the next section of the book examines evidence for trends in system support and the distribution and size of any democratic deficits. The study seeks to understand aspirations to democracy, in particular, whether support for democratic values and principles is now widespread in many regions of the world, as earlier studies suggest, as well as considering what people understand when they express support for democratic governance. We also contrast support for democratic ideals with evaluations of democratic practices, to explore the tensions between these sets of attitudes.

PART II

SYMPTOMS

4

Trends in the United States and Western Europe

The assumption that the general public in established democracies has become deeply disillusioned with government and politics is so pervasive today that many accounts jump straight into the discussion of consequences and solutions without questioning the evidence. To understand these claims, Part I summarizes what is known about system support from the previous research literature, where concern about trust and confidence in governing institutions has usually waxed and waned over the years, with scholarly accounts reflecting the impact of contemporary political events, realpolitik, and global waves of democratization. Part II sets out the interpretive framework used for describing and interpreting trends in citizens' orientations, emphasizing the importance of paying close attention to the *when*, *where*, and *what* has changed. This chapter focuses upon comparing established democracies, as the longest and richest time-series survey data is available in these societies. Longitudinal trends are documented in the United States and Western Europe, all affluent societies with extensive historical experience of democracy. Using the Eastonian framework discussed earlier, the chapter first compares developments in the most specific levels of support, including attitudes toward particular government agencies, and then moves upward to consider more diffuse indicators of satisfaction with the general performance of democratic regimes and the strength of core attachments to the nation-state.

The longitudinal evidence available within the United States and Western Europe challenges conventional claims that an inevitable downward spiral of public disenchantment with politics has occurred across all established democracies. In particular, when changes in system support do occur, it is usually far more common to observe fluctuations over time in successive surveys rather than straightforward linear or uniform decline. Some cross-national changes in system support do occasionally occur simultaneously – symbolized by the events of 9/11, after which support for government appears to peak simultaneously across many countries – but these are the exception, not the rule. In terms of *where* changes occur, persistent cultural differences can be observed over many years even among relatively similar nations, such as contrasting levels of confidence in government in Italy and Spain, different levels of trust in parties in the Netherlands and Belgium, and diverse patterns of national pride in Germany and France. During the last decade, a few established democracies (notably the UK and Portugal) experienced a rising tide of mistrust about government institutions, which should raise concern in these particular countries, although during the same period, Belgium and Finland experienced the reverse.[1] Last, in terms of *what* changes occur, instead of a uniform general pattern, contrasts in public attitudes toward different branches of government are apparent within each country, including the United States, exemplified by different levels of trust and confidence in the legislature and in the courts. Perhaps most important for an accurate diagnosis, at the most diffuse level, public satisfaction with the general performance of democracy in Western Europe has usually strengthened over time, not weakened. Affective attachments to the nation-state remain strong and stable.

This complexity indicates the need for differentiated and nuanced arguments that can account for cross-national *variance* and the *dynamics* of longitudinal flux in political support. The diagnosis suggests that it would probably be most fruitful to investigate short- and medium-term explanations of any changes in indicators of system support, abandoning over-simple claims about steadily growing public disenchantment with politics across all established democracies – or indeed across the world.[2] Hence, the most promising hypotheses concern the instrumental performance of governments and public sector institutions rather than propositions that posit glacial, long-term social trends, such as processes of human development and cultural evolution. The next chapter builds upon these conclusions by comparing cross-national patterns in the far broader range of countries, cultural regions, and types of regimes included in the 2005 wave of the World Values Survey, setting developments in the United States and Western Europe within a global perspective.

I: THE DEBATE ABOUT CRITICAL CITIZENS IN ESTABLISHED DEMOCRACIES

The earliest surveys of American public opinion about government were conducted during the decade after the end of World War II, at a time when the role and functions of the federal government had expanded greatly under the New Deal Roosevelt administration, and when the United States had recently emerged as victorious and economically dominant in the world. It was often assumed that during this era American public opinion was relatively favorable toward the role of government. Rather than a 'golden age,' however, the earliest studies conducted by Hyman and Sheatsley in 1954, McClosky in 1958, and Mitchell in 1959 described American postwar attitudes as ambivalent toward government; public opinion typically expressed pride in U.S. democracy and yet considerable skepticism about the morality and honesty of elected politicians. The American, Mitchell concluded, "tends to expect the worst in politics but hopes for the best."[3]

Systematic comparative work on public opinion toward government originated during the late 1950s and early 1960s, with Almond and Verba's landmark study, *The Civic Culture*. The theoretical impetus for this work reflected contemporary concern in understanding the underlying causes of regime instability during the second great reverse wave of democracy.[4] The context included the historic rise of Nazi Germany and Italian fascism and the global disruption of the Second World War, as well as the collapse during the 1960s of fledgling parliamentary democracies in many newly independent African states emerging from colonial rule and the checkered political experience of Latin America, due to a succession of military coups, populist dictators, and communist revolution.[5] The central message emerging from *The Civic Culture* emphasized that political stability required congruence between culture and structure. Almond and Verba argued that the democratic public needed to be finely balanced in equilibrium between the dangers of either an excessively deferential, apathetic, and disengaged citizenry, on the one hand, or an overly agitated, disenchanted, and heated engagement, on the other. An optimal level of political trust was posited in stable democratic states, such as Britain and the United States, where active and watchful citizens checked the powerful, without succumbing to the destabilizing forces of either excessive loyalty and deference, at one pole, or excessive disaffection and alienation, at the other extreme. The idea that societies differed in their political culture was hardly novel; indeed, it had been the subject of philosophical speculation for centuries, in classic works from Montesquieu to de Tocqueville. But one of the more radical aspects of the civic culture study was the way that support for the theory was derived from a pathbreaking cross-national opinion survey, demonstrating that citizens' orientations could be examined empirically. The study analyzed the mass publics in Mexico, the United States, Italy, Britain, and Germany during the late 1950s.

Almond and Verba concluded that the United States (and to a lesser extent, Britain) exemplified their notion of a *civic* culture:

Respondents in the United States, compared with those in the other four nations, are very frequently exposed to politics. They report political discussion and involvement in political affairs, a sense of obligation to take an active part in the community, and a sense of competence to influence the government. They are frequently active members of voluntary associations. Furthermore, they tend to be affectively involved in the political system: they report emotional involvement during election campaigns, and they have a high degree of pride in the political system. And their attachment to the political system includes both generalized system affect as well as satisfaction with specific government performance.[6]

By contrast, Italy (and to a lesser extent, Mexico) exemplified an *alienated* political culture: "The picture of Italian political culture that has emerged from our data is one of relatively unrelieved political alienation and distrust. The

Italians are particularly low in national pride, in moderate and open partisanship, in the acknowledgment of the obligation to take an active part in local community affairs, in the sense of competence to join with others in situations of political stress, in their choice of social forms of leisure activity, and in their confidence in the social environment."[7] *The Civic Culture* therefore emphasized the cross-national variations, even among relatively similar postindustrial societies, such as Italy and Germany. This influential study did much to establish the conventional view that during the Eisenhower era, a period of economic abundance and cold war politics, Americans held positive views about their political system.

The mid-1960s and early 1970s, however, saw mounting concern about the capacity of democratic institutions to serve as an outlet to contain public dissent in the United States and in Western Europe. The era experienced the outbreak of tumultuous protest politics, with urban riots in Philadelphia, Watts, Newark, and Detroit symbolizing a radicalization of race relations and a breakdown of social control in the United States. Mass demonstrations on the streets of London, Paris, and Bonn catalyzed similar concerns in Western Europe. These events triggered new cross-national survey research seeking to understand the causes of protest activism.[8] The gloomier prognostications that became common during these decades received their strongest endorsement from Crosier, Huntington, and Watakuki, who published a major influential report written during the mid-1970s for the Trilateral Commission, which diagnosed a 'crisis' of democratic legitimacy afflicting not just America but also many similar post-industrial societies.[9]

This wave of concern ebbed somewhat during the early 1980s, reflecting some subsidence of radical social movements and the more quiescent mass politics characteristic of the Thatcher-Reagan era. During these years, Lipset and Schneider compared a wide range of American public opinion polls reflecting respondents' attitudes toward government, business, and labor.[10] The research concluded that mass support for many types of political institutions in the United States had indeed eroded over time, but Lipset and Schneider argued that most criticisms were leveled at the behavior and performance of specific power holders rather than expressing doubts about the underlying structure and function of American institutions. The more positive interpretation was reinforced by the *Beliefs in Government* project, a multivolume comparison examining broader trends in Western Europe from the early 1970s until the mid- or late 1990s. A thorough and detailed collaborative study, the *Beliefs in Government* project dismissed talk of a 'crisis of democracy' as exaggerated. In particular, chapters in these volumes that examined institutional confidence and trust in politicians concluded that little evidence pointed to a steady secular erosion of systems support in Europe during these three decades. Instead, the authors arrived at relatively sanguine conclusions that emphasized the existence of persistent cross-national differences in systems support across different European member states and a pattern of trendless fluctuations over the years.[11]

The debate over the depth of any problem was far from settled, however, and during the early to mid-1990s, as already noted, a host of American scholars continued to express worries about 'disenchanted democrats,' 'critical citizens,' and growing civic disengagement. Similar concern about political mistrust, voter apathy, and democratic disaffection echo among commentators in many other post-industrial societies as well.[12] Russell Dalton provided the most comprehensive recent summary of the cross-national survey evidence from the 1960s until the late 1990s across a range of established democracies and post-industrial societies. Dalton concluded that during these years citizens became increasingly detached from political parties, more skeptical toward governing elites and institutions, and less confident about parliaments, although public support for democratic ideals has not flagged.[13] Scholarly research mirrors popular commentary focused on contemporary phenomena in Western societies that appear to underline citizen anger, exemplified during 2009 by the public reaction to the Westminster expenses scandal in Britain, and in the United States by the simmering rage and breakdown of civility toward elected representatives expressed by 'tea party' activists at town hall meetings debating health care reform, the federal deficit, and the stimulus package.[14]

II: THE INTERPRETIVE FRAMEWORK: WHAT HAS DECLINED, WHEN, AND WHERE?

Before analyzing the causes of any democratic deficits, as a preliminary step it is important to establish a clear picture of trends in the descriptive evidence. Analysts need to pay attention to the depth, breadth, and timing of any changes in citizens' orientations toward democratic politics and government in the United States and Western Europe. What has declined, where, and when?

In terms of *what*, bearing in mind the Eastonian framework already discussed, it needs to be established whether any erosion of support has occurred only at the most *specific* level of trust in politicians, party leaders, elected officials, and public sector workers, or whether any rot has spread upward to damage confidence in many core political institutions and state agencies, and even, at the most diffuse level, to fragment common identities within multinational communities.

In terms of *where*, we need to demonstrate whether general patterns of declining trust and confidence are evident across many comparable established democracies – suggesting general causes – or whether any serious problem of eroding system support is confined to just a few nations. The largest research literature on this topic concerns the United States, but the American constitution was founded upon classical liberal principles, emphasizing mistrust of government. Lipset notes that American culture may prove exceptional in this regard, as in so much else.[15]

Last, in terms of *when*, close attention needs to be paid to the exact timing of any fluctuations in systems support. It is insufficient to look at net changes in different societies, since countries may all arrive at a similar end point through divergent pathways. Moreover, the starting and ending date for many series of observations is often arbitrary, yet this can clearly color interpretations of the trends – for example, if the series of survey measurements commences on a relatively high or low point. It is more rigorous to examine whether any changes happen simultaneously across states, or whether trends vary in their timing.

Prior attention to the *what, where* and *when* helps to select the most plausible competing theoretical hypotheses that can then be analyzed further in subsequent chapters. For example, any evidence of a glacial erosion of political support for parties and parliaments that persists over successive decades in many similar Western societies would suggest looking for evidence of long-term causes, such as processes of social psychological change in cultural value occurring among individual citizens or the impact of societal modernization, human development, the penetration of the mass media, and globalization at the macro-level. On the other hand, if patterns of trendless fluctuations and short-term volatility can be observed, with dynamic peaks and troughs that vary across relatively similar types of societies and among different branches of government, this points more clearly toward the need for investigating specific performance and event-based explanations within each country, such as the government's success or failure in handling the economy, the outbreak of a major parliamentary scandal, the end of an unpopular war, the rise of new parties, polarization of party politics, or an election throwing the governing party out of office.

The longest continuous time-series evidence is available from the American National Election Study (ANES), allowing us to track half a century of trends in the standard American indicators of trust in government officials. The U.S. General Social Survey (GSS) has also regularly monitored institutional confidence in public and private sector agencies from 1972 to 2006. To see whether similar trends are apparent in other established democracies, we can draw upon the series of bi-annual Eurobarometer surveys conducted since the early 1970s. The Eurobarometer survey regularly monitors confidence in national institutions, satisfaction with the performance of democracy, and feelings of national pride and identity. It should be noted, however, that often cross-national European trends can only be examined for shorter periods, and the results of any estimates of net change and linear trends remain sensitive to the particular years and countries under review. It remains possible that rising European disaffection occurred in the longer term period, but the evidence is too limited to allow researchers to refute or confirm these claims.

Given the immense outpouring of scholarly research and popular commentary, what is there new to say? Surprisingly, perhaps, a lot. Many studies of the empirical evidence provide a partial view by selecting only one aspect of the underlying multidimensional concept of systems support or by focusing upon only a few countries, or a single global region. Much of the literature lacks a clear and comprehensive conceptual framework focused on support for the political system. In studies of the empirical evidence, both attitudinal and behavioral indicators are commonly mixed together. Equally important, even half a century after the original *Civic Culture* survey, items carried in the time-series survey evidence used for identifying trends is often of limited duration and cross-national breadth, making it impossible to determine with any accuracy whether general trends have indeed occurred. To update the analysis, we can start by monitoring developments in the United States and Western Europe, which possess the longest series of indicators and the largest body of previous research. This sets the context for the broader comparison of contemporary societies worldwide presented in the next chapter.

III: LONGITUDINAL TRENDS IN THE UNITED STATES AND WESTERN EUROPE

Trust in Public Officials in the U.S. Federal Government

As discussed earlier, the standard American National Election Study questions about political trust ask whether the 'government in Washington' or 'people running the government' can be trusted to '*do what is right*,' whether they '*waste taxes*,' whether government is run '*for a few big interests*,' or whether public officials are '*crooked*.' These items seek to tap public orientations toward the national government including perceptions about the ethical standards, probity, and integrity of elected officials. The questions have also been carried in other American and cross-national surveys.[16] As Russell Hardin points out, however, these items are often used in empirical studies without reflecting upon whether they actually relate to the underlying notion of political *trust*.[17] For Hardin, trustworthiness rests on both motivations and competencies; do government officials seek to act in the public interest and, if so, do they actually have the capacity to do so? For example, people may believe that elected officials are trustworthy in their motivations for public service (for example, that the local congressional representative from their local district is honest and hardworking, or that the president is well-meaning and likable), and yet they may also feel that these individuals often prove generally incompetent or ineffective, for example, when managing a major economic or foreign policy crisis. Or conversely, citizens could logically believe that politicians are usually competent and effective but also venal, if thought to line their own pockets or those of special interests. The standard ANES battery of items mostly concerns the trustworthiness of the motivations of public officials (to 'do the right thing'), but not their competencies.

Reflecting a long-standing debate, the meaning of these indicators is also open to alternative interpretations. Hence for Jack Citrin, they provide signs of *specific* support for incumbent officeholders, with limited consequences. The erosion of American political trust that occurred during the 1960s can be best understood in this view as an expression of public dissatisfaction with the performance of particular incumbent political leaders and public policies, representing part of the regular cycle of normal electoral politics and real-world events.[18] From this perspective, the public popularity of members of Congress and particular presidents can be expected to ebb and flow over time, without indicating that Americans are willing to support constitutional reforms. For Arthur Miller, however, the ANES indicators tap into diffuse support. Any erosion suggests that the roots of public dissatisfaction extend more deeply to indicate a crisis of legitimacy in American democracy, representing a loss of faith that U.S. political institutions are the most appropriate ones for American society.[19] Others suggest that because government institutions are operated by incumbents, in practice it is difficult, if not impossible, to disentangle support for agencies and actors.[20] The ambiguity and potential measurement error when operationalizing the complex concept of political trust means that relying solely upon these indicators is unwise, and it would be prudent to see whether similar trends are evident in support for institutions using alternative data.[21] If the dynamics of public confidence in the executive, legislative, and judicial branches of American government reflect the peaks and troughs of confidence in the federal government, this would lend greater confidence to time-series trends, as well as indirectly supporting the Miller interpretation. If, however, there are marked variations in citizens' reactions toward different institutions, then this suggests the need to search for more performance- and event-driven explanations.

The first item in the ANES battery comes closest to the notion of general trust in public sector officials working within the federal government, relating to Easton's notion of specific rather than diffuse support. This item also provides the longest time-series. If we compare trends over time in the proportion of the American public reporting that they trusted the federal government to do what is right 'most of the time' or 'just about always,' as shown in Figure 4.1, the evidence suggests that American trust in government leaders plummeted steadily every election year from the mid-1960s to the late 1970s, during the period of hot button politics and dissent over race relations, Vietnam, the war on poverty, and Watergate.[22] Yet the subsequent trend line displays considerable volatility, with dynamic peaks and troughs rather than a simple linear or continuous fall. According to this series of observations, a sharp revival of American trust in the federal government occurred during the first Reagan administration from 1980 to 1984, despite the anti-government rhetoric of this administration, the deep recession in the U.S. economy during the early 1980s, and the growing polarization of party politics as the GOP moved sharply toward the right on certain moral and economic issues. Citrin and Green suggest that this happened because economic indicators for employment and inflation improved markedly after 1982, and President Reagan's leadership style exuded confidence and sunny optimism.[23] Trust in the federal government revived again from 1994 to 2002, a period of sustained economic growth that started under President Clinton and continued under President George W. Bush. Support peaked again after the dramatic events of 9/11, which Hetherington attributed to a 'rally around the flag' effect associated with any foreign policy crisis and the priority given to security issues.[24] Support then fell back again during the next

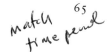

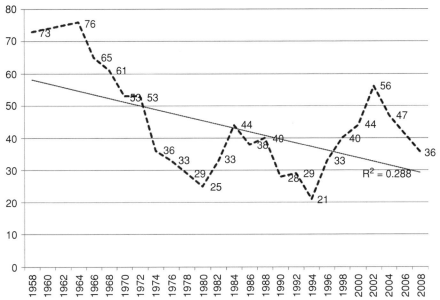

FIGURE 4.1. American trust in the federal government, 1958–2008. The standard ANES question is *"How much of the time do you think you can trust the government in Washington to do what is right – just about always, most of the time or only some of the time?"* The unstandardized beta regression coefficient proved significant (>001). *Source:* The American National Election Surveys, 1958–2008.

three national elections. Nor is this simply a product of the ANES survey measurement as similar volatility among the American public is evident when the same question was asked in a series of Gallup polls and New York Times/CBS News polls conducted since the early 1970s.[25] The overall volatility indicates that there are clearly periods when American trust in the federal government has revitalized, as well as periods when it has plummeted, and comprehensive explanations need to account for dynamic fluctuations over time.

Are similar trends evident elsewhere? Some of the ANES items on trust in politicians have been asked in national election surveys conducted in some other established democracies, but as a previous review by Listhaug emphasized, comparisons of trends are limited because of considerable variations in the item wording and the lack of continuity of items over successive national surveys.[26] The most thorough and comprehensive recent review of trends in sixteen established democracies using these types of items, by Dalton, concluded that these indicate a net decline in confidence in politicians in recent decades: "Regardless of recent trends in the economy, in large and small nations, in presidential and parliamentary systems, in countries with few parties and many, in federal and unitary states, the direction of change is the same."[27] The evidence that the public has become more skeptical about elected officials presented by Dalton is certainly suggestive and important, but nevertheless some caution is needed when interpreting the results of the regression analysis used in his study, since out of forty-three separate items, only seventeen items saw a statistically significant fall in trust over time. Moreover, any erosion of support that has occurred at the most specific level of elected officials may have few important consequences; in democracies with regular multiparty elections allowing the removal of incumbents, less public trust in politicians may generate higher turnover of elected representatives without necessarily affecting more diffuse levels of public confidence in government institutions.

Institutional Confidence in the United States

The U.S. General Social Survey monitors trends in confidence in public sector agencies, including the three branches of the American federal government. Any sustained erosion of faith in these institutions has potentially far more serious consequences than loss of trust in particular presidents, congressional leaders, or elected representatives. In democratic states, the popularity of elected leaders and governing parties is expected to rise and fall according to citizens' evaluation of their performance. Where opinions are overwhelmingly negative, multiparty democracies with alternating parties in government provide a safety valve for dissatisfaction through periodic opportunities to 'throw the rascals out' via the ballot box. But institutional confidence reflects more enduring and diffuse orientations than the popularity of specific leaders; any severe and persistent loss of legitimacy for the U.S. Congress, the Supreme Court, or the executive branch is not easily remedied, and it has broader ramifications. The GSS also examines attitudes toward the private sector as well, including confidence in major companies as well as in banks and financial institutions. This helps to establish whether the American public has increasingly lost faith in many established pillars of authority or whether this particular problem is confined mainly to the image or performance of government agencies and bureaucrats working in the public sector.

The U.S General Social Survey, conducted by NORC, has monitored confidence in institutional leaders since the early 1970s by asking: "*I am going to name some institutions in this country. As far as the people running these institutions are concerned, would you say you have a great deal of confidence, only some confidence, or hardly any confidence at all in them?*" Figure 4.2 shows the trends in American confidence in the executive branch and the Supreme Court. The dotted trend line and the R^2 coefficient summarize the overall strength and direction of any linear trends. The trend in public confidence in both the executive branch and the Supreme Court clearly demonstrates patterns of trendless fluctuation around the mean; in particular, and most striking, *no significant overall fall in institutional confidence occurred for either of these institutions from 1972 to 2008*. The executive

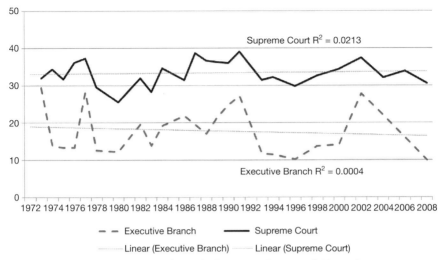

FIGURE 4.2. American trust in the U.S. Supreme Court and Executive, 1972–2008. *"I am going to name some institutions in this country. As far as the people running these institutions are concerned, would you say you have a great deal of confidence, only some confidence, or hardly any confidence at all in them?"* Chart shows the proportion reporting 'a great deal' of confidence in each institution. The linear trends summarize each series. *Source:* U.S. General Social Survey cumulative file 1972–2008 http://publicdata.norc.org/webview/.

branch, in particular, displays considerable volatility over time, for example, with the sharp peaks registered temporarily in 1977 (temporarily restoring levels of confidence under the Carter administration to the pre-Watergate era), in 1988–92 (under the presidency of George H. W. Bush), and again in 2001, under George W. Bush, following the events of 9/11. The highs and lows are rarely sustained, however, although the White House saw lower than average confidence during Clinton's first term, before public revelations surrounding the Lewinsky affair. The trend lines for the Supreme Court and the executive branch roughly mirror each other, although the Supreme Court retains higher public confidence and more stable evaluations.

Confidence in the U.S. Congress, illustrated in Figure 4.3, displays parallel periods of rising and falling public confidence, providing a fainter mirror of trends in the executive. Similar fluctuations can be observed in other surveys – for example, in June 2008, the Gallup poll found that just 12% of Americans expressed confidence in Congress, the worst rating the organization had measured for any institution in the thirty-five-year history of the question. Following the election of President Obama and the return of a Democratic-led Congress, the March 2009 Gallup poll saw congressional approval jump to 39%. After an initial honeymoon period, approval fell back again to 25% by the end of 2009.[28] Overall, however, compared with presidential approval, there is a flatter line for congressional approval in the GSS series, suggesting less

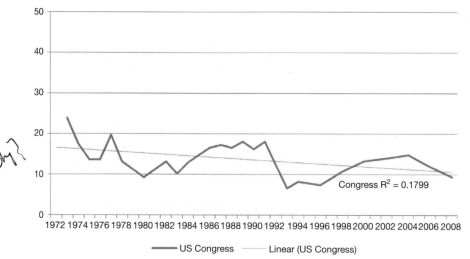

FIGURE 4.3. American trust in the U.S. Congress, 1972–2008. *"I am going to name some institutions in this country. As far as the people running these institutions are concerned, would you say you have a great deal of confidence, only some confidence, or hardly any confidence at all in them?"* Chart shows the proportion reporting 'a great deal' of confidence in each institution. The linear trends summarize each series. *Source*: U.S. General Social Survey cumulative file 1972–2008 http://publicdata.norc .org/webview/.

pronounced volatility for the legislature than the executive branch. Moreover, and most important, the overall trend line since the early 1970s to 2008 shows falling net support for Congress during these decades, as many commentators have noted.[29] It appears that in evaluations about the leadership among the core institutions of the U.S. federal government, the public has expressed the most consistent growing doubts about the legislative branch.

But does this long-term fall in congressional approval mean a crisis of legitimacy for American *government* – suggesting the need to search for potential political explanations – or are similar trends apparent for other established institutions in the private sector as well? If there is a more generic trend affecting attitudes toward those in authority, then cultural or social reasons might provide more plausible explanations. For comparison, the bottom graph in Figure 4.4 shows parallel trends in confidence in the private sector for banks and financial institutions as well as for major companies. Most striking, both these private sector institutions show overall trends of falling confidence from the start to the end of this era, with declines that are similar in strength to that experienced during the same era by Congress. It is also notable that banks and financial institutions show sharper peaks and troughs than confidence in major companies.

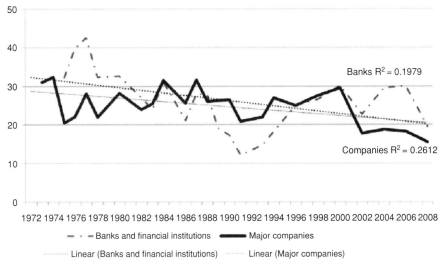

FIGURE 4.4. American trust in banks and major companies, 1972–2008. *"I am going to name some institutions in this country. As far as the people running these institutions are concerned, would you say you have a great deal of confidence, only some confidence, or hardly any confidence at all in them?"* Chart shows the proportion reporting 'a great deal' of confidence in each institution. The linear trends summarize each series. *Source:* U.S. General Social Survey cumulative file 1972–2008 http://publicdata.norc.org/webview/.

The GSS evidence concerning institutional trust in the United States therefore suggests several important points, which challenge the conventional wisdom. First, the time-series evidence suggests that any trends in American public opinion are not simply directed toward loss of faith in all three branches of the U.S. federal government; instead, the most consistent net loss of confidence during more than three decades focuses upon Congress. Second, the legislature is not alone in this regard, and the issue is broader than simply a crisis of faith in government; other major private sector institutions like American banks and companies have experienced an equivalent net loss of public confidence as well. Last, these data reinforce the point that any persuasive explanations need to account for the dynamics of public support in attitudes toward government institutions, with attention to the precise timing of particular short-term fluctuations rather than assuming a net erosion of political trust and confidence. Often, studies have simply focused upon net percentage point change derived from the starting and end points for any time-series data, but inevitably this approach assumes certain arbitrary benchmarks; it is unclear, for example, what confidence in these institutions was like prior to the early 1970s. It is equally important analytically to understand the dynamic variance in the trends over time.

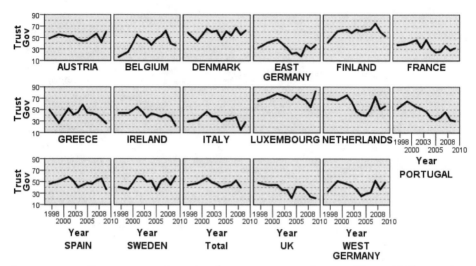

FIGURE 4.5. European trust in national government, 1998–2009. *"I would like to ask you a question about how much trust you have in certain institutions. For each of the following institutions, please tell me if you tend to trust it or tend not to trust it. The national government."* Chart shows proportion responding 'Tend to trust.' *Source:* Eurobarometer surveys 1998–2009.

INSTITUTIONAL TRUST IN WESTERN EUROPE

For comparison with other long-established democracies and affluent post-industrial societies, the Eurobarometer allows us to compare the United States with Western Europe. The survey monitors longitudinal trends in trust and confidence in a wide range of public and private sector institutions, including governments, parliaments, and parties, as well as satisfaction with the general performance of democracy and the strength of national identities. The Euro-barometer now covers public opinion in all twenty-five current member states. For a consistent time-series, however, the longest trend analysis from these surveys is limited to the countries that have been member states since 1973.

European Trust in Government

We can start by comparing the annual trends in institutional trust in the national government across seventeen European societies where attitudes have been monitored during the last decade. The data illustrated in Figure 4.5 and sum-marized in Table 4.1 show the proportion of the public who express trust in their national government every year (allowing *comparisons* of persistent con-trasts across countries, such as between Italy and Luxembourg) and the overall net change that occurred from the start to the end of this decade (showing any overall *net losses or gains*). The final columns in Table 4.1 measure the strength and significance of the unstandardized OLS regression beta coefficients (which summarizes the *direction* of linear trends).

TABLE 4.1. *European Trust in National Government, 1997–2009*

	1997	1999	2001 Spr	2001 Fall	2002	2003	2004	2005	2006	2007	2008	2009	Net change 1997–2009	Year	Sig
UK	48	44	35	44	36	36	22	41	41	34	24	22	−26	−1.83	**
Greece	50	27	39	52	41	45	59	44	43	41	34	26	−24	−.821	N/s
Portugal	52	65	50	55	52	47	36	33	37	46	32	30	−22	−2.46	**
Ireland	44	44	48	55	47	37	43	41	38	41	37	22	−21	−1.39	*
Netherlands	69	67	66	76	65	47	41	40	51	73	51	56	−13	−1.42	N/s
Spain	46	50	48	58	51	40	44	47	46	52	55	37	−9	−.327	N/s
France	38	40	37	46	32	46	31	25	26	36	28	32	−6	−1.05	N/s
Italy	29	32	33	47	39	38	29	35	35	37	15	29	−1	−.712	N/s
Denmark	59	44	54	66	60	62	47	61	54	67	55	62	3	.458	N/s
East Germany	32	41	40	47	40	32	22	24	18	37	30	38	5	−.759	N/s
Finland	42	61	56	64	59	64	61	64	65	75	61	53	11	.957	N/s
Austria	48	56	47	52	53	46	44	46	51	57	42	60	12	.108	N/s
West Germany	34	51	47	54	43	37	25	30	31	52	37	48	15	.188	N/s
Luxembourg	65	71	77	78	76	72	68	76	70	66	55	82	17	−.101	N/s
Sweden	41	37	49	59	59	50	51	35	51	55	45	60	19	.805	N/s
Belgium	16	25	45	55	49	46	37	47	52	62	40	37	21	1.83	N/s
TOTAL	44	47	47	56	49	46	40	43	44	52	40	43	−1	−.346	N/s

Note: "I would like to ask you a question about how much trust you have in certain institutions. For each of the following institutions, please tell me if you tend to trust it or tend not to trust it. The national government." Proportion responding 'Tend to trust.' OLS regression analysis was used to monitor the effects of time (the survey year) on trust in the national government, generating the unstandardized beta coefficient and its significance.

* = > .05 ** = > .01 *** = > .001

Source: Eurobarometer surveys 1997–2009 downloaded from Gesis ZACAT.

Trends in Europeans' trust in their national government indicate several important points. First, (1) *during the last decade the net change in European confidence in government varied in direction and size by country.* For example, the UK, Portugal, and Ireland experienced the sharpest significant net drop in the proportion trusting government during the last decade (down by 20 percentage points or more).[30] This finding would give support to the conventional assumption of steadily eroding trust but for the fact that other European societies experienced trendless fluctuations and *no* significant linear change over time, or even, in a few cases (Sweden and Belgium), a 19- to 21-point net *rise* in political trust during the same period (although this was not statistically significant as a linear trend). The assumption that trust in government has eroded consistently across established European democracies receives no support from this cross-national survey evidence. Now of course the time series is relatively short, and it may be that trust in government eroded during earlier eras; we simply cannot determine this with the available Eurobarometer evidence, but neither can others. It is also important to emphasize that there are substantial persistent contrasts among EU member states that need to be explained; for example, just as Almond and Verba observed half a century ago, the Italian public remains deeply skeptical in their orientation toward their government.[31] By comparison, citizens in Luxembourg and Finland are generally more trusting than average. The precise reasons for the restoration of political trust in Sweden and Belgium, and the simultaneous fall in Britain and Portugal, also deserve further scrutiny when we consider alternative explanations later in this volume. But the overall comparison suggests that performance-based explanations that affect specific government policies appear more plausible candidates than any account proposing systematic shifts in cultural values toward politics and public affairs.

As Figure 4.5 illustrates, however, this does not mean that European trust in government was steady; instead (2) *sharp fluctuations in trust in government can be observed in many countries,* such as the peaks and troughs occurring in Denmark, Sweden, and France. Last, and equally important, (3) *two period effects register a short-term peak in trust in government occurring simultaneously across many European countries,* notably in the survey taken in October–November 2001, shortly after the events of 9/11, when average trust jumped by 9 percentage points from the spring to fall, and another clear but smaller average peak in April–May 2007, which cannot be so easily attributed to any particular event or terrorist incident.

European Trust in Parliaments

As with the U.S. data, however, we also need to establish whether there are general trends in Europe across all major branches of government. As in the United States, it may be that European publics continue to support the executive branch in their national government, but that any erosion of confidence has occurred in the legislature and in political parties. Dalton suggests that

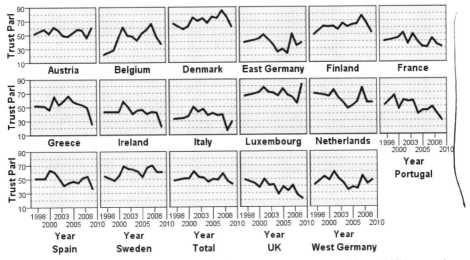

FIGURE 4.6. European trust in national parliaments, 1998–2009. *"I would like to ask you a question about how much trust you have in certain institutions. For each of the following institutions, please tell me if you tend to trust it or tend not to trust it. The national parliament."* Chart shows proportion responding 'Tend to trust.' *Source:* Eurobarometer surveys 1998–2009 downloaded from Gesis ZACAT.

public support for both institutions has fallen in a wide range of advanced industrialized democracies.[32] Evidence of eroding confidence in parliament in his study is based on regression analysis derived from four waves of the World Values Survey, as well as trends in Gallup, Harris, and related commercial polls, but in fact only six of the twenty-one coefficients in the Dalton study prove statistically significant and negative. Figure 4.6 and Table 4.2 show the Eurobarometer evidence when citizens were asked directly about their trust in parliament during the last decade.

The results largely confirm the observations already made concerning government. Again the data show that most countries have experienced trendless fluctuations in trust of parliaments, with the UK and Portugal again showing a significant growth of cynicism toward these institutions since the late 1990s (reflecting the pattern already observed for trust in government), while Denmark, Sweden, and Belgium experienced growing public trust toward their national legislatures. The overall mean trust in parties across the EU shows no significant change. Overall, there are also marked and persistent contrasts between European societies, with only one-fifth (19%) of British citizens expressing trust in their parliament in 2009, compared with three-quarters of Danes (78%). This strengthens the conclusion that specific cultural or institutional factors need to be explored in subsequent chapters to account for long-term contrasts among countries, while the dynamics of short-term fluctuations in trust over time may plausibly relate to variations in the perceived performance of governments, parliaments, and elected representatives.

TABLE 4.2. *European Trust in Parliament, 1997–2009*

	1997	1999	2000	2001 Spr	2001 Fall	2002	2003	2004	2005	2006	2007	2008	2009	Net change 1997–2009	Year	Sig
UK	49	44	38	36	50	41	42	28	39	33	41	27	19	−30	−1.796	**
Greece	52	51	46	50	65	53	59	66	58	55	53	49	34	−18	−0.909	N/s
Ireland	43	43	43	49	58	50	40	45	46	40	43	42	26	−17	−1.088	N/s
Spain	51	51	63	52	60	51	41	45	47	45	52	54	35	−16	−0.934	N/s
Portugal	52	66	46	58	59	57	58	39	44	44	49	39	39	−13	−1.949	**
Netherlands	69	67	65	68	74	63	56	47	51	57	77	56	58	−11	−0.978	N/s
France	40	43	45	41	52	36	50	39	32	31	44	35	36	−4	−0.953	N/s
Italy	33	34	37	38	50	43	47	38	41	38	39	16	30	−3	−0.835	N/s
East Germany	39	42	44	39	50	43	36	25	29	23	51	34	38	−1	−0.724	N/s
West Germany	42	53	48	52	60	50	44	34	38	36	54	43	50	8	−0.453	N/s
Austria	52	58	52	53	61	57	49	48	53	58	57	46	61	9	−0.027	N/s
Luxembourg	66	69	71	75	78	71	70	66	76	67	64	55	77	11	−0.116	N/s
Finland	50	62	61	57	62	57	66	61	64	65	77	66	61	11	0.762	N/s
Denmark	66	58	62	60	75	70	74	67	76	74	85	76	78	12	0.948	N/s
Sweden	54	48	55	57	69	65	64	61	53	67	70	60	68	14	0.784	N/s
Belgium	22	28	46	48	61	49	48	42	52	57	66	48	43	21	1.668	N/s
TOTAL	48	51	51	51	61	53	52	46	50	49	58	47	47	−1	−0.360	N/s

Note: "I would like to ask you a question about how much trust you have in certain institutions. For each of the following institutions, please tell me if you tend to trust it or tend not to trust it. The national parliament." Proportion responding 'Tend to trust.' OLS regression analysis was used to monitor the effects of time (the survey year) on trust in the national parliament, generating the unstandardized beta coefficient and its significance.

* = >.05 ** = >.01 *** = >.001

Source: Eurobarometer surveys 1997–2009 downloaded from Gesis ZACAT.

European Trust in Political Parties

What about political parties? There is a wealth of literature showing important changes in citizens' social psychological orientations toward political parties, as well as behavioral measures such as falling party membership rolls, but the implications of these trends for systems support is not straightforward. There is indeed good evidence that party membership has declined in many established democracies.[33] But this may happen for multiple reasons, however, such as organizational changes in how much parties seek to recruit grass-roots voluntary supporters and local activists, whether parties rely increasingly upon public funding and paid professionals, as well as broader shifts in more general patterns of social and political activism. As argued earlier, interpreting motivational attitudes directly from behavioral measures can be highly misleading. More directly, Dalton compares attitudes toward political parties derived from trends in the strength of party identification in a range of advanced industrialized democracies. Based on this evidence, Dalton concludes: "If party attachments reflect citizen support for the system of party based representative government, then the simultaneous decline in party attachments in nearly all advanced industrial democracies offers a strong sign of the public's affective disengagement from political authorities."[34] Yet it is not clear whether party identification is the most appropriate measure of trust and confidence in these institutions, since this orientation could weaken for many reasons, including the growth of more educated and rational voters choosing parties based upon policies and performance rather than habitual loyalties toward specific parties, without meaning that citizens have necessarily lost faith with the party system as a whole.

To look more directly at the evidence, Table 4.3 and Figure 4.7 show the Eurobarometer evidence when citizens were asked directly about their trust in political parties. Contrary to the declinist thesis, party trust fell significantly during the last decade only in the UK. In most European nations there were trendless fluctuations, while in three cases (Sweden, Belgium, and Denmark) party trust strengthened significantly by eighteen to twenty-six points during this era. The consistent erosion of institutional trust in government, parliament, and parties observed under the Labour government in the UK and the strengthening of institutional trust during the same decade in Belgium are clearly cases requiring further exploration later in the book. It may be that particular incidents of party polarization, policy failure, and corruption reduced faith in the government in Belgium.[35] In Britain, as well, there has been much concern about these developments, which came to a peak in the 2009 parliamentary expenses scandal.[36] Many reasons have been offered to account for British trends, generating public concern and parliamentary debate about the role of declining standards in public life.[37] Overall, however, contrary to much commentary, the net change in European trust in political parties proved significantly positive during these years.

TABLE 4.3. *European Trust in Political Parties, 1997–2009*

	1997	1999	2000	2001 Spr	2001 Fall	2002	2003	2004	2005	2006	2007	2008	2009	Net change 1997–2009	Year	Sig
UK	20	19	15	18	18	17	15	12	15	14	13	13	12	−7	−0.613	***
Greece	21	19	19	19	26	17	18	30	16	18	17	17	16	−5	−0.401	N/s
Netherlands	43	45	44	36	40	38	37	29	35	41	40	40	42	−1	−0.329	N/s
Ireland	22	23	24	28	32	26	22	27	25	25	27	27	21	−1	0.062	N/s
Spain	22	21	30	25	25	26	24	29	23	23	40	40	24	2	0.820	N/s
Portugal	16	23	19	20	23	23	22	17	31	27	19	19	18	3	0.130	N/s
France	12	12	15	12	16	13	16	14	10	12	10	10	14	3	0.184	N/s
East Germany	14	16	19	15	18	16	10	9	18	20	18	18	14	3	0.225	N/s
Italy	14	17	14	12	14	16	16	14	21	21	13	13	20	6	0.250	N/s
West Germany	15	21	19	21	18	20	13	13	20	16	19	19	27	12	0.350	N/s
Austria	28	25	22	26	27	27	22	21	21	29	30	30	41	13	0.755	N/s
Luxembourg	39	32	41	42	35	34	33	36	41	41	29	29	55	16	0.386	N/s
Finland	15	24	23	25	25	23	28	22	12	9	31	31	31	16	0.633	N/s
Belgium	11	18	22	19	21	24	23	22	24	30	28	28	29	18	1.269	***
Sweden	18	20	17	20	24	26	21	22	28	29	28	28	38	20	1.321	***
Denmark	34	30	34	36	38	38	42	36	38	44	50	50	60	26	1.996	***
TOTAL	21	22	23	23	25	24	22	21	24	25	26	26	29	8	0.368	*

Note: "I would like to ask you a question about how much trust you have in certain institutions. For each of the following institutions, please tell me if you tend to trust it or tend not to trust it. Political parties." "Proportion responding 'Tend to trust.'" OLS regression analysis was used to monitor the effects of time (the survey year) on trust in political parties, generating the unstandardized beta coefficient and its significance.

* = >.05 ** = >.01 *** = >.001

Source: Eurobarometer surveys 1997–2009 downloaded from Gesis ZACAT.

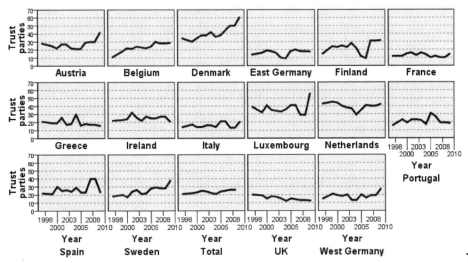

FIGURE 4.7. European trust in political parties, 1998–2009. *"I would like to ask you a question about how much trust you have in certain institutions. For each of the following institutions, please tell me if you tend to trust it or tend not to trust it. Political parties."* Chart shows proportion responding 'Tend to trust.' *Source:* Eurobarometer surveys 1998–2009 downloaded from Gesis ZACAT.

European Satisfaction with the Performance of Democracy

We can also compare trends in satisfaction with democracy, one of the standard indicators used in the research literature in many global regions.[38] This item has been carried in many cross-national surveys, including in the Eurobarometer since the early 1970s. As discussed earlier in Chapter 2, however, there remain ongoing debates about the precise meaning of this measure.[39] On the one hand, the item can be seen to tap approval of 'democracy' as a value or ideal, analogous to support for the principles of human rights or gender equality. In this study, however, we agree with Linde and Ekman that the phrasing of the question (by emphasizing how democracy is *performing*) makes it most suitable to test public evaluations of the actual workings of democratic regimes and assessments of democratic practices, rather than principles.[40] Satisfaction with the performance of democracy can also be regarded as a more diffuse level of support than trust in institutions or authorities, and therefore evidence of any deepening dissatisfaction would be real cause for genuine concern.

The comparison of trends in satisfaction with democracy illustrated in Figure 4.8 and Table 4.4 share certain aspects of the findings already presented concerning trust in state institutions; there remain diverse trends in democratic satisfaction in different European countries, annual volatility in public evaluations, and some persistent contrasts among societies, notably the low satisfaction registered in Italy.[41] But the overall direction of satisfaction with the performance of democracy among most European countries is usually positive

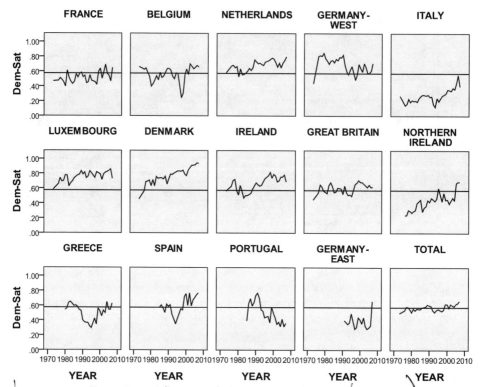

FIGURE 4.8. European satisfaction with democratic performance, 1973–2009. *"On the whole, are you very satisfied, fairly satisfied, not very satisfied, or not at all satisfied with the way democracy works in your country?"* Chart shows proportion who are 'fairly' or 'very' satisfied. *Source:* The Mannheim Eurobarometer Trend File 1970–2002; Eurobarometer surveys 2002–2009 downloaded from Gesis ZACAT.

over time. Table 4.4 demonstrates that today across Western Europe, on average two-thirds of the European public expresses satisfaction with the workings of democracy in their own country. In half of the nations under comparison, from 1990 to 2007 these attitudes become more positive, not less. Satisfaction is exceptionally low in Italy – but persistently so – and even here, satisfaction with democracy grew since the early 1990s. Regression analysis of the linear trends, summarized in Table 4.4, summarizes the direction and significance of linear changes over time. Of the societies registering a significant change, five become more positive in evaluations of the performance of their democracy (with major improvements in Northern Ireland, Denmark, Luxembourg, and Italy), two become progressively more negative (with less satisfaction over time in Portugal, Ireland, and West Germany), while the remainder show more modest net change. The overall pattern across all these EU member states is one showing that satisfaction grows significantly. Far from any signs of a general crisis of European states, or even spreading disaffection or disenchantment, the overall pattern shows that the public's satisfaction with the workings

TABLE 4.4. *European Satisfaction with Democratic Performance, 1973–2009*

	1973	1980	1990	2000	2009	Net change 1990–2009	Year	Sig
Portugal			74	50	40	−34	−0.015	***
Ireland	56	51	68	79	56	−12	0.007	***
Germany – West	44	78	82	64	72	−10	−0.005	**
Belgium	66	40	64	63	62	−2	0.002	N/s
Netherlands	58	53	73	77	72	−1	0.005	***
France	47	40	52	64	51	−1	0.003	**
Spain			59	76	58	−1	0.010	**
Great Britain	45	55	53	69	58	6	0.003	*
Germany – East			60	41	68	8	0.002	N/s
Greece		54	40	52	49	9	−0.002	N/s
Luxembourg	59	78	79	79	90	11	0.004	***
Italy	27	21	26	36	44	18	0.007	***
Denmark	46	63	73	77	91	18	0.010	***
Northern Ireland		27	42	45		27	0.011	***
TOTAL	50	51	60	62	62	6	0.002	***

Note: "*On the whole, are you very satisfied, fairly satisfied, not very satisfied, or not at all satisfied with the way democracy works in your country?*" Proportion responding 'fairly' or 'very' satisfied. OLS regression analysis was used to monitor the effects of time (the survey year) on trust in political parties, generating the unstandardized beta coefficient and its significance. Selected years presented. For the full annual trends, see Figure 4.6.

* = >.05 ** = >.01 *** = >.001

Source: Mannheim Eurobarometer Trend File 1970–2002; Eurobarometer surveys 2002–2009, downloaded from Gesis ZACAT.

of democracy has progressively strengthened during recent decades in many countries.

European National Pride

Last, we can also compare trends in the strength of national pride, operating at the most diffuse level of systems support. Lasting bonds to the nation-state are exemplified by feelings of national pride and identity, representing a sense of community within shared common territorial boundaries. Such feelings are important for every nation-state but they are thought to have particularly significant consequences for social cohesion and state legitimacy in multicultural communities and plural societies. The European evidence is also important because the growing powers and functions of the European Union, and the process of economic and social integration across the borders of member states, might be expected to have eroded national pride and identities more strongly within this region than in other parts of the world, although previous empirical studies provide little support for this claim.[42]

Figure 4.9 and Table 4.5 show the proportion of the European public who express national pride in their country, and the trends over time. It is striking

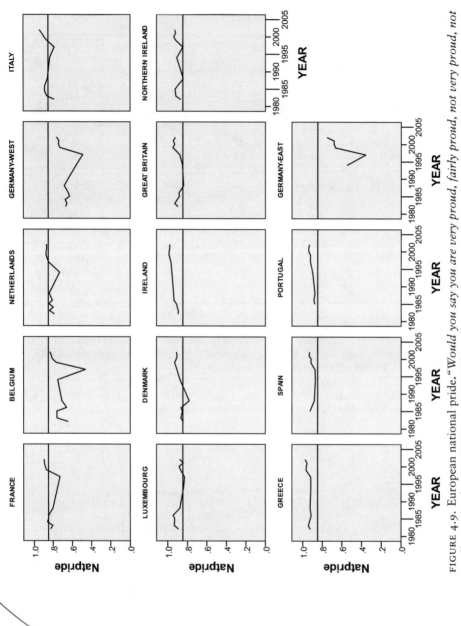

FIGURE 4.9. European national pride. "Would you say you are very proud, fairly proud, not very proud, not at all proud to be (NATIONALITY)?" Chart shows proportion who say that they are 'fairly' or 'very' proud. *Source:* The Mannheim Eurobarometer Trend File 1970–2002.

TABLE 4.5. *European National Pride*

	1982	1994	2000	2007	Net change 1994–2007	Year	Sig
Portugal		90	94	86	−4	0.002	N/s
Northern Ireland	87	91	94	89	−2	0.001	N/s
Spain		87	91	85	−2	0.000	N/s
Ireland	90	96	99	96	0	0.004	***
Italy	79	83	89	84	1	0.001	N/s
Denmark	84	88	91	90	2	0.004	**
Great Britain	90	85	93	89	4	0.001	N/s
Greece	92	92	96	97	5	0.002	**
Luxembourg	89	84	89	90	6	−0.002	N/s
Belgium	64	75	81	85	10	0.005	N/s
Germany – East		55	68	68	13	0.021	N/s
France	83	75	88	89	14	0.002	N/s
Netherlands	79	73	87	87	14	0.003	*
Germany – West	67	56	74	72	16	0.003	N/s
TOTAL	82	81	88	86	6	0.002	*

Note: "*Would you say you are very proud, fairly proud, not very proud, not at all proud to be (NATIONALITY)?*" Proportion who say that they are 'fairly' or 'very' proud. OLS regression analysis was used to monitor the effects of time (the survey year) on trust in political parties, generating the unstandardized beta coefficient and its significance. Selected years presented. For the full annual trends, see Figure 4.7.

* = >.05 ** = >.01 *** = >.001

Source: The Mannheim Eurobarometer Trend File 1970–2002; Eurobarometer surveys 2002–2007 downloaded from Gesis ZACAT.

that most European societies display consistently high levels of national pride, with eight out of ten Europeans reporting that they are very or fairly proud of their country. The most notable exception is East and West Germany, a pattern that can perhaps best be accounted for by cultural awareness of the particular historical experience of Germany's role in World War II. Elsewhere national pride remains strong and stable even in societies such as Italy where we have observed little public faith in political institutions or satisfaction with democracy. Unlike the previous tables, no European societies saw a significant drop in national pride during these years.

CONCLUSIONS AND DISCUSSION

Numerous commentators assume that support for the political system has gradually weakened in many established democracies, generating widespread public and scholarly concern about the rise of public disaffection (Torcal and Montero), mistrust of government (Dogan), or 'dissatisfied democrats' (Pharr and Putnam).[43] This chapter has sought to describe time-series survey evidence about public opinion within established democracies. Based on the analysis, this chapter arrives at an interpretation that challenges the over-simple views of an inevitable downward spiral of public disenchantment and steadily growing hostility toward government actors, institutions, and feelings of attachment to the nation-state. The evidence reinforces the conclusion that it is essential to distinguish trends in public attitudes that operate at different levels, rather than treating 'political support' as though it is all of one piece. Careful attention to the precise timing and breadth of any trends is also critical for an accurate diagnosis of developments.

The most diffuse level concerns the most fundamental orientations toward the nation-state, exemplified by deep-rooted feelings of national pride and national identity. Membership in the European Union might be expected to have eroded these attachments, generating more cosmopolitan attitudes as Europeans are increasingly bound together through ties of trans-border communication flows, labor force mobility, and trade.[44] Nevertheless, the evidence confirms that nationalism remains strong and relatively stable, even among West European societies that are long-standing members of the EU.[45] Trust in political institutions such as national governments, parliaments, and parties shows systematic and persistent contrasts among established democracies in Western Europe and the United States. Overall fluctuations over time usually prove far more common than straightforward linear or uniform downward trends. The conclusions lend further confirmation to Levi and Stoker's observation: "despite all the verbiage decrying the decline in trust, there is little actual evidence of a long-term decline, either in the United States or in Western Europe across the board."[46] Contrasts are also evident in public attitudes toward different branches of government within each country; for example, the United States has seen a long-term significant erosion of support for the legislature, but this has not affected public support for the Supreme Court or the Executive. Persistent differences in institutional trust can also be observed among relatively similar nations, such as between Italy and Spain, or Germany and France. A few European countries have experienced growing trust in state institutions, while a few have seen the reverse situation. Perhaps most important, in Europe diffuse support for the nation-state remains strong and stable, and satisfaction with the performance of democracy has usually strengthened over time, not weakened.

The conventional wisdom assumes that public support for government has eroded significantly and consistently over time in established democracies. If symptoms of trendless fluctuations are evident in recent decades in Western countries, however, this suggests the need to revise the standard interpretation. The complexity observed in this chapter calls for a diagnosis that can account for the dynamic fluctuations and the persistent cross-national variations in political support. Before examining these explanations, however, it is important to cast the net wider by comparing many other countries. Even though it often remains more difficult to explore time-series trends elsewhere, contemporary contrasts in systems support can be compared among rich and poor nations, as well as among many democratic and autocratic regimes worldwide.

5

Comparing Political Support around the World

The previous chapter established trends in public opinion in Western Europe and the United States – all affluent post-industrial societies, long-standing liberal democracies, and stable states. Instead of a tidal wave of growing political disaffection, the evidence demonstrates fluctuating support for the nation-state, its agencies, and its actors. Some enduring contrasts in public opinion persist for decades, such as those distinguishing confidence in government in Norway and Italy, Britain and France, or the Netherlands and Belgium, maintaining cultural diversity among European nations.[1] European satisfaction with the performance of democracy fluctuates over time, gradually moving upward during the last thirty-five years. Even in the United States – where the loudest alarm bells can be heard about a supposed rising tide of political cynicism and voter anger – in fact, American support for government has both risen and fallen periodically, and public confidence varies among the major branches of the federal government. The diagnosis suggests that much of the conventional prognosis turns out to be mistaken. This diagnosis does not imply that democracy has a clean bill of health. There remains genuine cause for concern in the disparities observed between public expectations and evaluations of how democracy works in practice. The next part of the book analyzes how far size and distribution of the democratic deficit can be explained by cultural shifts among citizens, by processes of political communications, and by the actual performance of democratic governance.

Yet post-industrial societies in Western Europe and the United States are all stable states and wealthy economies where the culture of liberal democracy has deep-seated roots that have grown over centuries, where any substantial deficit is unlikely to destabilize the regime. At the same time, as explored in the final section of the book, fluctuations in support may still have important consequences. The democratic deficit may tie policy makers' hands.[2] Deeply unpopular governments may fall through periodic election upsets, where prime ministers are replaced by rival political leaders. Presidents who have fallen

out of favor can face demands for impeachment. Pervasive public dissatisfaction with how successive governments work can also catalyze support for
constitutional reform movements, spurring demands for strengthening public
participation and government accountability.[3] Enduring dissatisfaction with
government is widely believed to fuel contentious politics, exemplified by violent acts of rebellion and sporadic outbreaks of street protest. Periods when
confidence in government sharply plummets should indeed raise red flags when
this occurs in particular countries. For all these reasons, many observers have
expressed mounting anxiety about these issues.[4]

Nevertheless, even with the worst-case scenario, the institutional inertia of
long-standing democracies makes them highly unlikely to experience a major
legitimacy crisis, far less serious threats of regime change or state failure, due
to any public disaffection. In Italy, for example, as observed in the previous
chapter, the majority of the public has persistently lacked confidence in public
sector institutions and satisfaction with democracy, a pattern that can be traced
back half a century to *The Civic Culture* survey in the late 1950s.[5] In the 2008
Eurobarometer, remarkably few Italians said that they tended to trust the
national government (15%), the parliament (16%), or political parties (13%).
It remains to be determined, however, whether this pattern is an underlying
cause or a consequence of the polity. Over the years, Italian politics has been
characterized by numerous tensions, exemplified by outbreaks of contentious
politics and episodic street protests by students and workers, the disintegration
of the once-predominant Christian Democrats and the emergence of radical
nationalist parties, and the repeated occurrence of corruption scandals in the
public sector. These tensions are believed to have catalyzed major reforms to
the electoral system and the emergence of what some have seen as the 'Second
Republic.'[6] But the Italian state has not collapsed.

The same is not necessarily true elsewhere. In regimes classified as electoral autocracies or electoral democracies, which have not yet fully consolidated the transition from absolute autocracy, a serious and enduring lack
of democratic legitimacy can be expected to have more serious consequences
for political stability. Huntington emphasizes that previous historical waves of
democratization during the twentieth century have been followed by periods of
widespread reversal.[7] There are numerous cases – such as in Kenya, Thailand,
Honduras, Bangladesh, or Fiji – where regular democratic processes have been
undermined by inconclusive or disputed election results, deep-rooted partisan
strife and factional violence, outbreaks of major political scandals, and coups
d'état by opposition forces or the military.[8] Regimes have proved relatively
short-lived in some other cases; for example, many Latin American constitutions have been frequently overhauled or amended.[9] Moreover, in exceptional
cases the most severe legitimacy crises have catalyzed state failure; in late-
twentieth century Africa, in particular, rapacious and predatory rulers, deep-
rooted communal violence, civil wars and conflict, and endemic poverty have
fueled insurgency movements that have challenged the authority and power
of the central government and sometimes the common boundaries of the

nation-state.[10] Some fear that the sluggish progress in the growth of liberal democracies during the early twenty-first century – and some major reversals in countries such as Russia, Venezuela, and Thailand – has been accompanied by growing weariness or ennui among the general public with this form of governance, by a wave of nostalgia supporting strong-man populist autocracy, or by a popular backlash against democracy promotion.[11]

This chapter therefore seeks to expand the country coverage worldwide to understand global public opinion. Again for an accurate diagnosis the survey evidence needs to be described and interpreted by paying close attention to *where, when,* and *what* has changed. If system support is relatively low or steadily eroding in many countries worldwide or in states sharing similar characteristics in their type of regime, levels of economic development, or regional cultures, these patterns would suggest searching for generic causes. On the other hand, specific cases that are outliers to global patterns also help to isolate particular causes. The timing of any fluctuations in system support is also particularly worthy of attention, with case studies of regime change and transitions from autocracy providing important natural 'before' and 'after' experiments. The comparisons across multiple indicators of system support help to determine if any changes have occurred at more specific levels (representing the normal ups and downs in political fortunes experienced by parties and political leaders) or whether any developments have affected more diffuse levels of system support, for example, if strong feelings of national identity have been eroded in many societies by processes of globalization. This mapping cannot determine causal patterns by itself, but description provides the essential foundation for theory building, generating plausible analytical propositions that can be analyzed in subsequent chapters, grounding our understanding in real-world conditions and places.

This chapter uses data derived from the fifth wave of the World Values Survey, with fieldwork conducted from 2005–7 in more than fifty countries, to map the broadest cross-national patterns under a wide range of political conditions. This allows us to replicate and update previous studies, to establish *where* system support is strongest. The seminal global comparison by Hans-Dieter Klingemann, conducted based on survey data from the 1990s, first documented the significant number of 'dissatisfied democrats' around the world. Klingemann found no major decline in support for democracy in the abstract, although citizens in established and younger democracies expressed considerable dissatisfaction with the performance of their regimes.[12] Accordingly, this chapter can see whether this phenomenon remains evident roughly a decade later. For comparison with the trends already observed in established democracies in Western Europe and the United States, five dimensions of systems support are examined, ranging from specific to diffuse levels, focusing upon (1) public trust and confidence in regime institutions; (2) evaluations of democratic performance; (3) endorsement of regime principles, including attitudes toward democratic political systems and the rejection of autocratic alternatives; (4) support for democratic values; and also, at the most diffuse level,

(5) orientations toward the nation-state, including feelings of national identity and pride.[13] In recent decades, the study of public opinion has gone global.[14] The fifth wave of the World Values Survey includes states differing substantially in their historical traditions, religious cultures, physical and population size, degree of globalization, and levels of economic development. The analysis in this chapter focuses upon comparing public opinion under different types of contemporary regimes. Countries are classified based on the regime typology and classification outlined earlier in Table 3.3 including a range of seventeen *older liberal democracies* (such as Canada, Italy, and Japan), nineteen *younger liberal democracies* (e.g., Brazil, Bulgaria, and Mali), nine *electoral democracies* with more limited political rights and civil liberties (exemplified by Burkina Faso, Colombia, and Morocco), and seven *autocracies* (including China, Iran, and Russia).[15]

The diagnosis of the descriptive evidence leads us toward three principal findings. First, not surprisingly, older liberal democracies that have experienced this form of governance over many decades, or even centuries, have developed slightly stronger democratic cultures by many indices, whether measured by satisfaction with democracy, endorsement of democratic attitudes, or rejection of autocracy. Second, the evidence also demonstrates that not all forms of system support fall into this pattern; autocracies display the strongest levels of institutional confidence and feelings of nationalism. Last, despite these contrasts, in general the variance across indices of system support is greatest among countries *within* each regime category rather than among types of regimes. Today, public endorsement of democratic attitudes and values is almost universal, even in repressive regimes. This evidence therefore suggests that the process of democratization, and the contemporary type of regime, is only part of any comprehensive explanation of contemporary patterns of system support around the world.

GLOBAL PATTERNS OF SYSTEM SUPPORT

Confidence in Regime Institutions

As observed earlier, at the more specific level, the issue of declining public confidence in the core institutions of representative democracy, including parliaments, political parties, and governments, has attracted widespread concern in Western Europe and the United States.[16] Some of the angst is exaggerated in popular commentary; the evidence presented earlier showed trendless volatility in institutional confidence in most West European states. Admittedly, a few of these countries have indeed experienced a loss of public confidence in certain state institutions during the last decade, notably in parliaments, but other societies have witnessed the reverse. Confidence in public sector institutions, however, is arguably far more critical for regime stability elsewhere in the world, especially in electoral democracies that have recently transitioned from repressive dictatorships or one-party states, as well as in deeply divided societies that have experienced deep-rooted conflict, such as in Iraq, Sudan, the Democratic Republic of the Congo (DRC), or Afghanistan. These issues are also important for poor developing states with minimal resources to deliver basic public services, such as clean water, health care, and schooling. For example, Mali and Burkina Faso hold multiparty competitive elections that meet international standards, but nevertheless the public sector remains poorly institutionalized. Prospects for democratic consolidation would seem poor in these countries if the public expresses minimal faith in the core representative institutions, if ministers and civil servants are widely regarded as deeply corrupt and self-serving, and if the legitimacy and authority of the central government is widely challenged.

To compare global patterns, an institutional confidence scale was constructed from the fifth wave of the WVS. The composite scale measured attitudes toward seven types of public sector organizations, including political parties, the national government, the national parliament, the civil service, the courts, the police, and the armed forces. The factor analysis presented in Chapter 3 demonstrated that responses to all these items were strongly intercorrelated, meaning that people who trusted parties or parliaments, for example, often usually also trusted governments and the civil service. When the pooled sample was broken down further by the type of regime and the factor analysis run separately for each, the public living in the older liberal democracies distinguished between the institutions closely associated with representative government (including parties, parliaments, the government, and the civil service) and those institutions closely associated with maintaining security, rule of law, and social order (the armed forces, the police, and the courts). Elsewhere in the world, however, no such dimensions emerged from the factor analysis, suggesting that the scale based on aggregating confidence in all seven types of public sector institutions is the most appropriate one for comparison across all societies. The composite institutional confidence scale was constructed and then standardized to 100 points for ease of comparisons across all indices.

Table 5.1 describes the distribution of the institutional confidence scale within each type of contemporary regime, in descending rank order by nation, without any prior controls. Overall, the comparison demonstrates that autocracies displayed significantly higher institutional confidence than all other types of regimes, although it is also striking that considerable variance among countries exists *within* each category. Among the older liberal democracies, for example, an 11- to 12-point gap separates the positive attitudes toward public sector institutions in Finland and Norway compared with the situation in France and the Netherlands. More substantial contrasts of 20 points or more are displayed among the publics living in the younger liberal democracies, as exemplified by the confident sentiments recorded in India, Mali, and Ghana compared with far greater skepticism expressed in Slovenia, Serbia, and Argentina. Similar substantial gaps separated different electoral democracies and autocracies, as well; for example, overwhelming levels of confidence in public sector institutions were expressed in Vietnam and China, compared with relatively weak

TABLE 5.1. *Institutional Confidence by Regime and Nation, 2005–2007*

Older liberal democracies		Younger liberal democracies		Electoral democracies		Autocracies	
Finland	69.2	India	71.9	Jordan	77.9	Vietnam	91.1
Norway	67.1	Mali	70.6	Malaysia	72.5	China	80.2
Cyprus	66.9	Ghana	68.9	Turkey	69.4	Iran	62.5
Switzerland	66.1	South Africa	66.3	Morocco	64.1	Thailand	61.1
Sweden	64.6	Indonesia	63.1	Burkina Faso	60.8	Russia	56.9
United States	63.9	Korea, South	59.4	Zambia	60.6		
Canada	63.9	Uruguay	57.5	Colombia	55.6		
Australia	62.7	Brazil	57.2	Ethiopia	54.4		
United Kingdom	61.9	Bulgaria	56.0	Moldova	49.9		
New Zealand	61.2	Chile	55.8				
Spain	60.9	Mexico	54.0				
Japan	60.1	Romania	53.8				
Italy	59.2	Trinidad &	53.3				
Germany	59.0	Tobago					
France	57.5	Ukraine	53.2				
Netherlands	56.0	Taiwan	52.8				
		Poland	52.7				
		Slovenia	51.5				
		Serbia	51.2				
		Argentina	46.0				
Mean	62.0		57.9		62.8		70.3

Notes: All indicators are standardized to 100-point scales, for ease of comparison, and derived from the fifth wave of the WVS. The index includes confidence in seven public sector institutions (parliament, political parties, the national government, the civil service, justice, police, and the military). The regime typology and classification of nations is described in Chapter 3. For more details, see Technical Appendix A.

Source: World Values Survey 2005–2007.

support in Thailand and Russia. In general, there is no support from this evidence for the contention that liberal democracies gradually accumulate a much stronger and deeper reservoir of confidence toward public sector institutions, such as parliaments, governments, and parties. Instead, levels of institutional confidence proved to be remarkably similar in many older and younger liberal democracies, for example, if we compare Switzerland and South Africa, or if we look at contrasts between the United States and Indonesia.

Evaluations of Democratic Performance

How do people evaluate the democratic performance of their own government? This represents a more diffuse level of support that is arguably more important as an indicator; people can express increasingly skeptical attitudes toward parliamentary representatives, political parties, and government leaders, but in competitive democratic states, regular elections provide periodic opportunities to 'throw the rascals out,' providing a release valve for any dis-affection. If the public loses faith in the quality of their democracy, however, this can have potentially far more significant consequences for regime stabil-ity. The 'regime' represents the overall constitutional arrangements and rules of the game governing any state, where the legislative, judicial, and executive branches of central government are the main components. As discussed earlier, the Eurobarometer surveys of EU member states regularly gauge satisfaction with the performance of democracy (see Chapter 4), and similar measures are carried elsewhere in the International Social Survey Program and the Global Barometers. The results have been widely analyzed in the research literature, with studies analyzing the impact of institutional design, indices of good gov-ernance, the policy performance, and the legacy of regime histories on public satisfaction with democracy.[17] Nevertheless, the precise meaning of the stan-dard survey measure of democratic satisfaction remains ambiguous and open to interpretation. The standard survey question asks: *"On the whole, are you very satisfied, fairly satisfied, not very satisfied, or not at all satisfied with the way democracy works in your country?"* The question may indeed cap-ture public assessments of democratic practices and performance (including the emphasis on 'the way democracy *works* in your country'). Responses to the standard question, however, have also been seen as endorsing normative approval about the general legitimacy of democratic principles ('are you sat-isfied with democracy'?).[18] Using an alternative phrasing, the fifth wave WVS asks the following question: *"And how democratically is this country being governed today? Again using a scale from 1 to 10, where 1 means that it is 'not at all democratic' and 10 means that it is 'completely democratic,' what posi-tion would you choose?"* The way this question emphasizes evaluations of how democratically each country is being *governed* makes it more suitable than the standard question to test public evaluations of the perceived democratic perfor-mance of regimes in each country.[19] The use of the 10-point scale also provides respondents with a more subtle range of choices than the standard question's 4-point scale. Moreover, evaluations of democratic performance using the WVS item are strongly correlated at the national level with other WVS survey items asking respondents to evaluate respect for human rights in their own country ($R = 0.78$, $p > .000$) and to express confidence in government ($R = .51$, $p > .000$). This general pattern increases confidence that the WVS democratic eval-uation measure taps into how people regard the workings of their own political system more generally. The democratic performance scale was standardized to 100 points, for comparison with other indices of systems support.

The comparison presented in Table 5.2 demonstrates that citizens living in the older liberal democracies expressed the most positive assessments of how democratically their own country was being governed. At the same time, the comparisons highlighted the wide range of responses among these countries, with Scandinavians, in particular, proving exceptionally happy with the demo-cratic performance of their own states, in marked contrast to far lower levels of satisfaction expressed in the UK, the United States, and Italy. The ranking

TABLE 5.2. *Satisfaction with Democratic Performance by Regime and Nation,*
2005–2007

Older liberal democracies		Younger liberal democracies		Electoral democracies		Autocracies	
Norway	81.3	Ghana	84.8	Jordan	28.2	Vietnam	79.5
Switzerland	76.2	Uruguay	77.3	Malaysia	70.0	Thailand	70.4
Sweden	75.1	South Africa	73.5	Zambia	67.1	China	67.4
Spain	74.2	Mali	70.2	Colombia	62.7	Iran	52.0
Finland	74.0	Chile	69.8	Turkey	59.2	Russia	43.7
Germany	72.1	Argentina	69.7	Burkina Faso	56.8		
Australia	71.4	Taiwan	69.2	Moldova	50.9		
Canada	70.7	Mexico	65.7	Morocco	49.9		
Japan	68.6	India	65.3	Ethiopia	42.1		
France	65.7	Indonesia	65.2				
Cyprus	64.9	Korea, South	64.3				
Netherlands	64.8	Brazil	61.9				
United Kingdom	64.1	Trinidad &	61.1				
United States	63.1	Tobago					
Italy	57.9	Slovenia	58.3				
		Romania	58.1				
		Poland	57.2				
		Andorra	53.7				
		Serbia	51.8				
		Bulgaria	43.3				
		Ukraine	42.3				
Mean	69.1		63.2		59.6		62.6

Notes: All indicators are standardized to 100-point scales, for ease of comparison, and derived
from the fifth wave of the WVS. The index measures evaluations of the performance of democracy
in each country. The regime typology and classification of nations is described in Chapter 3. For
more details, see Technical Appendix A.
Source: World Values Survey 2005–2007.

of European countries on this WVS index lends further confirmation to the
robustness of similar patterns observed earlier in the Eurobarometer surveys
(see Table 4.4). Even stronger contrasts were evident among the younger liberal democracies; the post-communist societies in particular, namely, Ukraine,
Bulgaria, and Serbia, proved far more critical about how their own democracy
works compared with the more favorable evaluations expressed in Ghana,
Uruguay, and South Africa.[20] Ethiopians, Moroccans, Russians, and Iranians
also rated their own governments extremely poorly by democratic standards,
judgments in accordance with the evaluative reports of independent observers
and expert judgments provided annually by the Freedom House and Polity IV
indices.

At the same time, certain major contrasts can be observed between the negative assessments of the regimes in Jordan, Vietnam, and China provided by

Freedom House and Polity IV independent experts, and the relatively satisfied public reactions observed in these cases. These disparities raise important
questions about the reliability and interpretation of the survey data and what
people in these countries understand by the notion of democratic governance.
Democracy is a complex and abstract concept, open to several alternative
interpretations; Chapter 7 explores how citizens understand the meaning of
this idea, particularly in closed autocracies lacking experience of this form
of governance, to establish whether public judgments are based on informed
knowledge.

Attitudes toward Democratic Governance and Autocratic Rule

The concept of 'attitudes' refers to approval or disapproval of certain types
of regime principles and ideals, such as whether governments derive legitimate
authority from the ballot box, from spiritual authority, or from monarchical
descent. Here there is an important distinction to be drawn between values,
or more abstract priorities and societal goals, and more specific attitudinal
statements; hence, for example, people can agree that a high priority should
be placed on democracy, as the most desirable goal or value, but there is still
room for legitimate debate about which institutional arrangements are most
likely to maximize opportunities for political participation and competition,
and hence differing attitudes toward alternative types of electoral systems or
the appropriate division of powers between the executive and legislature.

Surveys have sought to tap public attitudes toward democratic principles
and autocratic forms of governance in several ways.[21] Perhaps the most common approach has relied upon questions that ask the public to express their
direct or overt preferences for democratic rule as a normative ideal, using the
'd' word but without providing a more specific context, concrete principles, or
further elaboration of its meaning. For example, surveys have typically asked
people whether they approve of democracy as the 'best form of government,'
whether democracy is 'preferable to any other form of government,' whether it
is important 'to live in a country that is governed democratically,' or whether
they approve of having a democratic system 'as a good or suitable way of
governing their own country.' The direct or overt approach allows survey
respondents to reply using their own understanding of these terms rather than
imposing a common meaning. Similar methods have often been used to gauge
opinions toward other complex normative concepts, such as notions of equality, freedom, or human rights. At the same time, direct questions suffer from
certain important limits that put their face validity into question. It is therefore
important to explore the underlying meaning, as well as the depth, of any overt
support for democracy.[22]

Research based on the Global Barometer and the World Values Surveys during the 1990s reports that when asked directly, many citizens around the globe
expressed widespread aspirations for democratic principles as the best system
of government.[23] The 'Asian values' thesis propounded by Lee Kuan Yew,

former prime minister of Singapore, claimed that democracy was a Western cultural artifact.[24] Confucian values, the thesis stressed, emphasize community rather than individualism, duties rather than rights, and the importance of harmony, consensus, respect for authority, and an orderly society.[25] Despite these claims, orientations toward authority, as well as support for democracy, have been found to be remarkably similar in East Asia and Anglo-American societies.[26] Indeed Diamond notes that almost universal public approval for the abstract idea of democratic governance has been expressed even in some of the most rigid East Asian autocracies, including Communist China and Vietnam, where the public lacks any direct experience of living under this type of rule.[27] In the Middle East, as well, the region that lags furthest behind the rest of the world in transitions from autocracy, it might be expected that support for democratic ideals and values would be relatively scarce. Yet the 2006 Arab Barometer survey reported that eight or nine out of ten respondents in Jordan, Algeria, Morocco, and Kuwait believe that 'democracy is the best form of government' and that 'having a democratic system of government would be good for our country.'[28] As Diamond summarized the Global Barometer evidence: "Strikingly, the belief that democracy is (in principle at least) the best system is overwhelming and universal. While there is a slightly higher preference for the Western industrialized countries, in every region – even the former Soviet Union and the Muslim Middle East – an average of at least 80 percent of people polled say that democracy is best."[29]

The World Values survey monitors direct or overt attitudes toward democratic governance using the following question: "*I'm going to describe various types of political systems and ask what you think about each as a way of governing this country. For each one, would you say it is a very good, fairly good, fairly bad or very bad way of governing this country? Having a democratic political system.*" The comparison of survey results presented in Table 5.3 confirms that support for democracy as an ideal form of governance proves ubiquitous; almost nine out of ten respondents worldwide approved of democratic governance as a 'very' or 'fairly' good political system for their own country. Moreover positive attitudes were expressed among the public living under every type of regime, including in autocracies, and also in every cultural region, including in the Middle East and sub-Saharan Africa. Hence 97% of Swedes and Norwegians expressed overt approval of democratic values, but similar levels of endorsement were recorded in Indonesia, Ghana, Ethiopia, Morocco, China, and Vietnam. Far from being a Western phenomenon, as the 'Asian values' thesis argued, the WVS survey evidence indicates that overt approval of democratic governance is widespread and universal. This lends further confidence to the findings reported from previous studies based on the Global Barometer surveys in almost sixty countries.[30] Democratic states have not produced 'the end of history' and the inexorable triumph of liberal democracy, as optimists once hoped, although it seems as though the overt idea of democracy has remarkably broad appeal, even in unlikely places.[31]

TABLE 5.3. *Overt Approval of Democratic Attitudes by Regime and Nation,*
2005–2007

Older liberal democracies		Younger liberal democracies		Electoral democracies		Autocracies	
Sweden	97%	Andorra	97%	Ethiopia	98%	China	95%
Norway	97%	Indonesia	96%	Morocco	96%	Vietnam	94%
Italy	96%	Ghana	96%	Burkina Faso	95%	Thailand	93%
Germany	96%	Uruguay	93%	Jordan	95%	Iran	90%
Cyprus	96%	Taiwan	93%	Turkey	92%	Iraq	90%
Spain	95%	Argentina	92%	Zambia	92%	Russia	66%
Switzerland	95%	Romania	92%	Malaysia	92%		
Netherlands	94%	India	92%	Guatemala	87%		
New Zealand	92%	Trinidad &	90%	Moldova	83%		
Japan	90%	Tobago		Colombia	62%		
France	89%	South Africa	90%				
Canada	89%	Mali	88%				
United States	89%	Serbia	88%				
United Kingdom	89%	Brazil	88%				
Australia	88%	Slovenia	88%				
Finland	85%	Chile	87%				
		Bulgaria	87%				
		Poland	84%				
		Korea, South	83%				
		Ukraine	81%				
		Mexico	81%				
Mean	92%		89%		89%		88%

Notes: Q: "*I'm going to describe various types of political systems and ask what you think about*
each as a way of governing this country. For each one, would you say it is a very good, fairly good,
fairly bad or very bad way of governing this country? Having a democratic political system."
The table presents the proportion responding 'very' or 'fairly' good. The regime typology and
classification of nations is described in Chapter 3. For more details, see Technical Appendix A.
Source: World Values Survey 2005–2007.

The ubiquity of overt approval of democracy around the world, however,
also raises important questions about the measurement and interpretation of
these results. In particular Schedler and Sarsfield argue that the validity of direct
or overt measures of abstract support for democracy can be questioned due
to the potential problems of interviewer effects generating 'politically correct'
responses, as well as problems associated with the vague, shifting, and con-
troversial meaning associated with ideas of democracy.[32] Instead, they argue,
abstract measures should be compared with attitudes toward more specific,
concrete, and detailed procedures, rights, and institutions associated with this
form of governance. Testing this argument in the context of a Mexican survey,
they examined public approval of the specific principles of freedom of speech,

freedom of assembly, political equality, and tolerance of minority rights, without mentioning the term 'democracy' directly in these questions, to avoid cueing respondents. The study reported that Mexicans who expressed the strongest support for democracy also continue to manifest illiberal convictions concerning at least some specific principles, suggesting that Mexican attitudes lack coherence.

Moreover if overt approval of democratic governance is tapped, without considering alternatives or trade-off values, then the relative preferences for different forms of rule cannot be determined. Hence, support for democracy may be widely endorsed by Jordanians, the Chinese, or Moroccans, but it remains unclear how important this is to respondents compared with, for example, the desire to maintain social stability and order, the value of respecting traditional authorities, or the substantial risks of regime change. In the same way, if people are asked by pollsters whether they value health care and also whether they want lower taxes, then it is likely that both statements will be widely endorsed. If trade-off questions are used instead, so that people are asked whether they prefer more public spending on health care or more tax cuts, then this presents respondents with more realistic and complex choices that force them to prioritize options. A more effective way to explore whether democratic attitudes are robust and to measure more nuanced choices is to use trade-off items that ask citizens to express their preference for different types of democratic *and* autocratic regimes. This strategy has been widely used in countries that have experienced a recent watershed transition, notably in post-communist Europe, where surveys have commonly compared people's evaluation of the current against the previous regime.[33] This is a useful approach in the context of revolutionary upheaval or a watershed constitutional change involving a sharp break from the past regime, exemplified by the end of apartheid in South Africa, the reversion to civilian rule in Chile, or the fall of the Berlin Wall signaling a newly unified Germany. It is less appropriate, however, in countries where democratization has been a more evolutionary process involving a series of incremental linear reforms, or indeed for many states such as Russia, Pakistan, and Nigeria which have veered back and forth in their human rights record over the years. In the light of these considerations, the Global Barometer surveys used a trade-off question to monitor regime preferences, as follows: *"Which of the following statements do you agree with most? Democracy is preferable to any other kind of government. In certain situations, an authoritarian government can be preferable to a democratic one. It doesn't matter to people like me whether we have a democratic government or a non-democratic government."* The results of the analysis of responses in almost fifty countries confirmed widespread popular support for democratic rule in the abstract; majorities in forty-three out of forty-nine societies preferred democracy over any other kind of government. Most people also exercised a clear choice; few responded that the type of regime didn't matter.

For comparability, to see whether the results remain robust and consistent with other indicators, the World Values Survey monitored preferences

TABLE 5.4. *Endorsement of Democracy and Rejection of Autocracy by Regime and Nation, 2005–2007*

Older liberal democracies		Younger liberal democracies		Electoral democracies		Autocracies	
New Zealand	83.3	Andorra	78.3	Morocco	71.6	Iraq	70.5
Norway	83.0	Ghana	75.6	Zambia	71.0	China	67.5
Germany	82.2	Trinidad &	74.8	Ethiopia	68.7	Russia	67.1
Sweden	80.5	Tobago		Moldova	65.4	Iran	61.9
Canada	80.1	Uruguay	74.2	Colombia	64.0	Thailand	57.7
Italy	80.1	Slovenia	73.8	Burkina Faso	63.9	Vietnam	57.1
Switzerland	79.4	Argentina	73.7	Turkey	62.3		
Australia	79.4	Korea, South	73.1	Guatemala	62.1		
United Kingdom	78.4	South Africa	70.8	Jordan	58.2		
Japan	78.4	Chile	70.4	Malaysia	57.7		
United States	77.5	Serbia	70.0				
Netherlands	77.3	Poland	67.3				
France	76.3	Ukraine	66.7				
Spain	76.2	Taiwan	66.0				
Finland	75.2	Mexico	64.7				
Cyprus	69.2	Bulgaria	64.1				
		Romania	62.4				
		India	61.3				
		Indonesia	59.7				
		Brazil	59.1				
		Mali	57.5				
Mean	78.3		67.8		64.5		63.6

Notes: All indicators are standardized to 100-point scales, for ease of comparison, and derived from the fifth wave of the WVS. The index measures endorsement of democratic political systems and rejection of autocratic principles. The regime typology and classification of nations is described in Chapter 3. For more details, see Technical Appendix A.
Source: World Values Survey 2005–2007.

for democratic governance, military rule, rule by bureaucratic elites, and also strong-man leadership unchecked by parliament and elections. The standardized democratic-autocratic values scale is constructed by recoding these items to reflect the endorsement of democratic rule and the rejection of autocratic forms of governance, and then combining these responses and standardizing the resulting scale to 100 points. Table 5.4 shows the distribution of attitudes using this standardized index. The trade-off democracy-autocracy scale employed in the World Values Survey, where respondents express preferences for democracy and autocracy, generated a less overwhelming consensus than simply monitoring direct or overt approval of democracy. Nevertheless the results continue to confirm the widespread appeal of the idea of democracy as well as the public's widespread rejection of autocratic forms of government. Democratic attitudes and the rejection of autocracy proved strongest in older liberal democratic states, as might be expected, given their longer experience of this form of governance. But there was little difference in preferences among the other types of regimes.

Democratic Values

The public's preference or desire for democracy can be captured in several ways. The expression of democratic attitudes and the rejection of autocratic alternatives can be used, as discussed earlier, but by itself this is still essentially 'costless' and hence it remains difficult to estimate the weight that should be given to these responses. Thus although general approval of the idea of democratic governance and the rejection of autocracy appear remarkably widespread, it is unclear from this evidence whether democracy is regarded as vital and urgent to people's lives or whether it is seen as generally desirable but as less important than other more immediate priorities facing poorer developing societies, such as the need to improve economic growth, basic living standards, or domestic security.

In addition to attitudes toward democratic and autocratic types of regimes, therefore, we must also compare whether people value democracy. The concept of *'values'* refers to personal, societal, or global goals that are regarded as desirable, for example, concerning the importance of freedom and autonomy, of security and avoiding risk, of respecting traditional sources of authority, or of material gains in living standards.[34] Values can apply to the individual or to broader units such as the family and household, social group, the community and society, the nation-state, or even the world. Values can be understood as the normative benchmarks or standards of evaluation that can be used to judge how well actions, policies, and events meet desirable goals – for instance, where there is a trade-off, whether it is regarded as more important for governments to pursue economic growth or environmental protection, and whether societies should seek to reward entrepreneurial success or to share public goods more equitably among all members.

The value of democracy can be gauged from the World Values Survey 2005– 7 by the question: *"How important is it for you to live in a country that is governed democratically? On this scale where 1 means it is 'not at all important' and 10 means 'absolutely important' what position would you choose?"* This item is arguably superior to asking simply about approval of democratic attitudes and the rejection of autocracy, as it seeks to measure the depth or strength of any support. The results compared in Table 5.5 demonstrate that living in a democracy was almost universally regarded as important, although this was given slightly higher priority in the older liberal democracies with the most extensive historical experience of this form of rule. Democratic values were strongly endorsed by Scandinavian citizens, as well as by the Swiss, Germans, and Canadians, although strong preferences for living in a democracy were also expressed among citizens living in other types of regimes, such as in Ghana, Turkey, and Argentina, as well as in Ethiopia, Vietnam, and Jordan.

TABLE 5.5. *Democratic Aspirations by Regime and Nation, 2005–2007*

Older liberal democracies		Younger liberal democracies		Electoral democracies		Autocracies	
Sweden	9.5	Ghana	9.2	Jordan	9.4	Vietnam	9.2
Norway	9.3	Argentina	9.1	Ethiopia	9.2	China	8.5
Switzerland	9.3	Uruguay	8.9	Turkey	9.1	Thailand	8.2
Germany	9.2	Taiwan	8.9	Morocco	8.9	Iran	7.9
Australia	9.1	Andorra	8.9	Zambia	8.8	Russia	7.5
Cyprus	9.1	South Africa	8.7	Burkina Faso	8.0		
Canada	9.0	Mexico	8.7	Malaysia	7.9		
United States	8.8	Trinidad & Tobago	8.7	Colombia	7.9		
Italy	8.8	Poland	8.7	Moldova	7.9		
Spain	8.7	Korea, South	8.6				
Finland	8.7	Romania	8.6				
Netherlands	8.7	Indonesia	8.5				
United Kingdom	8.6	Chile	8.2				
Japan	8.5	Brazil	8.2				
France	8.5	Bulgaria	8.0				
		Ukraine	8.0				
		Slovenia	7.9				
		Mali	7.7				
		Serbia	7.5				
		India	7.1				
Mean	8.9		8.4		8.6		8.4

Notes: Democratic aspirations: V162. *"How important is it for you to live in a country that is governed democratically? On this scale where 1 means it is 'not at all important' and 10 means 'absolutely important' what position would you choose?"*

Source: World Values Survey 2005–2007.

Strength of Nationalism

The final dimension that can be compared concerns the strength of nationalism, operating at the most abstract or diffuse level of systems support. Enduring bonds to the nation reflect a sense of community within common territorial boundaries. National identities underpin the nation-state and its institutions exercising legitimate political authority within a given territory, although there are many multinational states and also stateless nations. Such feelings are believed to be important for binding together every nation-state, but they are thought to play a particularly important function by strengthening social cohesion and state legitimacy in multicultural communities, in deeply divided societies, and in fragile states emerging from long-lasting conflict.[35] Nationalism is a highly complex concept, with different dimensions, such as ties of physical land, religious faiths, historical traditions, and shared languages that remain difficult to gauge. One way to assess its strength is through WVS survey items measuring feelings of national pride as well as the willingness of citizens to

TABLE 5.6. *Nationalism by Regime and Nation, 2005–2007*

Older liberal democracies		Younger liberal democracies		Electoral democracies		Autocracies	
Finland	86.9	Ghana	96.3	Turkey	94.9	Vietnam	95.5
New Zealand	86.3	Mali	95.6	Burkina Faso	93.3	Thailand	94.8
Norway	86.1	Trinidad &	91.3	Jordan	92.7	Rwanda	94.6
United States	85.8	Tobago		Guatemala	90.4	Iran	87.2
Cyprus	85.6	Mexico	90.6	Malaysia	88.6	Iraq	83.1
Canada	85.5	India	90.4	Ethiopia	88.4	Russia	82.7
Australia	85.3	South Africa	87.0	Morocco	85.1	China	76.6
Sweden	83.4	Poland	86.8	Zambia	82.9		
United Kingdom	81.3	Indonesia	86.2	Moldova	69.7		
Spain	79.5	Slovenia	85.3				
Switzerland	77.7	Uruguay	85.1				
Italy	74.9	Argentina	82.6				
France	74.8	Chile	81.8				
Netherlands	71.4	Serbia	79.1				
Germany	64.1	Romania	77.9				
Japan	60.2	Bulgaria	76.5				
		Brazil	75.9				
		Korea, South	75.4				
		Andorra	73.6				
		Ukraine	73.3				
		Taiwan	69.9				
Mean	80.0		82.6		87.3		87.8

Notes: All indicators are standardized to 100-point scales, for ease of comparison, and derived from the fifth wave of the WVS. The nationalism scale combines items measuring willingness to fight for one's country in a war and feelings of national pride. The regime typology and classification of nations is described in Chapter 3. For more details, see Technical Appendix A. *Source:* World Values Survey 2005–2007.

defend their own country in case of war. The factor analysis developed in Chapter 3 showed that these items formed one attitudinal dimension. These items can therefore be combined into a standardized nationalism scale using a 100-point index.

The global comparison illustrated in Table 5.6 shows that feelings of nationalism were exceptionally weak in the special cases of Germany and Japan, which can be attributed to the historical legacy of World War II on their contemporary cultures. Compared by type of regime, nationalism was usually stronger in the electoral democracies and in autocracies than in older liberal democracies. Hence, nationalist sentiments proved particularly widespread in a range of emerging economies and developing societies, including in Ghana, Mali, Turkey, Burkina Faso, Vietnam, Thailand, and Rwanda. One of the most plausible explanations for these patterns concerns the impact of globalization on the most cosmopolitan societies with open borders, which is related to the control of the mass media and the manipulation of nationalism by autocratic regimes in closed societies. Elsewhere it has been established that nationalist identities are *weaker* in the most globalized societies, such as the Netherlands, Switzerland, and Sweden, which are characterized by dense networks of cosmopolitan communications with easy access to foreign television channels, as well as international communication networks.[36] Moreover, multilevel analysis demonstrated that national identities are especially weaker among news users in these cosmopolitan societies. As some hope, and others fear, denser and faster interconnections across territorial borders seem to gradually erode older allegiances and promote a more multicultural ethos. Media use is not the strongest factor in this process, but it is a significant contributory agency, interacting with direct experience of living in an increasingly globalized world.

CONCLUSIONS AND DISCUSSION

Therefore, the descriptive evidence presented in this chapter helps to dispel many pervasive myths about a systematic erosion of system support experienced by democratic states. This chapter leads to several major conclusions, with the evidence summarized in Table 5.7.

First, although perhaps not surprising, older liberal democracies that have experienced this form of governance over many decades, or even centuries, have slightly stronger democratic cultures, whether measured by satisfaction with democracy, endorsement of democratic attitudes, or rejection of autocracy (see Table 5.7). It is not possible to determine the causal direction of this relationship, however, on the basis of the cross-national comparisons taken at one point in time, and we suspect that reciprocal factors are probably at work. Ever since Almond and Verba, cultural theories have long argued that stronger endorsement of democratic values and attitudes among the mass public strengthens the capacity of democracies to consolidate, so that state institutions rest upon a broad foundation of public legitimacy. Hence in younger liberal democracies, where citizens are strongly committed to democratic values, elites seeking to challenge the authority of elected leaders and governments seeking to restrict human rights will face stronger constraints from public opinion, generating more stable regimes. Yet socialization theories also predict that citizens growing up in democratic states will gradually acquire habitual norms, cultural values, and political practices, learning from parents and siblings, teachers, neighbors, and work colleagues, and the media and local community leaders during the formative years of childhood, adolescence, and early adulthood. Hence, citizens are thought to acquire attitudes such as social tolerance, partisan orientations, and interpersonal trust, all of which strengthen processes of democratic governance.

Second, compared with other types of regimes, autocracies display stronger confidence in public sector agencies and also feelings of nationalism. In previous research this pattern has been attributed to globalization and cosmopolitan communications.[37] Repressive autocracies in parochial societies exercise

TABLE 5.7. *Summary of Systems Support Indices by Regime, 2005–2007*

	Institutional confidence (i)	Democratic performance (ii)	Democracy-autocracy scale (iii)	Democratic aspirations (iv)	Feelings of nationalism (v)	# (vi)
Older liberal democracies	61.9	69.0	73.3	89.1	80.0	17
Younger liberal democracies	57.9	63.2	67.8	84.1	82.6	19
Electoral democracies	62.8	59.6	64.4	85.5	87.3	9
Autocracies	70.3	62.6	63.6	83.7	87.8	7
TOTAL	61.5	6.44	70.1	85.8	83.2	52
Coefficient of association (sig)	.457**	.357	.407*	.658***	.395*	

Notes: All indicators are standardized to 100-point scales, for ease of comparison, and derived from the fifth wave of the WVS. (i) Includes confidence in seven public sector institutions (parliament, political parties, the national government, the civil service, justice, police, and the military). (ii) Evaluations of the performance of democracy in each country. (iii) Endorsement of democracy and rejection of autocratic principles. (iv) Importance of democracy scale. (v) The nationalism scale combines items measuring willingness to fight for one's country in a war and feelings of national pride. The regime typology and classification of nations is described in Chapter 3. (vi) = Number of nations. For more details, see Technical Appendix A. The coefficient of association (eta) and significance of the difference between regimes is calculated using ANOVA.

* = >.05 ** = >.01 *** = >.001.

Source: World Values Survey 2005–2007.

greater control over the mass media, facilitating one-sided messages and more positive framing of their governments. The manipulation of nationalist senti-ments is one mechanism such regimes can use to deter opposition threats.

Last, despite these patterns, in general the variance in political cultures is greater among countries within each regime category rather than among types of regimes, as exemplified by the marked contrasts evident between Russia and China, Uruguay and Ukraine, or Norway and Italy. Although democratic attitudes and values are commonly assumed to be deepest and most widespread in long-standing democratic states in Western Europe and North America, in fact the cross-national picture shows that democratic aspirations are almost universal today, irrespective of the type of regime governing the state. The longitudinal evidence during the third wave era needs to be analyzed further in the next chapter to explore the dynamics of system support over time. Less than a dozen countries are included across all waves of the World Values Survey but we can analyze these particular cases to see whether there is any indication of a significant and sustained erosion of confidence in government, satisfaction with democracy, or support for democratic values and attitudes, as many commentators fear.

6

Trends in Democratic Deficits

The previous chapter established cross-national patterns in system support, but it did not examine trends or compare the size and distribution of the democratic deficit under a wide range of political conditions. This chapter starts by establishing longitudinal analysis of selected case studies to monitor if and *when* any changes occurred. The pooled World Values Survey 1981–2007 contains time-series survey data for a more restricted subset of eleven nations included in all five waves of the survey conducted over twenty-five years. This includes five states (Spain, South Africa, Mexico, South Korea, and Argentina) that have experienced transitions from diverse types of autocratic rule and the rapid consolidation of democratic regimes during this era. Mexico, Argentina, South Korea, and South Africa are also emerging market economies, characterized by moderate levels of per capita GDP. The effects of democratization on public opinion are examined by examining trends 'before' and 'after' the year when regime changed in these particular case studies, exemplified by the fall of the Argentinean military junta in 1983, the collapse of South African apartheid in 1994, and the end of the PRI's predominance in the 2000 Mexican presidential elections. The number of cases under comparison is admittedly limited, but nonetheless the results of the analysis serve to confirm the picture already familiar; during the last quarter century, no significant erosion of system support was detected from the indices of composite institutional confidence (with the notable exception of declining public confidence in parliaments), attitudes toward democratic governance and rejection of autocracy, or feelings of nationalism. Instead, trendless fluctuations over time (suggesting explanations based on either actual or perceived performance) or a relatively stable pattern can be observed.

Building on this foundation, the second part of this chapter compares the size and distribution of democratic deficits among regimes and nations. This phenomenon is conceived as the tensions that arise from the imbalance between the public's demand for democracy (measured by strong adherence to democratic values and rejection of authoritarian alternatives) and the perceived supply of

democracy (monitored by public dissàtisfaction with the democratic performance of governments in each country). Scholars have conceptualized similar
disparities as the phenomenon of 'disaffected,' 'dissatisfied,' or 'disenchanted'
democrats.[1] Operationalizing the conceptual framework more precisely with
the empirical indicators already developed allows the distribution of democratic deficits to be compared among different types of contemporary regimes,
as well as within each global region. The analysis suggests that the older liberal
democracies display strong endorsement of the importance of this form of governance, but also relatively positive perceptions of how democracy works in
their own country. Younger liberal democracies are far more dispersed on these
dimensions, with the most congruence between aspirations and performance
displayed in cases such as Ghana, Uruguay, and South Africa, all countries that
independent observers emphasize have experienced rapid progress in democratization during the third wave era. By contrast, a far larger disparity between
expectations and performance is evident in the post-communist states. Many
puzzles remain and the conclusion speculates about some of the reasons for
these disparities, analyzed further in subsequent chapters, including the role of
changing cultural values, political coverage by the news media, and government
performance.

I: TRENDS OVER TIME IN SYSTEM SUPPORT

By itself, the cross-national evidence cannot determine whether any signs of
system support have gradually eroded over time, as commentators fear. For
this, the available longitudinal evidence from the pooled World Values Survey
needs to be examined, comparing the eleven countries included in all five
survey waves from 1981 to 2005. These countries cannot be treated as a
representative sample of democracies by any means. Nevertheless, they do
include some important cases of regime change and they reflect a variety of
cultural traditions, types of regime, and patterns of democratization. Figure 6.1
illustrates the process of democratization in these societies during the third wave
era, including some long-established democracies, such as Sweden, Britain, and
Japan where trends remain flat, and other states such as Spain, South Africa,
and South Korea, which made rapid progress in democratization during the
last quarter century.

  Most are rich nations but the comparison also includes three emerging
market economies with moderate levels of human development – Mexico,
Argentina, and South Africa. During the late twentieth century, economic
growth remained relatively flat in Mexico, Argentina, and South Africa,
although democracy made rapid strides following the restoration of constitutional rule in 1983 in Argentina, the end of apartheid in South Africa in
1994, and the demise of the PRI's long predominance in Mexico, following the
victory of President Vicente Fox in 2000. Today these three economies are classified as middle income, with average per capita GDP around $9,000–$10,000
in 2005, about one-third the level of the United States. The comparison also

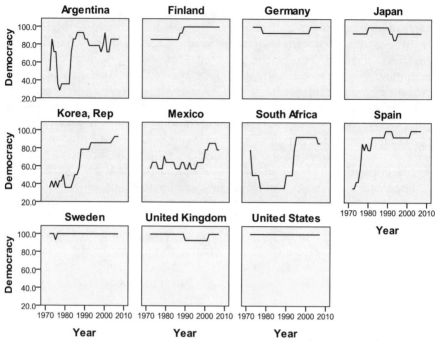

FIGURE 6.1. Changes in democracy during the third wave era, selected states. The selected societies include the eleven countries included in all five waves of the World Values Survey 1981–2007. The figure shows the annual rating based on Freedom House's classification of political rights and civil liberties in each society from 1972 to 2007, standardized to a 100-point liberal democracy scale. *Source*: Freedom House. *Freedom around the world*. www.freedomhouse.org.

includes one transitional case – South Korea – which has been transformed by rapid social, economic, and political change in recent decades. During the late twentieth century, the country shifted from an agrarian/industrial to a post-industrial service sector economy, and politically from autocracy to democracy. Today the population enjoys affluent and secure lifestyles; for example, average incomes for South Koreans roughly quadrupled during the last quarter century (measured by per capita GDP in constant dollars in purchasing power parity). Using each wave of the WVS for the eleven countries, with the results aggregated at the societal level, generated fifty-five nation-wave observations in total as the units of analysis.

Institutional Confidence

Figure 6.2 shows how the composite institutional confidence index, operationalized in the previous chapter, varies during the last twenty-five years. For

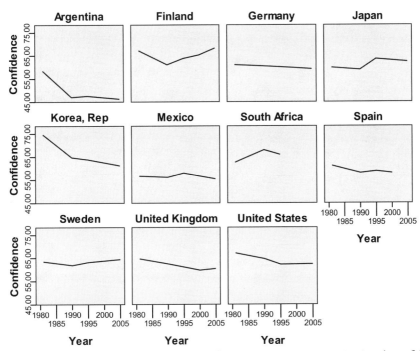

FIGURE 6.2. Trends in institutional confidence, 1981–2005. Institutional confidence scale (8) 1981–2005. V146–147: *"I am going to name a number of organizations. For each one, could you tell me how much confidence you have in them: is it a great deal of confidence (4), quite a lot of confidence (3), not very much confidence (2) or none at all (1)? (Read out and code one answer for each): The armed forces; The police; The courts; The government (in your nation's capital); Political parties; Parliament; The Civil service."* The standardized 100-point institutional confidence scale, where high represents most confidence, combines these items. The table describes the mean distribution by nation. For more detail about the survey items contained in each indicator, see the factor analysis in Table 3.2 and Technical Appendix A. Observations = 43. To test for the slope (beta) and statistical significance, the year was regressed on institutional confidence (b = −.127 N/s). *Source*: Pooled WVS 1981–2005.

comparison, Figure 6.3 focuses upon the trends in confidence in parliaments in these nations, since much of the concern emphasizes that the public has lost faith in legislatures.[2] Moreover, there may well be contrasts between trust in all public sector institutions, including the army and security forces, and those agencies most closely linked with representative democracy. There are only five time-points, so that any observations remain limited and it is not possible to establish the degree of annual flux in support. Nevertheless, the extended time period means it should be possible to detect any steady and consistent flows, especially any changes that occurred before or after the decisive period of regime change which occurred in Argentina (1983), South Korea (1987), South Africa (1993), and Mexico (2000). To test the direction and significance

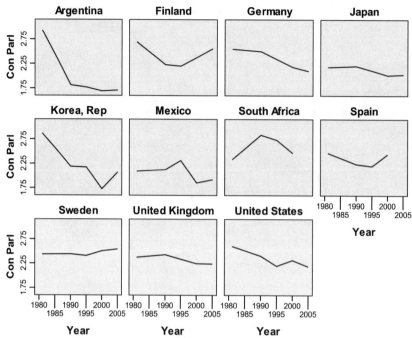

FIGURE 6.3. Trends in confidence in parliament, 1981–2005. Confidence in parliament, 1981–2005. *"I am going to name a number of organizations. For each one, could you tell me how much confidence you have in them: is it a great deal of confidence (4), quite a lot of confidence (3), not very much confidence (2) or none at all (1)? Parliament."* Observations = 50. To test for the slope (beta) and statistical significance, the year was regressed on institutional confidence (b = −.015, p = ∗∗∗). *Source*: Pooled WVS 1981–2005.

of any change over time more systematically, the year of the survey wave was regressed on political attitudes.

Among the younger liberal democracies, there are a few specific cases of decline across both indicators of institutional confidence, notably during the 1980s in Argentina and in South Korea. Constitutional rule was restored in Argentina in 1983; the presidency of Raúl Alfonsín saw the re-establishment of civilian command over the military and strengthened democratic institutions, although there were persistent economic problems in controlling hyperinflation. During this era, however, Argentinean institutional confidence fell sharply before stabilizing at a lower level. The Sixth Republic of South Korea began in 1987 with democratic elections that marked the transfer of power from the authoritarian President Chun Doo-hwan; despite this, and growing economic prosperity prior to the Asian economic crisis of 1997, confidence in public sector institutions gradually slipped among Koreans, and confidence in the National Assembly fell sharply. In South Africa, however, rising institutional confidence peaked in both indicators during the first post-apartheid election and then fell back (especially for the parliament) after the initial honeymoon period.

Overall, confirming our earlier observations, however, there is no support from the available time-series evidence for the argument that institutional confidence progressively eroded – or indeed strengthened significantly – during the third wave era among the democracies under comparison.[3] Despite the radical regime changes that have occurred during recent decades – including the restoration of civilian rule in Argentina, the end of apartheid in South Africa, and the breakdown of the hegemony of the ruling party in Mexico – any historical processes of cultural change in citizens' orientations toward state institutions appear to operate on a far longer time-scale.

In the remaining countries, the composite institutional confidence scale generally shows a fairly stable pattern from the start to the end of the series; the regression coefficient proved insignificant. The trends in confidence in parliament, however, do display a significant fall over time. The WVS evidence confirms the erosion in public confidence in the U.S. Congress that we have already observed from the GSS data, and a similar decline occurred in Germany, Argentina, and South Korea. Despite the limited number of observations (50 year-country units), the erosion of confidence in parliament since 1981 in the eleven countries under comparison proved statistically significant. The diagnosis, therefore, suggests that any loss of institutional confidence is more clearly related to the legislative body rather than to all public sector institutions, and this finding needs to be examined further in subsequent chapters to determine the underlying reasons.[4]

Endorsement of Democratic Attitudes

For comparison, trends in the endorsement of democratic values and the rejection of autocracy scale can also be compared from 1995 to 2005 across these eleven countries, using the same scale developed in Chapter 5. The available data provide a limited range of observations but nevertheless the results in Figure 6.4 show a fairly flat pattern; the regression of year of the survey on the democratic values index proved insignificant. Only in South Korea does there appear to be a slight erosion of support for democratic attitudes during this decade, but this trend is not evident elsewhere.

Nationalism

What about feelings of nationalism since the early 1980s? Using the WVS measure discussed earlier, Figure 6.5 shows either trendless fluctuations or a fairly stable level of nationalist orientations across most of the eleven countries under comparison. Nationalist feelings were persistently low in Germany and Japan, probably reflecting the enduring legacy of World War II, in comparison to all the other countries. The major changes in the series involved South Korea,

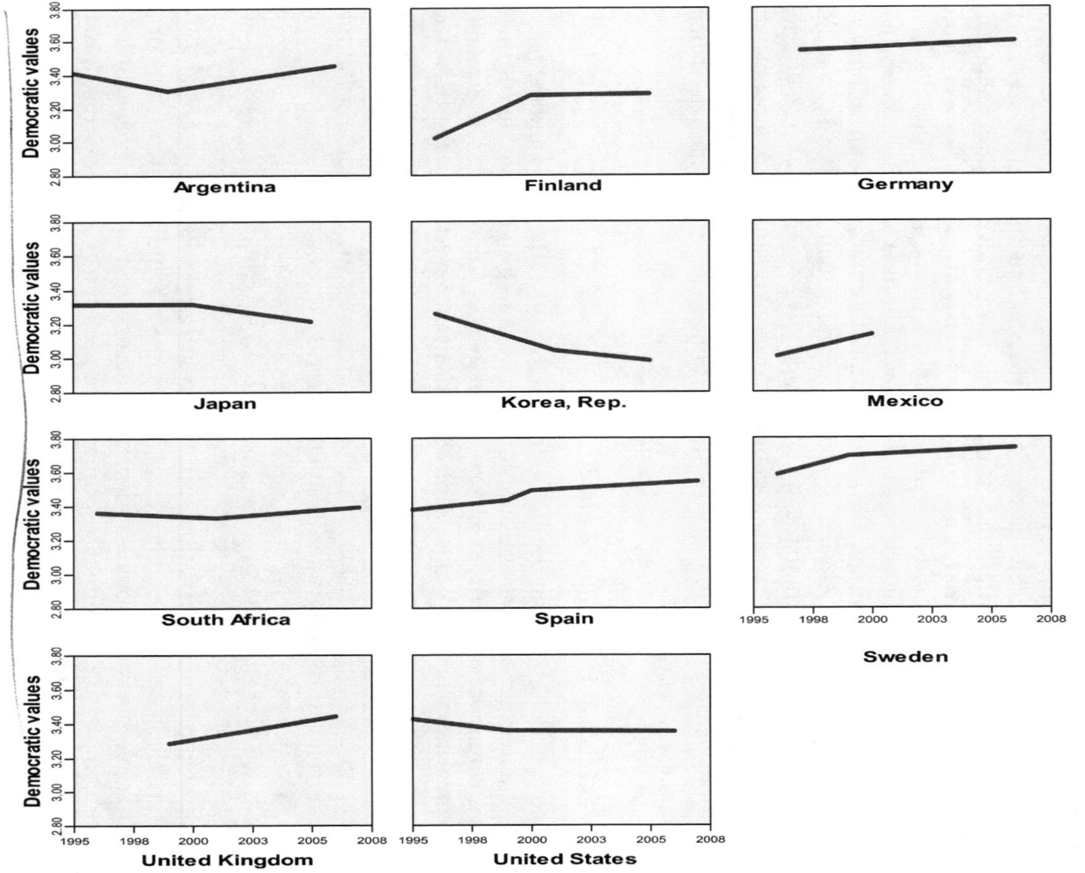

FIGURE 6.4. Trends in support for democratic values, 1981–2005. *Source:* Pooled WVS 1981–2005.

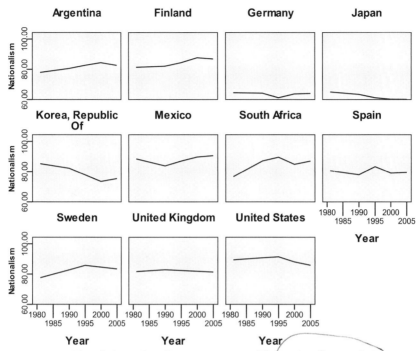

FIGURE 6.5. Trends in nationalism, 1981–2005. The nationalism scale is constructed from two items: (V75) Willingness to fight for one's country in a war, and (V209) Feelings of national pride. These items are summed and standardized to a 100-point scale. To test for the slope (beta) and statistical significance, the year was regressed on the nationalism scale (b = .071 N/s). *Source*: Pooled WVS 1981–2005.

where nationalism fell over the years, whereas by contrast the indicator became more positive in South Africa, peaking around the time of the end of apartheid and the first fully democratic elections in the early 1990s. Again there are a limited number of observations but the regression coefficient proved weak and insignificant.

Nationalism is also expected to weaken progressively under the forces of globalization and the process of growing regional integration. Hence in the European Union the experience of growing economic and political integration within the EU, with people working, living, studying, and traveling across the borders in different member states, has dissolved traditional geographic national barriers. European identities are also expected to have gradually strengthened most clearly among citizens of the founding states that have lived under European institutions for a long time, such as Italy, France, and Germany.[5] Despite the dramatic process of regional unification and the single market which have deepened and widened the European Union, in fact the empirical evidence presented here provides no support for the claim that nationalism has progressively weakened during the last quarter century among the EU member states under comparison (Germany, Spain, the UK, or Sweden).

II: ESTIMATING THE SIZE AND DISTRIBUTION
OF THE DEMOCRATIC DEFICIT

The evidence considered so far challenges any over-simple claims about a uniform erosion of systems support experienced across older liberal democracies in recent decades – or indeed more widely around the world. Ideas of a democratic crisis should be rejected as an oversimplification of more complex developments. Based on this foundation, we can focus more narrowly on the evidence for distribution and size of any democratic deficit. Using the World Values Survey 2005, the relationship between satisfaction with democratic performance and adherence to democratic values can be examined. Regimes that fail to meet public expectations over long periods of time can lose their legitimacy, risking instability. The dangers exist for all regimes but it is thought to be particularly risky for younger democracies, which have not yet developed a deep reservoir of mass support and where government authority depends to a large degree upon voluntary compliance, such as in the willingness of citizens to pay taxes and obey the law.

As discussed in the previous chapter, democratic satisfaction, reflecting citizens' evaluations of the performance of democratic governance in their own country, is measured by the question: *"And how democratically is this country being governed today? Again using a scale from 1 to 10, where 1 means that it is 'not at all democratic' and 10 means that it is 'completely democratic,' what position would you choose?"* Democratic aspirations, or the value of democracy, are gauged from the World Values Survey 2005 by the question: *"How important is it for you to live in a country that is governed democratically? On this scale where 1 means it is 'not at all important' and 10 means 'absolutely important' what position would you choose?"* This item is arguably superior to asking simply about approval of democratic attitudes and the rejection of autocracy, as it seeks to measure the depth or strength of any support.

Overall, based on the difference between these indicators, as shown in Table 6.1, the net democratic deficit is therefore relatively similar in size across each type of regime, but for slightly different reasons. Hence in autocracies, electoral democracies, and younger liberal democracies, the deficit ranged from −2.1 to −2.6 overall. In the older liberal democracies, democratic values were regarded as slightly more important, but there was also slightly greater satisfaction with the performance of democratic governance, generating a net deficit of −2.0. At the same time, as observed earlier, there are more substantial differences among countries within each type of regime, such as a relatively modest deficit in Thailand and Vietnam compared with Russia. Among the electoral democracies, similar variance could be observed between Malaysia and Ethiopia, with the latter country displaying high democratic aspirations but exceptionally poor marks for performance. As shown in Figure 6.6, contrasts

TABLE 6.1. *The Democratic Deficit by Regime and Nation, 2005–2007*

	Older liberal democracies				Younger liberal democracies				Electoral democracies				Autocracies		
	Values	Performance	Deficit		Values	Performance	Deficit		Values	Performance	Deficit		Values	Performance	Deficit
Norway	9.3	8.1	-1.2	India	7.1	6.5	-0.6	Malaysia	7.9	7.0	-0.9	Thailand	8.2	7.0	-1.2
Spain	8.7	7.4	-1.3	Mali	7.7	7.0	-0.6	Colombia	7.9	6.3	-1.6	Vietnam	9.2	8.0	-1.2
Finland	8.7	7.4	-1.3	Ghana	9.2	8.5	-0.7	Jordan	9.4	7.8	-1.6	China	8.5	6.7	-1.8
Japan	8.5	6.9	-1.6	Uruguay	8.9	7.7	-1.2	Zambia	8.8	6.7	-2.0	Iran	7.9	5.2	-2.7
Switzerland	9.3	7.6	-1.7	Chile	8.2	7.0	-1.2	Burkina Faso	8.0	5.7	-2.3	Russia	7.5	4.4	-3.1
Canada	9.0	7.1	-1.9	South Africa	8.7	7.4	-1.3	Moldova	7.9	5.1	-2.8				
France	8.5	6.6	-1.9	Indonesia	8.5	6.5	-2.0	Turkey	9.1	5.9	-3.2				
Australia	9.1	7.1	-1.9	Taiwan	8.9	6.9	-2.0	Morocco	8.9	5.0	-3.9				
Germany	9.2	7.2	-2.0	Brazil	8.2	6.2	-2.1	Ethiopia	9.2	4.2	-5.0				
Sweden	9.5	7.5	-2.0	Slovenia	7.9	5.8	-2.1								
United Kingdom	8.6	6.4	-2.2	Mexico	8.7	6.6	-2.1								
Netherlands	8.7	6.5	-2.2	Korea, South	8.6	6.4	-2.1								
United States	8.8	6.3	-2.5	Argentina	9.1	7.0	-2.1								
Cyprus	9.1	6.5	-2.6	Serbia	7.5	5.2	-2.4								
Italy	8.8	5.8	-3.0	Trinidad & Tobago	8.7	6.1	-2.6								
				Romania	8.6	5.8	-2.8								
				Poland	8.7	5.7	-3.0								
				Andorra	8.9	5.4	-3.5								
				Bulgaria	8.0	4.3	-3.7								
				Ukraine	8.0	4.2	-3.8								
Mean	8.9	7.0	-2.0		8.4	6.3	-2.1		8.6	6.0	-2.6		8.4	6.3	-2.1

Notes:
(i) **Democratic values:** V162. "How important is it for you to live in a country that is governed democratically? On this scale where 1 means it is 'not at all important' and 10 means 'absolutely important' what position would you choose?"
(ii) **Democratic performance:** V163. "And how democratically is this country being governed today? Again using a scale from 1 to 10, where 1 means that it is 'not at all democratic' and 10 means that it is 'completely democratic,' what position would you choose?"
Democratic deficit: Mean difference between (i) and (ii).
Source: World Values Survey 2005–2007.

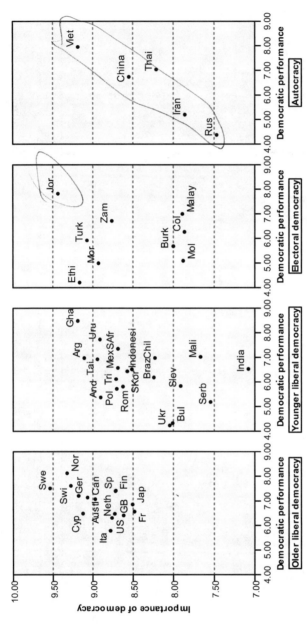

FIGURE 6.6. The democratic deficit by regime type, 2005–2007. **Democratic values:** *V162. "How important is it for you to live in a country that is governed democratically? On this scale where 1 means it is 'not at all important' and 10 means 'absolutely important' what position would you choose?"* **Democratic performance:** *V163. "And how democratically is this country being governed today? Again using a scale from 1 to 10, where 1 means that it is 'not at all democratic' and 10 means that it is 'completely democratic,' what position would you choose?"* **Democratic deficit:** *Mean difference between columns (i) and (ii). Source:* World Values Survey 2005–2007.

TABLE 6.2. *The Democratic Deficit by World Region, 2005–2007*

Global region	Values	Evaluations	Democratic deficit	#
	Importance of democracy (i)	Satisfaction with democratic performance (ii)	(i–ii)	
Scandinavia	9.19	7.68	−1.53	3
Asia-Pacific	8.43	6.90	−1.55	11
South America	8.34	6.57	−1.78	7
Africa	8.65	6.71	−1.91	7
North America	8.81	6.62	−2.20	3
Western Europe	8.87	6.64	−2.25	9
Middle East	8.59	5.79	−2.77	5
Central & Eastern Europe	7.99	5.06	−2.96	8
TOTAL	8.54	6.44	−2.10	53

Notes: For details, see Table 5.7.
Source: World Values Survey 2005–2007.

can also be observed among younger liberal democracies between the modest gap evident in India and Mali, compared with the more substantial deficit in Bulgaria and Ukraine. As consistently noted, among the long-established democracies, the disparities between aspirations and satisfaction with performance were smallest in Norway, Spain, and Finland, compared with larger gaps in the United States, Cyprus, and Italy.

Comparison of these indicators across global regions, presented in Table 6.2, demonstrates that the largest democratic deficit is evident among the postcommunist states in Central and Eastern Europe, especially in Ukraine, Bulgaria, Poland, Romania, and Russia, where the public expresses widespread aspirations for democracy and yet also minimal satisfaction with how democratic governance is actually performing in their own countries. The deficit is also substantial in the five countries under comparison in the Middle East. By contrast, widespread satisfaction with democratic governance means that the smallest democratic deficit exists in the Scandinavian nations under comparison. Relatively modest deficits are also registered among states in Asia-Pacific and South America. The challenges facing democracy in Latin America have been widely discussed, especially political turmoil and instability among states in the Andean region (Peru, Venezuela, Bolivia, and Colombia), as well as the presidential coup in Honduras and popular pressures ousting elected presidents earlier in Ecuador, Argentina, and Peru.[6] But in fact, the overall gap between democratic expectations and perceived performance in the seven Latin American nations contained in the 2005 WVS survey is relatively modest when compared with other world regions.

CONCLUSIONS AND DISCUSSION

This chapter leads to several major conclusions. Limited cross-national survey evidence is available to establish systematic longitudinal trends in political attitudes during the third wave era. Nonetheless, the result of the time-series analysis of successive waves of the World Values Survey data presented here, comparing a range of liberal democracies, serves to confirm the picture already familiar; during the last quarter century (except for confidence in parliaments), no significant erosion of system support can be detected from the indices of composite institutional confidence, attitudes toward democratic governance and rejection of autocracy, or feelings of nationalism. Instead, trendless fluctuations over time are apparent, or else a relatively stable pattern.

Tensions between almost universal public aspirations for democracy and more skeptical evaluations of how democratically governments work in practice have been widely observed in the previous literature, but nevertheless many puzzles remain. These components are most commonly analyzed separately, rather than being integrated.[7] Moreover, systematic research has not yet established the underlying reasons for the democratic deficit and why this varies across different types of societies and regimes. The analysis suggests that the older liberal democracies display strong endorsement of the importance of democracy but also relatively positive perceptions of how democracy works in the respondents' own country. Countries that have only democratized during the third wave era are far more diverse in their orientations, with the greatest congruence between aspirations and perceived performance displayed in cases such as Ghana, Uruguay, and South Africa, all relatively successful democracies. By contrast, larger disparities between expectations and perceived performance are evident in many post-communist states, including Russia, Ukraine, Bulgaria, and Serbia.

The descriptive evidence clears away some popular myths but it still leaves multiple puzzles to explain. Several general theories could help to account for the variations in the democratic deficit among countries, as well as the exceptionally positive attitudes observed in the Communist one-party states of Vietnam and China, furnishing several plausible propositions to be analyzed in subsequent chapters.[8] One potential explanation, derived from theories of political communication, focuses upon the news media's framing of politics and government. In particular, human rights observers report that many repressive autocracies routinely deploy techniques designed to suppress independent journalism, manipulate and slant news selectively in their favor, and limit critical coverage of the regime.[9] In this context, state-controlled media coverage generates one-sided messages. Any effects arising from one-sided messages should be apparent in countries with state-controlled broadcasting where regular television news users would be expected to display more positive system support. Some previous studies have started to document this process.[10] By contrast, in countries with an independent news media where the public is exposed to two-sided messages (with both positive and negative framing of public affairs), regular news media use would not be expected to have a dramatic impact upon evaluations of the performance of government. Under conditions where the proportion of negative news about politics and government increases, however, such as the outbreak of a major political scandal, then this would be expected to erode specific levels of system support. To test the impact of political communications, the attitudes of regular news users can be compared with non-users in each of these countries and types of regimes, including examining a few national case studies where changes in the directional tone of the news coverage of political scandals can be analyzed over time.

Yet rational choice theories suggest alternative propositions, relating public opinion more directly to the instrumental performance of the government rather than the role of the media in framing perceptions. In the cases of China and Vietnam, for example, positive perceptions of government could be driven by the remarkable economic record these societies have experienced during recent decades; today China is the fourth largest economy in the world. It has sustained average economic growth of over 9.5% for the past quarter century, becoming the manufacturing powerhouse of the globe, lifting millions out of poverty and producing dramatic improvements in living standards. The reformed mixed market economy in Vietnam has also achieved remarkably strong economic growth, expanded foreign trade, and sharp reductions in poverty. Vietnam has been one of the fastest growing economies in the world, averaging around 6.5% to 8% annual gross domestic product (GDP) growth since 1990. Per capita income rose from $220 in 1994 to $1,024 in 2008.[11] If institutional confidence is generally related to public assessments of the government's management of the economy and welfare services, then attitudes toward state agencies and more diffuse indicators of system support should be strongly linked to levels of economic satisfaction within each society, as well as to macro-level indicators of national economic performance.[12]

In addition, cultural theories suggest that other values and beliefs could also be expected to shape attitudes toward the political system – for example, in the cases of China and Vietnam, left-right ideological beliefs in Communist states are predicted to influence attitudes toward the market and state, reinforcing confidence in public sector agencies, while strong affective feelings of national pride found in these societies could also spill over to influence positive support toward the national government and its agencies.[13] Subsequent chapters build upon this foundation by using the market model to analyze the democratic deficit, monitoring the interaction concerning public demands for democracy, the impact of information conveyed by the mass media, and the instrumental performance of regimes.

PART III

DIAGNOSIS

7

Rising Aspirations?

For more than half a century following Almond and Verba's classic *The Civic Culture* (1963), scholars have debated the complex relationship between cultural values and democratic regimes. Two strands of literature have dominated contemporary discussion.[1] One builds upon modernization theories of cultural change. The intellectual roots of these ideas originated in nineteenth- and early twentieth-century political sociology, becoming the mainstream account of political development during the 1950s. These notions have been revived for the contemporary era and developed most extensively in the seminal work of Ronald Inglehart.[2] Processes of societal modernization and human development, Inglehart theorizes, encourage the growth of 'post-materialist' and 'self-expression' values in post-industrial societies, including rising levels of tolerance and trust, direct forms of political activism, and demands for personal and political freedoms. In turn, Inglehart argues, the diffusion of self-expression values among the mass public shapes the cultural conditions under which democratic institutions are most likely to spread and flourish. "The emergence of post-industrial society is conducive to rising emphasis on self-expression, which in turn brings rising mass demands for democracy."[3] If societal modernization and value change is at the heart of the democratization process, as theories claim, this suggests a series of testable propositions. Democratic values should be endorsed most strongly by populations living within affluent post-industrial societies, as well as by the younger generation, by the highly educated and more affluent, and by those expressing 'post-materialist' and 'self-expression' values.

The other development sweeping through cultural studies in recent years has been the modern renaissance of interest in social capital. Theorists from de Tocqueville and John Stuart Mill to Durkheim, Simmel, and Kornhauser have long emphasized the importance of civic society and voluntary associations as vital to the lifeblood of democracy. There is nothing particularly novel about praising the virtues of civic associations, especially for their capacity to perform many functions where states and the market fail. Pluralist theories popular during the 1960s emphasized the role of interest groups in aggregating and articulating public demands, providing multiple alternative channels of political participation linking citizens and the state.[4] Modern theories of social capital originated in the work by Pierre Bourdieu and James Coleman, both emphasizing the importance of social ties and shared norms to societal well-being and economic efficiency.[5] Contemporary study of these topics was transformed following publication of Robert Putnam's seminal accounts of civic engagement in Italy and the United States, in *Making Democracy Work* (1994) and *Bowling Alone* (2000).[6] Putnam's version of social capital theory emphasizes that typical face-to-face deliberative activities and horizontal collaboration within voluntary associations far removed from the political sphere, such as sports clubs, agricultural cooperatives, or philanthropic groups, promote interpersonal trust, fostering the capacity to work together in the future, creating the bonds of social life that are the basis for civil society and democratic governance. Organized groups not only achieve certain instrumental goals, it is claimed, but in the process of so doing, they also create the conditions for further collaboration, or social capital. If social capital underlies political cultures, then democratic aspirations and evaluations should be closely tied to macro- and micro-level patterns of interpersonal trust and associational activism.

Theories of post-materialism and social capital differ sharply in many important regards, but they both emphasize the cultural drivers of democratic governance, reflecting the 'demand' side of the equation in the general market model. From this perspective, societies are regarded as unlikely to maintain stable democratic regimes over the long term, or to deepen legitimacy, unless this form of governance has solid support among the mass public. Cultural attitudes cannot and do not guarantee the success of the rocky road of transitions from autocracy, and regimes may always revert back for multiple reasons, whether elite push-back or leadership coup, the destabilizing effects of external conflict spilling over national borders or internal ethnic tensions, sudden deep shocks to the economy, the violent outcome of deeply disputed election results, or the impact of many other catalytic events.[7] But third wave democratic regimes are regarded by these theories as more likely to endure, overcoming the hazards and seismic shocks of political earthquakes, if mounted on the cushioning understructure of democratic cultural foundations.

After outlining these alternative theories and propositions, this chapter compares descriptive data and uses multilevel regression models to test the cross-national evidence for each of these claims, drawing again upon the fifth wave of the World Values Survey (2005). Multilevel models examine the impact of selected modernization and social capital variables on democratic aspirations, democratic satisfaction, and the net democratic deficit, controlling for other standard national and social characteristics commonly related to political attitudes. The broader range of countries and conditions under comparison, covering more than fifty societies, provides a more comprehensive analysis than previous studies. Other work has often been limited to comparing public opinion in the United States and Western Europe, or comparing developing nations and emerging economies within specific cultural regions around the world. The modernization thesis, in particular, can be most thoroughly evaluated by comparing contemporary societies that differ sharply in their levels of economic and human development. Four key points emerge. (1) The evidence suggests no confirmation for the bolder claims in the societal modernization theory; in particular, *democratic aspirations are not associated with processes of human development nor with age effects.* Nevertheless, (2) cultural theories furnish a partial answer to some of the issues at the heart of this study; *educational levels, self-expression values, social trust, and associational activism all help to predict higher democratic aspirations.* Yet, most important, (3) *only the effects of education widened the democratic deficit*; self-expression values, social trust, and associational activism were significantly linked with *greater* democratic satisfaction, not less. Last, (4) limits arising from the use of cross-sectional analysis complicate how far this chapter can disentangle the direction of causality underlying cultural accounts. Let us first discuss the theoretical arguments and then demonstrate these claims with the empirical evidence.

I: MODERNIZATION THEORIES OF VALUE CHANGE

Modernization theories originated in the work of Karl Marx, Max Weber, and Emile Durkheim. These ideas were revived and popularized by political sociologists during the late 1950s and early 1960s to account for patterns of political development and political behavior during the era of de-colonization, as exemplified by the work of Seymour Martin Lipset, Daniel Lerner, Walt Rostow, and Karl Deutsch.[8] Traditional societies are characterized by subsistence livelihoods largely based on farming, fishing, extraction, and unskilled work; they have low levels of literacy and basic education, predominantly rural populations, endemic insecurity and minimum standards of living, and restricted social and geographic mobility. Citizens in agrarian societies are strongly rooted to local communities through ties of 'blood and belonging,' including those of kinship, family, ethnicity, and religion, as well as long-standing social bonds, governed through traditional forms of political authority. Modernization theories are based on the observation that the shift from agrarian-based economies toward industrial production generates massive structural changes in society. This includes growing prosperity, wider access to basic schooling and literacy, expanding access to tertiary education, and processes of urbanization and geographic mobility. These developments, in turn, were understood to lay the social foundations for mass participation in democratic political systems.

The shift from traditional agrarian society toward industrialized society concerns the move from agricultural production to manufacturing, from farms to factories, from peasants to workers. Social trends accompanying these developments include population migration to metropolitan conurbations, the rise of the working class and urban bourgeoisie, rising living standards, the separation of church and state, the increasing penetration of the mass media, the growth of Weberian bureaucratization and rational-legal authority in the state, the foundations of the early welfare state, and the spread of primary schooling and literacy. This phase was sparked by the Industrial Revolution in Britain during the mid- to late eighteenth century and then spread throughout the Western world during the nineteenth and early twentieth centuries. The early developmental theorists emphasized a range of social trends that commonly accompanied the process of industrialization, including the growing authority and legitimacy of European parliamentary democracies as a check on absolute monarchies, and critical changes in political cultures, exemplified by growing demands from the bourgeoisie, the urban working class, and women for the universal franchise and thus inclusive representation in parliamentary government.

During the early 1970s, Daniel Bell popularized the view that after a certain period of industrialization, a further distinct stage of development could be distinguished, as a non-linear process, in the rise of post-industrial societies.[9] For Bell, the critical tipping point was reached when the majority of the workforce moved from manufacturing into the service sector, employed as lawyers, bankers, financial analysts, technologists, scientists, and professionals in the knowledge industries. The familiar social and economic shifts characterizing post-industrial societies include the rise of a highly educated, skilled, and specialized workforce; the population shifts from urban to suburban neighborhoods and greater geographic mobility, including across national borders; rising living standards and growing leisure time; rapid scientific and technological innovation; the expansion and fragmentation of mass media channels, technologies, and markets; the growth of multilayered governance with power shifting away from the nation-state toward global and local levels; market liberalization and the expansion of non-profit social protection schemes; the erosion of the traditional nuclear family; and growing equality of sex roles within the home, family, and workforce. There is little doubt that processes of human development have been sweeping across many contemporary societies. Considerable controversy remains, however, concerning the political consequences of these changes and the causal linkages – in particular, the impact of societal modernization on democratic cultures. Behavioralism gradually fell out of fashion in political science during the 1980s, challenged by alternative rational choice and historical theories of institutionalism that emphasized the 'return of the state' and the autonomous role of constitutional structures. The determinist claims and linear sequential models of progressive change as a mechanical process of steps, favored by the early theorists, also gradually fell out of favor in studies of political economy and development.

Yet ideas of political culture, which never faded away, have experienced a contemporary revival since the early 1990s, not least due to the renewal of interest in the process and drivers of democratization, coupled with new opportunities for cross-national survey research offered by more open societies and by processes of globalization.[10] The most prominent contemporary account of how modernization affects cultural change has been developed in the seminal work of Ronald Inglehart, with evidence drawn from successive waves of the World Values Surveys/European Values Surveys.[11] In his work, Inglehart argues that the evolution from agrarian to industrial to post-industrial societies brings about two coherent, predictable, and interrelated dimensions of change: (1) socioeconomic shifts in the process of production and levels of human development, as Bell claimed, and also (2) a transformation in societal cultures, including rising emphasis in post-industrial societies on the values underpinning democracy, including growing social tolerance, trust, political efficacy, and demands for human rights and fundamental freedoms.[12]

Theories of value change and post-materialism were originally developed by Inglehart to account for the turbulent politics and new social movements that developed during the 1960s and early 1970s in the United States and Western Europe.[13] He argues that historical traditions are remarkably enduring in shaping cultural worldviews; nevertheless glacial shifts are taking place that move away from traditional orientations, toward more post-materialism and self-expression values. These shifts are intimately related to the long-term processes of human development, increasing people's economic, cognitive, and social resources in post-industrial societies as well as attributable to patterns of generational turnover within each society. Rising aspirations for democracy and the spread of attitudes such as social tolerance and trust are not an ad hoc and erratic process, according to this account; instead, patterns of societal modernization underpin attitudinal shifts. The broad direction of value change is predictable although the pace is conditioned by the cultural legacy and institutional structure in any given society, such as the enduring legacy of attitudes toward the state in post-Soviet Central Europe, the role of an Islamic heritage in the Middle East, and the egalitarian traditions predominating in Scandinavia. In contrast to earlier versions, Inglehart's account of modernization theory suggests that economic, cultural, and political changes go together in coherent ways, so that industrialization brings broadly similar trajectories for democracy, even if situation-specific factors make it impossible to predict exactly what will happen in any given society: certain changes become increasingly likely to occur, but the changes are probabilistic, not deterministic. Reversals are also possible, for example, following the impact of global economic shocks as well as advances.

Based on traditional accounts of socialization processes, Inglehart emphasizes that each generation acquires their cultural values from parents and siblings, teachers and spiritual authorities, and the formative events and conditions that people experience when growing up. For the interwar generation living in post-industrial societies, Inglehart theorizes that the key experiences were conditions of mass unemployment, hunger, and poverty during the era of the Great Depression as well as the wrenching experience, insecurities, and social dislocation caused by conflict in two world wars. As a result, the interwar generation is predicted to prioritize core values reflecting the need for improvements in material living standards, exemplified by the importance of government management of the economy to generate the conditions of full employment, economic growth, and welfare protection. By contrast, the postwar generation living in post-industrial societies, growing up during the 1950s and 1960s under conditions of existential security, economic affluence, material well-being, and full employment, as well as the cradle-to-grave welfare safety net available for health care, pensions, and unemployment benefits, and rapidly expanding access to higher education, is predicted to emphasize 'post-materialist' values. These are exemplified by prioritizing opportunities for direct forms of demo-cratic participation, for example, through protest demonstrations, petitions, and consumer politics, as well as valuing quality-of-life issues of environmen-tal protection, gender equality, and sexual liberalization.

In more recent work, Inglehart and Welzel have broadened the conceptu-alization of value change by emphasizing a generational shift toward 'self-expression' or 'emancipative' values, a syndrome of pro-democratic attitudes of which post-materialism is only one component.[14] Self-expression values are seen to emphasize individual choice and autonomy, including tolerance, trust, subjective well-being (happiness), and civic activism. Its polar opposite is the survival syndrome, which emphasizes economic and physical security, intoler-ance of minorities (homosexuality), the insistence on traditional gender roles, lack of social trust, and an authoritarian political outlook. Inglehart and Welzel demonstrate that self-expression values among the younger generation in richer nations are associated with elite-challenging behavior, exemplified by mass demonstrations and declining respect for government and hierarchical institu-tions. Any sustained erosion of deference toward political leaders, parliaments, and parties that has occurred in modern societies, in this theory, is in line with more searching scrutiny of other traditional sources of hierarchical authority, such as churches and the military. These cultural shifts, which should be most apparent among the younger generation in affluent post-industrial societies, are thought to have many consequences for civic orientations. In particular, Welzel argues that pro-democratic attitudes will lend support to activists and reforms struggling to expand human freedoms.[15] It should be noted that the direct endorsement of democratic values and evaluations of democratic performance are not an explicit part of Inglehart and Welzel's self-expression syndrome, nor are these particular items claimed to be directly correlated with the self-expression scale.[16] Indeed, these two survey questions were only included in the fifth wave of the WVS, and hence they were unavailable for earlier analysis. The logic of their theoretical argument, however, implies that if individuals strongly favor autonomy and freedom, they should also regard democratic governance as important and rising expectations should also shape how people evaluate democratic performance.

To support the claim that democratic cultures underpin democratic regimes, Inglehart and Welzel demonstrate that the strength of a composite emancipa-tive values index (measured in the 1990 World Values Survey) was significantly related to *subsequent* levels of democracy in any state (measured by Freedom House in 2000–2004).[17] By contrast, Inglehart and Welzel show that demo-cratic regimes (measured in 1981–86) have a more modest effect on subsequent self-expression values (measured in the early 1990s). The authors theorize that emancipative values undermine the legitimacy of authoritarian rule, so that these regimes become more vulnerable to being toppled by democratic reform movements and opposition forces.

Testing the Core Propositions

Modernization thesis therefore generates several propositions that can be tested against the macro-level and micro-level empirical evidence using the fifth wave of the pooled World Values Survey 2005. As in previous chapters, democratic '*aspirations*' are measured by the importance that is attached to living in a democracy, while democratic '*satisfaction*' refers to evaluations of the perceived performance of democracy in each country, with all dependent variables standardized to 100 points for ease of comparison. The 'deficit' represents the difference when satisfaction is subtracted from aspirations. The descriptive statistics can be compared to illustrate the data while multilevel regression models analyze the evidence for the relationships with the full battery of controls.

A note about how to interpret the results presented in this section of the book may be useful for those unfamiliar with multilevel analysis. A fuller technical description is provided in Appendix C. In brief, regression models are used for multivariate analysis to discover whether independent variables are having a genuine effect upon the dependent variable (so that the coefficients of any independent variables are really different from zero) or alternatively whether any apparent differences from zero are just due to random chance. The null (default) hypothesis is always that each independent variable is having absolutely no effect (that it thereby has a coefficient of 0) and we are looking for a reason to reject this proposition. In the past, many analysts relied upon standard ordinary least squares (OLS) regression models; for example, Anderson and Guillory merged national-level data derived from classifying the type of majoritarian or consensual political system into individual-level survey data measuring democratic satisfaction.[18] Rose, Mischler, and Haepfer used similar processes to examine the impact of changes in freedom, democratic traditions, levels of perceived corruption, and changes in GDP on support for democracy and rejection of authoritarianism in Eastern European countries.[19] Yet standard OLS regression models are now regarded as less appropriate for analyzing hierarchical data that includes both macro-level data (such as the mean level of economic development or the type of regime in a country) and micro-level data (such as individual attitudes toward democracy or autocracy).[20] Ordinary least squares regression can be particularly misleading for hierarchical data when national-level data are merged with very large-scale surveys; for example, the pooled World Values Survey 1981–2005 contains over 350,000 respondents but only ninety-three countries. An alternative strategy is to limit analysis to only one level, for example, by aggregating the survey data to national means, but this strategy has the disadvantage of discarding valuable information.[21] The multilevel regression analysis has the advantage of taking account of the appropriate number of macro-level cases (countries) included in the hierarchical data. This process thereby avoids Type I errors or false positives for the macro-level variables, where analysts conclude that a statistically significant difference exists when, in fact, there is no statistical difference between countries. The multilevel tests of significance are therefore more rigorous and conservative than those generated through OLS regression.[22]

Nevertheless, any interpretation of the standard regression coefficients generated by the multilevel models remains familiar for analysts. Interpretations look first at the statistical significance of any coefficients and, assuming a properly specified model, a probability of .05 or less is the generally accepted point at which to reject the null hypothesis. The lower the probability, the greater the confidence that the results would have come up in a random distribution. Since all the variables are standardized using mean centering (x-scores) prior to entry, the relative strength of each of the regression coefficients can be compared against each other, for example, to see whether educational qualifications, news media use, or household income play a stronger role when predicting democratic aspirations. The standard errors can also usefully be compared, reflecting an estimate of the standard deviation of the coefficient, the amount it varies across cases. It can be thought of as a measure of the precision with which the regression coefficient is measured. The standard errors can also be compared against each other, since all the independent variables are standardized to 1.0. The strength of the multilevel regression coefficients is also substantively meaningful; these can be interpreted intuitively as how much change in the dependent variable is generated by a 1% change in each independent variable. The direction of the sign indicates whether the change is positive or negative.

The Impact of Human Development

The central proposition at the heart of modernization theories is the claim that cultural shifts occur in response to long-term conditions of societal modernization, especially rising levels of human development associated with economic growth, expanding literacy, education, and access to information in post-industrial economies. Changes are probabilistic, not deterministic; nevertheless, more traditional security values are predicted to continue to prevail in poorer developing societies, while support for self-expression values is theorized to grow in post-industrial societies. Accordingly, at the macro-level, the first proposition arising from modernization theory predicts that *democratic aspirations will be strongest in affluent post-industrialized societies* rather than in emerging manufacturing economies or in poorer developing nations.

This proposition can be tested at macro-level by using two indicators of societal modernization. The UNDP's Human Development Index (HDI) is the standard composite 100-point index that measures a country's average achievements in three basic aspects of human development: health, knowledge, and a decent standard of living.[23] Health is measured by life expectancy at birth;

TABLE 7.1. *Social Characteristics, Cultural Values, and Democratic Orientations, 2005–2007*

	Democratic aspirations (i)	Democratic satisfaction (ii)	Deficit (i)–(ii)
INDIVIDUAL LEVEL			
Demographic characteristics			
Age (in years)	2.07***	.723***	−1.44***
	(.135)	(.163)	(.186)
Sex (male = 1)	.245*	−.105	−.351*
	(.122)	(.148)	(.169)
Socioeconomic resources			
Household income 10-point scale	−.117	1.486***	1.53***
	(.147)	(.178)	(.220)
Education 9-point scale	1.96***	−.660***	−2.62***
	(.106)	(.193)	(.220)
News media use 100-point scale	1.04***	−.037	−1.08***
	(.152)	(.184)	(.209)
Cultural values			
Self-expression values	1.77***	.580***	−1.24***
	(.151)	(.183)	(.208)
NATIONAL LEVEL			
Human Development Index	−1.07	−.820	1.64
	(.620)	(1.19)	(1.14)
Constant (intercept)	84.9	64.7	−20.2
Schwarz BIC	217,452	217,149	221,765
N. respondents	24,826	23,837	23,702
N. nations	39	39	39
Measurement	100-pts	100-pts	100-pts

Note: All independent variables were standardized using mean centering (z-scores). Models present the results of the REML multilevel regression models (for details, see Appendix C) including the beta coefficient (the standard error below in parenthesis) and the significance. See Appendix A for details about the measurement, coding, and construction of all variables. Significant coefficients are highlighted in **bold**.

p* = .05 ** = .01 *** = .001

Source: World Values Survey 2005–2007.

knowledge by a combination of the adult literacy rate and the combined primary, secondary, and tertiary gross enrollment ratio; and standard of living by GDP per capita (PPP US$). To see whether the results of the analysis remain robust, the models were also re-run by testing for the effects of economic development, measured by per capita GDP (PPP US$), substituted instead of the Human Development Index. Table 7.1 provides the full multilevel model analyzing the factors contributing toward these democratic orientations including the Human Development Index, demographic characteristics (age and sex),

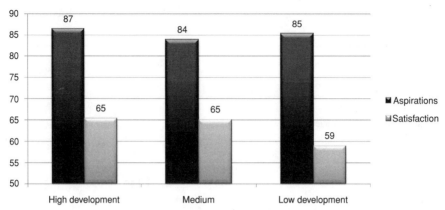

FIGURE 7.1. Democratic deficits by type of society, 2005–2007. (i) **Democratic aspirations:** V162. *"How important is it for you to live in a country that is governed democratically? On this scale where 1 means it is 'not at all important' and 10 means 'absolutely important' what position would you choose?"* Standardized to 100 pts. (ii) **Democratic satisfaction:** V163. *"And how democratically is this country being governed today? Again using a scale from 1 to 10, where 1 means that it is 'not at all democratic' and 10 means that it is 'completely democratic,' what position would you choose?"* Standardized to 100 pts. **Democratic deficit:** *Mean difference between (i) and (ii).* Source: The World Values Survey 2005–2007.

socioeconomic resources (household income, education, and news media use), and culture (self-expression values). It should be noted that these models do not control for the historical experience of democratic governance in each society, an issue examined in Chapter 10, but the results proved robust and the inclusion or exclusion of this variable did not affect the analysis. Models were also checked and confirmed to be free of problems of multi-collinearity.

The results of the multivariate models presented in Table 7.1 demonstrate that, contrary to expectations arising from modernization theory, social levels of human development (measured by the UNDP Human Development Index) fail to prove a statistically significant predictor of political attitudes (whether democratic aspirations, democratic satisfaction, or the democratic deficit). The results mean it is not possible to reject the null hypothesis. Moreover these patterns were not simply attributable to the specific measures used; the basic results remain robust when the models were re-run testing for the effects of economic development (per capita GDP), substituted instead of the more comprehensive Human Development Index. Moreover the core findings did not alter with alternative model specifications, for example if the historical index of democratization was included or excluded as a control.

The simple descriptive results also confirm these patterns; Figure 7.1 and Table 7.2 illustrate how attitudes compare across societies at different levels of human development. Today the richest and poorest developing societies share roughly similar democratic aspirations, as observed in many previous studies.

TABLE 7.2. *Societal Development and Democratic Orientations, 2005–2007*

		Democratic aspirations	Democratic satisfaction	Democratic deficit
All	Mean	86	64	−22
Human development	High development	87	65	21
	Medium	84	65	19
	Low development	85	59	25
Economic development	High income society	89	69	20
	Medium income society	74	63	21
	Low income society	84	63	22

Notes:
(i) Democratic aspirations: V162. *"How important is it for you to live in a country that is governed democratically? On this scale where 1 means it is 'not at all important' and 10 means 'absolutely important' what position would you choose?"* Standardized to 100 points.
(ii) Democratic satisfaction: V163. *"And how democratically is this country being governed today? Again using a scale from 1 to 10, where 1 means that it is 'not at all democratic' and 10 means that it is 'completely democratic,' what position would you choose?"* Standardized to 100 points.
Democratic deficit: *Mean difference between (i) and (ii).*
Source: The World Values Survey 2005–2007.

Far from being a 'Western' phenomenon, as the Asian values thesis suggested, in fact democratic values are widely endorsed in diverse countries and cultural regions around the globe.[24] People living in low-development societies prove slightly more critical when evaluating the democratic performance of their own country, but the mean differences among rich and poor nations are extremely modest. The empirical evidence therefore provides no support for the first and most important proposition arising from modernization theory; contrary to expectations, *no statistically significant contrasts in democratic aspirations or in satisfaction with democratic performance can be observed when comparing affluent post-industrialized societies, emerging manufacturing economies, or poorer developing nations.* Given the contrasts in democratic orientations and system support found even among relatively affluent societies, exemplified by the contrasts in the attitudes typically expressed towards government and politics in Italy and Norway which were observed in previous chapters, the lack of macro-level patterns associated with human development is less surprising. At the same time, democratic cultures in each society can be expected to be affected by many complex factors beyond macro-levels of development, so before dismissing the account, several micro-level propositions which also arise from modernization theory deserve further scrutiny.

Educational and Socioeconomic Effects

The impact of education on democratic attitudes and values is expected to be particularly strong. Modernization theories emphasize that economic

development is accompanied by rising levels of literacy, numeracy, and formal primary, secondary, and tertiary education, all of which expand the civic
skills, knowledge, and capacities of citizens.[25] The social structure of developing societies and emerging economies has been transformed by the spread of
primary schooling, for girls as well as boys, as well as by the expansion of the
secondary and tertiary sectors. Higher education develops cognitive skills and
thus the capacity to organize and make sense of the flood of information available in contemporary societies, strengthening political knowledge.[26] In democratic societies, classes in civic education in particular are explicitly designed to
provide young people with practical information and skills that facilitate active
citizenship and community service, while the general curriculum (especially in
social studies, history, and geography) can be expected to shape broader attitudes toward democracy, government, and the nation-state.[27] Education is also
closely related to political interest, increasing the motivation to seek out information, such as paying regular attention to civic affairs covered in the news
media and on political Web sites. Educational attainments also help to predict
subsequent employment opportunities in the workforce and thus patterns of
socioeconomic status and household income.

An extensive literature has confirmed the general impact of education on
civic cultures, although there is greater dispute concerning the links between
education and democratic values. In a long series of studies, Verba and colleagues demonstrated that levels of formal education are closely associated with
social tolerance and trust, as well as consistently proving one of the strongest
predictors of political participation. More educated citizens typically display
far greater political interest, civic knowledge, internal efficacy, and activism in
public affairs.[28] Verba suggests that the link between education and internal
efficacy is particularly important for political participation; formal schooling
strengthens confidence in the ability of citizens to affect the public policymaking
process. Education also provides important communication and organizational
skills, which facilitate engagement in local community associations, voluntary
groups, and political parties, as well as running for elected office.

Other studies have also examined the more direct impact of social structural
characteristics (age, sex, and education) and post-material values on several
of the indicators at the heart of this study, including satisfaction with democracy, institutional confidence, and levels of trust in politicians. The large-scale
multi-author Beliefs in Government project provided the most thorough analysis of European trends in these cultural indicators from the mid-1970s until
the early 1990s, based on analyzing Eurobarometer data covering a dozen
EU member states. The research concluded that relationships were complex
and not always in accordance with the assumptions of modernization theory;
for example, post-materialists, young people, and the more educated Europeans were found to become increasingly *satisfied* with democracy, not more
critical.[29] Education and age were only weakly related to European patterns
of political trust and institutional confidence.[30] To update the analysis, more
recently Dalton compared the impact of education and age upon indicators of

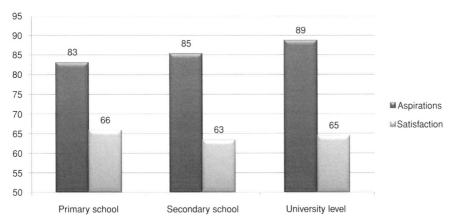

FIGURE 7.2. Democratic orientations by education, 2005–2007. Categorized by the highest educational level attained. (i) **Democratic aspirations:** $V162$. *"How important is it for you to live in a country that is governed democratically? On this scale where 1 means it is 'not at all important' and 10 means 'absolutely important' what position would you choose?" Standardized to 100 pts.* (ii) **Democratic satisfaction:** $V163$. *"And how democratically is this country being governed today? Again using a scale from 1 to 10, where 1 means that it is 'not at all democratic' and 10 means that it is 'completely democratic,' what position would you choose?" Standardized to 100 pts.* **Democratic deficit:** *Mean difference between (i) and (ii).* Source: The World Values Survey 2005–2007.

specific-level support toward political authorities in a range of post-industrial societies. The research established that over time the better educated in these countries have become slightly less trusting of politicians. Accordingly, modernization theories suggest the proposition that *the endorsement of democratic values will be strongest among the well educated.* If growing cognitive skills and political knowledge generate rising aspirations for democracy, as Inglehart suggests, then it also follows that *democratic deficits will be larger among the better educated.* According to modernization theory, education should have a direct effect upon democratic orientations as well as exerting an indirect effect through encouraging the endorsement of self-expression values that underpin democratic cultures.

The multivariate analysis presented in Table 7.1 confirms that, as predicted, education is strongly and significantly related to democratic orientations. Indeed, out of all the variables reinforcing aspirations for democracy, education plays the second strongest role. Education also simultaneously encourages significantly more critical evaluations of how democratically countries are being governed, and the combined effect thereby exacerbates the democratic deficit. University graduates have democratic deficits that are typically about 9 percentage points larger than those with only primary school education. Figure 7.2 and Table 7.3 illustrate the contrasts by levels of formal education, highlighting the impact of aspirations for democracy. Basic literacy, numeracy, and

TABLE 7.3. *Social and Demographic Characteristics and Democratic Orientations, 2005–2007*

		Aspirations	Satisfaction	Deficit
All education	Mean	86	64	−22
	High education	89	65	−24
	Medium	85	63	−22
	Low education	83	66	−17
Age (in years)	18–29	84	63	−21
	Thirties	85	64	−21
	Forties	86	65	−21
	Fifties	86	65	−22
	Sixties	87	66	−22
	70s+	87	67	−21
Socioeconomic status	Professional/managerial	89	65	−24
	Other non-manual	87	63	−24
	Skilled manual	85	62	−22
	Unskilled manual	84	67	−17
Household income	High household income	87	66	−21
	Low household income	84	63	−22

Notes:
(i) Democratic aspirations: V162. *"How important is it for you to live in a country that is governed democratically? On this scale where 1 means it is 'not at all important' and 10 means 'absolutely important' what position would you choose?" Standardized to 100 points.*
(ii) Democratic satisfaction: V163. *"And how democratically is this country being governed today? Again using a scale from 1 to 10, where 1 means that it is 'not at all democratic' and 10 means that it is 'completely democratic,' what position would you choose?" Standardized to 100 points.*
Democratic deficit: *Mean difference between (i) and (ii).*
Source: The World Values Survey 2005–2007.

cognitive skills derived from schooling make it easier to absorb, organize, and process political information derived from the news media, especially coverage of public affairs available from printed newspapers and the internet. Formal education also strengthens civic knowledge, including information about the role of citizens and the structure of government, which is essential for informed participation in democratic societies.[31] As shown in the next chapter, cognitive mobilization and information derived from formal education and the news media also expand the capacity of citizens to understand the complex concept of liberal democracy and to distinguish some core features of this type of governance from the characteristics of autocratic states. Steadily expanding access to educational opportunities, particularly but not exclusively in contemporary post-industrial societies, is therefore one of the factors encouraging the growing gap between citizens' evaluations and expectations about how democracy should work.

Educational qualifications are also closely related in later life to subsequent socioeconomic status and household income, so similar effects might be expected to be observed. Yet in fact, as shown in the models in Table 7.1, household income typically has no significant impact on aspirations although it strongly boosts democratic satisfaction. The poorest quintile of households in each society usually has levels of satisfaction with the performance of democracy that are about 8 percentage points lower than those of the top quintile. In contrast to the effects of education, the impact of income therefore reduces the deficit. The profile of attitudes by socioeconomic status presented in Table 7.3 does show a clearer association, however, with the net democratic deficit 7 percentage points higher for the professional and managerial middle class than for unskilled manual workers. The way that education is linked with political attitudes is therefore probably partly associated with socioeconomic status, although the civic orientations, political information, and cognitive skills learned through schooling seem to play a more direct role in shaping rising expectations about how democracy should work.

Age Effects

Modernization theory also emphasizes that much cultural change is intergenerational, reflecting the accumulated effects of population replacement. In this perspective, basic values do not change overnight; instead, modernization theories suggest that a substantial time lag occurs between economic development and the impact of this process on prevailing cultural values, because adults retain the norms, values, and beliefs that were instilled by socialization processes during their formative pre-adult years.[32] Generational accounts emphasize that values evolve in society as younger birth cohorts, shaped by distinctive formative experiences, gradually replace their elders. Socialization theory has long suggested that people learn from parents and siblings in childhood, adolescence, and early adulthood, as well as absorbing the prevailing social norms and values transmitted by the mass media, teachers, and religious authorities, and within local communities.[33] Longitudinal studies of social learning report that core political predispositions tend to be highly stable through the life span, with attitudes relatively flexible in youth but crystallizing as people age, infusing core predispositions with increasing psychological strength over time.[34] Dalton confirmed that generational effects on specific levels of political trust were found in six out of the nine post-industrial societies he compared. The contrasts between younger and older cohorts were relatively modest in size, but cumulatively, through processes of generational turnover, they could be expected to have a substantial impact in transforming social cultures: "Over time older and more trustful citizens are gradually replaced by younger and more cynical individuals."[35]

The results of the multivariate analysis presented in Table 7.1 demonstrate that the age of respondents was significantly associated with democratic aspirations and satisfaction, but in the *contrary* direction to that predicted by modernization theory. Hence, compared with the youngest birth cohort, the oldest expresses significantly higher expectations of democracy and also slightly greater satisfaction with how democratically their own government works in practice (see Table 7.3). The age effects in these models proved robust, and indeed the coefficients even strengthened when the models were re-run with the country coverage restricted to post-industrial societies (defined as highly developed by the HDI index), as well as when the analysis was restricted to older electoral democracies.

Post-Materialism and Self-Expression Values

Last, what of the direct effects of cultural values on democratic orientations? Democratic performance commonly falls short of citizens' aspirations, according to this perspective, mainly due to the rising *expectations* of citizens, especially in affluent societies. In this regard, even if regime performance remains constant, governments are nevertheless being judged against more stringent and rigorous standards. "In the short run," Inglehart argues, "economic development tends to bring rising levels of political satisfaction; in the long run, however, it leads to the emergence of new and more demanding standards by which government performance is evaluated – and to lower levels of respect and confidence in their authorities."[36] Value change in post-industrial societies is expected to encourage stronger adherence to a wide range of cultural changes, including a cluster of attitudes such as social trust and tolerance of minorities, support for freedom and autonomy, endorsement of democratic ideals and a rejection of autocracy, and rising public demands for more participatory and direct involvement in decision-making processes.

The multivariate models in Table 7.1 confirm that even with a battery of prior controls, self-expression values are significantly related to higher democratic aspirations, as the theory predicts. Yet at the same time, self-expression values are also linked with *greater* democratic satisfaction, not less. Similar patterns can be observed for the narrower measure of post-materialism, as Figure 7.3 shows. A modest relationship can be observed, with democratic aspirations rising with the endorsement of post-materialism, although evaluations of democratic performance stay relatively constant. Hence, the net deficit is 20 points for materialists, but 25 points for post-materialists.

When interpreting this evidence, however, it is important to avoid the tautological fallacy of circular reasoning. In particular, the standard four-item materialism/post-materialism index includes one item measuring the priority given to '*Giving people more say in important government decisions.*' Since this statement reflects the essence of democratic participation and citizen empowerment, assuming that political attitudes are coherent and well structured, any link between the standard four-item post-materialism scale and other survey items measuring the importance of democratic values would not be wholly unexpected. The post-materialism index is also one component of the survival-self expression index, which also includes feelings of national pride, respect

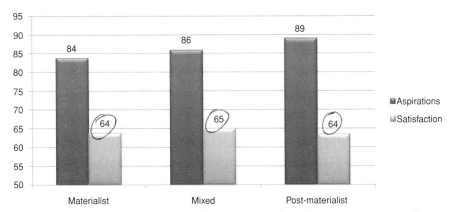

FIGURE 7.3. Democratic orientations by post-materialist values, 2005–2007. (i) Democratic aspirations: V162. *"How important is it for you to live in a country that is governed democratically? On this scale where 1 means it is 'not at all important' and 10 means 'absolutely important' what position would you choose?" Standardized to 100 pts.* (ii) Democratic satisfaction: V163. *"And how democratically is this country being governed today? Again using a scale from 1 to 10, where 1 means that it is 'not at all democratic' and 10 means that it is 'completely democratic,' what position would you choose?" Standardized to 100 pts.* Democratic deficit: *Mean difference between (i) and (ii).* Source: The World Values Survey 2005–2007.

for authority, subjective well-being, and willingness to sign a petition, among other items. Again, if citizens hold coherent and well-structured belief systems, given the construction and meanings of the items used in the scale's construction, self-expression values would be expected a priori to be strongly related to democratic values.

Overall we can conclude that democratic aspirations are strongly related to individual-level educational qualifications and to post-material and self-expression values, lending some limited support to the core claims at the heart of modernization theories. Yet only education was consistently associated with the democratic deficit, since post-materialism, self-expression values, and subjective well-being were all related to greater democratic satisfaction, not less. Moreover, the lack of any significant link between levels of human development and democratic orientations, as well as the stronger democratic aspirations and satisfaction found among older cohorts, means that the evidence does not support the broader cultural claim that processes of population turnover and societal modernization are driving a growing democratic deficit. Indeed, modernization theory also fails to provide an adequate explanation for the trendless fluctuations in system support observed in both established democracies and other countries worldwide. Modernization theories are most powerful when seeking to account for the long-term evolution of cultural attitudes, such as the persistent erosion of religiosity in affluent nations, or the growth of more egalitarian attitudes toward sex roles in the home, family, and workplace. But these theories are not well designed to account for the dynamic ebb and flow of attitudes toward political regimes.

II: SOCIAL CAPITAL THEORIES OF DEMOCRATIC CULTURES

The alternative cultural explanation relates democratic attitudes and values to patterns of social capital. Theorists from de Tocqueville and John Stuart Mill to Durkheim, Simmel, and Kornhauser have long emphasized the importance of civic society and voluntary associations as vital to the lifeblood of democracy.[37] The leading proponent is Robert Putnam, who argues that social capital represents both horizontal social networks, connecting individuals face-to-face within communities, and norms of reciprocity and interpersonal trust, which are thought to cement these bonds.[38] Dense social ties are believed to foster the conditions for collaboration, coordination, and cooperation to create collective goods within local communities. Social capital theories therefore emphasize that dense community networks foster interpersonal trust and civic engagement and, ultimately, such cultures underpin democratic governance. People who are closely tied together are more likely to join forces and build social movements, facilitating the expression of collective preferences in democratic polities.

The original evidence presented by Putnam to buttress this argument focused upon Italy and America. The erosion of social capital in the United States, and its consequences for declining political trust and civic engagement, is the leitmotif of *Bowling Alone*. In this study, Putnam uses a range of U.S. social survey evidence to demonstrate that Americans with low generalized social trust are also significantly less satisfied with government.[39] Building upon this foundation, the body of scholarly and policy research has expanded the comparative framework and applied these ideas to many other societies worldwide.[40] The cross-national evidence allowing us to generalize more broadly about the linkages between social and political trust, however, generates inconclusive and mixed results. Hence, research by Newton and Norris, based on comparing post-industrial societies in the 1981–1995 waves of the World Values Survey, detected that at the macro-level, social trust was positively related to confidence in public and private institutions; societies where people tend to trust each other also usually have more confidence in public and private institutions.[41] The individual-level association between social and political trust, on the other hand, has usually been found to be either very weak or statistically insignificant. More recent analysis by Zmerli and Newton, using the 2002 European Social Survey in two dozen nations, however, reported a stronger association at the individual level among generalized social trust, confidence in political institutions, and satisfaction with democracy. The authors suggest that analysis of these relationships may be sensitive to measurement issues, including the use of dichotomous items or continuous scales to monitor generalized social trust.[42] Alternatively, different comparative frameworks may well generate alternative results.

Nevertheless, if we assume that generalized social trust is indeed the root cause behind fluctuating levels of *political* trust, the exact reasons are neither straightforward nor self-evident. After all, people can easily trust their neighbors or work colleagues, without necessarily trusting the state, and vice versa. Based on the analysis of the performance of Italian regional government, Putnam claims that communities with abundant and dense skeins of associational connections and rich civic societies encourage more effective democratic governance. Dense networks of voluntary associations, Putnam theorizes, should instill norms and values such as collaboration and shared responsibilities among their members, while also affecting the wider polity, as pluralists have long argued, through interest articulation and aggregation.[43] In democracies rich in social capital, Putnam argues, watchful citizens are more likely to hold elected leaders accountable for their actions, and leaders are more likely to believe that their acts will be held to account. Social capital is thus believed to encourage better government performance, and this, in turn, is thought to strengthen public satisfaction with democratic governance.[44] The complicated linkage mechanisms in the extended chain that is thought to connect social and political trust have not been demonstrated conclusively, however, and many other theorists have reversed this relationship or regarded it as reciprocal.[45] Hence Bo Rothstein argues that when the performance of representative government is seen as effective, then this strengthens public confidence in the working of legislatures, the judiciary, and the executive.[46] Rothstein suggests that effective democratic states that promote social justice and equality, successfully maintain public security and rule of law, and deliver comprehensive welfare services that meet social needs are also likely to maximize well-functioning societies and thus social trust. Zmerli and Newton also suggest a virtuous circle or reciprocal relationship, as democracy and good government may reinforce the conditions in which social and political trust can flourish, enabling citizens to cooperate together.[47]

To examine the cross-national empirical evidence, Table 7.4 describes the distribution of democratic orientations by social trust and associational activism, while Table 7.5 presents the multivariate model of analyzing these attitudes. The item on generalized social trust is the standard dichotomous measure, originally designed for the U.S. General Social Survey, which has been used in many previous studies: *"Generally speaking, would you say that most people can be trusted or that you need to be very careful in dealing with people?"* This measure is analyzed for comparison with many other studies in the research literature. Associational activism was gauged by summing active or inactive membership in a range of nine voluntary associations, such as arts and recreational societies, sports clubs, and religious organizations.[48] The results presented in Table 7.5 confirm the importance of social capital; generalized social trust and associational activism were both positively linked with stronger democratic aspirations and also with greater democratic satisfaction. The net democratic deficit was slightly reduced by the effects of social trust. The multilevel models are designed to test the effects of social capital on democratic

TABLE 7.4. *Cultural Values, Social Capital, and Democratic Orientations, 2005–2007*

		Democratic aspirations (i)	Democratic satisfaction (ii)	Deficit (i)–(ii)
All	Mean	86	64	−22
Post-materialist values	Materialist	84	64	−20
	Mixed	86	65	−21
	Post-materialist	89	64	−26
Social trust	Not trusting	84	62	−22
	Socially trusting	88	69	−19
Associational activism	Not active in any association	84	62	−22
	Active in one or two associations	85	64	−21
	Active in more than two associations	87	67	−20

Notes:

(i) Democratic aspirations: V162. *"How important is it for you to live in a country that is governed democratically? On this scale where 1 means it is 'not at all important' and 10 means 'absolutely important' what position would you choose?" Standardized to 100 points.*

(ii) Democratic satisfaction: V163. *"And how democratically is this country being governed today? Again using a scale from 1 to 10, where 1 means that it is 'not at all democratic' and 10 means that it is 'completely democratic,' what position would you choose?" Standardized to 100 points.*

Democratic deficit: *Mean difference between (i) and (ii).*

Source: The World Values Survey 2005–2007.

orientations with multiple controls; however, one important limitation should be noted. Given the use of cross-sectional data derived from the 2005 wave of the WVS, the research design is unable to disentangle the causal direction of any reciprocal linkages. This issue can be addressed in future research once the survey items monitoring democratic aspirations and satisfaction are carried in subsequent waves of the WVS, facilitating time-series analysis.

CONCLUSIONS AND DISCUSSION

Cultural accounts emphasize that major changes in system support are driven by sociological changes, whether these are glacial processes of value change eroding respect for traditional authorities and fueling emancipative demands for democracy, or the wearing away of generalized social trust and the face-to-face bonds of community associations. These accounts provide some of the most popular approaches to understanding the complex relationship between culture and democracy, each generating a substantial literature. Neverthe-less, the analysis of the empirical evidence provides, at best, only partial

TABLE 7.5. *The Impact of Social Capital on Democratic Orientations, 2005–2007*

	Democratic aspirations (i)	Democratic satisfaction (ii)	Deficit (i)–(ii)
INDIVIDUAL LEVEL			
Demographic characteristics			
Age (in years)	**1.73*****	**.600*****	**−1.20*****
	(.130)	(.113)	(.130)
Sex (male = 1)	.142	−.040	−.150
	(.086)	(.102)	(.117)
Socioeconomic resources			
Household income 10-pt. scale	**.565*****	**2.03*****	**1.38*****
	(.102)	(.121)	(.139)
Education 9-pt. scale	**2.09*****	**−.630*****	**−2.69*****
	(.111)	(.132)	(.152)
News media use 100-pt. scale	**1.17*****	.012	**−1.14*****
	(.107)	(.127)	(.145)
Social capital			
Social trust (trusting = 1)	**.906*****	**2.04*****	**1.15*****
	(.094)	(.112)	(.128)
Associational activism scale	**.576*****	**.309****	−.167
	(.099)	(.119)	(.136)
NATIONAL LEVEL			
Human Development Index	−.214	1.45	1.42
	(.635)	(1.20)	(1.16)
Constant (intercept)	85.7	64.7	−21.2
Schwarz BIC	408,002	409,333	417,709
N. respondents	46,929	45,436	45,040
N. nations	43	42	42
Measurement	100 pts.	100 pts.	100 pts.

Note: All independent variables were standardized using mean centering (z-scores). Models present the results of the REML multilevel regression models (for details, see Appendix C) including the beta coefficient (the standard error below in parentheses) and the significance. See Appendix A for details about the measurement, coding, and construction of all variables. Significant coefficients are highlighted in **bold**.
$p^* = .05 \ ^{**} = .01 \ ^{***} = .001$
Source: World Values Survey 2005–2007.

confirmation for the predicted effects arising from cultural accounts. Three key points emerge.

1. The evidence suggests no confirmation for the bolder claims in the societal modernization theory; in particular, *democratic aspirations are not associated with processes of human development nor with age*

effects. Contrary to theoretical expectations, democratic aspirations were slightly stronger among the older generation, not the young. Even more striking, these values were not related to contemporary levels of human development in each society; today both rich and poor nations emphasize the importance of living in democratic states. The next chapter considers some of the reasons for these patterns, including the way that education and access to the news media shape political knowledge about the principles and processes of liberal democracy.

2. Nevertheless, *cultural theories furnish a partial answer to some of the issues at the heart of this study; in particular, educational levels, self-expression values, social trust, and associational activism all help to predict higher democratic aspirations.* It should be emphasized that cultural variables exerted only a modest impact on democratic aspirations, and many other factors, considered in subsequent chapters, are likely to determine these attitudes as well. For example, the models in this chapter have not yet analyzed indicators of the quality of governance and the type of regime (discussed in Chapter 10).

3. At the same time and most important, *only the effects of education widened the democratic deficit.* Democratic aspirations were positively associated with education. And the well educated were also less satisfied with the way that democracy works. Contrary to theoretical expectations, however, self-expression values, subjective well-being, social trust, and associational activism were significantly linked with *more* democratic satisfaction, not less.

Nevertheless, certain important qualifications should be emphasized when one considers the interpretation of these findings. The use of cross-sectional analysis limits how far this chapter can disentangle the direction of causality underlying cultural accounts of societal modernization on democratic aspirations and democratic satisfaction. Issues of reciprocal causation complicate the analysis of the results. Questions remain unresolved concerning how best to interpret and disentangle the links among variables, particularly if an interdependent relationship or 'virtuous circle' bundles together government policies and performance, social capital, and democratic orientations.

In particular, Putnam's original account presented the argument that historical and contemporary patterns of social capital found in different Italian regions underlay the policy performance of Italian local government.[49] Similar arguments underlay claims in *Bowling Alone* about the impact of social trust on the policy performance of U.S. states, such as the contrasts in levels of schooling, health care, and violent crime typically found in Mississippi and Minnesota, or in Louisiana and Vermont.[50] The theoretical linkages between generalized interpersonal trust, associational activism, and the quality of governance remain complex. There are many plausible reasons to make us expect this relationship to reverse; for example, as discussed in Chapter 10, rational choice accounts suggest that public trust is most widespread where governments are trustworthy. A number of scholars have noted that many of the smaller Nordic and West European social democratic states are widely regarded as highly accountable, honest, and transparent in their decision-making processes, scoring well on indices of good governance, with low levels of perceived corruption, as well as proving effective and responsive to social needs through the provision of egalitarian and generous welfare policies.[51] These states are also characterized by relatively high levels of public satisfaction with the way democratic government works, strong adherence to democratic values, and the presence of cultures emphasizing strong bonds of informal solidarity and generalized interpersonal trust.

Therefore, Putnam's theory of social capital suggests that social trust and associational activism encourage democratic values, and the empirical evidence presented here partially supports this relationship; however, the findings remain open to alternative interpretations. An agnostic conclusion remains the wisest strategy until the issue of government performance can be analyzed in more depth in later chapters. The evidence therefore suggests that culture provides a partial explanation for this phenomenon, but a lot more needs to be considered in any comprehensive understanding of democratic orientations. The dynamics of system support also suggest that alternative explanations need to be scrutinized, including communication theories emphasizing the way that the media reports politics and frames public perceptions of government, and rational choice theories emphasizing evaluations of the government's policy record when managing the delivery of public goods and services as well as any improvement or deterioration in the quality of democratic governance. It is also critical to establish what people understand when they express support for democracy, especially in societies such as China, Russia, and Mali that lack a long historical tradition of this form of governance, an issue explored in the next chapter.

8

Democratic Knowledge

Previous chapters have demonstrated that overt support for democracy as an ideal form of governance proves almost universal today; almost nine out of ten respondents in the WVS survey approved of democratic governance as either a 'very' or 'fairly' good political system for their own country. The majority of citizens in every country under comparison say they wish to live in a democracy. These sentiments are not restricted by levels of development or the type of regime in power. If taken at face value, this worldwide pattern could be celebrated as indicating popular aspirations for democracy, indeed possibly signaling the end of normative debate about the best type of governance. If attitudes shape actions, then these sentiments have the potential to fuel enthusiasm for mass reform movements in Western nations as well as strengthening the legitimacy of fragile democracies and catalyzing 'people power' street protests, opposition uprisings, and dissident movements challenging repressive autocracies, such as those in Iran and Kyrgyzstan. The ubiquity of democratic aspirations cannot be dismissed as simply a technical artifact of the World Values Survey research methods or measurement error; similar findings have been widely reported by many other studies.[1]

Yet it would be unwise to treat the meaning of the survey evidence as straightforward and unproblematic without first establishing what people in diverse cultures understand when they express the desire for democracy as an ideal principle or when they approve of the performance of democratic governance in their own country. After all, earlier chapters also demonstrated that positive evaluations of how well democracy works proved remarkably high in certain states with poor human rights records, including the one-party communist regimes of Vietnam and China, as well as the monarchy-dominated electoral autocracy of Jordan. Democratic deficits could rest upon irrational, inflated, uninformed, or inaccurate expectations about this form of governance – and thus low levels of political knowledge – especially in societies that lack historical experience of how democracies work.

Accordingly this chapter builds upon a substantial literature that has examined what people know and how people learn about democracy within particular contexts and regions. This includes studies comparing the public of the unified Germany (Rohrschneider), societies within post-communist Europe (Rose, Mishler, and Haerpfer), and states in sub-Saharan Africa (Mattes and Bratton).[2] Part I considers the long-standing debate about levels of political knowledge and the capacity of the public to make rational and informed judgments when expressing political aspirations and when evaluating the performance of democracy in their own country. Four perspectives are compared. In contrast to these approaches, this chapter builds upon traditional theories of social learning through socialization processes. The study predicts that as a result, democratic knowledge is usually strengthened by levels of formal education and literacy, by access to the independent news media, and by the historical legacy of democratic traditions within each nation. Societies and groups not meeting these conditions lack the necessary awareness and information to evaluate the quality of democratic regimes with any degree of accuracy.

Part II establishes the research design used to test these propositions. '*Enlightened democratic knowledge*' is defined and measured by awareness of some basic principles at the heart of liberal democratic regimes – as well as the ability to distinguish those principles which are incompatible with this form of governance. The fifth wave of the World Values Survey (2005–2007), covering more than fifty societies, is again the source of evidence used to analyze the distribution of enlightened democratic knowledge. The results of the multilevel regression analysis models presented in Part III support the core propositions derived from socialization theories of political learning; at the macro-level, enlightened democratic knowledge in any society is significantly strengthened by three factors: *longer historical experience of democratic governance, cosmopolitan communications,* and levels of *economic development.* Each of these expands information about how democracy works. Moreover, at the micro-level, enlightened democratic knowledge is significantly strengthened by the cognitive skills and knowledge derived from *education* and by access to information from *the news media.* The results of the multilevel regression analysis prove significant after controlling for the effects of age, sex, and income. The conclusion discusses the implications of these results for understanding the reasons behind the democratic deficit.

I: THEORETICAL PERSPECTIVES ON DEMOCRATIC KNOWLEDGE

Traditional Socialization Theories of Political Learning

This chapter builds upon classic accounts of learning processes provided by socialization theories. This mainstream approach in the disciplines of educational studies, social psychology, political sociology, and cultural anthropology has long emphasized that political knowledge, behavioral norms, and cultural values are acquired from formative experiences occurring during earliest childhood through adolescence and beyond.[3] The primary role models and sources of learning include the immediate family and peer groups as well as the school, local community, mass media, civic institutions, and other agencies of cultural transmission. Traditional theories of socialization emphasize that people's enduring social and political values, attitudes, and beliefs are gradually acquired during the formative years in childhood and adolescence, due to early experiences. Socialization processes are thought to shape the ways in which individuals acquire their attitudes, beliefs, and values of the political culture from their surrounding environment, and how they take on a role as citizens within that political framework. Longitudinal panel surveys are the most effective technique to establish socialization processes; studies of the American public using this approach established that distinctive generational differences could be attributed to certain events occurring at the early, formative life stages.[4]

The type of regime in power and contemporary political conditions are expected to play a significant role in a person's acquisition of political learning during the formative years. According to socialization theory, once established, cultural orientations are likely to crystallize and persist, even if the regime changes through the breakdown of autocracy and the gradual consolidation of democratic states. Therefore, past political conditions, decisive historical events, and formative political experiences within each society should have stamped an enduring imprint that should remain evident today in contemporary political cultures. At the macro-level, citizens living in cultures with experience of democratic governance over many years, or even decades and centuries, are therefore expected to display more informed attitudes and familiarity with how democracy works than the public growing up under autocracy. Accordingly, the cumulative historical index of democratization, used earlier, should prove an important predictor of enlightened democratic knowledge.

In addition to direct experience, people are also expected to learn about democracy through political information provided by the independent news media in their own country as well as via channels of cosmopolitan communications flowing from abroad. Elsewhere previous comparative studies have demonstrated that individual use of the news media is positively associated with many types of civic engagement, including strengthening support for democratic values.[5] These results are consistent with the 'virtuous circle' thesis, where media use and civic engagement are regarded as complementary processes.[6] In addition, living in a more cosmopolitan society – with borders open to information flows, where people can learn about the rights, principles, and procedures that characterize this type of governance – has been found to be positively associated with support for democratic values, with use of the news media within cosmopolitan societies reinforcing these effects.[7]

Therefore, traditional socialization theories suggest a series of testable propositions. At the macro-level, enlightened knowledge about liberal democratic regimes is predicted to be most common (1) in states with extensive historical democratic traditions, as well as (2) in the most cosmopolitan societies, where political information is easily available from the independent mass media, and (3) in affluent post-industrial societies, characterized by high levels of literacy and education, with multiple communication channels and widespread public access to the news media. Given the strong interrelationship between these macro-level factors, each is entered separately in separate models, to avoid problems of multi-collinearity. At the individual level, information and awareness of the core procedures associated with liberal democracy should be greater (4) among citizens with formal education and (5) among regular news media users. Multiple studies have reported that political knowledge gaps within societies are consistently associated with levels of education, although the size of this gap is typically conditioned by the type of media system (whether predominantly commercial or public sector), the type of media channels people use, and the dimensions and level of knowledge that is tested.[8]

Skeptical Theories of Political Knowledge

Nevertheless, all these propositions derived from socialization theory are challenged by alternative perspectives about levels of political knowledge. Perhaps the most common approach emphasizes the limits of citizens' cognitive awareness, even in long-standing democratic states and highly educated societies. More than forty years ago Converse suggested that many citizens lack meaningful beliefs and enduring preferences about many basic political facts, even on topics of public policy that have been the subject of intense debate among elites.[9] Yet, when interviewed in the artificial context of social surveys and opinion polls, Converse argues, the public often offers responses to questions, in the attempt to avoid appearing ignorant or negligent. These statements, Converse suggests, commonly reflect 'non-attitudes' rather than deeply held convictions, sophisticated knowledge, and enduring beliefs. By contrast, well-educated and informed political elites are thought to display more abstract, coherent, and well-organized belief systems. To support his argument, Converse emphasized that many statements of public opinion recorded by polls often proved unstable, inconsistent, and superficial, vacillating across repeated interviews, and responding to trivial methodological differences in fieldwork practices, questionnaire construction, and item phrasing in each survey.[10] This approach fueled concern about the consequence of asking the public to express their opinions in social surveys on many complex topics to which they have previously given little attention and which are beyond their immediate daily experience.

The long-standing debate about non-attitudes has given rise to a substantial literature in public opinion research, with scholars generating alternative models seeking to understand the rationality, coherence, and sophistication of social psychological decision-making processes involved in voting choice and public policy preferences, as well as the role of measurement error.[11] In an influential study that revised the Converse thesis, Zaller emphasized that ordinary people who are asked survey questions do not lack opinions; instead, they often have to shuffle through a wide range of conflicting considerations. The artificial interview process prompts respondent to offer what Zaller calls 'top-of-the-head responses' triggered by the specific question wording and order and other related contextual framing cues, without necessarily attaching any deeper meaning to their answers.[12] The replies offered by respondents may be perfectly genuine and sincere in the context, but at the same time, repeated surveys with the same respondents are likely to prompt different answers reflecting alternative questionnaire designs. In this regard, when asked to express the meaning or the characteristics of democracy, the answers are expected to depend upon the survey context and question framing.

The skeptical interpretation of opinion polls therefore implies that survey data about mass attitudes toward democracy are not necessarily based on a sophisticated, informed, and coherent grasp of the main principles of democracy. This perspective is in line with Schedler and Sarsfield's argument that abstract notions of democracy are a social valence issue, similar to concepts such as personal success and happiness, which provoke positive reactions although people are often unable to define more concrete meanings of these terms.[13] Popular misconceptions, irrational beliefs, and lack of awareness of some basic facts concerning political events, issues, persons, and institutions have been widely documented in many social surveys, particularly among politically disengaged and uninterested citizens.[14] In the United States, for example, public opinion polls have demonstrated limited knowledge, such as being able to identify the name of the vice president, rights guaranteed by the First Amendment, the size of the federal budget deficit, which party controls Congress, or the proportion of minorities in the American population.[15] Lack of understanding about the fundamental principles of democracy is reported even in long-established liberal democratic states, such as the United States and Western Europe. This general problem can be expected to be exacerbated in countries that lack historical experience of this form of governance, and in developing societies with restricted access to information from the independent news media, as well as among the less educated and literate sectors of the population. Although the issue of limited knowledge is widely recognized in social psychological studies of decision-making processes shaping consumer choices, voting behavior, and public policy preferences, less is known about the extent of public awareness about democracy, for example, when surveys ask respondents to rate the importance of living in a democracy, to evaluate the democratic performance of their own government, and to express their preferences toward democracy and autocracy. These sorts of questions are also potentially vulnerable to prompting politically correct answers that are perceived to be socially acceptable to the interviewer. This danger is common everywhere but it is particularly acute in autocracies such as China, Belarus, and Iran, which severely limit freedom of expression, encouraging respondents to disguise the expression of their true opinions.

In a related argument, Inglehart and Welzel suggest that although most people around the world say that they like the general idea of democracy and that they support democratic values, this does not necessarily indicate strong motivations or deep-rooted coherent orientations.[16] Inglehart and Welzel reason that in many societies a marked disjuncture is evident between overt public expressions of support for democracy and the actual type of regime in power (measured historically by Freedom House). By contrast, they argue, the presence of more deeply rooted 'emancipative' or 'self-expression' attitudes, values, and behaviors in society, exemplified by feelings of social (interpersonal) trust, tolerance of out-groups, and political participation, prove a more accurate cultural predictor of the persistence of democratic regimes.[17] For Inglehart: "Although lip service to democracy is almost universal today, it is not necessarily an accurate indicator of how deeply democracy has taken root in a given country. The extent to which a society emphasizes a syndrome of tolerance, trust, political activism and Post-materialist values is a much stronger predictor of stable democracy."[18] Yet it may be highly misleading to assume that strong democratic aspirations, by themselves, would be directly related to either the attainment or the persistence of democratic regimes. Public opinion can overwhelmingly favor democratic rule, as can be observed in the cases of China, Vietnam, and Iran, and yet citizens in these states may be powerless to overthrow long-established autocracies.[19] Democratic aspirations may be genuine but unrealized or even repressed. For example, in Iran, days of street protests after the disputed June 2009 presidential election were followed by a security crackdown resulting in almost a dozen deaths and the arrest of hundreds of demonstrators, including activists, journalists, academics, and lawyers.[20] In a context where states are willing to imprison opponents and suppress opposition reform movements, it is a flawed logic to expect that public opinion, no matter how favorable toward democracy, would reflect the type of regime in power. Even in more liberal regimes that respect human rights, both institutional structures and also levels of human development may prove more powerful drivers of democratization than cultural values alone.[21] The meaningfulness of public expressions of support for democracy, like other types of attitudes and values, can be explored by seeing whether public opinion remains stable over time where conditions are also relatively unchanged, and whether attitudes and values are coherently structured, displaying a consistent underlying logic.

Relativism

An alternative interpretation offered by the relativistic view emphasizes that the concept of democracy holds culturally specific meanings in different contexts, with the word changing its connotation in translation and in everyday usage. One major challenge in understanding public opinion on this issue, especially in comparative perspective, is that democracy is an essentially contested, multidimensional, normative concept that is open to multiple meanings. Thus, assessing the factual basis for any understanding of democracy is different from, for example, testing how many citizens can correctly identify the name of their local elected representative or the number of members in the Senate, where there are unambiguous factually right or wrong answers. With the essentially contested concept of democracy, it is difficult to establish an appropriate clear-cut factual baseline of agreed truth against which to assess levels of knowledge. Hence, theorists have long argued about the alternative virtues of participatory, direct, deliberative, cosmopolitan, liberal, associational, social, and representative versions of democracy.[22] Following Lijphart, institutionalists continue to debate the pros and cons concerning consensus and majoritarian democracies.[23] More recently, a plethora of adjectives has been used to try to account for contrasts among regimes in the 'gray' area located between the most clear-cut cases of absolute autocracies and established liberal democracies. Alternative approaches have struggled to categorize these regimes variously as 'semi-democracy,' 'semi-free,' 'partly democratic,' 'electoral democracy,' 'hybrid democracy,' 'electoral autocracy,' or 'illiberal democracy.'[24] According to relativists, the language, institutions, and meaning of democracy is remade and evolves within each society, so that classical liberal notions based on Western political thought are not fixed in stone when transported to other cultures.[25] For example, Keane argues that a process of 'indigenization' means that democracy adapts to its specific local environment. As such, focusing on formal institutions such as elections and party competition, or the existence of human rights, represents a relatively narrow Western prism that excludes democratic evolutions in other societies and cultures. In terms of empirical measurement, as well, continuing debate among scholars advocating minimalist and maximalist approaches also reflects deeper arguments about conceptual definitions and underlying meanings.[26] Not surprisingly, where experts and scholars disagree, there is considerable latitude for different understandings of ambiguous terms in ordinary language and popular discourse.

Moreover, claims about the performance of democracy are themselves political and thus subject to contestation. Politicians, governments, the mass media, and advocacy organizations can all attempt to manipulate citizens' judgments by providing misleading information.[27] The general public may be particularly muddled or ill-informed about the idea of democracy in states where powerful elites in autocratic regimes restrict the free flow of information across national borders, censor internal dissent, and propagate Orwellian rhetoric by claiming that their states are already democratic; for example, Kim Jung Il rules the country officially entitled the Democratic People's Republic of North Korea. In China, Chairman Mao proclaimed that the Communist Party served democracy by acting *for* the people, while by contrast he argued that competing interest groups represented narrow cliques rather than the public good.[28] The cultural meaning of democracy therefore deserves closer scrutiny, most especially among publics in long-standing autocracies, such as in China, Vietnam, Belarus, and Saudi Arabia, where the independent news media are restricted and where ordinary people lack historical experience of this form of governance.

The relativistic perspective was emphasized by Schaffer, based on evidence derived from in-depth interviews conducted in Senegal, a mostly Islamic and agrarian country with a long history of electoral politics. He discovered that ideas of "demokaraasi" held by Wolof-speakers often reflect concerns about collective security rather than the standard liberal concepts of free and fair elections, accountable executives, and respect for human rights.[29] Elsewhere it has been suggested by other scholars that the Confucian tradition that predominates in the Chinese culture has translated the idea of democracy into 'government *for* the people,' meaning rule in their general interests, rather than 'government *by* the people,' as conventionally understood in Western cultures.[30] If so, then the meaning of democracy in China, Vietnam, Taiwan, and other East Asian societies sharing a common Confucian tradition may display a distinctive understanding of the characteristics of this form of government. If this is indeed the pervasive understanding in East Asia, then the performance of the state in delivering record economic growth in the 'East Asian Tigers,' lifting millions out of poverty, could help to explain why an instrumental evaluation would lead citizens in these countries to award high marks to their governments. Another indicator of the culturally specific meaning of democracy was derived from comparisons within the newly united Germany. After the fall of the Berlin Wall, Hofferbert and Klingemann found that the attitudes of West and East Germans shared certain common notions about what defines democracy in terms of procedures and processes, such as the association of this form of governance with freedom of speech and competitive elections. Nevertheless, during the 1990s, West and East German citizens differed significantly in their understanding of the social and economic features of democracy.[31]

If the relativistic perspective is correct, then people in societies as diverse as the United States, China, Ghana, Jordan, and Sweden may endorse democratic values in the abstract, but cultures will differ sharply in how the term is understood. As a result, there may be no agreed factual yardstick against which to judge the rationality of mass (or, indeed, elite) opinions about democracy.[32] Conceptual equivalence is a constant challenge for cross-national questionnaires and it extends far beyond matters of linguistic translation. Languages are not just ways to communicate the same ideas and values; instead, they may carry alternative ways of thinking and understanding.

Open-ended questions tapping the meaning of democracy help to establish whether understandings of the concept of democracy are shared around the world. Using Global Barometer surveys conducted in more than fifty countries, Dalton, Shin, and Jou analyzed the result of open-ended responses when ordinary people were asked to describe the meaning of democracy.[33] The study found that in most places, democracy was broadly associated with ideas of freedom and civil liberties. This response was far more common than defining the meaning of democracy in terms of institutions and procedures, such as elections or rule of law, or describing it in terms of instrumental social benefits, such as peace, stability, and social equality. At the same time, roughly one-fifth of the public could not offer any substantive definition of democracy.

The use of 'anchoring vignettes' is an alternative methodology designed to generate more accurate survey measurement of complex notions, especially those involving differences among respondents on normative issues, such as democracy, freedom, privacy, and corruption. This approach measures responses to hypothetical examples, allowing analysts to arrive at an inductively derived understanding of the common usage of a core concept and reducing interpersonal incomparability (where survey questions hold different meanings for each respondent).[34] Using vignettes allows analysts to examine the meaning of democracy, then to use this measure to rescale the rating of democracy in their own country. The logic of the relativist argument, however, challenges the ability of many existing standard survey instruments to capture cognitive awareness of democracy, if the essential meaning and definition of democracy vary cross-culturally. Where truth is contested, no agreed-on yardstick is available to evaluate whether views are more or less informed about democracy, as societies lack a common understanding of the core concept.

Instrumental Support for Governance

Yet another viewpoint suggests that support for democracy often reflects calculations about the quality of governance, such as ideas of efficiency and effectiveness, rather than reflecting intrinsic commitment to democratic ideals. For example, Bratton and Mattes emphasize that most citizens in Africa favor democracy for its ability to guarantee basic political rights, but some provide instrumental reasons, where this type of regime is associated with economic prosperity, improvements in living standards, the alleviation of poverty, and the provision of health clinics and schools.[35] Moreno also compared what Costa Ricans, Chileans, and Mexicans regarded as the main task of democracy, concluding that instrumental benefits (notably fighting crime and redistributing wealth) were often cited as major priorities by many citizens, while elections and the protection of minorities were not regarded as so important.[36] Moreno found that both news media use and political knowledge consistently strengthened the focus on procedural characteristics.

Instrumental support for democracy is important and real, but it is also limited and conditional. If governments fail to deliver jobs, prosperity and social services, then public enthusiasm for democracy may fade.[37] Democratic governance has long predominated in Western nations, and hence it may have become associated in the public's mind with the world's richest and most powerful nations. Nevertheless, instrumental approval does not mean that citizens possess detailed knowledge about the complex principles, practices, and procedures underlying how this form of governance works, or that they approve of these characteristics. Moreover, the idea that democracy inevitably leads to greater affluence, social equality, or improved public services is a deeply contested normative claim rather than a universally accepted scientific truth. Research remains divided; some studies suggest that poor democracies usually outperform poor autocracies in economic growth and the delivery of social services, as shown by indicators of maternal mortality, education spending, or poverty, but other scholars continue to cast doubt on these claims.[38] The widespread belief in the instrumental benefits of democracy can therefore be regarded as a contested truth that may prove to be factually incorrect. Instrumental aspirations for democracy are meaningful and genuine but also probably misplaced and erroneous, if founded upon the belief that democratic reforms will automatically generate certain material benefits.

To summarize these arguments, socialization theories are widely popular accounts of social learning but they are also challenged. Skeptical interpretations emphasize that political knowledge is usually limited, so that many citizens commonly lack the capacity to distinguish some of the basic features of democratic and autocratic regimes. Relativists suggest that the meaning of many complex concepts is usually culturally specific, including ideas about democracy. Instrumentalists claim that public satisfaction is often based primarily upon judgments about the quality of governance rather than adherence to basic democratic principles. Democratic states evolved during earlier centuries in some of the world's most stable and affluent societies, so the reverse logic infers that democratic governance will be more effective at generating these qualities elsewhere.

II: EVIDENCE ABOUT LEVELS OF DEMOCRATIC KNOWLEDGE

The empirical survey evidence can be scrutinized to establish what people in diverse societies know and understand by the idea of democracy. But what is the most appropriate way of conceptualizing and measuring 'political knowledge'? The simple true-false factual knowledge approach, or the so-called civics test approach, exemplified by Delli Carpini and Keeter, assumes that voters need to grasp the basic institutional arrangements in any regime (typified in American studies by being able to identify the name of the U.S. vice president or which party controls Congress), comprehensive and detailed information about the policy platforms of the main contenders for office, and familiarity with the fine print of the government's record.[39] The main problem with the encyclopedic approach is that even in long-established democracies and highly educated societies, the majority of citizens appear to fail these test most of the time. Often the trivial is weighted equally with the important in knowledge scores, and no allowance is made for whether it makes any difference or whether there are any consequences if citizens get the answers right or wrong.

In contrast, the *relativist* approach acknowledges that people have a limited reservoir of political information but suggests that this can be sufficient for citizens.[40] Relativists argue that cognitive shortcuts, such as ideology or 'schema,' like a handy ready reckoner, reduce the time and effort required to make a reasoned choice about the performance of government with imperfect information. In this view, citizens are capable of making good low-information decisions because the costs of keeping fully informed are high, whereas the rewards for engaging in politics in contemporary democracies are low. Relativists lower the necessary information hurdles, producing a more realistic assessment so that most citizens get at least a passing grade. Yet one major difficulty with this approach is that the cognitive shortcuts that voters use to decide may be helpful in reducing the buzzing clutter of multiple messages, or they may be based on serious factual inaccuracies – or 'false knowledge' – especially if the public is not paying attention when evaluating the quality of democracy.

The last approach, associated with the work of Lupia and McCubbins, focuses on the importance of *practical knowledge*.[41] In this view, citizens need to acquire sufficient information, primarily from the news media, for them to be able to estimate how their democracy works. People need practical knowledge – in domains that matter to them – to connect their political preferences for democracy accurately to how democracy works. This approach strikes a middle way on the assumption that citizens do not need to know everything about democratic governance, as if cramming for a school civics test. Nor do they need to rely upon ideological shortcuts, such as feelings of national pride, to evaluate the performance of democracy in their own country, as such shortcuts may prove misleadingly dated or inaccurate. Instead, the practical knowledge approach, which is adopted in this study, implies that for rational judgments, citizens need sufficient practical information to connect their preferences for living in a democratic state with how well their government meets democratic standards.

Accordingly, the concept of *enlightened democratic knowledge* is defined and measured in this study by whether citizens can accurately identify a few of the core principles, institutions, and processes that are most closely associated with liberal democracy, as well as applying the more rigorous test of whether they can also clearly distinguish characteristics that are incompatible with this form of rule. In terms of the core procedures of liberal democracy, the benchmark adopted in this study for measuring an accurate understanding is defined by Dahl's notion of polyarchy, emphasizing the importance of the institutions leading toward political participation and contestation.[42] In particular, knowledgeable citizens should be aware that democratic states use regular, competitive, multiparty elections with universal suffrage to fill the major legislative and executive offices. But this, by itself, sets the knowledge benchmark test fairly low. In addition, knowledgeable citizens should also recognize that liberal democracies respect a wide range of fundamental freedoms and civil liberties, so that contending interests can be expressed and compete through processes of articulation and representation, including freedom of belief, speech and publication, assembly, and association. Knowledgeable citizens should also recognize that liberal democratic states are based on the rule of law and judicial independence so that legal rules are applied fairly and consistently across equivalent cases and all citizens have equal access to justice.

This form of governance also respects the principle of equal rights for women and for ethnic, religious, and cultural minority groups, not restricting the participation and representation of minorities in political processes.[43] Conversely, as well as getting the 'true' statement correct, knowledgeable citizens should also be able to distinguish the 'false' statements in any multiple-choice test, by rejecting certain practices that are incompatible with liberal democracy. Hence knowledgeable citizens should be able to recognize that democracies incorporate civilian control of the military, where the army stays in the barracks in any political crisis, as well as understanding the principle of the separation of church and state, maintaining the distinction between governmental and spiritual authority.

To analyze democratic knowledge, this chapter draws upon a battery of items included in the 2005–7 wave of the WVS. The survey asked people to identify the essential characteristics associated with democracy, using a 10-point scale to rank the importance of a list of ten items shown in Table 6.1, with the following question:

Many things may be desirable, but not all of them are essential characteristics of democracy. Please tell me for each of the following things how essential you think it is as a characteristic of democracy. Use this scale where 1 means "not at all an essential characteristic of democracy" and 10 means it definitely is "an essential characteristic of democracy."

Four characteristics in the list reflect an understanding of the procedures associated with democratic governance, including the idea that democracies respect civil rights to protect people against oppression, and under this form of governance people typically choose their leaders through a process of free elections, women and men have equal rights, and people can change laws through referenda. The design of these items unfortunately contains certain ambiguities that make them less than ideal. Respect for equal rights for women is not exclusively associated with liberal democracies, by any means; for example, gender quotas for parliamentary office were used in many communist states before they became widely adopted elsewhere. Only certain democracies, not all, allow the use of legally binding referenda.[44] In parliamentary democracies, electors choose parties as collectivities, but prime ministers and party leaders are usually selected through other indirect mechanisms. Nevertheless, these four survey items serve as proxy measures for some of the basic components of Dahl's notion of polyarchy and thus best fit a procedural understanding of democratic governance.[45]

The idea that elections are at the heart of any liberal democracy sets the knowledge bar relatively low, however, as this notion is so widely endorsed. Being able to distinguish characteristics that are *not* an integral and essential part of liberal democracy provides a more stringent and rigorous test of knowledge. Another four items listed in the battery of characteristics tap *instrumental* notions of the quality of governance, including whether democracy is characterized by economic prosperity, punishment of criminals, state aid for unemployment, and redistributive taxation/welfare states. Again, the design of these items is not ideal, but they reflect the general notion that democratic governance is usually more effective and efficient in delivering material benefits through improved living standards, economic growth, and the alleviation of poverty; maintaining law and public safety against crime; and managing an efficient and equitable delivery of public goods and services. People may come to regard democratic governance favorably on instrumental grounds if this type of regime becomes associated in their minds with the world's most powerful states, affluent post-industrial societies, and advanced economies. This perception is not uninformed; historically, most democratic states *have* typically displayed these characteristics. Instrumental notions of governance reflect genuine attitudes and perceptions, not non-attitudes. Nevertheless, this type of support does not imply any durable commitment to the procedures and principles associated with how democratic governance works, nor does it display any awareness of the institutional characteristics and processes of democracy. The last two items contained in the list are closely associated with certain types of *authoritarian* governance, namely, a situation in which the army takes over when the government is incompetent (through military rule or a coup d'état), and states where religious authorities interpret the law (theocracy). Knowledgeable citizens should be capable of rejecting principles that are, in fact, antithetical to conventional notions of liberal democracy. This form of governance requires, at a minimum, that the military is always kept under civilian control and that religious and state authorities are clearly separated. Citizens with a fuzzier understanding will be less capable of distinguishing how different types of regimes work.

Using the complete battery of closed-ended items allows us to examine the characteristics that the public thought were most closely associated with the concept of democracy. The procedural knowledge scale was constructed by adding together scores on each of the four institutional characteristics of liberal democracy (standardized to construct a 0–10-point scale). Similar processes were followed by adding together the scores that identified the instrumental and the authoritarian understanding of the characteristics of democracy to construct standardized instrumental and authoritarian scales. Last, to summarize the patterns, an enlightened awareness of liberal democracy scale was constructed by deducting the scores on the combined instrumental and authoritarian scales from the procedural scale. That is to say, a more knowledgeable grasp of liberal democracy was defined as (1) understanding some of the core principles and practices of how liberal democratic states work and (2) rejecting the idea that democracy generates certain instrumental benefits, and that democracy is compatible with certain autocratic practices. In examining knowledge, models need to control for the standard individual-level social characteristics most closely associated with access to education and the media, namely, sex, household income, and socioeconomic status. Multilevel models allow us to monitor simultaneously both the societal and the individual characteristics of the most knowledgeable citizens.

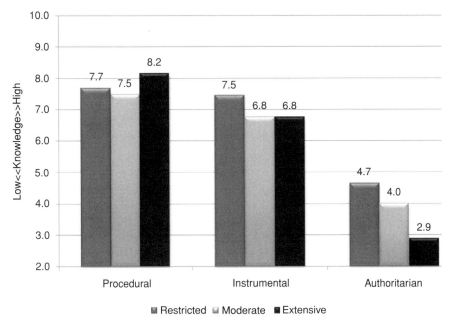

FIGURE 8.1. Perceived characteristics of democracy, 2005–2007. Q: *"Many things may be desirable, but not all of them are essential characteristics of democracy. Please tell me for each of the following things how essential you think it is as a characteristic of democracy. Use this scale where 1 means 'not at all an essential characteristic of democracy' and 10 means it definitely is 'an essential characteristic of democracy.'"* "Don't know" is coded as 0. See Table 6.1 for details of the perceived characteristics classified into the procedural, instrumental, and authoritarian 10-point scales. The *historical experience of democratization* is measured by the cumulative Freedom House index for political rights and civil liberties 1972–2006, standardized to a 100-point scale, then categorized into restricted, moderate, or extensive experience. N. 70,930. Tested with ANOVA, the mean differences among groups are all statistically significant. *Source*: World Values Survey 2005–2007.

III: AWARENESS OF THE PROCEDURAL CHARACTERISTICS OF DEMOCRACY

Figure 8.1 and Table 8.1 show the perceived characteristics of democracy by countries with extensive, moderate, and restricted historical experience of democracy. Several important findings emerge. First, *the procedural understanding of democracy proves the most widespread and popular interpretation across all types of societies.* Hence, for most people democracy is closely associated with the principles and procedures of equality for women and men in human rights, the use of free elections to choose political leaders, the existence of civil liberties as protection against oppression, and the use of referenda. People in countries with the longest historical experience of democracy give the greatest emphasis to these procedures, providing some initial support for the

TABLE 8.1. *Understanding of Democracy by Historical Experience of Democracy*

Country's historical experience of democracy	Procedural understanding				Instrumental understanding				Authoritarian understanding	
	Women have the same rights as men	People choose their leaders in free elections	Civil liberties protect against oppression	People can change laws through referenda	The economy prospers	Criminals are severely punished	People receive state aid for unemployment	Governments tax the rich and subsidize the poor	Army takes over when government is incompetent	Religious authorities interpret the laws
Extensive	8.76	8.39	7.66	7.33	6.98	7.04	6.86	6.05	3.26	2.86
Moderate	8.00	8.08	7.06	6.95	7.25	7.04	6.53	5.86	3.88	3.83
Restricted	8.38	7.95	7.59	7.16	7.88	7.68	7.17	6.53	4.37	3.88
TOTAL	8.32	8.14	7.36	7.11	7.31	7.19	6.78	6.07	3.80	3.56

Note: Q: *"Many things may be desirable, but not all of them are essential characteristics of democracy. Please tell me for each of the following things how essential you think it is as a characteristic of democracy. Use this scale where 1 means 'not at all an essential characteristic of democracy' and 10 means it definitely is 'an essential characteristic of democracy.'"* 'Don't knows' are coded 0. N. 55.485. The *historical experience of democratization* is measured by the cumulative Freedom House index for political rights and civil liberties 1972–2006, standardized to a 100-point scale, then categorized into restricted, moderate, or extensive experience.

Source: World Values Survey 2005.

experiential thesis, but the public in other types of regimes also recognize these characteristics. The instrumental understanding of the characteristics of democratic governance proves slightly less popular, although not uncommon. The instrumental benefits are emphasized most often by citizens living in autocracies, such as China, Russia, Iraq, and Jordan, with little or no historical experience of other regimes. Last, the authoritarian understanding is far less common, especially in democratic states.

If we look at the regional patterns, in Table 8.2, overall the procedural conception of democracy – including the principles of women's equal rights, free election, civil liberties, and referenda – was seen by respondents in all world regions as the most essential characteristic of democracy. Indeed, although Scandinavia led the way in regarding these features as essential, a broad consensus about the importance of these characteristics for democracy was found worldwide. Many people also agreed that democracy was characterized by the instrumental benefits, albeit slightly less strongly. Hence people in Vietnam, Taiwan, and Ethiopia were particularly likely to say that democracy was important but for instrumental reasons, because of the improved governance it was assumed to bring. But this understanding was not confined to developing countries, by any means; for example, the majority of West Europeans also thought that democracies were characterized by economic prosperity, rule of law, state welfare, and progressive taxation. Last, the majority of people in all world regions reject the notion that either military rule or theocracy is compatible with democracy. But authoritarian notions of democracy were particularly common in highly religious Muslim societies, such as Jordan, Iran, Ethiopia, Mali, and Iraq, where many people believed that it was not inconsistent with democracy for religious authorities to interpret the law or for the security forces to intervene if the government proved incompetent.

To explore the underlying factors helping to explain these alternative understandings of the characteristics of democracy, multilevel regression models were used, controlling for age, sex, and income at the individual level, all standard factors commonly associated with social and political attitudes and beliefs. The models seek to test how far political knowledge is influenced by historical experiences of democracy at the societal level, and by education and news media use at the micro-level. These models were run for the procedural, instrumental, and authoritarian perceptions of democracy, each standardized to 100-point scales. Moreover, an overall summary measure of enlightened knowledge was constructed by subtracting the instrumental and authoritarian scales from the procedural scale. All independent variables were standardized using mean centering, as is conventional in multilevel models. This helps to reduce the dangers of multi-collinearity, as well as to facilitate comparison of the strength of the regression coefficients across all variables, as discussed in the previous chapter.

Table 8.3 demonstrates that at the micro-level, a procedural understanding of the characteristics of democracy was most strongly predicted by education and use of the news media, and, to a lesser extent, by age, sex, and income.

TABLE 8.2. *Understanding of Democracy by World Region*

World Region	Procedural understanding				Instrumental understanding				Authoritarian understanding	
	Women have the same rights as men	People choose their leaders in free elections	Civil liberties protect against oppression	People can change laws through referenda	The economy prospers	Criminals are severely punished	People receive state aid for unemployment	Governments tax the rich and subsidize the poor	Army takes over when government is incompetent	Religious authorities interpret the laws
Africa	8.22	8.36	7.34	8.03	7.71	7.81	6.86	6.03	4.87	4.84
Asia-Pacific	8.49	8.51	8.11	7.72	8.24	8.13	7.00	7.40	4.62	4.59
Central & Eastern Europe	8.92	8.67	8.39	8.14	8.53	8.07	7.84	6.53	4.43	3.86
North America	8.68	8.41	7.69	6.91	6.92	6.51	6.53	5.59	4.28	3.49
South America	8.76	8.63	7.77	7.98	7.49	6.82	7.19	5.69	4.03	4.03
Scandinavia	9.50	9.20	8.72	7.94	6.17	6.15	7.35	6.71	2.81	2.16
Western Europe	8.98	8.62	8.25	7.90	7.46	7.58	7.43	6.43	3.00	2.82
TOTAL	8.69	8.56	8.00	7.82	7.80	7.60	7.19	6.46	4.21	3.95

Note: Q: "*Many things may be desirable, but not all of them are essential characteristics of democracy. Please tell me for each of the following things how essential you think it is as a characteristic of democracy. Use this scale where 1 means 'not at all an essential characteristic of democracy' and 10 means it definitely is 'an essential characteristic of democracy.'*" 'Don't knows' are coded 0. N. 55,485.

Source: World Values Survey 2005.

TABLE 8.3. *Explaining Perceptions of Democracy*

	Perceptions of democracy's characteristics			
	Procedural (i)	Instrumental (ii)	Authoritarian (iii)	Enlightened (i–(ii+iii))
INDIVIDUAL LEVEL				
Demographic characteristics				
Age (years)	.060*	.030***	−.113***	.078***
	(.009)	(.009)	(.012)	(.008)
Gender (male = 1)	.093*	.062***	.017	.047***
	(.008)	(.008)	(.010)	(.007)
Socioeconomic resources				
Household income 10-point	.059***	.025***	.035***	.069***
scale	(.010)	(.010)	(.012)	(.009)
Education 9-point scale	.319**	.075***	−.206***	.337***
	(.011)	(.011)	(.013)	(.011)
Media use				
News media use scale	.125***	.057***	.058***	.068***
	(.010)	(.010)	(.012)	(.011)
NATIONAL LEVEL				
Historical experience of	.097	−.213***	−.658***	.493*
democracy	(.095)	(.095)	(.126)	(.103)
Constant (intercept)	7.90	6.94	3.63	2.05
Schwarz BIC	233,854	234,671	243,775	216,945
N. respondents	54,649	54,678	53,722	53,625
N. nations	44	44	43	43

Note: All independent variables were standardized using mean centering (z-scores). Models present the results of the REML multilevel regression models (for details, see Appendix C) including the beta coefficient (the standard error below in parenthesis) and the significance. The 100-point scales are constructed from the items listed in Table 6.1. The 100-point media use scale combined use of newspapers, radio/TV news, the internet, books, and magazines. See Appendix A for details about the measurement, coding, and construction of all variables. Significant coefficients are highlighted in **bold**. The *historical experience of democratization* is measured by the cumulative Freedom House index for political rights and civil liberties 1972–2006, standardized to a 100-point scale.

*= >.05 **= >.01 ***= >.001

Source: World Values Survey 2005–2007.

Thus as socialization theory predicts, an understanding of some of the basic processes within liberal democracy is strengthened both by formal education and by use of the media for information, as well as proving greater among the older generation and the more affluent sectors of the population. After controlling for all these factors, however, contrary to expectations, the historical experience of democracy in each society did *not* help to predict a correct procedural understanding. Figure 8.2 illustrates the national comparisons, showing that although some long-established democracies such as Sweden and Switzerland emphasized the procedural understanding, this understanding was widely shared by younger democracies such as Argentina and Romania, as well as

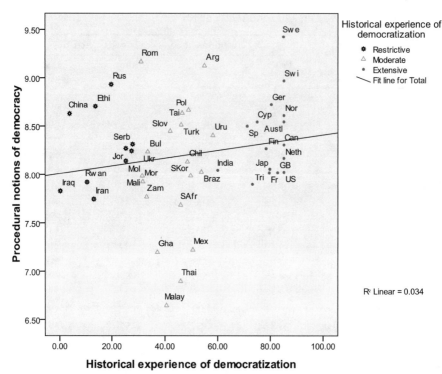

FIGURE 8.2. Procedural notions of democracy, 2005–2007. Q: *"Many things may be desirable, but not all of them are essential characteristics of democracy. Please tell me for each of the following things how essential you think it is as a characteristic of democracy. Use this scale where 1 means 'not at all an essential characteristic of democracy' and 10 means it definitely is 'an essential characteristic of democracy.'"* "Don't know" is coded as 0. See Table 6.1 for details of the perceived characteristics classified into the procedural, instrumental, and authoritarian 10-point scales. The *historical experience of democratization* is measured by the cumulative Freedom House index for political rights and civil liberties 1972–2006, standardized to a 100-point scale, then categorized into restricted, moderate, or extensive experience. *Source:* World Values Survey 2005–2007.

by Russians and the Chinese. At the same time, some other younger democracies, such as Ghana, Mexico, and Malaysia, regarded these characteristics as more weakly linked with democracy. It appears that democratic regimes are so closely associated with elections and civil liberties that awareness of these defining features has become almost universal today.

In the multilevel model, an instrumental understanding of democracy was significantly predicted by all the factors expected to prove important, including (negatively) the historical experience of democracy in each society, as well as (positively) by individual-level education and use of the news media, as well as varying by age and sex. As shown in Figure 8.3, in the simple correlations

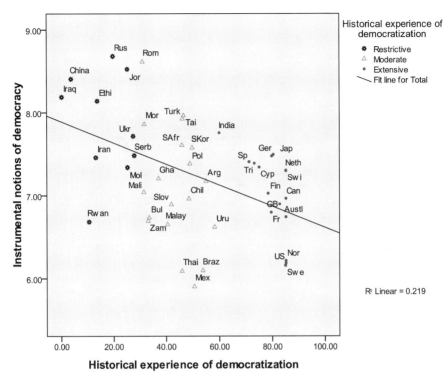

FIGURE 8.3. Instrumental notions of democracy, 2005–2007. Q: *"Many things may be desirable, but not all of them are essential characteristics of democracy. Please tell me for each of the following things how essential you think it is as a characteristic of democracy. Use this scale where 1 means 'not at all an essential characteristic of democracy' and 10 means it definitely is 'an essential characteristic of democracy.'"* "Don't know" is coded as 0. See Table 6.1 for details of the perceived characteristics classified into the procedural, instrumental, and authoritarian 10-point scales. The *historical experience of democratization* is measured by the cumulative Freedom House index for political rights and civil liberties 1972–2006, standardized to a 100-point scale, then categorized into restricted, moderate, or extensive experience. *Source*: World Values Survey 2005–2007.

without any controls, longer historical experience of democracy in each society weakened instrumental conceptions; people living in autocracies such as China, Russia, and Iraq were most likely to perceive democracy in terms of instrumental characteristics, such as economic growth or improved living standards. Although far from negligible, this conception was generally less common in long-established democracies, especially in Sweden, Norway, and the United States. Democratic experience therefore undermines instrumental understandings of democracy. This finding has important implications for understanding the meaning of the widespread demand for democracy, observed in previous chapters. Hence, people living in Iraq, China, Sweden, and Norway all say that

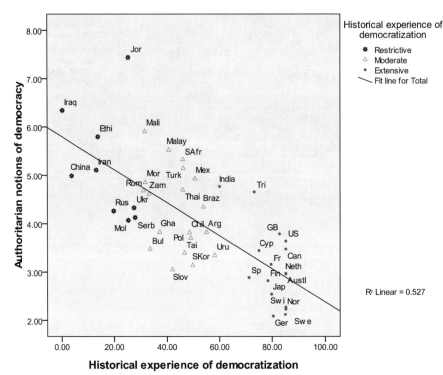

FIGURE 8.4. Authoritarian notions of democracy, 2005–2007. Q: "*Many things may be desirable, but not all of them are essential characteristics of democracy. Please tell me for each of the following things how essential you think it is as a characteristic of democracy. Use this scale where 1 means 'not at all an essential characteristic of democracy' and 10 means it definitely is 'an essential characteristic of democracy.'*" "Don't know" is coded as 0. See Table 6.1 for details of the perceived characteristics classified into the procedural, instrumental, and authoritarian 10-point scales. The *historical experience of democratization* is measured by the cumulative Freedom House index for political rights and civil liberties 1972–2006, standardized to a 100-point scale, then categorized into restricted, moderate, or extensive experience. *Source*: World Values Survey 2005–2007.

they strongly endorse the importance of living in a democracy, but the cultural meaning and understanding of this statement appears to differ substantially among these countries. The Chinese and Iraqis, for example, are more likely to express democratic aspirations because they believe that this regime will strengthen governance (by improving living standards and economic growth). By contrast, Scandinavians typically desire democracy because they think it will bolster human rights and fundamental freedoms.

Last, authoritarian perceptions of the characteristics of democracy, where the military takes over in case of need or religious leaders define the law, are also far stronger among those societies lacking the historical experience of democracy (see Figure 8.4). Hence, few citizens subscribed to these notions in Germany, Switzerland, and Japan, although the authoritarian view proved widespread in Iraq, Jordan, Ethiopia, Iran, and China. In the multilevel models, the authoritarian perception of democracy was greater in societies lacking historical experience of democracy or having limited education. This pattern helps to explain some of the anomalies observed earlier, for example, why Jordanians see their state as more democratic than the standard expert perceptual indicators; the authoritarian notion of democracy, which is widespread in this culture, could lead logically to these evaluations. In this regard, historical democratic experience sharpens an accurate awareness of what liberal democracy is and is not, and thus undermines authoritarian understandings.

To summarize the overall patterns, the enlightened knowledge of democracy is calculated by measuring the perception that procedural features are important, minus the identification of the instrumental or authoritarian characteristics. The final column in Table 8.3 shows that an enlightened understanding of liberal democracy was most strongly predicted by the historical experience of democracy in each society and by education, as well as by news media use. As predicted by socialization theory, knowledge of democracy is far from randomly distributed. Instead, citizens who have grown up in long-standing democratic states have learned how democratic procedures and principles do and do not work, a process reinforced by the cognitive skills and civic knowledge acquired through education and by political information about public affairs derived from the independent news media. In particular, democratic experience strongly undermines instrumental and authoritarian understandings. Enlightened knowledge of democracy also strengthens with age, among men more than women, and in more affluent households (which is closely associated with education and literacy).

Figure 8.5 illustrates the proportion of citizens in each country who reported an enlightened understanding of the characteristics of democracy plotted against each country's historical experience of democracy, on the horizontal axis, measured by the standardized cumulative score derived from Freedom House's index of civil liberties and political rights from 1972 to 2008. The scattergram demonstrates that enlightened knowledge of democracy rises in a curvilinear pattern with the length of experience of living in such a regime (R^2 cubic = 0.49). Hence, people in Iraq, Jordan, and Iran score exceptionally poorly on this scale. Typically, many third wave electoral democracies and middle-income economies display a moderate understanding of these concepts, such as Argentina, Poland, and South Korea. By contrast, citizens in long-established democracies, such as Sweden, Switzerland, and Australia, recognize these principles most fully.

Nevertheless, it is difficult to establish that it was the historical experience of democracy, per se, that generated awareness of democracy, rather than the many other factors commonly associated with long-standing democratic states. To test whether other societal conditions also predict awareness of democracy, Table 8.4 compares a series of multilevel models for the effects

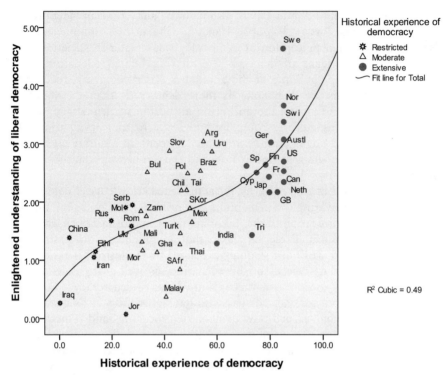

FIGURE 8.5. Enlightened awareness of democracy, 2005–2007. Q: *"Many things may be desirable, but not all of them are essential characteristics of democracy. Please tell me for each of the following things how essential you think it is as a characteristic of democracy. Use this scale where 1 means 'not at all an essential characteristic of democracy' and 10 means it definitely is 'an essential characteristic of democracy.'"* "Don't know" is coded as 0. See Table 6.1 for details of the perceived characteristics classified into the procedural, instrumental, and authoritarian 10-point scales. The measure of enlightened understanding was constructed by subtracting the instrumental and authoritarian scales from the procedural scale. The *historical experience of democracy* is measured by the cumulative Freedom House index for political rights and civil liberties 1972–2006, standardized to a 100-point scale, then categorized into restricted, moderate, or extensive experience. *Source*: World Values Survey 2005–2007.

of the historical experience of democracy, human development (measured by the UNDP's 2006 Human Development Index), economic development (the World Bank 2006 measure of per capita GDP in purchasing power parity), and the Cosmopolitan Communications Index. The concept of cosmopolitan societies is defined as those that have the lowest external and internal barriers in access to information.[46] The Cosmopolitanism index, developed for the earlier study, allows us to test the impact of communication flows on knowledge about democracy. The index is constructed by combining indicators of Media Freedom (from Freedom House), Economic Development (GDP per

TABLE 8.4. *Explaining Enlightened Awareness of Democracy*

	Predictors of democratic knowledge			
	Historical democracy	Cosmopolitan communications	Economic development	Human development
INDIVIDUAL LEVEL				
Demographic characteristics				
Age (years)	.078***	.078***	.078***	.077***
	(.008)	(.008)	(.008)	(.009)
Gender (male = 1)	.047***	.048***	.046***	.046***
	(.007)	(.008)	(.008)	(.008)
Socioeconomic resources				
Household income 10-point scale	.069***	.072***	.071***	.070***
	(.009)	(.009)	(.009)	(.009)
Education 9-point scale	.337***	.338***	.336***	.343***
	(.011)	(.010)	(.010)	(.010)
Media use				
News media use scale	.068***	.066***	.067***	.063**
	(.011)	(.009)	(.009)	(.101)
NATIONAL LEVEL				
Historical experience of democracy	.493***			
	(.103)			
Cosmopolitan communications		.557***		
		(.098)		
Economic development (per capita GDP)			.452***	
			(.092)	
Human development (HDI)				.267***
				(.092)
Constant (intercept)	2.05	1.89	1.95	1.89
Schwarz BIC	216,945	208,785	213,345	200,564
N. respondents	53,625	51,545	52,691	49,381
N. nations	43	41	42	39

Note: All independent variables were standardized using mean centering (z-scores). Models present the results of the REML multilevel regression models (for details, see Appendix C) including the beta coefficient (the standard error below in parentheses) and the significance. The 100-point scales are constructed from the items listed in Table 6.1. See Appendix A for details about the measurement, coding, and construction of all variables. Significant coefficients are highlighted in **bold**. The *historical experience of democratization* is measured by the cumulative Freedom House index for political rights and civil liberties 1972–2006, standardized to a 100-point scale.

* = > .05 ** = > .01 *** = > .001

Source: World Values Survey 2005–2007.

capita in purchasing power parity), and the KOF Globalization Index (including economic, political, and cultural components). These indices were first standardized around the mean, with a standard deviation of 1, to give each component equal weighting, and then combined into a single Cosmopolitanism index. Since levels of historical democracy, human and economic development, and cosmopolitan communications are all closely correlated, they cannot all be entered into the same regression model. A series of rival multilevel models, however, allows us to examine each of these indicators.

The results in Table 8.4 confirm the expectations concerning societal-level predictors; after controlling for the individual factors, knowledge about democracy is indeed significantly stronger in nations with longer experience of democracy, as well as in societies that are more affluent, cosmopolitan, and developed. Among these factors, human development was most weakly associated with democratic knowledge, and the other factors proved roughly equal in importance. Overall, the historical experience of democracy, cosmopolitan communications, and economic development all proved stronger predictors of democratic knowledge than the effect of any of the individual-level variables, including the impact of education.

CONCLUSIONS AND DISCUSSION

Many scholars remain skeptical about the public's competency to make informed judgments about the quality of their own democracy with any degree of accuracy. Following Converse, skeptics have argued that many respondents express opinions in surveys even though they lack coherent and enduring attitudes toward government policies on the most important issues.[47] If the public often lacks meaningful and stable opinions on basic political matters featured in the daily news headlines, it seems unlikely that citizens will display a sophisticated grasp of more complex and abstract ideas, such as the principles and procedures of liberal democracy. Relativists suggest reasons to doubt whether a universally shared understanding of the notion of democracy exists in different cultures. Alternative instrumental interpretations suggest that people evaluate democracy based on the material benefits believed to flow from this form of governance, rather than endorsing the principles and ideals of democracy for intrinsic reasons.

The socialization theory of enlightened democratic knowledge presented here focuses on how people learn about democratic regimes, throwing new light on this old debate. In particular, according to this account, learning about democracy is predicted to be strengthened by growing up during childhood and early adult life in democratic societies, as well as by the cognitive skills and information derived from formal education and by access to information from the independent news media. By contrast, lack of awareness about democracy is expected to be particularly evident among citizens who are largely unfamiliar and inexperienced with this type of governance, such as those growing up in the former Soviet Union or in contemporary Arab states, as well as among poorer sectors of the population lacking literacy, formal educational qualifications, and access to the independent media to find out about democratic politics. The empirical analysis indicates several key findings that largely support the socialization thesis of social learning.

First, in the countries under comparison, *many people subscribe to a procedural understanding of the meaning of democracy*; therefore, democracy is most commonly associated with certain basic procedures, practices, and institutions, such as leadership elections, women's rights, and civil liberties.

In this regard, the public often shares a procedural understanding of liberal democracy that reflects the checklist of institutional arrangements developed by Robert Dahl. In some societies, however, particularly those less familiar with this type of regime, democratic governance is also widely regarded as generating concrete instrumental benefits, such as states that are more effective at fighting crime, reducing poverty, or redistributing wealth. Moreover, a minority of citizens also proved unable to distinguish between the principles of democracy and autocracy, for example, mistakenly regarding democracy as consistent with military rule. Enlightened knowledge about democracy (which emphasized procedural over instrumental or authoritarian notions) deepened at the macro-level with a country's historical democratic experience, as well as with citizens' exposure to cosmopolitan communications and economic development. Knowledge was further strengthened at the micro-level among social sectors with greater education and access to the news media.

What do these findings imply for the broader issues at the heart of this book? The way that enlightened knowledge of democracy is predicted by these conditions serves to undermine the more skeptical interpretation; learning about democracy should indeed be strongest among countries such as Sweden, Norway, and Australia, where cognitive skills and civics lessons are widely available through schooling; where awareness of public affairs, world events, and political leaders is absorbed from attention to the independent news media; and where people directly experience the processes and procedures associated with democratic citizenship. By contrast, less structured and coherent awareness about how liberal democracy works would be predicted in traditional societies, such as Iraq, Ethiopia, and Jordan, especially among the less educated and illiterate populations. Authoritarian perceptions of democracy were more commonly found in autocracies that lacked historical experience of this form of governance, in poorer developing societies, and in states that were more isolated from cosmopolitan communication flows of political information across national borders.

The results also suggest that public expressions of support for democratic principles, and evaluations of the democratic performance of the government in their own country, should be carefully interpreted, as people do endorse democracy for different reasons. The public in long-established democratic societies often displays an understanding that demonstrates an accurate grasp of some basic principles and processes embodied in liberal democratic theory, including the importance of civil liberties, equal rights, and holding government leaders accountable to the people through electoral processes, and an awareness of principles such as military rule that are clearly incompatible with any form of democracy. In this context, democratic aspirations should be understood to reflect a genuine desire for the procedures and ideals most closely associated with liberal democracy.

At the same time, the meaning of democratic aspirations and evaluations of democratic performance should indeed be regarded with considerable caution in autocracies where experience of liberal democracy remains limited, in developing societies where the mass population lacks literacy and formal education, and in states where the free flow of political information in the domestic media and from abroad is restricted. In this context, democratic aspirations are often widely expressed in the general public; many people say that living in a democracy is important to them. But this should *not* be taken to mean that people necessarily yearn deeply for democratic procedural reforms, or indeed that citizens have the capacity to draw a bright line between democracy and governance.

Many Western observers share an unconscious normative bias in that they want to believe that all people worldwide, shackled by repressive states, are yearning for freedom and human rights. In places such as Ukraine, Georgia, and Iran, opposition movements have mobilized mass protests under the rhetorical banner of democracy. Western commentators and policy makers have often taken the rhetorical claims at face value, interpreting these developments as 'color' revolutions seeking to expand democratic freedoms and civil liberties. In fact, however, the process of regime change in these societies may reflect the complex outcome of competitive power struggles among rival elites, where opposition forces seek to oust incumbent leaders but with little deep commitment to democratic principles per se.[48] Moreover, the mass publics engaged in street protests in Tehran, Kyiv, and T'bilisi may be driven by the desire for good governance, exemplified by a state capable of providing jobs, health care, security, and public services, far more than by the abstract and lofty ideals of democracy. We have seen that access to the news media facilitates more awareness about democracy. But does news media coverage of public affairs also shape public perceptions of government performance more directly? The next chapter considers this piece of the puzzle.

9

Negative News

One of the most popular explanations for any growth in public disaffection is based upon theories of political communications. Two alternative versions of this thesis can be distinguished in the literature. The first, arising from the theory of 'video-malaise,' focuses upon the *type* of media. This perspective argues that television broadcasting in general and the accumulated effects arising from the standard tone of TV news reporting in particular usually foster public mistrust of government and dissatisfaction with regime institutions, thus contributing toward civic disengagement.[1] A related argument shares similar concerns but it emphasizes the *tone* of media coverage, particularly the impact of watchdog journalism when covering scandals, malfeasance, and corruption in public life, irrespective of which media convey such news. A steady diet of negative news is thought to encourage a rising tide of political disenchantment.[2]

Although plausible and popular claims, the evidence supporting each of these arguments remains scattered and inconclusive. The concept of 'negative' news is far more complex in practice than is often assumed in popular commentary; for instance, studies have found that Americans distinguish between critical coverage of issues and 'mud-slinging' personal attacks.[3] Any impact from negative news may also prove highly contingent upon attitudinal predispositions; research suggests that the effects arising from strategic campaign news coverage and from negative campaign advertising in the United States are mediated by citizens' prior levels of political sophistication, partisanship, and involvement, as well as by their media habits and by the broader political climate.[4] Moreover, while many anecdotal cases of unethical behavior in public life are often cited – such as Watergate, Tangentopoli, and the Westminster expenses scandals – the impact of revelations about these events on public opinion, especially on more diffuse levels of system support, remains unclear. The public may also be capable of distinguishing the type of scandal; after all, for all the immense publicity and the congressional expressions of outrage over the Lewinsky affair, President Clinton's public popularity was found to have depended far more upon economic conditions than on his sexual behavior, with the public rejecting elite frames.[5]

Accordingly, this chapter considers the arguments of alternative theories of media effects – arising from habitual exposure to television news and from the amount of negative news coverage – and then analyzes empirical evidence to test these claims. The chapter concludes that the cross-national data considered here provide no support for the video-malaise theory; instead, contrary to this perspective, regular exposure to television and radio news strengthened democratic aspirations and satisfaction with democracy, thereby reducing the democratic deficit. In addition, two detailed case studies in Britain and the United States are used to examine the impact of the extent of negative news coverage upon subsequent political attitudes. The results showed that in Britain, neither the amount of scandal coverage nor the degree of negative news depressed satisfaction with government. In the United States, negative news also proved insignificant, although the amount of scandal coverage did depress approval of Congress. Complex patterns are therefore revealed in each country, rather than a simple narrative. The evidence from the British and American cases highlights the need for considerable caution in any sweeping claims about how journalism is to blame for any public dissatisfaction with government.

I: IS TELEVISION NEWS TO BLAME?

The news media are thought to play a particularly important role in system support by *priming* citizens about the criteria that are most appropriate for evaluating the quality of democratic governance, as well as by *framing* whether the performance of the government is perceived positively or negatively against these standards.[6] For many decades, theories of video-malaise have dominated the literature, especially in the United States, although during the last decade this approach has come under challenge from a growing body of literature emphasizing the alternative 'virtuous circle' thesis.

The modern idea of 'video-malaise' emerged in the political science literature during the turbulent 1960s. Kurt and Gladys Lang were the first to make the connection between the rise of network news and broader feelings of disenchantment with American politics. TV broadcasts, they argued, fueled public cynicism by overemphasizing political conflict and downplaying routine policymaking in the District of Columbia. This process, they suggested, had most impact on the 'inadvertent audience,' who encountered politics because they happened to be watching TV when the news was shown, but who lacked much interest in, or prior knowledge about, public affairs.[7] In this view the general accumulated effect of exposure to television news coverage about government, politics, and public affairs has negative consequences for system support. The idea gained currency during the mid-1970s since the rise of television seemed to provide a plausible reason for growing public alienation in the post-Vietnam and post-Watergate era. Michael Robinson first popularized the term 'video-malaise' to describe the link between reliance upon American television journalism and feelings of political cynicism, social mistrust, and lack of politi-cal efficacy. Greater exposure to television news, he argued, with its high 'neg-ativism,' conflictual frames, and anti-institutional themes, generated political disaffection, frustration, cynicism, self-doubt, and malaise.[8] This perspective was taken up again by a series of authors during the early 1990s, when Thomas Patterson highlighted a pattern of growing negative coverage of public affairs in the American news media, a shift he attributed to the move from descriptive to interpretive reporting.[9] Over time, he argues, U.S. journalists have provided increasingly critical and unfavorable coverage of politics, and these trends are correlated with rising political mistrust in American public opinion. Along similar lines, Capella and Jamieson argued that strategic frames, depicting U.S. election campaigns as competitive games by each candidate, damaged public trust in politicians and government, generating a 'spiral of cynicism,' a claim sparking an extensive debate in the literature.[10] In *Bowling Alone*, Putnam echoed these concerns, blaming TV entertainment for sapping American social trust and associational activism, and thus gradually eroding the reservoir of social capital.[11] Others have attributed declining American confidence in the military and organized religion with the growth of negative news coverage of these institutions.[12]

Scholars in other countries have also echoed these types of concerns. Hence, for example, research in the Netherlands argued that public cynicism was due to strategic campaign coverage by the press, focused on stories about spin and party tactics rather than issues.[13] Content analysis of the news media in sev-eral countries, not just the United States, suggests that journalism has become increasingly critical of politicians and the policymaking process, shifting from 'watchdog' to 'attack dog' mode. In Germany, for example, Kepplinger argues that increasingly negative press coverage led to the long-term decline in public esteem about politicians that has occurred since the late 1960s.[14] Content anal-ysis of leading German newspapers found that the growth in negativity was associated in particular with coverage of politicians' personal qualities (such as their honesty, credibility, and integrity) and their problem-solving skills (including their decision-making abilities and knowledgeability). In this regard, the media may encourage the public to regard elected officials as untrustwor-thy or, at least, incompetent and ineffective. The personal behavior of political leaders, which would have remained in the private domain a generation ago, has now become the fodder of front-page headlines. In Japan, Susan Pharr mon-itored reports on corruption in *Asahi Shimbun*, a major national newspaper, finding that this expanded over time, with peaks around specific scandals.[15] Pharr concluded that the amount of reporting about official misconduct during a period of more than two decades was strongly correlated with polls monitor-ing Japanese confidence in government.

Nevertheless, although video-malaise theories are common in the scholarly literature and in editorial commentary, the survey evidence supporting claims that television journalism generally undermines political trust and satisfaction with democracy remains inconclusive. Although a popular view, especially in the American literature, these claims have been strongly disputed over the years. In contrast, the theory of a 'virtuous circle' suggests positive reinforcement effects arising from frequently watching TV news, with similar effects to those derived from habitual use of newspapers and the internet.[16] Indeed, considerable survey and experimental evidence in established democracies has now accumulated suggesting that regular TV news users typically display more positive attitudes toward politics and government, not less. The alternative 'virtuous circle' thesis holds that prior political interest and knowledge stimulates exposure and attention to news and this process, in turn, gradually reinforces practical knowledge, political trust, and civic activism. Elsewhere I have presented a range of American and cross-national survey evidence demonstrating that news media exposure consistently leads toward greater political trust and engagement, not less.[17] Some recent studies in Britain, the Netherlands, and the United States have confirmed similar results.[18] Most of this body of work has focused upon the effects of news media exposure on political trust and activism, however, and it needs to be extended to see whether democratic aspirations and satisfaction fall into the same pattern. Some recent accounts also emphasize more complex conditional media effects on political trust, which depend heavily upon the type of news outlet, prior levels of political trust, the tone of campaign advertising, the types of issues, and the heated style of modern commentary.[19] The previous chapter in this book demonstrated that the information provided by news media use strengthened democratic knowledge; in a similar way, news media use may have beneficial effects by bolstering democratic aspirations and satisfaction with the way democracy works.

The debate between the video-malaise and the virtuous circle theses remains difficult to resolve, however, in part because of difficulties when disentangling media effects from cross-sectional and longitudinal comparisons. Even if the contents of routine political journalism and television commentary have indeed become increasingly negative and critical of government over time, as video-malaise theories claim, this does not prove that these developments necessarily *caused* any greater public disenchantment with politicians. Any correlations between these two time-series trends could always be spurious, for example, if a third factor, such as the recent deep and prolonged global economic recession arising from the banking sector, undermines both media evaluations of government performance and a sense of political trust. External events, such as a rally-around-the-flag effect from 9/11, can also spur a spike in confidence in the federal government and more supportive and patriotic journalistic commentary. Alternatively, it is also possible that the presumed direction of causality in any relationship could be reversed, for example, if the public's deepening disenchantment with political leaders and government gradually encourages news organizations competing in the marketplace to respond to readers' interests by expanding scandal coverage (thereby maximizing potential newspaper sales). Moreover, explanations based on the effects of historical trends in the culture of journalism, such as any shift thought to have occurred from descriptive reporting toward more interpretive commentary, fail to provide a convincing account of the dynamic *fluctuations* in systems support, which Chapter 4 documented are evident in the United States and in European democracies. If reporting practices have gradually altered in recent decades, this cannot account for sudden recoveries in confidence in political institutions or similar short-term improvements in satisfaction with democracy.

In the light of this debate, in this chapter we can reexamine the general effects of regular exposure to television news to see whether they either weaken or strengthen democratic orientations. In particular, the fifth wave of the World Values Survey covering a wide variety of media systems and societal contexts can be used to analyze the usual or habitual effects of watching or listening to broadcast television and radio news on the democratic deficit, compared with the impact of reading newspapers and surfing the internet. Table 9.1 presents the multilevel models, including micro-level exposure to newspapers, television and radio news, and the internet, controlling for the prior demographic and socioeconomic characteristics (age, gender, income, education, and knowledge) that are commonly associated with political attitudes, as well as predicting regular patterns of media use. The models, including forty-two societies where data are available from the fifth wave of the World Values Survey, also control at the macro-level for freedom of the press, on the grounds that the independent media could well serve to strengthen democratic orientations.

The results of the analysis confirm that all these types of habitual media exposure are positively related to democratic aspirations; the strength of the positive effects of television and radio news on political values is particularly striking. Contrary to the video-malaise thesis, the results demonstrate that the more often people tune into broadcast news, the more strongly they express aspirations for democracy. Regular use of television and radio news also strengthened democratic satisfaction, although no significant effects emerged from newspaper readership, while internet users proved significantly more critical about how democracy worked. In terms of the net effect on the democratic deficit, *use of all the media reduced the gap between democratic expectations and perceived performance,* and thereby shrank the size of the democratic deficit. There is no support for the video-malaise claims that exposure to broadcast news damages democratic orientations; instead this evidence further confirms the 'virtuous circle' thesis.

II: NEGATIVE NEWS AND SCANDAL COVERAGE

Yet general use of television news does not address the alternative argument that emphasizes the impact of negative news on political trust and confidence in government. It is commonly assumed that the reputation of particular public officials, and more diffuse attitudes toward the authorities, government institutions, and even the regime, can be deeply damaged through negative media coverage. The concept of negative news is often loosely defined in the literature, for example, where this is seen as skeptical, cynical, or hostile coverage of government, or as an adversarial journalistic tone toward political

TABLE 9.1. *Media Use and Democratic Orientations, 2005–2007*

	Democratic aspirations (i)	Democratic satisfaction (ii)	Democratic deficit (iii)
INDIVIDUAL LEVEL			
Demographic characteristics			
Age (years)	1.32***	.362**	–.956***
	(.091)	(.108)	(.124)
Gender (male = 1)	.057	–.208*	–.237*
	(.080)	(.096)	(.109)
Socioeconomic resources			
Household income 10-point scale	.315***	2.27***	1.92***
	(.096)	(.114)	(.131)
Education 9-point scale	1.50***	–.428***	–1.87***
	(.103)	(.011)	(.141)
Democratic knowledge	3.92***	.549***	–3.42***
	(.092)	(.101)	(.127)
Media use			
Newspaper use	.564***	.066	–.470***
	(.094)	(.111)	(.127)
Television and radio news use	1.10***	.733***	–.349**
	(.090)	(.108)	(.124)
Internet use	.368***	–.484***	–.831***
	(.097)	(115)	(.131)
NATIONAL LEVEL			
Freedom of the Press, 2005	.109	4.62**	4.47**
	(.840)	(1.56)	(1.41)
Constant (intercept)	84.8	62.7	–22.1
Schwarz BIC	455,203	465,358	474718
N. respondents	52,522	51,713	51,277
N. nations	42	42	42

Note: All independent variables were standardized using mean centering (z-scores). Models present the results of the REML multilevel regression models (for details, see Appendix C) including the beta coefficient (the standard error below in parentheses) and the significance. The 100-point scales are constructed from the items listed in Table 6.1. See Appendix A for details about the measurement, coding, and construction of all variables. Significant coefficients are highlighted in **bold**. Freedom of the Press is measured by the Freedom House index 2005, standardized to a 100-point scale.
*= >.05 **= >.01 ***= >.001
Source: World Values Survey 2005–2007.

leaders and institutions.[20] Negative news can be evident in all types of reporting but it is exemplified most dramatically by coverage of 'scandals,' defined as any action or event regarded as ethically or legally wrong that causes general public outrage, reproach, or disgrace, commonly, but not exclusively, arising from financial or sexual behavior. Scandals transgress social norms, especially regarding money, sex, or power. Corruption, understood as the abuse of entrusted office for private gain, can be seen as a subcategory of financial scandal, although also covering multiple types of behaviors, typified by bribery, extortion, inducements, malfeasance, fraud, racketeering, and illegal monetary contributions, services, or gifts given to parties, politicians, or public officials, and irregular financial receipt or payment for contracts, licenses or permits. The events themselves are the primary cause of any political disaffection but they can only shape public opinion if they come to the light of day.

Of course, incidents of sexual improprieties and financial malfeasance in public affairs are hardly new; one only has to reflect upon the eighteenth-century cartoons of Gillray or the depictions of politics in engravings by Hogarth to realize that the world of politics has often been held in low regard. But the impact of scandals is expected to be reinforced in contemporary societies characterized by a 24/7 media-saturated and personalistic news environment, emphasizing 'gotcha' headlines, combined with a dramatic increase in the role and powers of official monitoring agencies and special investigative prosecutors.[21] This process is most dramatically illustrated in the United States by the Watergate crisis in 1972, the House Banking scandal in 1992, and the Lewinsky imbroglio in 1998.[22] Similarly in Italy, public disaffection has been attributed to the Tangentopoli (bribesville) financial scandal that occurred in the early 1990s and a long series of charges against Prime Minister Silvio Berlusconi for tax evasion, judicial bribery, and sexual scandals.[23] In Britain, as well, trust in political parties and in the government is widely believed to have been badly damaged by the series of minor sexual and financial shenanigans that undermined the reputation of John Major's administration during the mid-1990s, leading to a series of ministerial resignations. Public trust was widely believed to be further eroded in Britain by the scandal surrounding the expenses claimed by members of Parliament, which came to light in May 2009, fueling the resignation of the Speaker and many incumbent MPs, the legal prosecution of several members, public outrage and protests about these practices, and a general disgust and ennui with Westminster politics.[24] In Latin America, as well, the rise of corrupt leadership, election fraud, bribery, and clientelism has also been regarded as deeply detrimental to the consolidation of democracy and to economic development.[25] For all these reasons, multilateral development agencies, including the World Bank, Transparency International, and Global Integrity, have prioritized the fight against political corruption in their programs designed to strengthen transparent governance around the world.[26]

In open societies, the news media has traditionally long played the role of 'watchdog' as the fourth estate of government.[27] As 'watchdogs,' the news media have a responsibility to help guard the public interest, ensuring the accountability of powerful decision makers by highlighting cases of malfeasance, misadministration, and corruption, thereby strengthening the transparency and effectiveness of governance. The defining feature of investigative journalism is not the political stance of the individual reporter, story, or media outlet but rather the role of asking hard or probing questions of the powerful in order to maximize transparency and to serve the public interest. On a routine basis, timely and accurate information provided by news coverage of public affairs should help citizens to evaluate the performance of political leaders and parties, for example, the government's record in reducing poverty or improving economic growth. Investigative reporting commonly highlights failures in government, especially those arising from cases of bribery, corruption, and malfeasance, from abuse of power, or from incompetent management of public service delivery. The notion of reporters as watchdogs is one common in many democratic states, as confirmed by surveys of journalists in Sweden, the United States, and Britain.[28] Yet many factors can inhibit the extent to which this is practiced; for example, a Nigerian study emphasized that journalists often engage in clientelistic practices and bribery due to poor pay and working conditions, lack of professional training, and limits on reporting imposed by owners and politicians.[29]

Corruption and scandal are therefore widely regarded today as one of the most important causes of political mistrust of incumbent officials. According to these accounts, the blame for any growing or pervasive lack of trust rests with the reckless behavior of politicians and low standards of public life, combined with negative coverage of scandals and politics in the news media. Despite the popularity of these claims, however, it remains difficult to document this process with systematic evidence. As Dogan notes, a substantial lag can occur between the time when a specific scandal occurs or breaks into the light of day and its cumulative impact in eroding public trust.[30] Major scandals are often both idiosyncratic and episodic. Particular scandals may prove to be ephemeral events, entertaining spectacles that rapidly fade from public consciousness, possibly damaging the reputations of the individuals concerned and generating public debate but leaving little lasting imprint upon public attitudes toward government.[31] Nevertheless, in general a long series of repeated scandals is widely expected to have a corrosive impact upon public trust in social institutions, such as the way that the rising tide of reported cases of child sex abuse by priests is believed to have undermined faith in the Catholic Church.[32] Moreover, most previous studies have examined evidence for the impact of negative news and particular scandal events on specific levels of political trust, such as confidence in the U.S. Congress, rather than looking for effects on more diffuse levels of system support, such as support for democratic values. The type and severity of any scandal may also matter; for instance, the public may prove more forgiving about the personal standards of sexual behavior of elected officials than problems of financial ethics.

The most systematic empirical studies have generally either focused upon analyzing time-series evidence within particular societies, to see whether scandal events influence subsequent trends in political trust, or they have compared patterns of corruption and political attitudes cross-nationally. Some of the most systematic longitudinal evidence supporting strong claims about the effects of scandals was demonstrated in an American study by Chanley, Rudolph, and Rahn measuring the impact of congressional and presidential scandal events on quarterly changes in trust in the American federal government.[33] The authors concluded that congressional (but not presidential) scandals significantly depressed trust in American government; events such as the House Banking scandal and the Post Office scandal each led to an approximately 4% decline in trust in the federal government. Some time-series studies also suggest that scandal events are capable of exerting an even stronger impact on changes in American presidential popularity, although there is no consensus in the scholarly literature, and other research indicates that compared with the role of economic conditions and foreign policy, these events often have minimal effect.[34]

Among the cross-national studies, Anderson and Tverdova compared Transparency International's (TI) 1996 Corruption Perception Index (estimated from expert elite judgments) against measures of macro-level institutional confidence among the general public, derived from the 1996 ISSP survey in sixteen post-industrial democracies. Transparency International's Corruption Perception Index was found to be related to lower trust in civil servants and more negative evaluations of the overall performance of the political system.[35] A similar comparison of fifteen industrialized societies by Andrain and Smith also reported that the Corruption Perception Index was linked with public support for democratic ideals, as monitored by the World Values Survey during the mid-1990s.[36] Yet the results are not conclusive as these multilevel studies used standard OLS regression models to analyze national contextual effects. This approach may have overestimated the appropriate degrees of freedom and thus generated potentially misleading tests of statistical significance. Wells and Krieckhaus carefully replicated the Anderson and Tverdova study using more conservative multilevel analysis methods, concluding that the Corruption Perception Index has no significant impact on citizens' satisfaction with democracy.[37]

Moreover, the CPI index is a noisy and imprecise measure; what matters for public attitudes is less the incidence or frequency of financial scandals per se than their reporting and media coverage in each society; after all, many cases of corruption remain unknown until investigative journalism headlines the evidence. Buried scandals may not come to light if corrupt practices are widely accepted in certain cultures; if journalists, broadcasters, and editorial gatekeepers are part of the problem rather than part of the solution; and if government or commercial pressures limit watchdog reporting by the independent media.[38] The coverage of corruption could also have grown without having any significant impact on public opinion – for example, if people are already deeply cynical about government so that further stories about malfeasance and sexual misconduct lose their ability to shock, or if attitudes toward democracy are shaped by long-term processes of values change, as cultural theories suggest. Moreover, the direction of causality is further complicated by the fact that news media coverage of corruption is also likely to influence corruption perceptions, measured by the TI index. Any correlation between the frequency of major scandals and public opinion could also be produced either by the *direct* impact of the experience of bribery and petty corruption – for example, on political trust, confidence in government institutions, and general satisfaction with democracy – or by the *indirect* role of the news media as an intermediary in this process. Therefore the general idea that public faith in politicians deteriorates when standards of public life worsen, especially when investigative reporters reveal major scandals, is a plausible proposition, but the independent evidence to corroborate this claim is far from simple and straightforward.

Correlating Corruption Perceptions and Democratic Satisfaction

Several approaches can be used to crack this nut. First, to start, we can replicate previous cross-national correlation studies. Data on the Corruption Perception Index (CPI) can be analyzed in countries worldwide, derived from Transparency International's annual surveys of experts in 2005, to measure the perceived incidence of corruption in each society. These data can be compared against the standardized Democratic Satisfaction scale in each country, derived from the World Values Survey 2005–2007. Moreover, since watchdog journalism is more likely to occur where there is an independent news media sector, the correlations are expected to strengthen in societies with a free press, as measured by Reporters without Borders World Press Freedom Index, 2005.

The simple macro-level correlations generated by this process are illustrated in Figure 9.1. The results display a strong and significant relationship between each society's perceived level of corruption and how satisfied citizens felt about the performance of democracy in their own country. Hence, countries in the top-right corner of the scattergram, such as Finland, Australia, and Switzerland, have the cleanest government, according to Transparency International's index, and also relatively high levels of public contentment with the way democracy works. By contrast, states in the bottom-left quadrant, such as Ethiopia, Ukraine, and Russia, score exceptionally poorly on both criteria. At the same time, the exact role of the news media as an intermediary in this process remains unclear; the regression models presented in Table 9.2 confirm that the Corruption Perception Index is a significant predictor of democratic satisfaction, but freedom of the press proved to be insignificant, either by itself or in alternative models testing interaction effects. Moreover, as discussed in the next chapter, it was not simply lower corruption that generates more positive political attitudes among citizens; as observed later (see Table 10.1), all the World Bank Institute indices of good governance (such as those measuring government effectiveness and rule of law) are linked with democratic satisfaction.

Trends in Public Opinion and the News Media

Overall, therefore, accounts blaming growing media negativity and scandal coverage for any supposed loss of trust and confidence in government are popular, calling attention to changes in the behavior of political elites, public expectations of public officials, and/or the role of the news media. The cross-national evidence to examine these propositions remains limited, however; ideally, to determine the linkages, studies need time-series data about the contents of the news media in many countries as well as survey data monitoring public

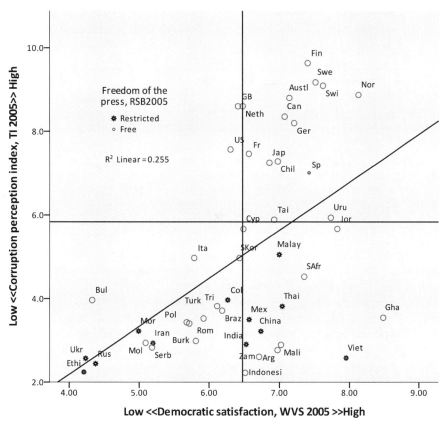

FIGURE 9.1. Corruption perceptions, the free press, and democratic satisfaction, 2005–2007. Democratic satisfaction: V163. *"And how democratically is this country being governed today? Again using a scale from 1 to 10, where 1 means that it is 'not at all democratic' and 10 means that it is 'completely democratic,' what position would you choose?* Corruption Perception Index, Transparency International, 2005. Freedom of the Press, Reporters without Borders, 2005. Countries were dichotomized around mean scores in Freedom of the Press. *Source*: World Values Survey 2005–2007; Transparency International, Reporters without Borders Press Freedom Index, http://www.rsf.org/en-classement554–2005.html.

opinion (and media use) during subsequent years. Unfortunately, such evidence is unavailable. As an alternative strategy, we can compare selected paired case studies in two countries, Britain and the United States. These countries share many cultural and social characteristics, as Anglo-American cousins, affluent post-industrial economies, and established democracies, although they also differ substantially in the structure of their broadcasting systems and newspaper industries, in their presidential and parliamentary political systems, and in their experience of particular financial and sexual scandals that occurred during these years. Hence, during the years of the Bush administration, America

TABLE 9.2. *Corruption, Press Freedom, and Democratic Satisfaction, 2005–2007*

	Beta	Std Error	Standardized beta	Sig
Corruption Perception Index, TI 2005	.234	.069	.533	***
Press Freedom, RSB 2005	−.002	.008	−.050	N/s
Constant	5.49			
N. countries	46			
Adjusted R²	.223			

Note: The dependent variable is the 100-point democratic satisfaction scale. Models present the results of the macro-level OLS regression model including the beta coefficient, the standard error, the standardized beta, and the significance. See Appendix A for details about the measurement, coding, and construction of all variables. Significant coefficients are highlighted in **bold**. Models were checked through tolerance statistics to be free of problems of multi-collinearity.

*= >.05 **= >.01 ***= >.001

Source: World Values Survey 2005–2007; Corruption Perception Index, Transparency International, 2005. Freedom of the Press, Reporters without Borders, 2005.

experienced 'Lawyergate,' the Jack Abramoff affair, and the Plame affair, while the British government had to cope with effects of the Kelly suicide and the Hutton Inquiry, Cash for Honors, and the Westminster expenses scandal.[39] Both administrations were also implicated in the 'sexed-up' Downing Street memo, which functioned as the 'smoking gun' in the run up to the invasion of Iraq. Content analysis data from Media Tenor Institute allows us to monitor detailed trends in news media coverage from 2000 to 2008, and this can be compared with indicators of system support derived from monthly public opinion polls conducted in these countries.

Media Content Analysis, 2000–2008

The Media Tenor Institute systematically content analyzed news coverage gathered from a series of major broadcast and print media outlets in both countries.[40] In Britain, this included all stories broadcast in the main BBC and ITV evening news programs, as well as coverage in three broadsheet Sunday newspapers (*Telegraph, Times,* and *Observer*). In the United States, Media Tenor analyzed stories broadcast in the NBC, ABC, CBS, and Fox main evening news programs, as well as stories reported in the *New York Times, USA Today,* and *Wall Street Journal,* and the magazines *Time* and *Newsweek.* From 2000 to 2008, Media Tenor monitored in total 1,260,401 stories in both countries, analyzing the content of all articles appearing in the politics, news, and business sections of the print media, and all stories featured in TV news programs. The content analysis coded (1) the directional tone of each news story (as positive [−1], neutral [0], and negative [1+]), as well as (2) the main subject of the story, and (3) the issue topic. The mean directional tone of stories and the amount of scandal coverage was estimated per month when the main subject concerned the government and government leaders. The directional tone was recoded to form a standardized 100-point scale, for ease of interpretation. The daily data points were aggregated to create monthly averages, to match against the public opinion polls, generating 106 monthly observation points in total. For analysis, the mean tone of news coverage and the amount of scandal coverage were both lagged by one month, on the assumption that the impact of negative news should gradually affect subsequent levels of public confidence and trust.

British Public Opinion

The monthly indicators of news coverage were compared against the available survey trend data in both countries monitoring indicators of systems support, such as trust in politicians, satisfaction with the performance of the government and party leaders, and confidence in core regime institutions. For Britain, Ipsos MORI Research provide a series of regular monthly surveys of public opinion measuring a range of social and political attitudes, including voting intentions and party leadership popularity, as well as trends in satisfaction with the government.[41] The latter is gauged in monthly polls by Ipsos MORI using the following question: *"Are you satisfied or dissatisfied with the way that the Government is running the country?"* This does not tap into more diffuse levels of attitudes toward democracy, the core issue at the heart of any democratic deficit, but it provides a suitable measure of public evaluations about regime performance. Throughout these years, the Labour Party was in government, first under the leadership of Tony Blair and then under Gordon Brown, who succeeded him as prime minister in June 2007. Public satisfaction with the prime minister, also monitored in the Ipsos MORI monthly polls, closely tracked ($R = 0.93$***) satisfaction with the British government.

Therefore, public opinion concerning satisfaction with the government and trust in politicians, drawn from Ipsos MORI polls, was compared against the monthly trends in the positive-negative directional tone of news coverage of the government, and also the amount of news stories about government scandals carried in the British media, as monitored by Media Tenor. First, to look at these patterns visually, Figure 9.2 illustrates the trends in both indicators. The graph shows some common fluctuations in both series, and some periodic peaks and troughs can also be observed. The most important periodic events during this period included the May 2001 and June 2005 general elections, returning Labour to power, as well as the events of 9/11, which reverberated across the Atlantic, and the replacement of Blair with Brown's leadership. Hence, the events of 9/11 saw a peak in public satisfaction with the British government along with a sharp uptick in positive news coverage about government. Similarly, the mid-term blues, which affect most governments cyclically, saw highly negative news coverage in the fall of 2003 and low public satisfaction as well. This period followed the Hutton inquiry, which examined the death of Dr. David Kelly, a Ministry of Defence official who apparently committed suicide after being identified as leaking that the Labour administration had 'sexed up' the report about Iraq and weapons of

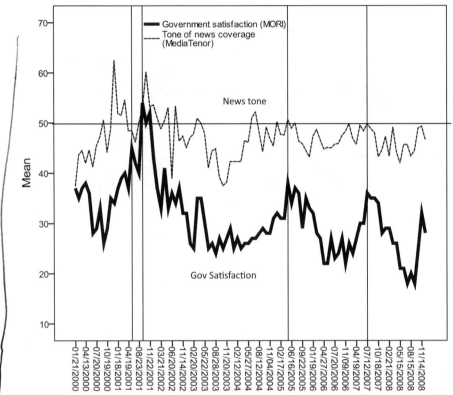

FIGURE 9.2. Tone of news coverage and government satisfaction, Britain, 2000–2008. *Government satisfaction* is monitored from Ipsos/MORI monthly polls: *"Are you satisfied or dissatisfied with the way (i) that the Government is running the country?"* *Tone of news coverage:* Media Tenor International: content analysis of the positive or negative tone of UK news media coverage of the Labour Party, Tony Blair, and Gordon Brown. The mean news tone per month was standardized to a 100-point scale, ranging from most negative (0) to most positive (100). Reference line events: (i) June 2001 General Election; (ii) events of 9/11; (iii) May 2005 General Election; (iv) Gordon Brown becomes prime minister. *Sources*: Ipsos/MORI Political Monitor Satisfaction Ratings; Media Tenor International.

mass destruction. At the same time, in other months there is clearly divergence between the series, for example, with public opinion becoming increasingly disenchanted with the government during the fall of 2008, although media coverage had not deviated from a mildly negative tone.

To analyze the data, following the approach of Betz and Katz, the multivariate ordinary least squares regression model was used with panel corrected errors.[42] The observable fluctuations in the series suggest the need to control for the periodic effects of general elections, events that typically generate an improvement in satisfaction with government, which gradually erodes over time, as well as the effects of leadership changes in any of the three major parties, and the rally-round-the-flag impact of terrorist shocks arising from the

TABLE 9.3. *British News Coverage and Satisfaction with Government,*
2000–2008

	Beta	Std Error	Standardized beta	Sig
Lagged tone of news coverage	.409	.122	.311	***
Lagged amount of scandal coverage	−3.31	2.52	−.122	N/s
Months since last election	−.090	.050	−.173	N/s
Election	8.39	4.33	.178	*
Leadership change in any major party	3.33	3.20	.099	N/s
Terrorist events (9/11 and 7 July, 2005)	10.0	4.54	.214	*
Constant	13.7			
N. monthly observations	93			
Adjusted R²	.278			

Notes: The dependent variable is government satisfaction, measured from Ipsos/MORI monthly polls: *"Are you satisfied or dissatisfied with the way (i) that the Government is running the country?"Tone of news coverage:* Media Tenor International: content analysis of the positive or negative tone of British news media coverage of stories about the British Labour government, Tony Blair, and Gordon Brown. The mean news tone per month was standardized to a 100-point scale, ranging from most negative (0) to most positive (100), and the scale was lagged by one month. The OLS regression analysis model used panel corrected standard errors.
*= >.05 **= >.01 ***= >.001
Sources: Ipsos/MORI Political Monitor Satisfaction Ratings; Media Tenor International.

aftermath of the dramatic events of 9/11 and the London bombings of July 7, 2005. The regression model of the British time-series analysis, incorporating these controls, is presented in Table 9.3. The results show that overall government satisfaction benefited most clearly by general elections and by the impact of 'rally-round-the-flag' effects arising in the aftermath of major terrorist events. The change in party leadership had a positive but insignificant effect, in part because this variable captured changes in each of the major parties, not just the Labour succession from Blair to Brown. Finally, after introducing all these controls, the lagged tone of news coverage proved to significantly improve satisfaction with government. This result is in the contrary direction to that predicted by the negative news thesis. The amount of scandal coverage proved to reduce government satisfaction, but this effect was statistically insignificant. Overall, then, despite the popularity of the claims, the results of the British time-series analysis are unable to provide conclusive confirmation of the negative news thesis.

U.S. Public Opinion

What of the situation in the United States? Although both countries share an Anglo-American culture, the institutional context differs in many important regards. The UK system of parliamentary democracy, cabinet government, programmatic parties, and a unitary state means that public satisfaction with government refers collectively to the major party in power. In contrast, the U.S. federal government, where power is divided among the presidential executive, the U.S. Congress, and the Supreme Court, makes it more difficult for the public to attribute *collective* praise or blame. Moreover, the media systems also differ substantially in both countries; the UK has a dual (public service and commercial) broadcasting system that is heavily regulated, with the British Broadcasting Corporation and ITV playing a major role in television and radio, and the daily tabloid and broadsheet newspapers serving a predominantly national audience. In America, by contrast, the commercial sector predominates in network and cable television news, and with a few notable exceptions, most broadsheet newspapers have a limited regional circulation. Moreover, the incidents and timing of major political scandals during the Bush and Blair administrations also differ in each case. As a result, the impact of negative news and scandals may well differ in each country. For comparison of satisfaction with government in the UK, the Gallup Polls in the United States have long provided a regular monthly series monitoring American public opinion, including job ratings for the legislative branch of the federal government, using the following standard question: *"Do you approve or disapprove of the way Congress is handling its job?"* These items allow us to track monthly fluctuations in popular approval at regime level.[43] Accordingly, American public opinion can be compared against the lagged monthly trends monitored by Media Tenor in the positive-negative directional tone, and the amount of stories about scandals, covered in the U.S. news media.

The visual illustration of trends in Figure 9.3 suggests that approval of Congress shows a dramatic surge following the events of 9/11, as many others have observed, before gradually falling back a year later to the level found before these events. Thereafter, approval erodes from fall 2003 until the end of the series in 2008. In contrast, the tone of news coverage shows fluctuations over time in the negative zone but no accompanying steady increase in negative news from 2003 to 2008.

The multivariate analysis presented in Table 9.4 demonstrates that the rally-round-the-flag effect following 9/11 was the greatest single factor affecting congressional approval ratings, reflecting even stronger effects than those recorded in the British analysis. At the same time, contrary to the British results, *congressional job ratings were sharply depressed by the lagged amount of news coverage of scandals*. The directional tone of American news coverage slightly reduced public satisfaction with Congress, but these results proved statistically insignificant. The U.S. analysis therefore does provide partial support for the claim that news stories about corruption and scandal can damage confidence in governmental institutions in some cases. It remains unclear, however, why there are contrasts between the British and American results. These differences could be attributed to contrasts in the specific types and severity of the financial and sexual scandals that occurred in politics during these years, or to the typical pattern of 'watchdog' journalistic coverage that followed these events

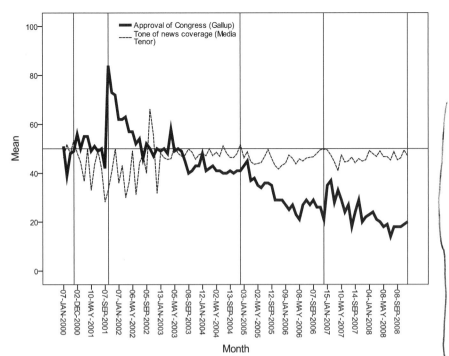

FIGURE 9.3. Tone of news coverage and congressional approval, United States, 2000–2010. *The tone of all news coverage* is defined as all the American news stories about the U.S. Congress, its members, and leaders, coded as positive, neutral, or negative in the content analysis conducted by Media Tenor International. The mean news tone per month was standardized to a 100-point scale, ranging from most negative (0) to most positive (100). *Approval of Congress* is derived from the monthly U.S. Gallup Polls: *"Do you approve or disapprove of the way Congress is handling its job?"* Reference line events: (i) Elections in November 2000, 2002, 2004, 2006, and 2008; (ii) terrorist events of 9/11. *Sources*: Gallup Polls; Media Tenor International.

TABLE 9.4. *U.S. News Coverage and Satisfaction with Congress, 2000–2008*

	Beta	Std Error	Standardized beta	Sig
Lagged tone of news coverage	−.201	.253	−.074	N/s
Lagged amount of scandal coverage	−37.0	10.3	−.312	***
Months since last election	−.322	.092	−.328	***
Election	−10.5	6.61	−.038	N/s
Major terrorist events	36.3	12.5	.257	**
Constant	57.9			
N. monthly observations	99			
Adjusted R²	.262			

Notes: The dependent variable is satisfaction with Congress, measured from Gallup monthly polls: *"Do you approve or disapprove of the way Congress is handling its job?"Tone of news coverage:* Media Tenor International: content analysis of the positive or negative tone of American news media coverage of stories about the U.S. Congress. The mean news tone per month was standardized to a 100-point scale, ranging from most negative (0) to most positive (100), and the scale was lagged by one month. The OLS regression analysis was used with panel corrected standard errors. * = > .05 ** = > .01 *** = > .001

Sources: Gallup Polls; Media Tenor International.

in each country, or to the way that the public attributes blame when evaluating responsibility for scandals under presidential and parliamentary political systems. Further research, ideally involving many cases, is needed to disentangle these sorts of factors.

CONCLUSIONS

The broadest data to examine the video-malaise thesis – and thus how far levels of democratic aspirations and satisfaction are affected by different types of news media use (comparing regular exposure to newspapers, television and radio news, and the internet) – are available from cross-national comparisons covering almost fifty societies contained in the fifth wave World Values Survey. Multilevel models examine these relationships controlling for the social characteristics typical of news users, as well as the societal or macro-level impact of the independent news media and corruption perceptions. The analysis demonstrates three main findings that undermine the video-malaise thesis. First, (1) general exposure to news and information from television and radio news, along with newspapers and the internet, usually *strengthened* democratic aspirations, even after controlling for factors such as age, income, and education, which typically characterize the news audience. (2) The effects on democratic satisfaction proved more mixed, but contrary to the core claim in the video-malaise thesis, users of television and radio broadcast news proved *more* satisfied with democracy, not less. Last, (3) regular use of all these news media, including television and radio, *reduced* the democratic deficit, or the size of the gap between expectations and perceived performance. The survey analysis therefore provides no support for the video-malaise claims about the damaging effects thought to arise from regular exposure to television news.

Yet this evidence cannot fully respond to the alternative thesis that public trust is damaged by regular exposure to negative news and to coverage of political scandals by any media outlet. Previous studies have examined these claims by comparing cross-national patterns of perceived corruption against levels of democratic satisfaction. This chapter replicates this approach, establishing that a moderate correlation does link perceived corruption with democratic satisfaction. At the same time, however, the precise role of the news media in this process remains unclear. Presumably the amount of coverage of political corruption reported by the news media may help to shape democratic orientations and political trust, but this linkage has not been fully established in existing research. It remains possible that direct experience of petty bribery in payment for goods and services in the public sector, such as contracts, licenses, and permits, could influence perceptions irrespective of journalistic coverage.

To go further, ideally studies need to compare the news coverage with public opinion in many countries and over time. The content analysis data across many countries are unavailable, but evidence from the selected case studies of Britain and the United States from 2000 to 2008 can throw some light on this issue. The longitudinal studies of the effect of negative news and scandal coverage on satisfaction with government in Britain and approval of Congress in America provided a partial test of these claims. In Britain, the results showed that neither the amount of scandal coverage nor the degree of negative news depressed satisfaction with government. In the United States, negative news proved insignificant, although the amount of scandal coverage did depress approval of Congress. Complex patterns rather than a simple narrative are therefore revealed in each country. Overall, while providing some limited support for the claims that scandal can damage confidence in government institutions, the lack of consistency among the two cases means that the results cannot be regarded as highly robust. The analysis therefore suggests the need for considerable caution and for further research into any general claims about how negative news or scandal coverage impacts public opinion.

IO

Failing Performance?

Earlier chapters documented how support for the political system in the United States and Western Europe typically has fluctuated during recent decades, including confidence in core regime institutions as well as satisfaction with democracy. The endorsement of democratic values is almost universal today, although satisfaction with democracy varied sharply over time and within each type of region, such as the contrasts found among Africans living in Ghana, Burkina Faso, and Ethiopia, or among Europeans in Italy, Austria, and Norway. What can explain these patterns?

The idea that regime performance matters, at least at some level, for public satisfaction with the workings of democracy, is the explanation favored by rational choice theories. This chapter considers how the underlying assumptions and claims embodied in these accounts differ from cultural explanations. At first sight, the rational choice argument appears straightforward, but what criteria might the public use to evaluate performance? Is the contemporary record of the regime compared against public expectations or independent indices? Party manifestos and leadership promises or the past performance of successive administrations? Neighboring countries or global conditions? There is no consensus in the research literature and several alternative factors may prove important in this regard, each generating certain testable propositions. Part I of this chapter focuses upon *process* accounts that emphasize that judgments of regime performance are based primarily upon retrospective evaluations of the quality of underlying democratic procedures, exemplified by the perceived fairness of elections, the responsiveness and accountability of elected representatives, and the honesty and probity of public officials. This goes beyond discontent with particular decisions or outcomes to tap more deep-rooted perceptions about how democracy works. Part II considers alternative *policy* accounts, suggesting that retrospective evaluations of the overall substantive policy record of successive governments are important, such as whether citizens experience effective public services for schools and health care, rising living standards, and domestic security. Last, Part III reviews *institutional* accounts, which theorize that regime evaluations based on either process or policy performance are conditioned by the intervening effects of power-sharing arrangements, determining the distribution of 'winners' and 'losers' in any state. This chapter reviews and unpacks the assumptions underlying each of these accounts in the literature and then lays out the empirical evidence and performance indicators suitable to test each of these claims.

The chapter demonstrates that process performance, measured by aggregate indicators of the quality of democratic governance, shapes public satisfaction with the way government works. Among the policy indices, economic development and a subjective sense of well-being also proved equally important, although most of the narrower economic, social, and environmental policy performance indicators were not significant. Last, among the institutional factors, the only measure that predicted satisfaction with democracy was support for the winning party.

CULTURAL VERSUS RATIONAL CHOICE THEORIES OF SYSTEM SUPPORT

Cultural explanations emphasize that democratic orientations are sentiments learned during the formative early years from parents, teachers, and neighbors, just as people acquire an enduring sense of the political legitimacy of authorities, government institutions, and the nation-state.[1] In some communities, many people are thought to acquire deep-rooted outlooks that make them instinctively trust authorities and prefer an expansive role for the state. In others, citizens learn from birth onward to be more wary about the power of the state and skeptical about how the public sector works, preferring market over state solutions. If attitudes toward the regime are largely affective, akin to enduring feelings of national pride and cultural identity, then levels of democratic satisfaction in each country would not be expected to be closely linked to the performance of regimes. The evidence scrutinized in earlier chapters established that cultural theories of societal modernization and social capital furnish *part* of the answer to the central issues in this book; in particular, educational levels, self-expression values, social trust, and associational activism are all significantly associated with rising democratic *aspirations*. Culture therefore appears to be linked to demand. Contrary to theoretical expectations, however, self-expression values, social trust, and associational activism were associated with *greater* democratic satisfaction, not less. Only the effects of education actually widened the democratic deficit. Moreover, in general, cultural accounts based on socialization processes are most plausible when explaining long-term secular trends in citizens' affective orientations and evolutionary shifts in enduring values rather than accounting for short-term volatile fluctuations.

The primary rival account in the literature draws upon rational choice theories. Scholars working within this tradition have focused most attention upon explaining the concept of social and political trust, but the general arguments and underlying premises of the rational choice approach can be applied to understand many dimensions of system support. Russell Hardin, one of the leading proponents of this perspective, theorizes that the basis of trust is cognitive, dependent upon knowledge about the *motivations* and the *competencies* of other people.[2] In this conception, as Hardin notes: "To say we trust you means we believe you have the right intentions toward us and that you are competent to do what we trust you to do."[3] The more citizens know, Hardin argues, the more reliably citizens can evaluate whether politicians have benevolent intentions, whether they are competent, and thus whether they are worthy of trust. If politicians or governments are usually demonstrably corrupt, inept, or self-serving, or perceived to be so, then rational citizens should conclude that they have become untrustworthy. Moreover, the default option for watchful citizens is to remain agnostic or skeptical in their judgments, suspending positive assessments (equivalent to the Popperian null scientific hypothesis) if lacking dependable information to evaluate the record and performance of elected representatives or leaders, if they have little awareness about how government agencies and processes work, or if they cannot fathom the effectiveness and impact of complex public policies.

Political trust is often conceptualized in this perspective as an individual relationship operating at the more specific levels of system support, typically shaping the dynamics of public approval of the U.S. president and confidence in members of Congress. But a similar logic can be applied to explain orientations toward the political system at more diffuse Eastonian levels, including evaluations of the collective government, the regime, and even general orientations toward the nation-state. From this perspective, satisfaction with the democratic performance of any regime is expected to reflect an informed assessment about the cumulative record of successive governments, whether judged by normative expectations about the democratic decision-making process or by the achievement of certain desired policy outputs and outcomes. Hence, in terms of process criteria, rational citizens who expect regimes to meet certain democratic standards – such as being transparent, accountable, equitable, and responsive to society's needs – should have little reason for satisfaction if the regime is perceived as failing to meet these benchmarks. Similarly, in terms of public policy outcomes, if politicians are elected on a platform promising to maintain security at home and abroad, improve living standards, and provide equitable welfare services, and if successive governments lack the capacity or will to fulfill these pledges, then again rational citizens should gradually become more critical of the regime's overall performance. If experience matters, however, this still leaves open the question about how the public forms judgments about regime performance and about how democracy works.

I: PROCESS PERFORMANCE

Working within this general theoretical framework, process accounts emphasize that citizens focus upon the intrinsic quality of democratic governance, exemplified by the state's record in respecting fundamental freedoms and universal human rights, expanding inclusive opportunities for public participation for women and minorities, and providing equitable and timely access to justice.[4] During the third wave era, the record of countries that transitioned from autocracy has proved extremely varied, with some far more successful than others.[5] States such as the Czech Republic, Ghana, South Africa, and Chile have rapidly consolidated the full panoply of democratic institutions during the third wave era, holding a series of free and fair competitive multiparty elections that have met international standards of transparency and openness. These contests paved the way for building the capacity and effectiveness of other core institutions of liberal democracy, including strengthening parliament, the judiciary, and public sector bureaucracy, as well as building effective political parties, the independent media, and civil society organizations. Many other states, including Russia and Venezuela, have stagnated in an ambiguous gray zone, however, with multiparty elections allowing limited competition, which legitimates the power of the ruling party or leader but without effective checks on the powers of the executive or rule of law. Such states often suffer from pervasive problems of corruption and clientelism in the public sector and occasional outbreaks of violent conflict. Still other cases such as Thailand and Fiji have enjoyed a brief democratic honeymoon period, but then floundered and reverted back to autocracy.[6] Moreover, a few regimes have proved largely impervious to global waves of democratization, beyond some strictly limited rhetorical gestures, retaining rule by absolute monarchies (Saudi Arabia), military juntas (Burma), personal dictatorships (Libya), or one-party states (Vietnam).

Beyond democracy, broader indicators of the quality of governance also vary substantially around the globe, whether in terms of perceived levels of corruption, rule of law, political stability and conflict, or public sector management. Process theories predict that rational citizens will be more satisfied with democratic performance where regimes perform well against the standard indicators of democratic governance, such as the expert evaluations provided by the Freedom House, Polity IV, and the World Bank Institute. By contrast, dissatisfaction will be far stronger in states where governments routinely perform poorly, exemplified by repressive regimes that employ rigid coercion, abuse basic human rights and imprison opponents, profit from endemic corruption and crony capitalism, and govern by arbitrary rule.

A series of empirical studies, in younger and older democracies, have provided some evidence favoring this general argument. Hence, Bratton and Mattes compared political attitudes in Ghana, Zambia, and South Africa, reporting that satisfaction with democracy in these countries is based on an appreciation of political reforms, perceptions of government responsibility and honesty, and guarantees of civil liberties, voting rights, and equal treatment under the law, as much as by perceptions of material benefits, improved living standards, and the delivery of economic goods.[7] A study among post-communist states in Central Europe during the mid-1990s by Evans and Whitefield also found that political experience influenced democratic satisfaction more strongly than the expansion of economic markets.[8] In Europe, Wagner and colleagues analyzed a series of Eurobarometer surveys from 1990 to 2000, demonstrating that quality of governance indicators for rule of law, well-functioning regulation, and low corruption strengthened satisfaction with democracy more strongly than economic considerations.[9] Similarly, multilevel analysis comparing forty nations, based on the Comparative Study of Electoral Systems (CSES) Module II survey, also concluded that political goods such as freedom, accountability, and representativeness were more important sources of democratic satisfaction than narrower indices of policy performance.[10] Moreover, process explanations can also be applied to help account for contrasts within particular countries; for example, Hibbing and Theiss-Morse argue that the U.S. Congress is unpopular relative to the other branches of the federal government because its decision-making processes are often bitterly partisan and divisive.[11] Nevertheless, Chapter 5 highlighted several cases that appear to challenge process accounts, exemplified by relatively high levels of satisfaction with the performance of democracy expressed in some countries with limited political rights and civil liberties, such as Vietnam and Jordan (see Table 5.2). Counter examples, where relatively low democratic satisfaction was expressed in some long-standing democratic states, can also be observed, such as in Italy, the United States, and the UK. This general theory therefore deserves further scrutiny and it can be tested most effectively where public opinion is compared across a broad range of countries rather than within a single global region in order to maximize variance in historical experiences, cultural traditions, and types of regimes.

Process Performance Indicators

There are, however, certain difficulties in measuring the process performance of regimes. At the micro-level, public opinion data allow satisfaction with democracy to be compared against subjective attitudes toward other dimensions of governance, such as the perceived quality of human rights or institutional confidence. This approach has been employed in the research literature, but even where a close association exists, it remains challenging, or even impossible, to disentangle the direction of causality from cross-sectional surveys – for example, to determine whether national pride is driving, or following, democratic satisfaction.[12] Moreover, unless independent evidence allows public judgments to be corroborated, the rationality of any subjective evaluations cannot be determined; for example, systematic perceptual biases are likely to arise in states where state propaganda and censorship prove effective in strengthening regime support and restricting explicit criticism of the government. In this context, as well, in places such as Zimbabwe, Belarus, China, and Saudi Arabia, survey respondents may be afraid of expressing negative views about the regime for fear of official reprisals, generating a 'spiral of silence.' Chapter 8 also established that awareness about democracy varies systematically worldwide according to respondents' historical experience of democracy, so that people with little knowledge of this form of governance in countries

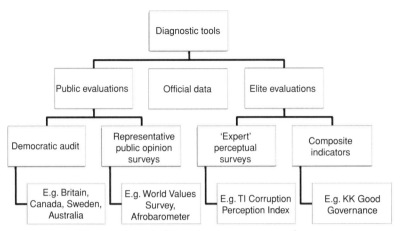

FIGURE 10.1. Diagnostic tools for evaluating process performance.

such as Jordan, Iraq, and Ethiopia will lack the capacity to form a rational assessment.

A more satisfactory strategy, also used in other previous studies, is to compare macro-level satisfaction with democracy, monitored by public opinion in any state, against independent 'objective' indicators of the quality of governance in each country.[13] Accordingly, for this study macro-level evidence is drawn from the burgeoning array of diagnostic tools monitoring the quality of governance that have become available in recent decades.[14] Political indicators are now widely used by the international community, by national governments, and by advocacy groups to evaluate needs and determine policy priorities, to highlight problems and identify benchmark practices, and to evaluate the effectiveness of programmatic interventions. Some of the earliest indicators, which became widely adopted in the academic and policy research communities, were developed to measure the state of civil liberties and political rights by Freedom House in 1972, as well as the Polity I data collection by Ted Robert Gurr and Harry Eckstein focusing upon patterns of democratic and autocratic regime change. Since then, dozens of indicators, of varying quality and coverage, have become widely available to gauge the quality of democracy in general, as well as multiple measures of 'good governance' and human rights. Some of the most commonly used measures, in addition to the Freedom House and Polity IV indices, focus on 'good governance,' corruption perceptions, women's empowerment, rule of law, levels of civic engagement, patterns of social capital, levels of conflict, and many related issues.[15] The expansion of indicators has been accompanied by gains in the level of conceptual sophistication, methodological transparency, scope, and geographic coverage of all these measures. The range of diagnostic tools is summarized in Figure 10.1. An important distinction can be drawn between public and elite evaluations, the former using deliberative democratic audits and representative public opinion polls while the latter relies upon 'expert' perceptual surveys and composite indices.

Elite-level perceptual judgments have become one of the most widely used sources of data, particularly for many areas of governance such as corruption where trustworthy 'aggregate' indicators are simply unavailable (although it should be noted that the accuracy and reliability of these estimates remain open to challenge). Organizations commonly use standardized questionnaires distributed to 'expert' sources, typically including scholars and researchers, country analysts, journalists, lawyers, business executives, independent consultants, human rights observers, and staff of non-governmental organizations (NGOs). This approach is exemplified by Freedom House's process of employing teams of researchers to assess the state of civil liberties and political rights worldwide, by Transparency International's use of experts to construct the Corruption Perceptions Index, and by the Reporters without Borders survey used to generate its annual Press Freedom Index.[16] Expert or elite-level surveys may prove unreliable for several reasons, including reliance upon a small number of national 'experts,' the use of business leaders and academic scholars as the basis of the judgments, variations in country coverage by different indices, and possible bias toward more favorable evaluations of governance in countries with good economic outcomes. Nevertheless, in the absence of other satisfactory indicators to compare the quality of governance worldwide, expert perception measures have been widely employed. Alternative macro-level indicators are compiled from official data based on administrative records collected by public officials, national statistical offices, and multinational organizations – for example concerning levels of voter turnout in national elections (collated by International IDEA), public access to the news media and new ICTs (UNESCO/International Telecommunications Union), and the proportion of women in national parliaments (Inter-Parliamentary Union).[17]

Given the numerous measures of the performance of democratic governance that are now available, which should be selected for analysis? Indicators can be set aside when they are restricted in the number of states and regions they cover, the frequency of the measures, or the time-period. Publicly available indicators, widely used in the comparative literature, also reflect the prevailing consensus among researchers, excluding more idiosyncratic approaches. Using these criteria whittles down the myriad choices to a selected list of standard elite-level indicators of democratic governance, each reflecting differing conceptions of the essential features of democracy, good governance, and human rights.

(1) Democracy: Freedom House

As discussed earlier in Chapter 3, the Gastil index of civil liberties and political rights produced annually by Freedom House is one of the best-known measures of liberal democracy and one of the most widely used in the comparative literature. The index provides comprehensive coverage of nation-states and independent territories worldwide and also establishes a long time-series of observations conducted annually since 1972. Despite methodological differences in the data collection, construction, and methodology, the Freedom House indices correlate strongly with those estimated independently by Polity IV

$(R = .904^{**})$.[18] Previous comparative studies have also reported that macro-level satisfaction with democracy is primarily affected by the age of each democracy.[19] To examine this proposition, the multivariate models control for the historical index of democratization. This index reflects the accumulated years citizens have lived under different types of regimes, as described in Chapter 3.

(2) Good Governance

The last decade has also seen a proliferation of alternative indicators that have sought to operationalize the related notion of 'good governance' and its components. The World Bank has used assessments of government performance when allocating resources since the mid-1970s. Focusing at first on macroeconomic management, the assessment criteria have expanded to include trade and financial policies, business regulation, social sector policies, the effectiveness of the public sector, and transparency, accountability, and corruption. These criteria are assessed annually for all World Bank borrowers. Among these, the issue of corruption has moved toward the center of the World Bank's governance strategy, as this is regarded as a fundamental impediment toward reducing poverty.[20] Many of the available indicators of good governance, political risk, and corruption are based on perceptual assessments, using expert surveys and subjective judgments. The most ambitious attempt to operationalize and measure 'good governance' concerns the indices generated by Kaufmann-Kraay and colleagues for the World Bank Institute. The Kaufmann-Kraay indicators (also known as the Worldwide Governance Indicators) have quickly become some of the most widely used measures of good governance. Compiled since 1996, these composite indices measure the perceived quality of six dimensions of governance for 213 countries, based on many data sources produced by more than two dozen organizations. The underlying data are based on hundreds of variables and reflect the perceptions and views of many types of 'experts' as well as mass survey respondents on various dimensions of governance. The World Bank does not generate these separate assessments; rather, it integrates them into composite indices. The measures specify the margins of error associated with each estimate, allowing users to identify a range of statistically likely ratings for each country.

The Worldwide Governance Indicators measure the quality of six dimensions of governance: *Voice and accountability* – the extent to which a country's citizens are able to participate in selecting their government, as well as freedom of expression, freedom of association, and free media. *Political stability and absence of violence* – perceptions of the likelihood that the government will be destabilized or overthrown by unconstitutional or violent means, including political violence and terrorism. *Government effectiveness* – the quality of public services, the quality of the civil service and the degree of its independence from political pressures, the quality of policy formulation and implementation, and the credibility of the government's commitment to such policies. *Regulatory quality* – the ability of the government to formulate and implement sound policies and regulations that permit and promote private sector development. *Rule of law* – the extent to which agents have confidence in and abide by the rules of society, and in particular the quality of contract enforcement, the police, and the courts, as well as the likelihood of crime and violence. *Control of corruption* – the extent to which public power is exercised for private gain, including both petty and grand forms of corruption, as well as 'capture' of the state by elites and private interests. The six indicators can also be combined into an integrated measure of good governance. The Kaufmann-Kraay indices are widely employed, especially in the econometric literature, in part because of their easy availability and geographic scope.[21] Unfortunately, these measures also face a number of criticisms. The core concept of 'good governance' remains under-theorized, especially compared with the long tradition of work developing the concept and indices of democracy.[22] Moreover, as Grindle has emphasized, the 'good governance' agenda is often poorly focused, over-long, and growing ever longer.[23]

(3) Human Rights

Another dimension that is important concerns universal human rights. The Cingranelli-Richards (CIRI) Database covers a wide range of human rights using standards-based quantitative information covering 191 countries annually from all regions of the world.[24] The index seeks to measure government human rights practices, not human rights policies or overall human rights conditions (which may be affected by non-state actors). It codes physical integrity rights – the rights not to be tortured, summarily executed, disappeared, or imprisoned for political beliefs – as well as civil liberties and rights. Out of all the CIRI items, factor analysis was used to select six measures falling into a single dimension. The CIRI Human Rights index included for comparison used a 10-point scale measuring freedom of movement, freedom of religion, freedom of association, freedom of speech, and political participation rights, all core components of the United Nations' Universal Declaration of Human Rights. Last, the UNDP's Gender Empowerment Measure (GEM) is also included for comparison to measure one important aspect of human rights, namely, how successfully women have achieved equality in the public sphere. GEM evaluates progress in advancing women's standing in political and economic forums. It examines the extent to which women and men are able to actively participate in economic and political life and take part in decision making. GEM measures political participation and decision-making power (the ratio of women to men in parliamentary seats), economic participation (female share of positions in management, administration, and professional positions), and command over resources (male and female ratio of earned income).[25]

Basic Correlation Results

How do these indices of democracy, good governance, and human rights compare with public satisfaction with democracy, monitored by the World Values

Survey? Assuming the accuracy and reliability of these indices, a strong correlation, where the underlying views of citizens within each state reflect elite-level estimates, would support the claim that public satisfaction is based upon a rational assessment of the process performance of regimes. On the other hand, any lack of correlation suggests the null hypothesis, either because of measurement error and noise or because other affective or evaluative factors are influencing citizens' judgments. As the appropriate time-period for comparison remains uncertain, to provide alternative tests of the evidence, the elite-level indices are compared for three periods: (1) *contemporary indices*, matching the period of fieldwork for the fifth wave World Values Survey conducted in 2005–7; (2) indices with five-year *lags*, and also (3) indices with ten-year lags, monitored roughly a decade earlier, to reflect the effect of cumulative experiences during this period. Any contemporary measure is inevitably fairly noisy – for example, specific events can push these up or down – but the lagged indices are expected to present a more stable relationship. We can first compare the simple macro-level correlations before then developing the multivariate models with the full battery of controls.

Table 10.1 presents the simple correlations between democratic satisfaction and the contemporary and lagged indices of democracy, good governance, and human rights in the roughly fifty nations under comparison. The results, without any prior controls, highlight that democratic satisfaction is significantly and positively correlated with nearly all the contemporary and lagged indices; hence, for example, citizens are usually far happier with how democracy works in regimes that experts rate as highly stable, clean, effective, and governed by rule of law. Previous work by Wagner et al. based on time-series analysis of countries in Western Europe during the 1990s also found that high-quality characteristics, such as low corruption and effective rule of law, had a positive impact upon satisfaction with democracy.[26] The findings in this chapter provide further confirmation of these patterns and allow us to generalize more broadly well beyond established European democracies. Attitudes were also significantly related to most of the available indices of democracy and human rights; in particular, people were more satisfied with the democratic performance of their government in states with a more liberal record of gender empowerment and freedom of the press. Democratic satisfaction was significantly related to the lagged, but not to the contemporary, Freedom House measures of democracy.

To examine some of these patterns in more detail, Figures 10.2 and 10.3 illustrate levels of democratic satisfaction compared with each society's experience of democracy and good governance. Figure 10.2 highlights the considerable variations in democratic satisfaction among long-standing democracies, notably, the relative contentment expressed in Norway and Switzerland, compared with more critical attitudes displayed in Italy and the United States. Among the states with moderate historical experience of democracy during the third wave era, once more marked contrasts can be observed between countries, such as the positive attitudes found among Africans in Ghana and South

TABLE 10.1. *Process Performance and Democratic Satisfaction, Macro-level Correlations, 2005–2007*

Indicators	Source	Performance measured with a 10-year lag (mid-1990s)		Performance measured with a 5-year lag (2000)		Performance measured with no lag (2005)	
		R	Sig	R	Sig	R	Sig
DEMOCRATIZATION							
Liberal democracy	Freedom House	.364	*	.335	*	.257	
GOOD GOVERNANCE							
Voice and accountability	Kaufmann-Kraay	.296	*	.316	*	.362	*
Political stability	Kaufmann-Kraay	.430	**	.377	**	.475	**
Government effectiveness	Kaufmann-Kraay	.500	**	.435	**	.447	**
Regulatory quality	Kaufmann-Kraay	.539	**	.465	**	.360	**
Rule of law	Kaufmann-Kraay	.451	**	.450	**	.459	**
Corruption perceptions	Kaufmann-Kraay	.444	**	.410	**	.419	**
Summary good governance	Kaufmann-Kraay	.489	**	.430	**	.443	**
HUMAN RIGHTS							
Gender empowerment	GEM, UNDP	.500	**	.562	**	.529	**
Human rights	CIRI	.286	*	.260		.253	
Freedom of the press	Freedom House	.315		.378	**	.365	**

Notes: The macro-level correlation coefficients measure the strength of the link between the democratic satisfaction scale in 2005–7 and the process indices monitoring the quality of democratic governance, with each time-period lag. * Correlation is significant at the 0.05 level; ** correlation is significant at the 0.01 level. Number of nations compared, 46–50.

Sources: World Values Survey 2005–2007; Freedom House. 2010. *Freedom in the World 2010.* Washington, DC: Freedom House. www .freedomhouse.org; Monty Marshall and Keith Jaggers. 2003. *Polity IV Project: Political Regime Characteristics and Transitions, 1800–2003.* http://www.cidcm.umd.edu/inscr/polity/; Daniel Kaufmann, Aart Kraay, and Massimo Mastruzzi. 2007. *Governance Matters VI: Aggregate and Individual Governance Indicators, 1996–2006.* Washington, DC: The World Bank, Policy Research Working Paper. www.worldbank.org; David L. Cingranelli and David L. Richards. 2004. The Cingranelli-Richards (CIRI) Human Rights Database Coder Manual. http://ciri.binghamton.edu/.

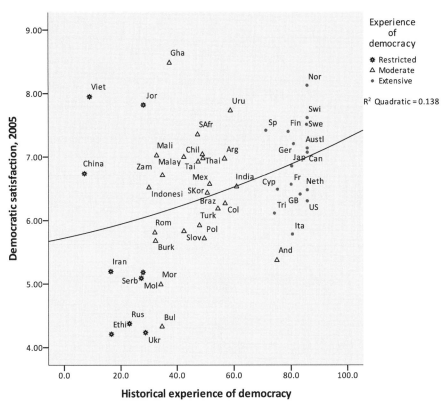

FIGURE 10.2. Democratic experience and democratic satisfaction, 2005–2007. Demo-cratic satisfaction: V163. *"And how democratically is this country being governed today? Again using a scale from 1 to 10, where 1 means that it is 'not at all democratic' and 10 means that it is 'completely democratic,' what position would you choose?"* The *historical experience of democratization* is measured by the cumulative Freedom House index for political rights and civil liberties 1972–2006, standardized to a 100-point scale. For comparison, these items were standardized to 100 points. For the survey items contained in each indicator, see Table 3.2 and Technical Appendix A. *Source*: World Values Survey, 2005–2007.

Africa, compared with the levels of deep discontent evident in post-communist Bulgaria and Moldova. The remaining countries, with little or no historical experience of democracy, showed the greatest variance, although again some of the countries in post-communist Europe proved the most disillusioned with how their government worked. Three cases – China, Vietnam, and Jordan – also illustrate the considerable disparity between the poor record of civil liberties and political rights, as estimated by Freedom House and by CIRI, and how the public in these societies evaluated the way their country was being governed. For comparison, Figure 10.3 illustrates how levels of democratic satisfaction relate to the composite good governance index, showing a slightly

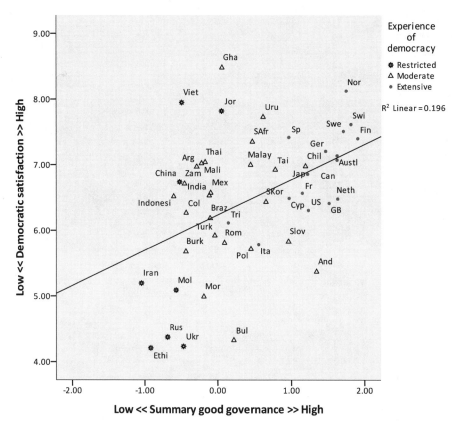

FIGURE 10.3. Good governance and democratic satisfaction, 2005–2007. Democratic satisfaction: V163. *"And how democratically is this country being governed today? Again using a scale from 1 to 10, where 1 means that it is 'not at all democratic' and 10 means that it is 'completely democratic,' what position would you choose?"* The summary good governance index is created by summing the six items (listed in Table 10.1) contained in the Kaufmann-Kraay indices, 2005. For more details see Technical Appendix A. *Source*: World Values Survey, 2005–2007.

closer fit, especially among both the autocracies and the longer established democracies. Countries such as Norway, Switzerland, and Germany score well on both indices, while by contrast, in the lower left-hand corner, Ethiopia, Russia, and Ukraine cluster together, showing a poor performance.

Many other macro- and micro-level factors may be influencing democratic satisfaction, however, such as education, income, and age. More rigorous scrutiny requires multiple controls. Rational choice theories emphasize that knowledge is the basis for informed judgments, and thus the role of higher educational attainment is expected to reinforce the link between citizens' satisfaction with democracy and the actual performance of the regime. As discussed in Chapter 8, enlightened knowledge about democracy is also predicted

TABLE 10.2. *Process Performance and Democratic Satisfaction, Multi-level Models, 2005–2007*

	Democracy	Good governance
CONTROLS		
Demographic characteristics		
Age (in years)	.486***	.524***
	(.102)	(.103)
Sex (male = 1)	−.189*	−.183*
	(.092)	(.093)
Socioeconomic resources		
Household income 10-point scale	2.20***	2.15***
	(.109)	(.110)
Education 9-point scale	−.470**	−.514***
	(.112)	(.113)
Democratic knowledge	.447***	.499***
	(.106)	(.107)
PERFORMANCE INDICES		
Liberal Democracy, 2006 (Freedom House)	3.24*	
	(1.53)	
Good governance index, 2006 (Kaufmann-Kraay)		4.94**
		(1.50)
Constant (intercept)	63.6	63.6
Schwarz BIC	504,283	494148
N. respondents	55,953	54,817
N. nations	44	43

Note: The dependent variable is the 100-point democratic satisfaction scale. All independent variables were standardized using mean centering (z-scores). Models present the results of the REML multilevel regression models (for details, see Appendix C) including the beta coefficient (the standard error below in parentheses) and the significance. See Appendix A for details about the measurement, coding, and construction of all variables. Significant coefficients are highlighted in **bold**. Models were checked through tolerance statistics to be free of problems of multi-collinearity.
*= >.05 **= >.01 ***= >.001
Source: World Values Survey 2005–2007.

to strengthen the linkage between satisfaction with democracy and independent indicators of the quality of governance. Standard demographic variables, such as age, sex, and income, also commonly influence political attitudes – for example, Chapter 7 reported that affluent and older citizens are usually more satisfied with regime performance. The process performance indicators are therefore added to multilevel models to see whether these measures contribute to democratic satisfaction, controlling for standard social and demographic characteristics. Since the process performance indices are strongly intercorrelated, separate regression models are run for each dimension.

The results in Table 10.2 demonstrate that after applying the battery of controls, *process performance indices prove strong and significant predictors of democratic satisfaction*; indeed, these measures were each more strongly linked with democratic satisfaction than any of the other demographic and socioeconomic indices, outweighing the effects of income. This confirms rational choice process theories; people are indeed happier with how democracy works in states characterized by good quality governance, where regimes respect the rule of law, prove effective in managing the delivery of public goods and services, and are open and transparent in policymaking processes. The supply-side part of the market model is therefore important for issues at the heart of this book, and democratic satisfaction is not simply an affective orientation learned through the socialization process.

II: POLICY PERFORMANCE

The results of these models need to be compared against alternative rational choice accounts suggesting that citizens' evaluations rely upon more instrumental criteria based on the regime's perceived record of policy outputs and outcomes over successive governments. Many studies of voting behavior and electoral choices have emphasized the role of retrospective evaluations of the economic record of successive governments, as well as prospective expectations of future economic conditions arising from party platforms.[27] Similarly, the general policy performance of governments has been seen as explaining the dynamics of confidence in government and satisfaction with democracy.[28] Such accounts emphasize that the public responds to the capacity of the state when managing the delivery of public goods and services demanded by citizens.

Performance has usually been conceptualized and operationalized fairly narrowly in the research literature as primarily economic – for example, where the public judges the government's record favorably when expanding GDP and living standards, maintaining full employment, and keeping prices low. Contemporary accounts give greater emphasis to a more complex and diverse policy agenda, however, when the public also cares about issues such as the quality of public services, the management of cultural diversity, immigration, and environmental protection, as well as foreign policies maintaining security at home and defending the country's interests abroad. Where successive governments have generally succeeded in meeting public expectations of peace, welfare, and prosperity, and representatives have responded sensitively to shifting public preference for 'more' or 'less' spending on different issues, it is believed that this record gradually builds a reservoir of generalized support toward the regime, which anchors support for democratic governance through bad times as well as good.[29]

Contemporary theorists have also emphasized that the heart of any problem of growing public disaffection in established democracies lies in the shrinking state; for example, Colin Hay emphasizes that processes of globalization and privatization have depoliticized many issues, reducing the role, power, and accountability of elected officials, representative bodies, and national governments.[30] Moreover Russell Dalton builds upon the performance-based explanation by emphasizing the growing complexity and fragmentation of multiple-issue publics in contemporary post-industrial societies, which he believes has increased the difficulties faced by political parties when trying to satisfy public expectations.[31] For this reason, for politicians genuinely seeking to serve the public interest, Dalton argues that state capacity to deliver has diminished, making governments appear less trustworthy. Moreover, the growing complexity of contemporary issue agendas, the more fragmented information environment in the digital age, the growth of multilevel governance, and the weakening of partisan cues, he suggests, all make it harder for even well-informed and attentive citizens to evaluate government and regime performance.

In North America and Western Europe, a series of empirical studies in political economy have used time-series data to predict confidence in governance and satisfaction with democracy based on national-level indicators of economic conditions as well as individual-level retrospective and prospective evaluations of the economy.[32] The evidence provides some support for the policy performance account; hence, an early study by Clarke, Dutt, and Kornberg examined pooled Eurobarometer time-series data for eight countries from the late 1970s to the mid-1980s, reporting that economic conditions affected feelings of satisfaction with democracy, although the effects were limited.[33] McAllister reviewed the comparative evidence among two dozen affluent post-industrial nations, also concluding that individual-level attitudes toward economic performance play a modest role in shaping confidence in political institutions in these countries, although the impact of policy performance is negligible compared with the effect of other factors, such as political culture and historical circumstances.[34] Lawrence examined the evidence for how far the economic record of successive governments in the United States mirrored trends in political trust, concluding cautiously that any links are not straightforward.[35] For example, it might be expected that the groups who were most affected by the loss of jobs from global labor markets, NAFTA, and free trade would have become significantly less trusting, but from 1958 to 1994 the erosion in the ANES trust in government index was widespread across different occupations, ages, and regions rather than being associated with poorer households, blue-collar workers, or union households.

The policy performance theory may also be more strongly related to democratic satisfaction if a wider range of non-economic aspects of government performance are incorporated in the equation, including salient issues such as security and defense, crime and justice, social services and welfare policies, and expressive moral values.[36] In poorer societies, for example, performance could be monitored by a nation's success in achieving the Millennium Development Goals, a range of internationally agreed-on specific targets covering issues such as poverty, schooling, gender equality, and health. Given the plethora of alternative indices and criteria available to gauge success, however, especially in any cross-national comparison among rich and poor nations, it becomes far harder to define any independent and objectively balanced scorecard of government 'performance.'[37] One of the most comprehensive attempts to monitor the performance of advanced industrialized economies, by Roller, uses a series of fourteen performance indices, based on outcome measures covering four policy dimensions: domestic security (e.g., rates of violent and property crime), economic policy (e.g., GDP, rates of inflation, and unemployment), social policy (e.g., infant mortality and poverty rates), and environmental policies (e.g., emission of carbon dioxide and rate of water consumption). It is true that many of the indicators chosen by Roller are indeed universal standards concerning certain desirable goals in any society; which state would *not* want to achieve lower crime, infant mortality, and rates of poverty? Nevertheless, the selection and operationalization of the core indices, the relative priority that should be given to each of them, and the exclusion of other policy dimensions cannot avoid the ideological nature of any judgments about government performance. Many central issues in politics also relate less to the overall goals than the policy means by which to achieve these.

An alternative approach to understanding the influence of policy performance on system support focuses upon comparing the dynamics of 'before' and 'after' case studies of the shocks arising from periods of severe and prolonged economic downturn, such as the 1997 Asian financial crisis, the 2001 debt crisis in Argentina, or the 2008 banking crisis in Iceland. Each of these provides potentially important natural experiments, where the economic performance thesis suggests that after these shocks, public dissatisfaction with governments and the regime should rise steeply. The contrary pattern should also be observed where living standards expand sharply in emerging markets, such as in Vietnam, Taiwan, and China, with a sustained period of economic growth encouraging positive assessments about the performance of the overall political system. At the same time, there remain grounds for caution, since certain case studies suggest that economic performance by itself may provide only a poor fit to account for trends in political trust observed in many countries. Among post-industrial societies, for example, both Italy and Japan experienced rapid economic growth during the postwar era, although we have already observed that political disaffection in both countries remains pervasive and enduring.[38] Moreover, earlier chapters demonstrated that American confidence in government declined throughout the 1960s despite the prosperous U.S. economy during this decade.[39] If the policy performance thesis is correct, then satisfaction with democracy should be predicted at the macro-level by a range of economic and social policy indicators, and further explained at the micro-level by public satisfaction with economic and political performance.

The choice of policy performance indices is clearly important for the interpretation of the analysis. There is no consensus in the research literature about the most appropriate choice of indices, although one of the most comprehensive studies, by Roller, suggests that any normative criteria for performance effectiveness should be multidimensional, involving the shared political goals of international security, domestic security, wealth, socioeconomic security and equality, and environmental protection.[40] The most comprehensive strategy therefore suggests that a wide range of empirical performance indicators should be compared against democratic satisfaction, first with simple correlation analysis, and then tested more rigorously through regression models using multiple controls. The literature in evaluation studies also suggests that subjective perceptions and independent outcome indices provide the most reliable cross-national measures of regime effectiveness, reflecting how far public policies achieve, or are perceived to have achieved, commonly agreed goals, rather than output instruments, such as patterns of government expenditure or the passage of legislation.[41] Hence, comparative studies of political economy commonly use micro-level subjective measures of well-being, such as financial satisfaction and happiness, as well as macro-level policy outcome measures, including national levels of growth, employment, and inflation rates. Similarly, cross-national health care studies routinely employ international developmental indices, such as rates of infant mortality, incidents of HIV/AIDS, and average life expectancy, as well as self-reported health of respondents. The policy mechanisms used to achieve common goals vary in each country, such as whether health care is delivered through private insurance providers versus a national health service, or some mix of the two, but the standardized outcome measures are more comparable across nations. The performance-based indicators are lagged at least a year prior to levels of democratic satisfaction monitored subsequently in the fifth wave World Values Survey. Checks using alternative lags did not substantially alter the interpretation of the results, suggesting that they remain robust irrespective of the particular year selected.

Following this strategy, Table 10.3 presents the results of the simple correlations across a series of selected macro-level output performance indicators of economic development, human development, and environmental sustainability, as well as survey-based measures of subjective well-being in each society, including life and financial satisfaction, self-reported health and happiness, and a combined subjective well-being index. The results demonstrate that *most (but not all) of the macro-level objective indicators usually prove to be poor predictors of democratic satisfaction*. The important exceptions to these patterns concern levels of per capita GDP and the Consumer Price Index, both of which were significantly associated with more positive political attitudes. The measure of the average growth of GDP also proved significant, although in the contrary direction to that expected theoretically; people were more satisfied with the performance of democracy in countries with lower rates of economic growth, and the results proved robust, whether measured for a single year or the accumulated rates of growth over a five-year period. Nearly all the other standard indicators of economic, social, and environmental policy performance, including rates of unemployment, the Human Development Index, and levels of income inequality, were not significantly linked with greater democratic satisfaction. By contrast, the subjective indices in each society were strongly and significantly related to democratic satisfaction, including life satisfaction, self-reported state of health, subjective happiness, financial satisfaction, and the summary subjective well-being index. Thus, those who were content with

	Sources	N.	Year	R	Sig
ECONOMIC					
Economic development	World Bank, GDP per capita in purchasing power parity	47	2004	.369	**
Economic growth	World Bank, GDP annual growth rate (%)	46	2000–2005	−.354	**
Economic growth	World Bank, GDP annual growth rate (%)	46	2004	−.308	*
Unemployment rate	World Bank, as % of total labor force	41	2004	−.158	
Inflation rate	World Bank, Consumer Price Index	46	2004	.346	*
GINI Index	UNDP, measures income inequality	45	2004	−.003	
Human poverty index	UNDP, % population living below the specified poverty line	21	2004	−.325	
Tax revenue	Tax revenue as % of GDP	35	2004	.256	
Public expenditure	Central government expenditure as % of GDP	40	2005	−.089	
SOCIAL POLICY					
Human Development Index	UNDP, Human Development Index	46	2004	.216	
Infant mortality	World Bank, rate (0–1 year) per 1,000 live births	48	2000	−.032	
Life expectancy	UNDP, average years at birth	46	2000–2005	.080	
Literacy rate	UNDP, adult literacy (15+)	46	2004	−.205	
Education	Combined gross enrollment ratio for primary, secondary, & tertiary schools	47	2002	.222	
HIV	Prevalence of HIV, total % population aged 15–49	45	2003	.064	
Measles	UNDP, one-year-olds fully immunized, %	48	2002	.037	
Health spending	Public health expenditure (% of GDP)	48	2001	.233	
ENVIRONMENTAL POLICY					
Carbon emissions	World Bank, per capita metric tons	47	2003	.044	
Commercial energy use	World Bank, per capita energy use, oil equivalent	44	2004	.134	
SUBJECTIVE WELL-BEING					
Life satisfaction	World Values Survey, 10-pt. scale (V20)	49	2005–7	.585	**
State of health	World Values Survey, 4-pt. scale (V11)	49	2005–7	.566	**
Subjective happiness	World Values Survey, 4-pt. scale (V10)	49	2005–7	.581	**
Financial satisfaction	World Values Survey, 10-pt. scale (V68)	49	2005–7	.660	**
Subjective well-being index	Combined life satisfaction, health, happiness, and financial satisfaction	49	2005–7	.684	**

Notes: The macro-level correlation coefficients measure the strength of the link between the democratic satisfaction scale in 2005–7 and the policy performance indices. * Correlation is significant at the .05 level; ** correlation is significant at the .01 level.

TABLE 10.4. *Policy Performance and Democratic Satisfaction, 2005–2007*

	Economic development	Human development	Subjective well-being
CONTROLS			
Demographic characteristics			
Age (in years)	**.484*****	**.458*****	**.618*****
	(.103)	(.105)	(.102)
Sex (male = 1)	**−.199***	−.172	−.096
	(.093)	(.095)	(.093)
Socioeconomic resources			
Household income 10-point scale	**2.15*****	**2.14*****	**.596****
	(.110)	(.112)	(.117)
Education 9-point scale	**−.507*****	**−.546***	**−.665*****
	(.113)	(.116)	(.112)
Democratic knowledge	**.450*****	**.468*****	**.433*****
	(.107)	(.109)	(.106)
PERFORMANCE INDICES			
Economic development	**3.24***		
	(1.39)		
Human Development Index, 2005		1.86	
		(1.29)	
Subjective well-being index			**4.45*****
			(.116)
Constant (intercept)	63.3	64.0	63.4
Schwarz BIC	495,565	474,666	438,254
N. respondents	54,987	52,676	54,494
N. nations	43	41	44

Note: The dependent variable is the 100-point democratic satisfaction scale. All independent variables were standardized using mean centering (z-scores). Models present the results of the REML multilevel regression models (for details, see Appendix C) including the beta coefficient (the standard error below in parentheses) and the significance. See Appendix A for details about the measurement, coding, and construction of all variables. Significant coefficients are highlighted in **bold**. Models were checked through tolerance statistics to be free of problems of multi-collinearity.

*= >.05 **= >.01 ***= >.001

Source: World Values Survey 2005–2007.

many aspects of their lives were also usually happier with how government works.

For more rigorous tests, levels of economic development, human development, and the subjective well-being index were entered into the models developed earlier, as shown in Table 10.4. The results in Table 10.4 confirm that economic development and subjective well-being continue to prove important even after controlling for other factors in the models. By contrast, human development appears to have no direct impact on political orientations. The effects of subjective well-being on democratic satisfaction are particularly strong; those

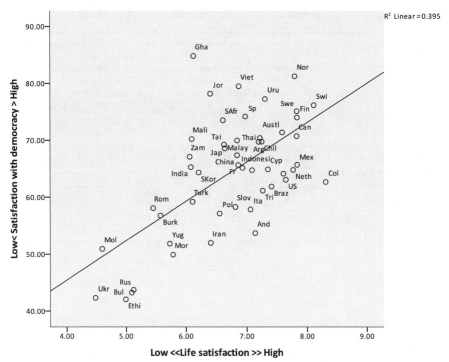

FIGURE 10.4. Satisfaction with democracy and subjective well-being, 2005–2007. **Democratic satisfaction:** *V163.* "*And how democratically is this country being governed today? Again using a scale from 1 to 10, where 1 means that it is 'not at all democratic' and 10 means that it is 'completely democratic,' what position would you choose?*" These items were standardized to 100 points.
Life satisfaction: *Q 22.* "*All things considered, how satisfied are you with your life as a whole these days? Using this card on which 1 means you are 'completely dissatisfied' and 10 means you are 'completely satisfied,' where would you put your satisfaction with your life as a whole?*" *Source:* The World Values Survey 2005–2007.

who feel happiest, healthiest, well-off, and most satisfied with life also prove most content with the way democratic governance works. The role of subjective well-being has generated a growing popular and scholarly literature in social psychology and economics during the past three decades.[42] Studies suggest that this broad syndrome links together many attitudes and feelings, including happiness and satisfaction with life, household finances, work, and family.[43] As illustrated in more detail by Figure 10.4, societies where subjective well-being is highest, including Norway and Switzerland, are also the ones that display the greatest contentment with the democratic performance of their regime. The opposite pattern can be observed in countries such as Ukraine, Russia, and Ethiopia. This suggests that subjective well-being is related to contentment with the way democracy works.

The theoretical interpretation of this pattern, however, remains to be determined. If understood primarily as a social psychological and affective phenomenon, reflecting a general feeling of contentment with life, then it could be argued that subjective well-being is part of any comprehensive cultural explanation. From this perspective, some people develop a general sense of well-being, which spills over into feelings about government, as an affective orientation acquired in early childhood from parents, family, and friends. In this view, also, people's personalities can have an important long-term influence on whether they are happy or unhappy, a reflection of inborn or learned traits.[44] Alternatively, if the measure of subjective well-being taps into cognitive evaluations about living conditions and social circumstances, reflecting how people evaluate their own state of happiness, health, and financial security, then it can be interpreted as a rational evaluation of regime performance. After all, many people may often find it hard to judge the outcome and impact of specific government decisions and public policy processes, especially in younger regimes, in societies with limited access to the independent news media, and in complex political systems with multilevel agencies of decision making. It also often proves difficult to evaluate the overall state of the national or local economy, and societal (socio-tropic) conditions of levels of unemployment or poverty. For example, an extensive literature on political knowledge in the United States has demonstrated that when asked about basic awareness of standard performance indices, such as the current rate of unemployment or the size of the public debt, few Americans manage to produce accurate estimates. Moreover, despite the growth of educational attainment and the proliferation of information and communication technologies, American knowledge about politics has not risen in recent decades.[45] By contrast, however, people are likely to be the best judge of their own life satisfaction. Subjective well-being can depend upon government performance for many reasons. For example, Helliwell argues that many services crucial to individuals and families, ranging from education and health to justice and transportation, are regulated and provided by governments.[46] He also suggests that a sense of human security depends considerably on the confidence with which people can rely on government services being available when and where they are needed. Understood in this light, subjective well-being can be interpreted as providing support for the rational choice perspective where those most satisfied with their lives are also observed to be happiest with how democratic governance works.

III: THE ROLE OF INSTITUTIONAL STRUCTURES

As mentioned earlier, the third perspective in rational choice theory is provided by *institutional* accounts, which emphasize that satisfaction with democracy is conditioned by the constitutional arrangements in any state, especially by power-sharing arrangements. The institutional view has become increasingly popular in the research literature, although little consensus has emerged about the evidence supporting these claims. If the thesis is correct, then satisfaction with democracy should be greater at the micro-level among electoral winners than losers, as well as being maximized at the macro-level in countries with power-sharing regimes that expand the number of electoral 'winners.'

Institutional explanations focus on the constitutional structure of the regime. The institutional thesis suggests that patterns of winners and losers in any political system are structured by constitutional arrangements, meaning the core institutions of state and the rules of the game, both written and unwritten. Some citizens win, some lose. Some parties and groups are mobilized into power, some are mobilized out. Over a long period of time, this accumulated experience is expected to shape general orientations toward the political regime. At the simplest level, if citizens feel that the rules of the game allow the party they endorse to be elected to power, they are more likely to feel that representative institutions are responsive to their needs, so that they can trust the political system. On the other hand, if citizens feel that the party they prefer persistently loses, over successive elections they are more likely to feel that their voice is excluded from the decision-making process, producing generalized dissatisfaction with the regime. Over time, when constitutional arrangements succeed in channeling popular demands into government outcomes, then we would expect this to be reflected in diffuse support for democracy. Institutional theories suggest that both process and policy performance may be judged through a *partisan prism*, where 'winners' supporting the parties in office express greater satisfaction with democracy than 'losers' supporting parties consistently excluded from power, and where regime power-sharing structures determine the overall distribution of 'winners' in any political system.[47]

What evidence is there that political institutions matter for political support? Since constitutional arrangements are relatively stable phenomena, usually characterized by incremental evolution, the most appropriate evidence concerns cross-national comparisons that maximize the variance in types of institutions, such as presidential or parliamentary executive, and majoritarian, mixed, or proportional electoral systems. In contrast, comparisons over time are less appropriate except in the exceptional natural experiments where democratic satisfaction is monitored 'before' and 'after' major constitutional reforms within nations, exemplified by changes to the electoral systems in Italy, Japan, and New Zealand. An extensive literature has explored the consequences of alternative constitutional designs. Theories about the virtues of power-sharing regimes, especially for multi-ethnic societies, have been developed in the work of Arendt Lijphart, Eric Nordlinger, Gerhard Lehmbruch, Klaus Armingeon, and others where it was conceptualized alternatively as 'consociational democracy,' 'consensus democracy,' 'proportional democracy,' or 'negotiation democracy.'[48] Today the more common concept focuses on 'power-sharing regimes,' a term used here since it has been widely adapted in international relations and political science. In a previous study, I defined power-sharing regimes most generally as those states that are characterized by formal institutional rules that give multiple political elites a stake in the decision-making process. The study classified some of the key characteristics of this type of regime such as type of electoral system, type of executive, degree of federalism and decentralization, and independence of the mass media.[49] Building on this study, democratic satisfaction arising from the policy and process performance indicators can be compared for power-sharing and power-concentrating regimes.

Anderson and colleagues conducted a very systematic analysis of the institutional thesis in Western Europe, comparing satisfaction with democracy among winners and losers in consensual and majoritarian democracies. Power-sharing electoral systems are expected to generate more positive attitudes toward government by maximizing the number of 'winners' in any contest.[50] The study hypothesized that (1) system support is consistently influenced by whether people are among the winners or losers in electoral contests, defined by whether the party they endorsed was returned to government; and (2) this process is mediated by the type of regime. Following Lijphart, nations were classified into *majoritarian* regimes (otherwise known as 'Westminster' or power-concentrating) or *consensual* regimes (consociational or power-sharing). Theories of responsible party government stress that majoritarian democracies empower the winners to impose their preferences over the losers. Accountability and effective government are valued more highly by these systems than the representation and inclusion of all viewpoints. Anderson et al. found that in power-concentrating regimes, winners (who supported the governing party) consistently expressed far higher satisfaction with democracy than losers (who supported the opposition). By contrast, power-sharing regimes seek to include political minorities in decision-making processes, giving less emphasis to accountability and the rotation of parties in government. Anderson and Guillory report that power-sharing systems produced a narrower gap in democratic satisfaction between winners and losers. Cross-national differences in system support could therefore be explained in this account as the product of the *type* of regime and the *distribution* of winners and losers in each country. Power-concentrating regimes, with fewer winners, were characterized by lower macro-levels of political support, while power-sharing regimes, with many winners, displayed greater satisfaction with democracy. It should be noted that this theory only takes account of the proportion of winners and losers (their distribution), not how much they win or lose (their strength).

The logic of our research design in exploring these issues is to test whether power-sharing regimes which maximize the number of 'winners' produce higher levels of institutional confidence than winner-take-all power-concentrating arrangements. Expanding the cross-national framework beyond the analysis of established democracies in Western Europe allows this account to be tested more broadly through two strategies. First we can compare how average national levels of democratic satisfaction vary according to the most important power-sharing constitutional arrangements in each regime, including the type of executive, the type of electoral system, and whether states are federal or unitary. Analysis draws upon the classification of institutions developed in previous studies.[51] Secondly, the democratic satisfaction of electoral

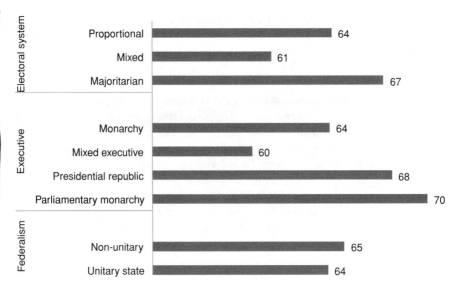

FIGURE 10.5. Political institutions and democratic satisfaction, 2005–2007. For the classification of institutions, see Norris (2008). The figure shows the mean levels of democratic satisfaction, measured by the standardized 100-point scale. *Source*: World Values Survey 2005.

'winners' and 'losers' can be compared under each of these institutional arrangements. These groups are defined by voting supporters of the largest party in the lower house of parliament in each country. Figure 10.5 presents the simple descriptive statistics, showing the average levels of democratic satisfaction in different types of institutional arrangement. The results demonstrate that the institutional arrangements in each regime generated only modest differences in average levels of public satisfaction. For example, proportional elections are the foundation of many other aspects of power-sharing arrangements, by lowering the electoral threshold facing minor parties seeking legislative and thus government office. Yet overall, among the fifty countries under comparison, democratic satisfaction proved marginally higher among countries with majoritarian electoral systems for the lower house of parliament. There were some greater disparities evident among electoral 'winners' and 'losers' within each type of institutional context, as shown in Figure 10.6, but the patterns were far from consistent.

As in previous models, however, any analysis of institutional effects also needs to control for various micro-level conditions that can influence democratic satisfaction in any society, including education (and thus cognitive skills), enlightened knowledge about liberal democracy, and the standard demographic and social characteristics that can affect political and social attitudes (age, sex, and income). When these factors are entered into the multilevel models as controls, Table 10.5 shows that the only institutional factor that proved a

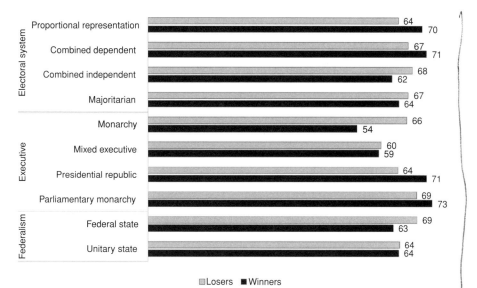

FIGURE 10.6. Political institutions and democratic satisfaction among winners and losers. For the classification of institutions, see Norris (2008). Electoral 'winners' and 'losers' are defined by voting support for the largest party in the lower house of the national legislature. *Source*: World Values Survey 2005.

significant predictor of democratic satisfaction was whether respondents had supported the winning party in parliamentary elections. As expected theoretically, 'winners' were more satisfied than 'losers.' Nevertheless, power-sharing institutions per se failed to determine overall levels of democratic satisfaction in any society.

CONCLUSIONS AND IMPLICATIONS

This chapter examined rational choice approaches that seek to explain satisfaction with democracy in terms of the process and the policy performance of governments, as well as by the institutional structure of regimes. This explanation, emphasizing how citizens evaluate the way governments perform, counterbalances the demand-side emphasis provided by cultural accounts. An accumulating research literature has explored these issues, but no consensus has yet emerged about the most significant performance factors that help to explain system support and thus the democratic deficit at the heart of this study. One reason for the lack of agreement is the varied range of performance indicators that can be examined, along with the intellectual division of labor, so that different disciplines have focused on different elements. Hence, institutionalists have often tested the 'winners and losers' thesis, while political economists have focused attention on some of the economic measures of good governance,

TABLE 10.5. *Institutions and Democratic Satisfaction,*
2005–2007

	Institutions
CONTROLS	
Demographic characteristics	
Age (in years)	**.470*****
	(.102)
Sex (male = 1)	−.202*
	(.092)
Socioeconomic resources	
Household income 10-point scale	**2.19*****
	(.109)
Education 9-point scale	−**.449****
	(.112)
Democratic knowledge	**.454*****
	(.106)
PERFORMANCE INDICES	
Proportional representation electoral system	.497
	(1.63)
Type of executive: Parliamentary monarchy	2.78
	(1.43)
Federal state	.715
	(.168)
Electoral support: Winning party	**1.45*****
	(.097)
Constant (intercept)	63.6
Schwarz BIC	504,060
N. respondents	55,953
N. nations	42

Notes: The dependent variable is the 100-point democratic satisfaction scale. All independent variables were standardized using mean centering (z-scores). Models present the results of the REML multilevel regression models (for details, see Appendix C) including the beta coefficient (the standard error below in parentheses) and the significance. See Appendix A for details about the measurement, coding, and construction of all variables. Significant coefficients are highlighted in **bold**. Models were checked through tolerance statistics to be free of problems of multi-collinearity.
*= >.05 **= >.01 ***= >.001
Source: World Values Survey 2005–2007.

such as the need for transparency, anti-corruption, rule of law, and property rights.

The results of the more comprehensive comparison of alternative measures presented in this chapter strongly suggest three main findings. First, process performance, including both measures of the quality of democracy and good governance, does count for how content people are with the way government works. In this regard, there is indeed a rational basis for public evaluations. Second, among the policy indices, economic development and a subjective sense of well-being proved equally important for satisfaction, although most of the narrower economic, social, and environmental performance indicators were not significant. Third, satisfaction with democracy was also reinforced by support for the winning party.

This chapter concludes by returning to the idea, first suggested by David Easton, that affective loyalties toward the authorities should be modified by our accumulated experience of how regimes work: "Members do not come to identify with basic political objects only because they have learned to do so ... from others – a critical aspect of socialization processes. If they did, diffuse support would have entirely the appearance of a non-rational phenomenon. Rather, on the basis of their own experiences, members may also judge the worth of supporting these objects for their own sake. Such attachment may be a product of spill-over effects from evaluations of a series of outputs and of performance over a long period of time. Even though the orientations derive from responses to particular outputs initially, they become in time disassociated from performance. They become transformed into generalised attitudes towards the authorities or other political objects."[52] Rational choice accounts emphasize that the way people experience democratic governance leads them to express negative or positive assessments of the way the regime works in their own country, and this chapter presents considerable support for this thesis. Thus, while culture helps to predict demand-side democratic aspirations, rational evaluations come into play with supply-side democratic performance. The interaction of supply and demand generates the deficit that is the heart of this study. But does the deficit matter? Whether for mass behavior, the authority and legitimacy of governments, or the process of regime transition and democratization? It is to these issues that we now turn.

PART IV

PROGNOSIS

The Consequences for Citizenship, Governance, and Democratization

Contemporary events highlight multiple reasons for concern about the underlying stability of many regimes that experienced transitions from autocracy during the third wave era. The heady hopes for the progressive spread of democracy worldwide, captured by Fukuyama's idea of the 'end of history,' a term coined immediately after the fall of the Berlin Wall, have flagged over the last two decades.[1] Freedom House reports that the number of electoral democracies grew globally during the third wave era but that further advances stalled around the turn of the twenty-first century, followed by four successive years of retreat.[2] Diamond suggests that the last decade saw the onset of a democratic recession.[3] Huntington emphasizes that ideas about steady progress are naïve; previous historical waves of democratization were followed by periods of sustained reversal.[4] In recent years, elected governments have often struggled to maintain stability following inconclusive or disputed contests (for instance, in Kenya and Mexico), partisan strife and recurrent political scandals (Bangladesh and Guatemala), and persistent outbreaks of violent ethnic conflict (Democratic Republic of Congo and Afghanistan). Contemporary setbacks for democracy have also occurred following dramatic coups against elected leaders (experienced in Honduras and Thailand) as well as creeping restrictions on human rights and fundamental freedoms (such as in Russia and Venezuela).[5]

In the light of all these developments, the initial high hopes and expectations for the further expansion and steady consolidation of democratic regimes around the world, commonly expressed in the early 1990s, have not come to fruition. It becomes even more vital to understand the conditions facilitating democratization – and the barriers to this process. The key issue in this chapter is how far political attitudes associated with the democratic deficit contribute toward the process of the transition from autocracy and the consolidation of sustainable democratic regimes. Accordingly, this chapter outlines cultural theories that suggest a series of reasons for why democratic deficits are expected to matter and then analyzes the systematic consequences of this phenomenon for (1) mass political participation at the micro-level, including patterns of conventional and protest politics; (2) processes of governance legitimacy and allegiant behavior, exemplified by the willingness to comply voluntarily with observing the law; and ultimately, (3) for processes of democratization, at the regime level. The chapter concludes that democratic orientations matter for many important components of democracy. In particular, the evidence presented here demonstrates that democratic aspirations play a significant role in strengthening forms of political participation, including both indicators of citizen interest and protest activism, as well as reinforcing compliance with the law, and ultimately contributing toward sustainable democratic regimes.

ACTIVE CITIZENSHIP

Active citizenship is one of the key defining features of democratic governance. Yet, as discussed in the first chapter, the conventional wisdom arising from a substantial scholarly literature suggests that during recent decades, many post-industrial societies have experienced a tidal wave of public withdrawal from the traditional channels of conventional political activism. Symptoms of this malady are widely thought to include sagging electoral turnout, rising anti-party sentiment, and the decay of civic organizations. The standard view emphasizes a familiar litany of civic ills that are believed to have undermined the democratic channels traditionally linking citizens to the state. Elections are the most common way for people to express their political preferences, and the half-empty ballot box is taken as the most common symptom of democratic ill health.[6] The idea of representative democracy sans parties is unthinkable, yet studies of party organizations suggest the desertion of grassroots members, at least in Western Europe, during recent decades.[7] An extensive literature on partisan dealignment has established that lifetime loyalties anchoring voters to parties have been eroding in many established democracies, contributing toward sliding turnout and producing a more unstable electorate open to the sway of short-term forces.[8] Political mobilization via traditional agencies and networks of civic society like unions and churches is believed to be under threat. Structural accounts emphasize that union membership is hemorrhaging due to the decline of jobs in the manufacturing industry, changing class structures, flexible labor markets, and the spread of individualist values.[9] Theories of secularization, deriving originally from Max Weber, suggest that the public in most modern post-industrial societies has been abandoning church pews for shopping malls.[10] The bonds of belonging to the plethora of traditional community associations and voluntary organizations may be becoming more frayed and tattered than in the past.[11] Putnam presents an extensive battery of evidence documenting anemic civic engagement in America, displayed in activities as diverse as community meetings, social networks, and associational membership.[12] In short, traditional political activities that arose and flourished in industrial societies during the late nineteenth and early twentieth centuries

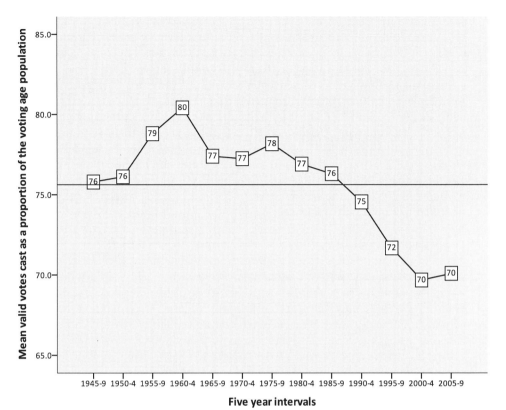

FIGURE II.I. Voting turnout in Western Europe, 1945–2009. The figure shows the number of valid votes cast in 380 national parliamentary elections as a proportion of the voting-age population in twenty-four West European nations during the post–World War II era. *Source*: International IDEA. *Voter Turnout since 1945*. www.IDEA.int.

are often thought to have peaked in the postwar era and waned in popularity today.

Anxiety about these issues is not confined to academe, as concern has also been expressed in numerous public speeches, editorial columns, and policy forums. These voices are heard most commonly in the United States, but similar echoes resonate in many other democracies. In particular, regimes are believed to face a hazardous and difficult pathway steering between the twin dangers of political activism where the public is neither too lukewarm nor overheated, the Scylla and Charybdis of contemporary politics. One potential danger is that citizens are becoming increasingly disengaged from conventional channels of public affairs. In West European national parliamentary elections, for example, overall levels of voting turnout have gradually fallen by 10 percentage points from 1960 to 2009 (see Figure 11.1). Signs of a glacial fall in voter turnout can also be found in the June 2009 elections to the European parliament, where more than half of the electorate (57%) stayed home, rising to almost two-thirds (61%) abstaining across the ten newest member states. Turnout in these contests dropped to a new low of 43% in 2009, down by 20 percentage points over four decades.[13] Many factors have contributed toward changing patterns of conventional civic engagement; not all indicators suggest a uniform decline over time, by any means; and comprehensive explanations remain complex. The macro-level institutional context and the structure of opportunities (such as the type of electoral system), the meso-level (including the role of organizational networks), as well as the micro-level role of resources and attitudes (such as political efficacy and social trust), are commonly regarded as the standard building blocks of any explanation of conventional political participation.[14] Previous studies have found that specific levels of political trust and institutional confidence positively correlate with conventional forms of political participation, such as voting and party activism, in the United States and other affluent societies.[15] It is unclear, however, whether more diffuse indicators of system support play a similar role. If the democratic deficit has grown, so that citizens' expectations of democracy have risen higher than democracy is capable of delivering, this is one additional attitudinal factor that could plausibly be expected to help account for any decline in conventional forms of participation expressed through the ballot box, political parties, and civic associations.

Besides apathy, the alternative risk arising from any democratic deficit is that citizens become intensely involved through protest politics in ways that may potentially destabilize the state, cause violent disruptions, and undermine democratically elected authorities. Seminal work of Ted Robert Gurr in the early 1970s regarded violent acts as a rebellious expression of discontent with the conventional channels of representative democracy and the search for alternative ways to challenge the regime, including the propensity to engage in riots damaging property or people, and in non-violent direct protest actions such as the willingness to block traffic or to occupy buildings.[16] Gurr theorized that protest politics represent an avenue to channel and express deep-seated feelings of frustration, anger, and alienation, not just with particular leaders or public policy issues but also with the political system as a whole. During the mid-1970s, similar views were echoed by Crozier, Huntington, and Watanuki in the widely influential Trilateral report *The Crisis of Democracy*, which regarded the May 1968 street uprisings and their subsequent reverberations as a serious threat to the underlying stability of the Trilateral democracies.[17] Protest politics, the authors suggested, challenged established sources of authority. More contemporary accounts on contentious politics are usually more sanguine about peaceful protest acts, which have become remarkably common. Nevertheless, where these events spark violence, there remains cause for concern. Many contemporary events in European democracies illustrate this process, from fuel strikes in London to urban riots among immigrants living in Paris suburbs, protests over the Muhammad cartoons in Copenhagen, farmers' dumping food on the streets of Brussels, firebombs outside parliament, and anarchist shop looting in Greece. Diverse cases in European democracies may or may not have similar underlying roots. There are few reasons to believe that even occasional violent outbreaks of this phenomenon pose a major risk today to the ultimate stability, cohesion, and unity of European democracies. Nevertheless, if democratic societies lack the capacity to contain sporadic outbreaks of contentious politics and if they are simultaneously unable to bring citizens to the ballot box, this becomes a societal challenge.

Threats to order and stability arising from violent street protests can be expected to prove a more serious problem for regime stability in states emerging from conflict, as well as those that have more recently experienced democratic transitions from autocracy, as exemplified by violent rioting and communal tensions following the closely fought January 2008 presidential elections in Kenya. At the same time, in repressive autocracies, protest uprisings can contribute toward the process of regime transition. Multiple cases of non-violent civil uprisings have had a decisive effect on processes of regime change – although sometimes they are brutally repressed. Some of the best-known historical cases include protests resulting in the Islamic revolution in Iran in 1979, huge demonstrations (especially organized by women and the Catholic Church) directed against General Pinochet's rule in Chile, outbreaks of 'people power' in the Philippines overthrowing President Ferdinand Marcos, the anti-apartheid struggles in South Africa, the long series of mass movements and street demonstrations overthrowing the Soviet powers, the 'color revolutions' in Ukraine and Georgia, and demonstrations and counter-demonstrations in Iran.[18] Many factors help to explain contentious politics through protest demonstrations, including the structure of opportunities, organizational networks, and the resources and attitudes that encourage a propensity to engage in these channels.[19] Previous research by Dalton found that specific support (attitudes toward incumbents and political institutions) failed to predict protest activism in post-industrial nations, although support for democratic values (without any prior controls) strongly correlated with protest activity.[20] To test this pattern more rigorously among a broader range of countries and types of regimes, here multilevel models can be used to examine the claim that *democratic deficits are likely to contribute to the underlying cultural conditions mobilizing protest politics.*

Although a common assumption in popular commentary, the claim that protest activism is strongly motivated by attitudes such as disaffection with government receives remarkably little systematic support from previous studies of the survey evidence within established democracies. For example, the earliest systematic survey evidence concerning protest activism was collected by the five-nation 1973–6 Political Action Study but this failed to establish a significant link between protest potential and feelings of 'external efficacy' or beliefs in the responsiveness of the political system.[21] In the follow-up study, Thomassen compared political attitudes in the Netherlands and West Germany and confirmed that support for the political regime was unrelated to protest potential.[22] A detailed case study found that protestors engaged in demonstrations were not significantly more critical of the political system, whether in terms of satisfaction with how democracy works, the responsiveness of government and politicians to social needs, or trust in government.[23] In Latin America, as well, the most thorough recent study by Booth and Seligson compared survey evidence in eight nations. The results challenged the claim that lack of system support generated protest politics; instead, they found that those with low institutional confidence and political trust were *more* likely to participate in conventional activism, not less.[24] The empirical literature therefore suggests the alternative *null hypothesis*, namely that *democratic deficits are unlikely to generate conditions favorable to the spread of protest politics.*

To examine the survey evidence, Table 11.1 uses two participation scales. One measures citizen interest, including interest in politics, the importance of politics, and whether respondents reported that they had voted in a recent parliamentary election. The other scale measures protest politics, including joining a lawful demonstration, signing a petition, and boycotting consumer products. Factor analysis showed that these items each formed distinct dimensions. The multilevel models entered the standard controls used throughout the book, including age, sex, household income, education, democratic knowledge (all at the micro-level), and the society's historical experience of democracy (at the macro-level). Each of these factors has commonly been found to be related to patterns of political activism. Last, the models entered democratic satisfaction and aspirations as well as the net democratic deficit.

The results clearly demonstrate a familiar general story that reflects the previous body of research literature; citizen interest is stronger among the older generation, men, and the more affluent, educated, and knowledgeable. As many previous studies have found, among all these factors, education proved most strongly associated with interest. The cognitive skills, capacities, and information provided by formal schooling make it easier for citizens to make sense of complex issues and government processes, and thus to follow public affairs and to become engaged. After entering all these controls, *citizens with stronger democratic aspirations and greater democratic satisfaction were also more interested in politics and civic affairs.* Protest activism was modeled using the same controls. Age had no effect on protest activism, in large part, as others have reported, because the greater propensity of the young to demonstrate has gradually faded over time, as protest politics moved mainstream.[25] As with citizen interest, however, men, and those more affluent, educated, and knowledgeable, were more likely to participate through these channels. Protest politics was also much stronger in countries with long experience of democracy where there are well-established traditional rights and freedoms to assemble and demonstrate peacefully. After entering all these factors, *those with democratic aspirations were significantly more likely to engage in protest politics.* This analysis provides further confirmation of the pattern that Dalton found in post-industrial nations; adherence to democratic values strengthens the propensity

TABLE 11.1. *The Impact of Democratic Orientations on Active Citizenship*

	Citizen interest		Protest activism	
INDIVIDUAL LEVEL				
Demographic characteristics				
Age (in years)	3.31***	3.48***	−.041	.021
	(.093)	(.093)	(.124)	(.124)
Sex (male = 1)	1.72***	1.72***	1.41***	1.41***
	(.084)	(.085)	(.113)	(.113)
Socioeconomic resources				
Household income 10-point scale	.833***	.997***	.841***	.903***
	(.099)	(.100)	(.134)	(.134)
Education 9-point scale	3.07***	3.25***	5.78***	5.84***
	(.104)	(.105)	(.140)	(.139)
Knowledge of democracy	.699***	1.10***	3.07***	3.24***
	(.100)	(.100)	(.134)	(.132)
Democratic attitudes				
Democratic aspirations	1.95***		2.15***	
	(.096)		(.129)	
Democratic satisfaction	1.30***		−1.22***	
	(.097)		(.131)	
Democratic deficit		−.088		−1.94***
		(.093)		(.124)
NATIONAL LEVEL				
Historic democracy index	−1.19	−.882	9.69***	9.81***
	(1.16)	(1.22)	(1.35)	(1.35)
Constant (intercept)	59.0	61.1	27.4	29.9
Schwarz BIC	411,225	411,988	444,025	444,087
N. respondents	47,450	47,451	47,940	47,941
N. nations	40	40	42	42
Measurement	100-pts.	100-pts.	100-pts.	100-pts.

Note: 'Protest politics' is a 100-point scale based on willingness or experience of joining a lawful demonstration, signing a petition, and boycotting consumer products. 'Citizen interest' is a 100-point scale based on interest in politics, the importance of politics, and voting.
* = >.05   ** = >.01   *** = >.001
Source: World Values Survey 2005–2007.

to demonstrate and to become engaged through unconventional channels.[26] At the same time, and in contrast to citizen interest, *those more dissatisfied with the way that democracy worked in their own country were also more willing to protest.* This combination of attitudes suggests that there is an important distinction between these types of activism; conventional participation reflects a broader contentment with the way democracy works. By contrast, protest acts were more strongly predicted by dissatisfaction with democracy. Overall, the models showed that the democratic deficit failed to predict citizen interest, which arose mainly from other factors such as educational skills and political knowledge. The deficit does have a significant effect, however, by *depressing* the propensity to engage in protest politics, not, as many fear, increasing it.

GOVERNANCE AND VOLUNTARY COMPLIANCE WITH THE LAW

In addition, any substantial democratic deficit may have broader consequences that reach beyond the political participation of citizens. In particular, there may well be implications for regime legitimacy and thus how far citizens are willing to comply voluntarily with laws, regulations, and government decisions without the threat of coercion and punishment. Easton theorized that political trust affected the ability of democratic states to raise revenues, to gain public consent for public policies, to implement decisions, and to ensure voluntary compliance with its laws.[27] In particular, he argued that systems support was associated with the willingness of citizens to obey the law and pay taxes without the penalty of coercion, thereby facilitating effective government. Previous research has found that trust in government institutions was significantly associated with the reported willingness to obey the law voluntarily and to pay taxes.[28] Political support is also thought to strengthen civic responsibilities and allegiant behaviors, such as serving on juries.[29] By contrast, people are thought more likely to engage in illegal acts, to sustain a black market economy, to cheat on their taxes, or to use bribery and corruption – and thus to undermine rule of law in fragile states – if they have little confidence in the integrity and legitimacy of their government and public officials.[30] Good governance has proved an issue of growing concern for the international development community, particularly for countries such as Russia, Colombia, and Mexico, which are characterized by widespread tax avoidance, rampant crime and corruption, and ineffective law enforcement.

Feelings of regime legitimacy are thus expected to strengthen allegiant behavior and thus more effective governance and rule of law.[31] To examine this thesis, we can draw upon two items in the World Values Survey that monitored how far people were willing to comply voluntarily with the law. The questions asked: *"Please tell me for each of the following statements whether you think it can always be justified, never be justified, or something in between, using this card.... Claiming government benefits to which you are not entitled.... Cheating on taxes if you have a chance."* Responses were gauged on a 10-point scale where those who rejected these sentiments, and thus expressed the strongest voluntary compliance with the law, scored highest. As with previous multilevel models, the standard demographic and socioeconomic factors were controlled. The results of the analysis of these items, shown in Table 11.2, provide partial confirmation of the legitimacy theory. In particular, *those with strong democratic values were significantly more likely to comply voluntarily with the law*, believing that it is wrong either to cheat on taxes or to claim government benefits fraudulently. Stronger satisfaction with democracy, however,

TABLE 11.2. *The Impact of Democratic Orientations on Allegiant Behavior*

	Wrong to cheat on taxes		Wrong to cheat on government benefits	
INDIVIDUAL LEVEL				
Demographic characteristics				
Age (in years)	.166***	.176***	.200***	.208***
	(.009)	(.009)	(.010)	(.124)
Sex (male = 1)	−.089***	−.089***	−.049***	−.049***
	(.008)	(.009)	(.009)	(.009)
Socioeconomic resources				
Household income 10-point scale	−.063***	−.054***	−.016	−.008
	(.010)	(.010)	(.011)	(.011)
Education 9-point scale	.014	.023*	.034*	.041***
	(.010)	(.010)	(.012)	(.012)
Knowledge of democracy	.201***	.225***	.289***	.309***
	(.010)	(.010)	(.011)	(.011)
Democratic attitudes				
Democratic aspirations	.159***		.166***	
	(.010)		(.011)	
Democratic satisfaction	.030*		−.014	
	(.010)		(.011)	
Democratic deficit		−.061***		−.096***
		(.009)		(.010)
NATIONAL LEVEL				
Historic democracy index	.064	.083	.268	.284
	(.174)	(.177)	(.154)	(.156)
Constant (intercept)	84.7	84.7	82.0	82.0
Schwarz BIC	411,225	411,988	244,391	244,536
N. respondents	54,606	54,606	54,341	54,336
N. nations	44	44	44	44
Measurement	100-pts.	100-pts.	100-pts.	100-pts.

Note: 'Cheat on taxes' is a 100-point scale based on the justifiability of cheating on tax payments. 'Cheat on government benefits' is a 100-point scale based on the justifiability of claiming benefits to which one is not entitled.
* = >.05 ** = >.01 *** = >.001
Source: World Values Survey 2005–2007.

was only significantly linked with willingness to pay taxes. Overall, *the net effect of the democratic deficit was to reduce voluntary compliance with the law significantly*, as legitimacy theory predicts. The effect of democratic orientations on compliance proved weaker than the impact of age or democratic knowledge, both of which greatly reinforced allegiant behavior. Nevertheless, democratic values also encouraged these behaviors and thus reinforced the capacity of the state to govern more effectively.

CULTURAL THEORIES OF DEMOCRATIZATION

The last and perhaps most important concern about any substantial and endur-ing democratic deficit are the implications for democratic reforms and democ-ratization. The research literature analyzing the factors leading to the break-down of autocratic regimes and the subsequent process of democratization has emphasized a lengthy catalogue of causes.[32] Among political economists and developmental sociologists, most attention has traditionally focused upon processes of industrialization and modernization (the classic Lipset thesis), which are thought to provide the structural foundation for building demo-cratic states.[33] Historians highlight the role of radical class struggles, mass mobilization, and negotiated elite pacts.[34] As an alternative view, institution-alists stress the importance of the design of constitutional structures, especially the impact of power-sharing institutions when bridging conflict within deeply divided societies (Lijphart).[35] International relations has emphasized the exter-nal forces shaping democratization, including the historical legacy of colonial-ism, the diffusion of human rights, the impact of conflict spilling over national borders, and the aid interventions of multilateral development agencies and regional associations.[36] By contrast to all these perspectives, ever since seminal work by Almond and Verba in the mid-twentieth century, cultural theorists have long assumed that citizen support for the nation-state, its agencies, and actors is essential for the sustainability of any democratic regime.[37] Cultural accounts have enjoyed something of a revival during the last decade, as the more deterministic versions of socioeconomic development have been seen as too limited and mechanistic to account for complex pathways of contemporary processes of democratization.[38] The global expansion of survey data has also allowed key propositions of cultural theories to be examined against empirical evidence in many diverse societies worldwide.

The argument that political culture is critical for sustainable processes of democratization and for effective democratic reforms is far from novel; indeed, its roots can be traced back more than half a century.[39] During the 1960s, memories of Weimar Germany and the collapse of parliamentary democ-racies following decolonization in Africa were the twin catalysts prompting many scholars to search for the underlying causes of sustainable democratic regimes. Cultural theories suggest that regimes in the initial stages of transition-ing toward electoral democracy – exemplified by contemporary states such as Thailand, Ukraine, Honduras, Kenya, and Russia – are particularly vulnerable to collapse under crisis conditions, reverting back to autocratic rule if they lack a broad reservoir of mass legitimacy, public support, and democratic values, such as a reservoir of social tolerance and interpersonal trust, respect for human rights, and the willingness to compromise.[40] The concept of 'legitimacy' repre-sents acceptance of the underlying 'rules of the game,' so that all actors, even electoral losers, willingly consent to rule by the regime without the sanction of force. The literature has stressed that fragile democracies may revert back to authoritarian rule or never progress beyond electoral autocracy unless they rest upon popular support for regime institutions over difficult times as well as periods of peace and prosperity.[41]

Why do some regimes break down while others persist? Congruence theory, originally developed by Harry Eckstein in the early 1960s, hypothesizes that regimes are most likely to endure if they are founded upon people's beliefs in legitimate authority.[42] Where citizens' preferences match the type of regime, this account predicts that institutional arrangements will prove long-lasting. It follows that the prospects for stable and enduring democratic regimes are regarded as more promising where democratic expectations are broadly in line with perceptions of democratic performance. In particular, democracies can function most effectively where there is a mass reservoir of popular legitimacy that can ensure voluntary compliance with the authorities, such as obeying the law, paying taxes, and complying with government decisions. A sense of popular legitimacy implies that the core institutions of the regime are widely regarded as appropriate and proper, so even if citizens dislike specific leaders, dissent from particular policies, or disagree vehemently with certain government decisions, they nevertheless accept the authority of officeholders and the processes that put them in power.[43] Maintaining a sense of legitimacy is critical in democracies, such as the sense that electoral processes are transparent, honest, and inclusive, so that all parties accept the outcome. The greater legitimacy a democratic regime accumulates, the more it will possess the potential to elicit compliance without excessive monitoring or punitive action, for example, to collect tax revenues or ensure observance of the law. Legitimacy is also important, however, for the authority exercised by many autocratic rulers. For example, repressive states, exemplified by North Korea and Turkmenistan, routinely deploy techniques of state propaganda and censorship and throw independent journalists, critics, and political opponents into jail to manipulate public opinion in support of the leader and to suppress any dissent.[44] Popular legitimacy is not essential for autocracies, however, since the threat, fear, or actual deployment of coercive methods of control through the security forces are available to rulers. If strongly challenged, repressive rulers can call the army out of the barracks.

When related to the core issues at the heart of this book, congruence theory therefore suggests several alternative propositions concerning the consequences of democratic orientations for democratic regimes. One proposition is that *societies with strong democratic aspirations will provide the most favorable conditions for democratization.* Alternatively, in some other cases it is possible that democratic supply can run ahead of demand – for instance, if multiparty elections are imposed by the international community as part of the peace-building process and constitutional settlement in fragile states such as in Afghanistan, DRC, and Iraq with deeply traditional cultures and little or no experience of this form of governance. This situation is less common, since we have already observed that overt adherence to democratic values is almost universal today, but nevertheless this pattern can occur, especially if the public is supporting democracy largely for instrumental reasons rather than intrinsic reasons. In this context, states in the early stages of democratic transitions face the serious risk of reverting back to authoritarian rule. Hence, Nancy Bermeo suggests that fragile democracies can be undermined if ordinary people are not willing to stand up and defend representative institutions when these are under threat.[45] Such threats can occur for diverse reasons, whether due to a military coup (such as in Thailand), the heady appeal of populist parties and the reassertion of executive power (as in Venezuela), thuggery, intimidation, and strong-man rule (as in Zimbabwe), or the more gradual erosion of human rights through a series of one-party manipulated electoral contests (as in Russia). Snyder and Mansfield also warn strongly against the imposition of competitive elections in fragile states emerging from conflict, which have not yet rebuilt the rule of law and where there is minimal demand for democracy, arguing that this process can produce perverse incentives for party leaders that exacerbate rather than mitigate societal ethnic tensions.[46] For all these reasons, another proposition is that *societies with weak democratic aspirations will provide unfavorable conditions for democratization.*

Alternatively, however, it remains the case that *democratic aspirations will have no major consequences for democratization* (the null hypothesis); after all, multiple factors beyond political culture contribute to processes of democratization. There are many plausible reasons that the impact of human development, political institutions, or elite pacts may outweigh the influence of public opinion. In a related argument, Booth and Seligson strongly challenge the claim that a long-term erosion of legitimacy has any serious consequences for regime stability in Latin America, noting that many states in the region have experienced declining support without any apparent effects on political stability, even in cases such as Argentina which have also seen deep-seated economic crises.[47] One possible reason the democratic deficit may have no major consequences at the macro-level is if citizens have the capacity to juggle and balance tensions between ideal aspirations and performance evaluations – for example, if they compartmentalize each dimension separately. The public has long been regarded as remaining fundamentally ambivalent about politics. Ever since seminal work by Philip Converse, social psychologists have recognized multiple dimensions of public opinion where individuals hold contradictory attitudes rather than displaying coherent and structured belief systems or consistent political ideologies.[48] Attitudes toward democracy may simply fall into this well-established pattern. Indeed, this was the conclusion of Hyman and Sheatley in one of the first empirical studies of U.S. attitudes toward government in the mid-1950s, who argued that Americans often hoped for the best from government but expected the worst.[49] If Americans are capable of holding incoherent and contradictory attitudes toward democratic governance, after centuries of experience, it would be foolhardy to assume that more systematic and coherent patterns of beliefs would be evident in countries with far less historical experience and everyday familiarity with this form of government – for example, among the publics living in Mali, Ukraine, or Indonesia. Moreover, previous studies by Inglehart and Welzel, which have emphasized the linkage between lagged cultural attitudes (in the early 1990s) and subsequent patterns of democracy (in 1997–2002), have focused upon the impact of the syndrome of 'self-expression' values. They have not examined the role of more direct and straightforward indicators of democratic aspirations.[50]

To test the evidence for the alternative propositions, the study needs to establish the impact of *prior* democratic attitudes on *subsequent* processes of democratization. The research design therefore needs to establish democratic orientations in t^1 prior to processes of democratization in t^2. Unfortunately, suitable items are unavailable in the World Values Survey prior to the fall of the Berlin Wall, which would have provided the most rigorous longitudinal test of the cultural thesis. Public opinion can be compared, however, by drawing upon the third wave of the WVS conducted in the mid-1990s, where data are available for forty-five countries around the world. Democratic aspirations are measured in this wave of the survey by support for democratic values and ideals, utilizing four items that fall into a consistent index: *"I'm going to describe various types of political systems and ask what you think about each as a way of governing this country. For each one, would you say it is a very good, fairly good, fairly bad or very bad way of governing this country? V164. Having a strong leader who does not have to bother with parliament and elections? V165. Having experts, not government, make decisions according to what they think is best for the country. V166. Having the army rule. V167. Having a democratic political system."* These items were recoded consistently, summed, and then standardized to create a 100-point democratic aspirations scale.

Subsequent processes of democratization occurring during the next decade can be examined by macro-level data. Many approaches to measuring processes of democratization exist in the literature and these broadly divide into either minimalist or maximalist conceptualizations, each with certain strengths and weaknesses. Minimalist notions reflect Schumpeterian notions where democracy is seen to exist in the competitive struggle for the people's vote.[51] Accordingly, Przeworski et al. define democratic types of regimes as those where two or more parties or candidates contest executive office through popular elections.[52] The advantage of minimalist definitions, proponents argue, is that this process helps to develop clear and unambiguous empirical indicators, precise operational definitions, and reliable and consistent classification procedures. In these conceptualizations, processes of regime change are seen as a stepped shift, where countries adopt competitive multiparty elections and thereby move from autocracy to democracy. Regime change implies the breakdown in the old constitutional settlement by which a state exercises its authority. Clear historic cases are exemplified by the fall of the Berlin Wall in 1989, ending decades of Soviet rule, or the bloodless coup d'état when Pervez Musharraf assumed power in Pakistan a decade later. Some regimes prove remarkably enduring, persisting in recognizable form over centuries, such as in the United States, Switzerland, and Britain. More commonly, regimes prove relatively short-lived, expiring for multiple reasons, whether triggered by a grassroots popular revolution, coup d'état or oligarchic challenge, military conquest or internal civil war, state failure, a major global or national economic crisis, or democratic process of constitutional revision.[53] Yet the capacity to identify a distinct watershed event signifying the end of the old regime and the birth of another is more ambiguous in cases where transitions from autocracy typically occur gradually, zig-zagging forward and backward in a non-linear fashion over an extended period. Most democracies in Africa, Asia, and Latin America are rarely born overnight as a simple result of a single decisive catalyst political event or a founding multiparty election. Moreover, the difficulties arising from the dichotomous approach are particularly problematic and prone to major measurement error when categorizing electoral autocracies, where the façade of multiparty competitive contests for legislative and executive office produce skewed outcomes serving to legitimate repressive regimes, such as Togo, Belarus, Egypt, Malaysia, Uzbekistan, and Zimbabwe.

Given these considerations, and for consistency with previous chapters, it is preferable to use 'thicker' conceptualizations reflecting Dahl's conception of liberal democracy, where the process of democratization is conceived as a continuous incremental process of a series of steps gradually expanding a range of fundamental freedoms and human rights, including, but not restricted to, competitive electoral processes. This conception is exemplified by the Freedom House continuous index, classifying regimes annually based on continuous scales. This approach facilitates more fine-grained distinctions across diverse types of regimes and more subtle gradations of states. This chapter therefore examines the Freedom House measure of political rights and civil liberties summed annually from 1995 to 2008, to provide the cumulative historical record of democracy in each state during these years, standardized to a 100-point scale for ease of comparison. Similar to the historical index used earlier covering the complete third wave era, the construction of this scale takes account of both regressions and advances in democratization during these years.

The simple correlation, illustrated in Figure 11.2, confirms the strong association between democratic aspirations, measured by the third wave of the WVS conducted in the mid-1990s and the subsequent record of democratization since this period. The scatterplot suggests that levels of economic development also play a role, which helps to account for the curvilinear pattern best captured by the cubic regression line. The OLS linear regression models in Table 11.3 test the relationship between democratic aspiration in 1995 and the subsequent historical record of democratization in each state, with additional controls for levels of economic and human development. Since the impact of cultural attitudes is being tested on levels of democracy in each state, the analysis is most appropriately conducted only at the macro-level. The results show that overall both economic development and human development are more strongly related to democratization than these cultural values, as the 'Lipset thesis' has long suggested.[54] But the models also confirm that lagged democratic aspirations remain significant predictors of democratization, even with these controls. The

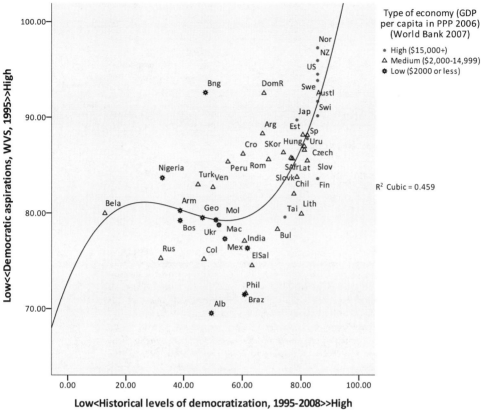

FIGURE 11.2. The impact of democratic aspirations on subsequent levels of democratization. Democratic aspirations are measured in the mid-1990s by a scale constructed from the following items. *"I'm going to describe various types of political systems and ask what you think about each as a way of governing this country. For each one, would you say it is a very good, fairly good, fairly bad, or very bad way of governing this country? V164. Having a strong leader who does not have to bother with parliament and elections? V165. Having experts, not government, make decisions according to what they think is best for the country. V166. Having the army rule. V167. Having a democratic political system."* The historical record of democratization is measured by summing the annual Freedom House index of civil and political liberties from 1995 to 2008, standardized to 100 points. The type of economy is classified by per capita GDP in 2006 measured in purchasing power parity by the World Bank. *Source*: World Values Survey third wave, mid-1990s; UNDP Human Development Report 2007; World Development Indicators, World Bank.

combined effects of both human development and cultural attitudes are impressive, as indicated by the adjusted R^2 coefficient of 0.510, explaining roughly half the variance in the historic record of democratization since the mid-1990s. This leads us to reject the null hypothesis. Instead, this evidence supports the

TABLE 11.3. *The Impact of Lagged Democratic Orientations on Subsequent Levels of Democratization*

	Historical record of democratization, 1995–2008	
MACRO-LEVEL		
Democratic aspirations, 1995	.797*	6.76**
	(.384)	(2.21)
Economic development, 2006	.001**	
	(.000)	
Human Development Index, 2006		87.3**
		(19.7)
Constant (intercept)	−7.68	−86.6
Adjusted R²	.399	.510
N. nations	45	44
Measurement	100-pts.	100-pts.

Notes: Democratic aspirations are measured in the mid-1990s by a scale constructed from the following items. *"I'm going to describe various types of political systems and ask what you think about each as a way of governing this country. For each one, would you say it is a very good, fairly good, fairly bad or very bad way of governing this country? V164. Having a strong leader who does not have to bother with parliament and elections? V165. Having experts, not government, make decisions according to what they think is best for the country. V166. Having the army rule. V167. Having a democratic political system."* Economic development is measured by GDP per capita in purchasing power parity, 2006, World Bank. The Human Development Index, 2006, is measured by the UNDP. The historical record of democratization is measured by summing the annual Freedom House index of civil and political liberties from 1995 to 2008, standardized to 100 points.
Sources: World Values Survey third wave, mid-1990s; UNDP Human Development Report 2007; World Development Indicators, World Bank.

first proposition: *societies with strong democratic aspirations provide the most favorable conditions for democratization.* Culture therefore cannot simply be reduced to patterns of societal modernization; instead, prior hopes for democracy play an independent role in helping to strengthen and sustain democratic regimes.

CONCLUSIONS AND DISCUSSION

This chapter has analyzed only a few of the many consequences that can be expected to flow from the tensions observed in this study between democratic aspirations and performance. For example, Dalton compares the impact of system support on American attitudes toward institutional reform and the implications for electoral and party change. The study found that U.S. states with more skeptical orientations toward government were more likely to pass limitations on the terms of legislators, suggesting that mistrust encouraged these reforms.[55] If people no longer feel that government policies are going to prove effective or well administered, then this could encourage neoliberal attempts to transfer many public services from the state to the non-profit or private sectors. Comparative evidence remains more limited, but elsewhere I have demonstrated that prior democratic aspirations are the strongest and most significant predictors of the subsequent passage and adoption of electoral reforms. Indeed, a series of multivariate regression models showed that democracy aspirations were stronger predictors of electoral reform than levels of economic or human development, the historical record of democracy in each country, or other cultural indicators, such as satisfaction with democratic performance and institutional confidence.[56] Moreover, the fact that public aspirations are followed by subsequent institutional changes, even in many non-democratic regimes, suggests that 'reform from below' is an important strategy that can succeed, even against elite interests. This chapter therefore only scratches the surface of a substantial research agenda in comparative politics examining how cultural values influence broader processes of democratic reforms, party politics, and electoral behavior, deserving scrutiny by future generations of scholars.

Nevertheless, the consequences of democratic orientations examined here on mass political activism, on allegiant behavior and compliance with the law, and ultimately on processes of democratization are some of the most important. Although long assumed by cultural theorists, systematic cross-national evidence that democratic orientations matter for how democracies work has often been lacking. Many previous empirical studies have also emphasized that democratization is shaped more by attitudes such as political efficacy, interpersonal trust, and social tolerance, or 'self-actualization' values than by the direct adherence to democratic ideals and values.[57] The result of the comparative evidence presented in this chapter confirms that democratic orientations matter; in particular, the evidence demonstrates that democratic aspirations play a significant role in strengthening forms of political participation, including both indicators of citizen interest and protest activism, as well as reinforcing compliant behavior in adhering to the law and ultimately also contributing toward sustainable democratic regimes. Moreover, we can theorize that these processes are likely to interact, with democratic aspirations improving voice and accountability as well as the capacity of the regime to govern effectively, thereby making democracies work better. Although there are many reasons to doubt whether cultural attitudes matter, in fact it turns out that they do.

12

Conclusions and Implications

More than a decade ago, the original *Critical Citizens* study brought together a distinguished group of international scholars and seminal thinkers to consider the state of support for the political system at the close of the twentieth century.[1] The core consensus emerging from contributors to the volume was that citizens in many countries had proved increasingly skeptical about the actual workings of the core institutions of representative democracy, notably political parties, parliaments, and governments. At the same time, however, public aspirations toward democratic ideals, values, and principles, or the demand for democracy, proved almost universal around the globe. The tensions between unwavering support for democratic principles but skeptical evaluations about democratic practices was interpreted in the study as the rise of 'critical citizens.' The passage of time means that the argument and evidence presented in *Critical Citizens* needed to be updated to show whether the central thesis continues to resonate today. The extensive anxieties that continue to be expressed about public support for democratic governance suggest that the core message from the earlier volume has not faded, but instead seems more relevant than ever to help explain contemporary developments. Updating and expanding the scope of the evidence and developing more systematic insights into the causes and consequences of the democratic deficit provide an important corrective to the misdiagnosis and exaggeration that is prevalent throughout so much of the literature. The conclusion recapitulates the standard concern about contemporary levels of political support, as expressed by numerous scholars and popular commentators over the years. It then summarizes the main arguments presented throughout the book, provides a series of reasons challenging the conventional wisdom, and finally concludes by reflecting upon the broader implications of democratic deficits for both theories and practices of democracy.

The Conventional Anxieties about Established Democracies

Concern about public support for the political system rises and falls periodically on the agenda, reflecting contemporary hopes and fears about real world events. Hence during the late 1950s and early 1960s, historical memories of the fall of the Weimar Republic, coupled with the failure and breakdown of many fledgling parliamentary democracies in post-colonial Africa, spurred the initial interest in cultural theories of democratization and regime stability among early scholars of political development.[2] Similarly during the late 1960s and early 1970s, the outbreak of urban riots, street protests, and counter-culture movements in the United States and Western Europe revived conservative anxieties about the root causes of protest politics and the consequences of radical challenges to the authority of democratic governments.[3] Apprehension faded somewhat during the subsequent decade, although the mid-1990s again saw renewed disquiet about these issues, uniting diverse concerns about a supposed erosion of civic engagement occurring in established democracies; as evidence, observers pointed to the half-empty ballot box, shrinking party loyalties and membership rolls, and a long-term fall in social capital.[4] Today a new wave of deep concern has arisen about public mistrust of politicians and government in both established democracies and in younger democracies elsewhere in the world.[5] The standard view today is encapsulated by Dalton's conclusions: "By almost any measure, public confidence and trust in, and support, for politicians, political parties, and political constitutions has eroded over the past generation."[6]

Anxiety about the root causes and consequences of any widespread erosion of political trust in Western societies resonates even more clearly outside of academe. Hence, in the United States, much journalistic coverage assessing the early years of the Obama administration has focused upon signs of public dissatisfaction with the federal government. Commentary has highlighted polls showing deepening political disaffection, notably low confidence in Congress, following partisan stalemate and gridlock in debate over health care reform, a deep economic recession characterized by eroding financial security, and collapsing home values.[7] Increasingly populist anti-government rhetoric has emanated from the 'Tea Party' movement, echoed by some leaders in the Republican Party and in parts of the news media. Sporadic acts of domestic and foreign terrorism in America are commonly linked in popular commentary with dissatisfaction with government, although the precise underlying connection has not been fully established. In Europe, as well, events such as the Westminster expenses scandal in Britain have been thought to have exacerbated a culture of pervasive public anger and mistrust, where the motivation and ethical standards of politicians are widely discredited.[8] Elsewhere, similar concerns echo about the declining image of the political class, for example, in Japan and Germany.[9]

Many reforms have been advocated to address public disaffection. Those who favor strengthening opportunities for collective deliberation and direct citizen engagement in decision-making processes have proposed expanding the use of citizen assemblies and juries, popular referenda and petitions, social audits, participatory budgeting, public consultation exercises, town hall meetings, and deliberative polls.[10] Other reformers concerned about strengthening governance transparency and accountability urge repeal of official secrecy acts and expanded rights to information, designing more open decision-making processes, reinforcing the independent news media, and utilizing e-governance. The role and powers of independent monitoring and regulatory agencies can also be strengthened, including anti-corruption institutions and electoral commissions, ombudsman institutions, human rights watch organizations, agencies regulating standards of public life, and budgetary auditors.[11] More radical changes include constitutional revisions, reforming electoral processes and campaign funding, increasing the social diversity of legislatures, and decentralizing decision making to local communities.[12] Despite extensive popular debate, however, it remains unclear whether any of these strategies will actually achieve their desired long-term objectives. These may all be intrinsically worthy initiatives in their own right. Reforms will fail, however, if the assumed problem of democratic legitimacy, or any so-called crisis of trust in government, has actually been exaggerated or misdiagnosed.

Concern about a Global Democratic Recession?

Outside of established democracies, developments around the world suggest more persuasive reasons for serious concern about the retrenchment of autocracy and an active push-back against the forces of democracy. Larry Diamond, a leading observer, suggests that the first decade of the twenty-first century is an era in which democracy has experienced little further advance (at best), or even the start of a new reverse wave (at worst).[13] Freedom House reports echo these worries.[14] Each global region has differed in the pace and extent of the transition from autocracy and the process of democratic consolidation during the third wave era. In Latin America democratic governance made sustained progress during the 1980s, although studies suggest that even in this region, dissatisfaction with the performance of government has encouraged political disillusionment and cynicism.[15] Other observers have detected evidence of a regional backlash against the way that liberal democracy and economic neoliberalism works, although not a rejection of democratic ideals per se.[16] For evidence of lack of progress, Venezuela experienced the return of strong-man populist rule under Hugo Chavez, Mexico and Colombia continue to be destabilized by violent drug cartels, while in the Caribbean, Cuba switched dictators from Fidel to Raul Castro, and fragile Haiti was devastated by the collapse of its buildings and government in the earthquake.

In sub-Saharan Africa, Freedom House estimates that human rights deteriorated in almost one-quarter of all states in recent years, including in Nigeria, Zimbabwe, and Mauritania. Many traditional dictatorships, military oligarchies, and strong-man rulers continue to rule African states.[17] Elsewhere on the continent, a series of bloody civil wars have led to the collapse of political order and failed states.[18] Some of the world's poorest nations on the sub-continent, including Mali, Liberia, Benin, and Ghana, have experienced a series of multiparty competitive elections and real gains in human rights since the early 1990s, but states still lack the capacity to lift millions out of poverty and to meet the targets for health care, education, and welfare in the Millennium Development Goals.[19] Among Arab states, some concrete but limited gains for human rights and freedoms have registered in recent years, yet the rhetoric of reform runs far ahead of realities.[20] Moreover, Carothers suggests that during the administration of President George W. Bush, the association of the rhetoric of democracy promotion with unpopular wars in Iraq and Afghanistan depressed public support for reform in the region and encouraged a more general push-back by oil-rich plutocrats.[21] Overall, most Middle East autocracies stagnated. In Eastern Europe, Russia has imposed renewed restrictions on human rights and challenges to the rule of law; Georgia has become less stable. Kyrgyzstan has experienced political turmoil but many Central Asian states seem frozen in Soviet-style dictatorships, seemingly isolated from global forces of regime change. The color revolutions in Georgia and Ukraine were commonly framed as the triumph of democratic forces, but it remains unclear whether these movements actually reflected more deep-rooted and widespread democratic sentiments or whether in fact they were triggered by elite contestation for power.[22] Afghanistan has registered mixed progress, experiencing flawed presidential elections and signs of renewed instability, which spill over its borders with Pakistan. Elsewhere occasional outbreaks of popular dissent seeking to topple autocratic regimes have also been brutally suppressed by the authorities, for example, most recently in Burma/Myanmar, Tibet, and Iran.[23] In Asia-Pacific, democratically elected leaders fell from power after military coups in Thailand (2006) and Fiji (2006). The Obama administration has downplayed ambitious neo-con talk of democracy building in Iraq and Afghanistan, in a backlash against the rhetoric of President Bush, as realists reasserted more pragmatic leadership in the U.S. State Department.[24]

Cultural attitudes toward democracy are expected to be important in all these cases but particularly so in countries that have experienced the initial transition from autocracy during the third wave era, but which have not yet firmly established the full panoply of legislative and judicial institutions associated with liberal democracy.[25] Many regime transitions have occurred in world regions lacking historical experience of democracy, as well as in low-income economies, post-conflict divided societies, and fragile states, all providing unfavorable soil for the seeds of democratization to flourish.[26] Theories of legitimacy suggest that regimes will prove most politically stable where they rest on popular support.[27] Hence, democratic constitutions built upon cultures that strongly endorse democratic ideals and principles are expected to weather shocks arising from any sudden economic crisis, internal conflict, or elite challenge more successfully than societies where the public remains indifferent, cynical, or even hostile toward the idea of democracy. Along similar lines, autocratic regimes are expected to endure where the general public endorses the legitimacy of this form of governance – for example, where citizens express deference to the authority of traditional monarchs and religious leaders, or where they are suckered by the heady appeals of populist dictators. If public legitimacy is lacking, however, regimes are thought to be more susceptible to mass and elite challenge. Democratic states, in particular, remain most vulnerable to this risk, as they rely upon a reservoir of popular legitimacy and voluntary compliance to govern. By contrast, brutal autocracies, if threatened by mass movements, reform factions, and opposition dissidents, can always reassert their grip on power by calling out the military.

Issues of regime change and progressive democratization, always difficult, have been compounded in recent years by the aftermath of the global financial crisis, which generated worsening economic conditions and poverty, falling employment and wages, and the largest decline in world trade for eighty years.[28] Even before this downturn, in the world's poorest societies, democratic governments faced particularly severe obstacles in delivering basic public services such as clean water, health clinics, and schools. The United Nations documents enduring and deeply entrenched poverty for the bottom billion in the least developed nations, raising doubts about whether the world can achieve the Millennium Development Goals by 2015, as planned.[29] Climate change exacerbates problems of food security and clean water scarcity and threatens new humanitarian disasters in low-lying coastal regions. In fragile or post-crisis states, the struggle to reduce conflict, build sustainable peace, and strengthen the capacity and legitimacy of democratically elected governments cannot be underestimated.[30] In this complex and difficult environment, it would be naïve to assume that the third wave era of democratization continues to advance steadily.

EXPLAINING THE DEMOCRATIC DEFICIT

In this context, understanding the cultural drivers of sustainable democratization represents one of the most fundamental challenges facing the international community, advocacy agencies seeking to advance universal human rights, and domestic reformers working to strengthen democratic governance. Often, separate disciplines and research sub-fields in the social sciences focus on one of the theoretical dimensions with partial empirical tests and without controlling for the full range of explanatory factors or examining whether the effects of models are robust when utilizing alternative dependent variables. Like the proverbial blind men and the elephant, each part of the puzzle is usually treated separately in the research literature. Survey analysts focus upon public opinion. Communication scholars scrutinize the news media. Policy analysts monitor government performance. And institutionalists examine power-sharing structures. A more comprehensive general theory provides a more satisfactory way of understanding this phenomenon. Multilevel analysis, with evidence derived from surveys of public opinion, media coverage of public affairs, and aggregate indicators of government performance, is the most appropriate technique to determine the most important causes for any democratic deficits. This book examined a wide range of empirical data, using a series of multilevel models, to analyze the strength of each of these potential explanations. This study seeks to integrate the separate approaches into a more coherent sequential framework where citizens, media, and governments interact as the central actors. The analysis presented throughout this study leads to several main conclusions, which deserve recapitulation here.

Trendless Fluctuations in System Support

Perhaps the most important simple message, challenging the conventional wisdom, is that *public support for the political system has not eroded consistently in established democracies, not across a wide range of countries around the world*. The 'crisis' myth, while fashionable, exaggerates the extent of political disaffection and too often falls into the dangers of fact-free hyperbole. In general, following in the footsteps of David Easton, support for the political system is best understood as a multidimensional phenomenon ranging from the most generalized feelings of attachment and belonging to a nation-state, through confidence and trust in the regime and its institutions, down to specific approval of particular authorities and leaders. Chapter 4 scrutinized and dissected time-series survey evidence about public opinion within established democracies. The chapter concluded that it is essential to distinguish trends in public attitudes that operate at different levels rather than treat 'political support' as though it is all of one piece. Careful attention to the precise timing and breadth of any trends is also critical for an accurate diagnosis of developments.

The most diffuse level of political support concerns the most fundamental orientations toward the nation-state, exemplified by deep-rooted feelings of national pride and national identity. Globalization might be expected to have weakened these feelings but the survey evidence demonstrates that nationalism remains strong and relatively stable, even among West European societies that are long-standing members of the EU. Trust in political institutions such as national governments, parliaments, and parties displays systematic and persistent contrasts among established democracies in Western Europe and the United States. The longitudinal evidence clearly demonstrates that fluctuations over time usually prove far more common than straightforward linear or uniform downward trends. Notwithstanding all the headlines exaggerating the decline in trust, there is little actual evidence of a long-term decline, either in the United States or in Western Europe across the board.[31] Contrasts are also evident in public attitudes toward different branches of government within each country; for example, the United States has seen a long-term significant erosion of support for Congress, but this has not affected public support for the Supreme Court or the Executive. Persistent differences in institutional trust can also be observed among relatively similar nations, such as between Italy and Spain, or Germany and France. A few European countries have experienced growing trust in state institutions, while a few have seen the reverse situation. Perhaps most important, in Europe diffuse support for the nation-state remains strong and stable, and European satisfaction with the performance of democracy has usually strengthened over time, not weakened.

Democratic Deficits

Nevertheless, the second major lesson arising from this study is that *in many states today, satisfaction with the performance of democracy continues to diverge from public aspirations.* This pattern was first observed in *Critical Citizens* and this book provides further confirmation about the persistence of the democratic deficit. The comparison of multiple dimensions of system support in contemporary societies worldwide, presented in Chapter 6, showed that compared with other types of regimes, autocracies display stronger confidence in public sector agencies and also feelings of nationalism. Yet if we focus upon pro-democratic attitudes, in particular, it is clear that these feelings are stronger among older liberal democracies that have experienced this form of governance over many decades, or even centuries, including levels of satisfaction with democracy, endorsement of democratic attitudes, and the rejection of autocracy. In terms of democratic aspirations, however, today these attitudes are almost universal, irrespective of the type of regime governing the state.

Building upon this foundation, the study compared the democratic deficit in each society, conceptualized as the tensions that arise from the imbalance between the public's demand for democracy (measured by strong adherence to democratic values and rejection of authoritarian alternatives) and the perceived supply of democracy (monitored by public dissatisfaction with the democratic performance of governments in each country). The evidence demonstrated that people living in older liberal democracies expressed strong endorsement of democratic values but they were also relatively content with how democracy works in their own country. States that have democratized only during the third wave era prove far more diverse in their orientations, with the greatest congruence between aspirations and perceived performance displayed in cases such as Ghana, Uruguay, and South Africa, which observers rate as relatively successful democracies. By contrast, larger disparities between expectations and perceived performance are evident in many post-communist states, including in Russia, Ukraine, Bulgaria, and Serbia.

The Causes of the Democratic Deficit

The 'market model' used for analysis in this book compared three distinct types of explanation for the democratic deficit. The most common account of rising aspirations toward democratic governance emphasizes long-term cultural developments among citizens, on the 'demand-side,' associated with the structural expansion in cognitive and civic skills related to rising educational levels and societal modernization (Dalton), generational shifts toward self-expression values in post-industrial societies (Inglehart and Welzel), and theories of social capital (Putnam).[32] The role of the news media as the intermediary channel of information between citizens and the state is another common explanation for levels of democratic knowledge and for public perceptions of government performance. Moreover, a range of 'supply-side' theories has also been suggested in the literature, emphasizing that public opinion is responding more rationally and instrumentally to the institutional context, including the enduring impact of historical political traditions on democratic cultures, government performance when delivering basic public goods and services, and the uneven distribution of partisan 'winners' and 'losers' arising from institutional structures.[33] Each explanation generates a series of testable propositions that are scrutinized against the available empirical evidence in Section III of the book.

Several main points arise from the autopsy. The book started from the premise that the democratic deficit could be best understood by a combination of rising aspirations (with the analysis suggesting that public demands are fueled strongly by education), the potential impact of negative news about government (although the evidence for this remains strictly limited), and perceived shortfalls in government performance (particularly *process* rather than policy performance).

Cultural accounts emphasize that major changes in system support are driven primarily by sociological changes, whether glacial processes of value change eroding respect for traditional authorities and fueling emancipative demands for democracy, or by the wearing away of generalized social trust and the face-to-face bonds of community associations. The extensive cross-national evidence examined in this study suggests no confirmation for the bolder claims in the societal modernization theory; in particular, *democratic aspirations were not found to be associated with processes of human development nor with age effects.* Contrary to theoretical expectations, democratic aspirations were slightly stronger among the older generation, not the young. Even more striking, these values were not related to contemporary levels of human development in each society; today both rich and poor nations emphasize the importance of living in democratic states. But the baby should not be thrown out with the bath water; cultural theories furnish a partial answer to some of the issues at the heart of this study; in particular, *educational levels, self-expression values, social trust, and associational activism all help to predict higher democratic aspirations. Only the effects of education, however, actually widened the democratic deficit.*

The study also reinforced the need for considerable caution when interpreting the almost universal support for democratic values, emphasizing that we need to establish what people understand by the complex concept of 'democracy.' Procedural, instrumental, and authoritarian notions of democracy can be distinguished. We develop the notion of 'enlightened democratic knowledge' that is defined and measured by awareness of some basic principles at the heart of democratic regimes – as well as the ability to distinguish those that are incompatible. Drawing upon socialization theories of political learning, Chapter 8 confirmed that enlightened democratic knowledge was significantly strengthened at the macro-level by longer historical experience of democratic governance in any state, by cosmopolitan communications, and by levels of economic development. At the micro-level, the cognitive skills and knowledge derived from education as well as access to news media information also strengthened enlightened political knowledge.

Communications theories provide an alternative perspective on the democratic deficit, emphasizing the type of media and the type of coverage. Scholars differ in whether they expect that exposure and attention to TV news will encourage more cynical attitudes toward politics, government, and democracy (the traditional video-malaise thesis), or whether they predict that this process will reinforce democratic orientations and civic engagement (the virtuous circle thesis). The analysis presented in Chapter 9 provides further confirmation of the latter perspective; exposure to news and information from newspapers, television and radio news, and the internet was found to have *strengthened* democratic values and aspirations, even after controlling for factors such as age, income, and education that characterize news users. The effects on democratic satisfaction proved more mixed, but contrary to the core claim in the video-malaise thesis, users of television and radio news proved more satisfied with democracy, not less. Moreover, regular use of all these media *reduced* the democratic deficit, or the gap between expectations and perceived performance. The study also tested the impact of the tone of coverage, with more negative news and scandal coverage expected to reduce public satisfaction with government. The evidence was limited to the cases of Britain and the United States, and the results of the analysis provided at best only limited and partial support for the tone thesis. Hence, the amount of scandal coverage about Congress in the news media did reduce public confidence in this institution, but similar effects were not detected in the British case. Further research is required to rule in, or indeed to rule out, the media tone thesis with more confidence.

An alternative account is provided by rational choice theories suggesting that regime performance matters, at least at some level, for public satisfaction with the workings of democracy. The underlying assumptions and claims embodied in these accounts were considered in Chapter 10, comparing the evidence supporting *process* accounts, which emphasize that judgments of regime performance are based primarily upon retrospective evaluations of the quality of underlying democratic procedures; *policy* accounts, suggesting that retrospective evaluations of the overall substantive policy record of successive governments are important; and *institutional* accounts, which theorize that regime evaluations are conditioned by the intervening effects of power-sharing arrangements, determining the distribution of 'winners' and 'losers' in any state. The results of analyzing a comprehensive range of measures suggest that process performance, including both indices of democracy and good governance, helps to explain satisfaction with the way democratic government works. Among the policy indices, economic development and a subjective sense of well-being also proved equally important, although most of the other more specific economic, social, and environmental performance indicators were not significant. Last among the institutional factors, satisfaction with democracy was indeed strengthened by support for the winning party. By contrast, the overall institutional arrangements in any regime did not appear to be important. Overall it appears that closing the democratic deficit is therefore largely about strengthening processes of democracy and the actual quality of governance so that the performance meets rising citizen expectations.

The Impact of Democratic Orientations

Scholars continue to debate the potential consequences of any democratic deficits both for political behavior at the individual level and for democratic governance in the nation-state. *Critical Citizens* concluded, somewhat cautiously and ambivalently, that the tensions between ideals and practices could be regarded in a positive light if the diffusion of democratic aspirations around the world will eventually spread downward to strengthen public confidence and generalized trust in the workings of representative institutions essential for democratic governance. Critical citizens may thereby be a positive force for reform in the world, fueling popular demands that states with poor human rights records come to embrace democratic principles more fully. A degree of skepticism about the trustworthiness of government authorities is healthy for democracy; after all, classical liberal political theory was founded on the need for citizen vigilance about the potential abuse of power by the state. These ideas led the framers of the U.S. Constitution to establish a set of institutions explicitly designed to limit government power.[34] As Hardin emphasizes, trust should be reserved for trustworthy actors. Yet substantial and enduring democratic deficits are more commonly regarded with concern, triggering alarm that prolonged and deep disenchantment with the performance of particular political leaders, lack of confidence with governing parties, and disillusionment with core representative institutions will eventually spread upward to corrode faith in democracy itself, like dry rot weakening the foundations from below, with the capacity to undermine popular support for fragile democratic regimes.

Although multiple puzzles remain, this book provides a more detailed examination about many of these issues, allowing firmer conclusions to be offered in this volume. The results presented in Chapter 11 demonstrate that democratic orientations matter – and matter a lot – including for patterns and types of political participation, for the willingness of citizens to comply voluntarily with the authorities (and thus for the capacity of states to implement decisions), and ultimately for strengthening processes of democratization. In particular, democratic aspirations played a significant role in bolstering indicators of citizen interest and protest activism, as well as reinforcing compliant behavior by citizens in accordance with the law. Last, the lagged model monitored the effects of culture on subsequent processes of democratization, showing that democratic aspirations contributed to sustainable democratic regimes. Therefore, as this book has demonstrated, democratic orientations are far from irrelevant to the real world; they matter for political participation, for the willingness of citizens to comply voluntarily with the authorities and thus to build capable states and rule of law, and ultimately for the process of strengthening democracy around the world.

Technical Appendix A

Concepts and Measures

Variable	Definitions, coding, and sources
MACRO-LEVEL INDICATORS	
Human Development Index	The Human Development Index (HDI) is based on longevity, as measured by life expectancy at birth; educational achievement; and standard of living, as measured by per capita GDP ([purchasing power parity] $US). Source: UNDP *Human Development Report*, various years.
Type of society	'*Post-industrial societies*' were defined as independent nation-states around the world ranking with an HDI score over .900. '*Industrial societies*' are classified as the nations with a moderate HDI (ranging from .740 to .899). Last, '*agrarian societies*' are the nations with lower levels of development (HDI of .739 or below). Source: UNDP *Human Development Report*, various years.
Economic development	Per capita GDP measured in constant international $ in purchasing power parity. Various years. Source: The World Bank. *World Development Indicators*. Various years.
Type of economy	'*High income*' economies were defined as the most affluent states around the world, ranking with a mean per capita GDP of $15,000+. '*Medium income*' economies are classified as the nations with a moderate per capita GDP of $2,000–14,999. Last, '*low income*' are those economies with a mean per capita GDP of $1999 or less. All are measured in constant international $ in purchasing power parity. Source: The World Bank. *World Development Indicators*.
Historical democratization index	The cumulative Freedom House annual ratings of political rights and civil liberties in each country during the third wave era, from 1972 to 2006. The index is standardized to 100 points. It is also subdivided into 'restricted experience' (scoring low through 29), moderate experience (30 through 69), and extensive experience (70 and higher). Source: Freedom House, various years www.Freedomhouse.com.

(*continued*)

Variable	Definitions, coding, and sources
Types of regime	'*Older liberal democracies*' are defined as independent nation-states with regimes which the Freedom House survey, *Freedom around the World,* classifies as "free" in terms of a wide range of political rights and civil liberties, scoring 70 and above on the 100-point Historical democratization index. '*Younger liberal democracies*' are defined as independent nation-states with regimes which the Freedom House survey, *Freedom around the World,* classifies as "free" in terms of a wide range of political rights and civil liberties, scoring 69 and below on the 100-point Historical democratization index. '*Electoral democracies*' are defined as contemporary independent nation-states which Freedom House defines as 'partly free.' '*Autocracies*' are defined as the countries classified as 'not free' by Freedom House.
Press Freedom indexes	The Reporters without Borders Press Freedom index. The index is 100 points. Source: www.rsf.org/. Also Freedom House *Media Freedom Index.* www.freedomhouse.org (various years).
Globalization index	The KOF Index of Globalization, 1970–2005. For methodological and technical details, see http://globalization.kof.ethz.ch/.
Cosmopolitanism index	The index is constructed from adding the standardized Freedom House Media Freedom index, the KOF Globalization Index, and per capita GDP (for sources, see above). The standardization means that each component is equally weighted. Source: Norris and Inglehart (2009).
Corruption Perception Index	Corruption Perception Index estimated by Transparency International. Source: www.**transparency**.org.
Good governance indices	Daniel Kaufmann, Aart Kraay, and Massimo Mastruzzi. 2007. *Governance Matters VI: Aggregate and Individual Governance Indicators, 1996–2006.* Washington, DC: The World Bank, Policy Research Working Paper. www.worldbank.org.
Human rights indices	David L. Cingranelli and David L. Richards. 2004. The Cingranelli-Richards (CIRI) Human Rights Database Coder Manual. http://ciri.binghamton.edu/.
Regime institutions	For the classification of types of electoral systems, types of executives, and federal or unitary states, see Norris (2008).

MICRO-LEVEL CULTURAL INDICATORS:

Democratic aspirations	V162. *"How important is it for you to live in a country that is governed democratically? On this scale where 1 means it is 'not at all important' and 10 means 'absolutely important' what position would you choose? Standardized to 100 points.* Source: World Values Survey 2005–2007.
Democratic satisfaction	V163. *"And how democratically is this country being governed today? Again using a scale from 1 to 10, where 1 means that it is 'not at all democratic' and 10 means that it is 'completely democratic,' what position would you choose?" Standardized to 100 points.* Source: World Values Survey 2005–2007.

Variable	Definitions, coding, and sources
Democratic deficit	*The mean difference between democratic aspirations and satisfaction.* Source: World Values Survey 2005–2007.
Confidence in institutions	V146–147. *"I am going to name a number of organizations. For each one, could you tell me how much confidence you have in them: is it a great deal of confidence (4), quite a lot of confidence (3), not very much confidence (2) or none at all (1)? (Read out and code one answer for each)*: The armed forces; The police; The courts; The government (in your nation's capital); Political parties; Parliament; The civil service." The 100-point institutional confidence scale, where high represents most confidence, combines these items. Source: World Values Surveys 1981–2007.
Political interest	V95. *"How interested would you say you are in politics? Are you... "* Very interested (*recoded* 4), Somewhat interested (3), Not very interested (2), Not at all interested (1). Source: World Values Surveys.
National pride	V209. *"How proud are you to be [**French**]*?"* Very proud (4); Quite proud (3); Not very proud (2); Not at all proud (1). *Substitute nationality. Source: World Values Surveys.
Subjective well-being	The index combined survey measures of life satisfaction, self-reported state of health, subjective happiness, and financial satisfaction, standardized to 100 points. Source: World Values Surveys.
Citizen interest	This scale combined interest in politics, the importance of politics, and whether respondents reported that they had voted in a recent parliamentary election. Source: World Values Surveys.
Protest politics	This scale combines whether respondents reported that they had joined a lawful demonstration, signed a petition, and boycotted consumer products. Source: World Values Surveys.
Traditional v. secular-rational values	The Traditional values scale is measured by support of the following items: God is very important in respondent's life; It is more important for a child to learn obedience and religious faith than independence and determination; Autonomy index; Abortion is never justifiable; Respondent has strong sense of national pride; Respondent favors respect for authority. In contrast, support for Secular-rational values is measured by the opposite position on all of above. Source: World Values Surveys.

INDIVIDUAL-LEVEL DEMOGRAPHIC, SOCIOECONOMIC, AND MEDIA USE INDICATORS:

Occupational class	Coded for the respondent's occupation. *"In which profession/occupation do you, or did you, work?"* The scale is coded into 4 categories: Professional/manager (1); Other non-manual (2); Skilled non-manual (3); Unskilled manual worker (4). Source: World Values Surveys.
Paid work status	V220. *"Are you employed now or not?"* Coded full-time, part-time, or self-employed (1), other (0). Source: World Values Surveys.

(continued)

Variable	Definitions, coding, and sources
Education	V217. *"What is the highest educational level that you have ever attained?"* Coded on a 9-point scale from no formal education (1) to university level with degree (9). Source: World Values Surveys.
Age	Age coded in continuous years derived from date of birth. Source: World Values Surveys.
Age group	Young = Under 30 years old; Middle aged = 30–59 years old; Older = 60 years and above. Source: World Values Surveys.
Household income	V253 *"On this card is a scale of incomes on which 1 indicates the 'lowest income decile' and 10 the 'highest income decile' in your country. We would like to know in what group your household is. Please, specify the appropriate number, counting all wages, salaries, pensions, and other incomes that come in."* (Code one number). Source: World Values Surveys.
Education scale	V238. *"What is the highest educational level that you have attained?"* [NOTE: if respondent is a student, code highest level he or she expects to complete]: (1) No formal education; (2) Incomplete primary school; (3) Complete primary school; (4) Incomplete secondary school: technical/vocational type; (5) Complete secondary school: technical/vocational type; (6) Incomplete secondary: university-preparatory type; (7) Complete secondary: university-preparatory type; (8) Some university-level education, without degree; (9) University-level education, with degree. Source: World Values Surveys.
Use of the media	*"People use different sources to learn what is going on in their country and the world. For each of the following sources, please indicate whether you used it last week (1) or did not use it last week (0) to obtain information."* (read out and code one answer for each):

		Used it last week	Did not use it last week
V223.	Daily newspaper	1	0
V224.	News broadcasts on radio or TV	1	0
V225.	Printed magazines	1	0
V226.	In-depth reports on radio or TV	1	0
V227.	Books	1	0
V228.	Internet, E-mail	1	0

Source: World Values Survey 2005–2007.

| *News media use scale* | Based on the above item, this scale is calculated by summing use of a daily newspaper, news broadcasts on radio or TV, printed magazine, books, and the internet/e-mail, transformed into a 100-point scale. Source: World Values Survey 2005–2007. |

Note: Full details of the World Values Survey codebooks and questionnaires can be found at www.worldvaluessurvey.com.

Technical Appendix B

Countries in the Pooled World Values Survey, 1981–2007

		Wave					
		1	2	3	4	5	
		1981–1984	1989–1993	1994–1999	1999–2004	2005–2007	Total
1	Albania	0	0	999	1000	0	1999
2	Algeria	0	0	0	1282	0	1282
3	Andorra	0	0	0	0	1003	1003
4	Argentina	1005	1002	1079	1280	1002	5368
5	Armenia	0	0	2000	0	0	2000
6	Australia	1228	0	2048	0	1421	4697
7	Austria	0	1460	0	1522	0	2982
8	Azerbaijan	0	0	2002	0	0	2002
9	Bangladesh	0	0	1525	1500	0	3025
10	Belarus	0	1015	2092	1000	0	4107
11	Belgium	1145	2792	0	1912	0	5849
12	Bosnia and Herzegovina	0	0	800	800	0	1600
13	Brazil	0	1782	1149	0	1500	4431
14	Bulgaria	0	1034	1072	1000	1001	4107
15	Burkina Faso	0	0	0	0	1534	1534
16	Canada	1254	1730	0	1931	2148	7063
17	Chile	0	1500	1000	1200	1000	4700
18	China	0	1000	1500	1000	2015	5515
19	Colombia	0	0	6025	0	3025	9050
20	Croatia	0	0	1196	1003	0	2199
21	Cyprus	0	0	0	0	1050	1050
22	Czech Republic	0	3033	1147	1908	0	6088
23	Denmark	1182	1030	0	1023	0	3235
24	Dominican Republic	0	0	417	0	0	417
25	Egypt, Arab Republic	0	0	0	3000	0	3000

(*continued*)

		\multicolumn{5}{c}{Wave}	
		1	2	3	4	5	
		1981–1984	1989–1993	1994–1999	1999–2004	2005–2007	Total
26	El Salvador	o	o	1254	o	o	1254
27	Estonia	o	1008	1021	1005	o	3034
28	Ethiopia	o	o	o	o	1500	1500
29	Finland	1003	588	987	1038	1014	4630
30	France	1200	1002	o	1615	1001	4818
31	Georgia	o	o	2008	o	o	2008
32	Germany	1305	2101	1017	1037	988	6448
33	Ghana	o	o	o	o	1534	1534
34	Greece	o	o	o	1142	o	1142
35	Guatemala	o	o	o	o	1000	1000
36	Hungary	1464	999	650	1000	o	4113
37	Iceland	927	702	o	968	o	2597
38	India	o	2500	2040	2002	2001	8543
39	Indonesia	o	o	o	1004	2015	3019
40	Iran, Islamic Republic	o	o	o	2532	2667	5199
41	Iraq	o	o	o	2325	2701	5026
42	Ireland	1217	1000	o	1012	o	3229
43	Israel	o	o	o	1199	o	1199
44	Italy	1348	2018	o	2000	1012	6378
45	Japan	1204	1011	1054	1362	1096	5727
46	Jordan	o	o	o	1223	1200	2423
47	Korea, Republic	970	1251	1249	1200	1200	5870
48	Kyrgyz Republic	o	o	o	1043	o	1043
49	Latvia	o	903	1200	1013	o	3116
50	Lithuania	o	1000	1009	1018	o	3027
51	Luxembourg	o	o	o	1211	o	1211
52	Macedonia, FYR	o	o	995	1055	o	2050
53	Malaysia	o	o	o	o	1201	1201
54	Mali	o	o	o	o	1534	1534
55	Malta	467	393	o	1002	o	1862
56	Mexico	1837	1531	2364	1535	1560	8827
57	Moldova	o	o	984	1008	1046	3038
58	Morocco	o	o	o	2264	1200	3464
59	Netherlands	1221	1017	o	1003	1050	4291
60	New Zealand	o	o	1201	o	954	2155
61	Nigeria	o	1001	1996	2022	o	5019
62	Norway	1051	1239	1127	o	1025	4442
63	Pakistan	o	o	733	2000	o	2733
64	Peru	o	o	1211	1501	o	2712
65	Philippines	o	o	1200	1200	o	2400
66	Poland	o	1920	1153	1095	1000	5168
67	Portugal	o	1185	o	1000	o	2185

| | | Wave | | | | | |
| | | 1 | 2 | 3 | 4 | 5 | |
		1981–1984	1989–1993	1994–1999	1999–2004	2005–2007	Total
68	Romania	0	1103	1239	1146	1776	5264
69	Russia	0	1961	2040	2500	2033	8534
70	Rwanda	0	0	0	0	1507	1507
71	Saudi Arabia	0	0	0	1502	0	1502
72	Serbia & Montenegro	0	0	1280	1200	1220	3700
73	Singapore	0	0	0	1512	0	1512
74	Slovak Republic	0	1602	1095	1331	0	4028
75	Slovenia	0	1035	1007	1006	1037	4085
76	South Africa	1596	2736	2935	3000	2988	13255
77	Spain	2303	4147	1211	2409	1200	11270
78	Sweden	954	1047	1009	1015	1003	5028
79	Switzerland	0	1400	1212	0	1241	3853
80	Tanzania	0	0	0	1171	0	1171
81	Thailand	0	0	0	0	1534	1534
82	Trinidad & Tobago	0	0	0	0	1002	1002
83	Turkey	0	1030	1907	4607	1346	8890
84	Uganda	0	0	0	1002	0	1002
85	Ukraine	0	0	2811	1195	1000	5006
86	United Kingdom	1167	1484	1093	1000	1041	5785
87	United States	2325	1839	1542	1200	2742	9648
88	Uruguay	0	0	1000	0	1000	2000
89	Venezuela	0	0	1200	1200	0	2400
90	Vietnam	0	0	0	1000	1495	2495
91	Zambia	0	0	0	0	1500	1500
92	Zimbabwe	0	0	0	1002	0	1002
93	Taiwan	0	0	780	0	1225	2005
	TOTAL nations	22	43	55	59	55	
	TOTAL respondents	29,373	61,131	75,865	96,993	76,088	339,450

Note: Contemporary independent nation-states (93), excluding regional samples such as surveys in Puerto Rico and Northern Ireland.

Technical Appendix C

Methods

As not all readers may be familiar with the multilevel analytical methods used in this study, a brief note helps to clarify the techniques. The general theory developed in Chapter 1 predicts that on the demand side, individual characteristics (such as education, age, and access to the news media) will have a *direct* effect on individual-level democratic orientations. In addition, the account predicts that on the supply side, certain contextual or societal-level factors in each nation-state will also have an important direct effect on these orientations, including the role of human development, the historical experience of democratization in each society, the process and policy performance of democratic regimes, the power-sharing structure of regimes, and levels of media freedom.

To operationalize these factors, the key models in the book involve measurement at two distinct levels. A representative sample of individual respondents (level 1) is nested within national-level contexts (level 2). The World Values Survey was conducted among a representative random sample of the adult population within each nation-state.

Many previous studies about political trust have employed ordinary least squares (OLS) regression for analysis. The danger of using this method is that the standard errors of the regression coefficients can be inaccurate for contextual variables, by overestimating the degrees of freedom (number of cases), and therefore tests of significance can prove misleading. OLS models can seek to control for national variations by using a pooled model, including dummy variables for each country, but this becomes inefficient with the coverage of many nations. Alternatively, OLS models can be run with no pooling, where separate models are run for each nation or type of media environment, but this is also clumsy.

Given the use of multilevel data, hierarchical linear models (HLM) are most appropriate for analysis, including multilevel regression analysis.[1] The models in this study use restricted maximum likelihood techniques (REML) to estimate direct and cross-level effects for hierarchical data. Individual respondents are thus grouped into nation-states. Each nation-state has a different set of

TABLE C.1. *Description of the core independent variables, WVS, 2005–2007*

	N	Unstandardized			Standardized (z scores)		
		Min	Max	Mean	Min	Max	Mean
INDIVIDUAL LEVEL							
Demographic characteristics							
Age (years)	78,017	16	89	42	−1.55	2.86	.000
Male gender	78,320	0	1	.48	−.96	1.04	.000
Socioeconomic resources							
Household income scale	78,416	1	10	4.7	−1.67	2.42	.000
Education scale	77,822	1	9	5.3	−1.84	1.55	.000
Media use							
Media use 100-point scale	65,729	0	100	38.5	−1.16	1.85	.000
Read newspaper (0/1)	70,692	0	1	.57	−1.15	.86	.000
Use radio/TV news (0/1)	70,306	0	1	.88	−2.72	.37	.000
Use internet/e-mail (0/1)	69,037	0	1	.29	−.65	1.53	.000
NATIONAL LEVEL							
Historical index of democratization	49	2.9	85.7	53.3	−2.06	1.32	.000
Development: GDP per capita in PPP	49	$155	$40,947	$10,499	−.82	2.40	.000

Source: World Values Survey 2005–2007.

parameters for the random factors, allowing intercepts and slopes to vary by nation.[2]

Level 1 in our core models includes the following *individual-level* measures: male gender (0/1), household income using a 10-point scale, age (in years), the education scale, and media use using a 5-point scale (or each of the separate dummy variables for use of newspapers, radio/TV, and the internet).

Level 2 includes many *national-level* variables, exemplified by the standardized Freedom House index of democracy and the standardized level of economic development (per capita GDP [2006] in purchasing power parity). In each case, unless lagged, the appropriate year of these indices was matched to the closest first year of fieldwork for the survey.

All variables are described in Technical Appendix A and Table C.1. In SPSS 18.0 Mixed Models, the iterative restricted maximum likelihood (REML) algorithm was used for estimating parameters. In hierarchical linear models, as is customary, all independent variables were centered, by subtracting the grand mean (which becomes zero). The standardized independent variables all have a standard deviation of 1.0. This process also helps to guard against problems of collinearity in the independent variables in the OLS models. The dependent variables are all converted into 100-point scales for ease of comparison across different tables. The independent variables were treated as fixed components, reflecting the weighted average for the slope across all groups, while nation was

TABLE C.2. *Comparison of OLS and multilevel regression models explaining democratic satisfaction*

	Model A: OLS regression				Model B: REML Multilevel regression		
	b	SE	Beta	Sig	b	SE	Sig
INDIVIDUAL LEVEL							
Demographic characteristics							
Age (years)	.142	.107	.006	N/s	.503	.104	***
Gender (male = 1)	.088	.102	.004	N/s	−.128	.094	N/s
Socioeconomic resources							
Household income 10-point scale	2.57	.115	.102	***	2.05	.112	***
Education 9-pt scale	−1.22	.120	−.051	***	−.373	.121	**
Media use							
Media use 100-point scale	−.446	.122	−.018	***	−.054	.116	N/s
NATIONAL LEVEL							
Historical index of democratization	3.65	.116	.143	***	3.87	1.44	*
Constant	64.5				63.7		
Goodness of fit: Adjusted R²	.027						
Goodness of fit: Schwarz BIC					491,891		
N. respondents	54,492				54,472		
N. nations	45				45		

Note: All independent variables have been standardized between 0 and 1 using mean centering (z-scores). *Model A* presents the results of OLS regression models while Model B presents the results of the REML multilevel regression models. The democratic satisfaction 100-point scale was the dependent variable. The 100-point media use scale combined use of newspapers, radio/TV, the internet, books, and magazines for information. Model A reports the unstandardized beta coefficients (b), the standard errors, the standardized betas, and their significance. The OLS models were checked by tolerance tests to be free of any multi-collinearity problems. See Appendix A for details about the measurement, coding, and construction of all variables. Significant coefficients are highlighted in **bold**.

*= >.05 **= >.01 ***= >.001

Source: World Values Survey 2005–2007.

treated as a random component, capturing the country variability in the slope. The strength of the beta coefficients (slopes) can be interpreted intuitively as how much change in the dependent variable is generated by a 1% change in each independent variable.

The treatment of missing data is also important. Mean substitution replaced missing data for individual-level income where this was omitted in the national surveys conducted in two countries. Models were tested with and without these treatments to check that they did not have a substantial effect on the interpretation of the results.

The multilevel regression models used in this study usually generate small differences in the size of the slope coefficient (b) compared with the results of OLS models, but the average standard errors for level 2 variables often tend to be slightly larger. *The process is thus more rigorous and conservative,* avoiding Type I errors (false positives, concluding that a statistically significant difference exists when, in truth, there is no statistical difference). The goodness of fit statistic in OLS is the adjusted R^2, where models with a higher coefficient indicate that it accounts for more of the variance. In the REML model, by contrast, Schwarz's Bayesian Criterion (BIC) is used, where the model with the *lower* value is the best fitting.

Table C.2 compares the results of using both the OLS and the REML models, where the 100-point 'democratic satisfaction' scale is used illustratively as the dependent variable. Comparison of the OLS and REML models in Table C.2 shows that many (but not all) of the estimates of the slope and intercept are very similar. Nevertheless, the OLS model can inflate the standard error and the appropriate degrees of freedom at the national level, whereas the REML model is preferable by providing a more rigorous and conservative estimate of significance at the national level.

The estimates of covariance suggest that the national intercepts were significant and strong, capturing the variability in the democratic satisfaction scale among countries.

Excluding the insignificant predictors generated the following equations. In the notation, $_1$ refers to level 1 (individual) and $_2$ to level 2 (national) variables.

Model A: OLS Regression Analysis

$$Y_{\text{DEMOSATISFACTION}} = 64.5 + .2.57 x_{\text{INCOME1}} - 1.22 x_{\text{EDUCATION1}}$$
$$- .446 x_{\text{MEDIAUSE1}} + 3.65 x_{\text{HISTDEMOCRACY2}}$$

Model B: REML Multilevel Regression Analysis

$$Y_{\text{DEMOSATISFACTION}} = 63.7 + .503 x_{\text{AGE1}} + 2.05 x_{\text{INCOME1}}$$
$$- .373 x_{\text{EDUCATION1}} + 3.87 x_{\text{HISTDEMOCRACY2}}$$

Notes

Chapter 1. Democratic Hopes and Fears

1. This concern generated an extensive American literature during the early to mid-1990s. See, for example, E. J. Dionne, Jr. 1991. *Why Americans Hate Politics.* New York: Simon and Schuster; Stephen Craig. 1993. *The Malevolent Leaders: Popular Discontent in America.* Boulder, CO: Westview Press; John R. Hibbing and Elizabeth Theiss-Morse. 1995. *Congress as Public Enemy.* New York: Cambridge University Press; Susan J. Tolchin. 1996. *The Angry American: How Voter Rage Is Changing the Nation.* Boulder, CO: Westview Press; Joseph S. Nye, Philip D. Zelikow, and David C. King, Eds. 1997. *Why People Don't Trust Government.* Cambridge, MA: Harvard University Press; John R. Hibbing and Elizabeth Theiss-Morse, Eds. 2001. *What Is It about Government That Americans Dislike?* Cambridge: Cambridge University Press; Peter Wood. 2004. *A Bee in the Mouth: Anger in America Now.* Encounter Books.
2. Ruy A. Teixeira. 1992. *The Disappearing American Voter.* Washington, DC: Brookings Institution; John H. Aldrich. 1995. *Why Parties? The Origin and Transformation of Party Politics in America.* Chicago: University of Chicago Press; Robert D. Putnam. 2000. *Bowling Alone: The Collapse and Revival of American Community.* New York: Simon and Schuster; Sidney Verba, Kay Schlozman, and Henry Brady. 1995. *Voice and Equality: Civic Volunteerism in American Politics.* Cambridge: Harvard University Press; Martin P. Wattenberg. 2002. *Where Have All the Voters Gone?* Cambridge, MA: Harvard University Press; Cliff Zukin, Scott Keeter, Molly Andolina, Krista Jenkins, and Michael X. Delli Carpini. 2006. *A New Engagement? Political Participation, Civic Life, and the Changing American Citizen.* New York: Oxford University Press.
3. Pippa Norris, Ed. 1999. *Critical Citizens: Global Support for Democratic Governance.* New York: Oxford University Press; Susan Pharr and Robert Putnam, Eds. 2000. *Disaffected Democracies: What's Troubling the Trilateral Countries?* Princeton, NJ: Princeton University Press; Russell J. Dalton. 2004. *Democratic Challenges, Democratic Choices: The Erosion of Political Support in Advanced Industrial Democracies.* New York: Oxford University Press; Mariano Torcal and José R. Montero. 2006. *Political Disaffection in Contemporary Democracies: Social Capital, Institutions, and Politics.* London: Routledge.

4. Colin Hay. 2007. *Why We Hate Politics*. Cambridge: Polity Press; Peter Mair and Ingrid van Biezen. 2001. 'Party membership in twenty European democracies 1980–2000.' *Party Politics* 7(1): 5–22; Ingrid van Biezen, Peter Mair, and Thomas Poguntke. 2009. 'Going, Going, . . . Gone? Party Membership in the 21st Century.' Paper presented at the Joint Workshops at the European Consortium for Political Research, Lisbon; Mark N. Franklin, Thomas T. Mackie, and Henry Valen. 1991. *Electoral Change: Responses to Evolving Social and Attitudinal Structures in Western Countries*. New York: Cambridge University Press; Russell J. Dalton and Marty P. Wattenberg. 2000. *Parties without Partisans: Political Change in Advanced Industrial Democracies*. Oxford: Oxford University Press; Mark N. Franklin. 2004. *Voter Turnout and the Dynamics of Electoral Competition in Established Democracies since 1945*. New York: Cambridge University Press; Colin Crouch. 2004. *Post-Democracy*. Cambridge: Polity Press; Susan Pharr and Robert Putnam, Eds. 2000. *Disaffected Democracies: What's Troubling the Trilateral Countries?* Princeton: Princeton University Press; Mariano Torcal and José R. Montero. 2006. *Political Disaffection in Contemporary Democracies: Social Capital, Institutions, and Politics*. London: Routledge; Mattei Dogan, Ed. 2005. *Political Mistrust and the Discrediting of Politicians*. Leiden: Brill; Jan Van Deth, Jose R. Montero, and Anders Westholm. 2007. *Citizenship and Involvement in European Democracies: A Comparative Analysis*. New York: Routledge.

5. Pippa Norris. 2005. *Radical Right: Voters and Parties in the Electoral Market*. New York: Cambridge University Press.

6. Colin Crouch. 2004. *Post-Democracy*. Cambridge: Polity Press; Guy Hermet. 2007. *L'Hiver de la Démocratie*. Paris: Armand Colin; John Keane. 2009. *The Life and Death of Democracy*. New York: W. W. Norton.

7. Russell J. Dalton. 2004. *Democratic Challenges, Democratic Choices: The Erosion of Political Support in Advanced Industrial Democracies*. New York: Oxford University Press.

8. Hans-Dieter Klingemann. 1999. 'Mapping political support in the 1990s.' In Pippa Norris (Ed.). *Critical Citizens: Global Support for Democratic Governance*. Oxford: Oxford University Press; Marta Lagos. 2003. 'Support for and satisfaction with democracy.' *International Journal of Public Opinion Research* 15(4): 471–487; Latinobarometro 2008 Report. http://www.latinobarometro.org/; Gabriela Catterberg and Alejandro Moreno. 2006. 'The individual bases of political trust: Trends in new and established democracies.' *International Journal of Public Opinion Research* 18(1): 31–48.

9. Larry Diamond. 2008. *The Spirit of Democracy: The Struggle to Build Free Societies throughout the World*. New York: Times Books; Arch Puddington. 2009. 'Freedom in the world 2009: Setbacks and resilience.' *Freedom in the World, 2009*. Washington, DC: Freedom House.

10. Jack Citrin. 1974. 'Comment: The political relevance of trust in government.' *American Political Science Review* 68: 973–988; Arthur H. Miller. 1974. 'Political issues and trust in government, 1964–1970.' *American Political Science Review* 68: 951–972.

11. For a related argument, see Richard Rose, William Mishler, and Christian Haerpfer. 1998. *Democracy and Its Alternatives: Understanding Post-Communist Societies*. Cambridge: Polity Press.

12. For the debate, see Andrew Moravcsik. 2002. 'In defence of the "democratic deficit": Reassessing legitimacy in the European Union.' *Journal of Common*

Market Studies 40: 603; Livia Door. 2008. *The Democratic Deficit Debate in the European Union.* Berlin: VDM Verlag; Peter Jancárik. 2009. *Understanding Democracy in the European Union: Democratic Deficit as a Powerful Myth?* Berlin: VDM Verlag; Jacques Thomassen, Ed. 2009. *The Legitimacy of the European Union after Enlargement.* Oxford: Oxford University Press.

13. Victor Bekkers, Geske Dijkstra, Arthur Edwards, and Menno Fenger, Eds. 2007. *Governance and the Democratic Deficit: Assessing the Democratic Legitimacy of Governance Practices.* Aldershot: Ashgate Publishing.

14. Pippa Norris, Ed. 1999. *Critical Citizens: Global Support for Democratic Governance.* New York: Oxford University Press.

15. Mark Bovens and Anchrit Wille. 2008. 'Deciphering the Dutch drop: Ten explanations for decreasing political trust in the Netherlands.' *International Review of Administrative Sciences* 74: 283–305.

16. Gary Orren. 1997. 'Fall from grace: The public's loss of faith in government.' In Joseph S. Nye, Jr., Philip D. Zelikow, and David C. King (Eds.). *Why People Don't Trust Government.* Chicago: University of Chicago Press.

17. Bruce Cain, Russell J. Dalton, and Susan Scarrow, Eds. 2003. *Democracy Transformed? The Expansion of Political Access in Advanced Industrialized Democracies.* Oxford: Oxford University Press; Russell J. Dalton. 2004. *Democratic Challenges, Democratic Choices: The Erosion of Political Support in Advanced Industrial Democracies.* New York: Oxford University Press, Ch. 9; John A. Booth and Mitchell A. Seligson. 2009. *The Legitimacy Puzzle in Latin America: Political Support and Democracy in Eight Nations.* New York: Cambridge University Press.

18. See, however, John A. Booth and Mitchell A. Seligson. 2009. *The Legitimacy Puzzle in Latin America.* New York: Cambridge University Press.

19. Marc J. Hetherington. 1998. 'The political relevance of political trust.' *American Political Science Review* 92(4): 791–808; Marc J. Hetherington. 2005. *Why Trust Matters.* Princeton, NJ: Princeton University Press; J. T. Scholz. 2000. 'Trust, taxes, and compliance.' In V. Braithwaite and Margaret Levi (Eds). *Trust and Governance.* New York: Russell Sage.

20. The 'crisis' alarm warnings are most clearly exemplified by Michel Crozier, Samuel P. Huntington, and Joji Watanuki. 1975. *The Crisis of Democracy: Report on the Governability of Democracies to the Trilateral Commission.* New York: New York University Press.

21. See Stephen Earl Bennett. 2001. 'Were the halcyon days really golden?' In John R. Hibbing and Elizabeth Theiss-Morse (Eds.). *What Is It about Government That Americans Dislike?* Cambridge: Cambridge University Press.

22. Michel Crozier, Samuel P. Huntington, and Joji Watanuki. 1975. *The Crisis of Democracy: Report on the Governability of Democracies to the Trilateral Commission.* New York: New York University Press. See also Samuel P. Huntington. 1981. *American Politics: The Promise of Disharmony.* Cambridge: Harvard University Press.

23. Pippa Norris, Ed. 1999. *Critical Citizens: Global Support for Democratic Governance.* New York: Oxford University Press.

24. David Easton. 1965. *A Framework for Political Analysis.* Englewood Cliffs, NJ: Prentice-Hall; David Easton. 1975. 'Reassessment of the concept of political support.' *British Journal of Political Science* 5: 435–457.

25. Susan Pharr and Robert Putnam (Eds.). 2000. *Disaffected Democracies: What's Troubling the Trilateral Countries?* Princeton, NJ: Princeton University Press;

Mariano Torcal and José R. Montero. 2006. *Political Disaffection in Contemporary Democracies: Social Capital, Institutions, and Politics*. London: Routledge; Richard I. Hofferbert and Hans-Dieter Klingemann. 2001. 'Democracy and its discontents in post-wall Germany.' *International Political Science Review* 22(4): 363–378.

26. Gabriel A. Almond and Sidney Verba. 1963. *The Civic Culture*. Princeton, NJ: Princeton University Press.

27. A comprehensive chronological list of comparative survey research resources and datasets is available at http://www.gesis.org/en/data_service/eurobarometer/handbook/index.htm; see also Wolfgang Donsbach and Michael Traugott. 2008. *The SAGE Handbook of Public Opinion Research*. London: Sage.

28. Pippa Norris. 2010. 'The globalization of comparative public opinion research.' In Neil Robinson and Todd Landman (Eds.). *The Sage Handbook of Comparative Politics*. London: Sage. See also the useful Web site maintained by GESIS. 'Tabular History of International Comparative Survey Research Projects.' http://www.gesis.org/en/services/data/portals-links/comparative-survey-projects/.

29. Jason M. Wells and Jonathan Krieckhaus. 2006. 'Does national context influence democratic satisfaction? A multi-level analysis.' *Political Research Quarterly* 59(4): 569–578.

30. Ronald Inglehart and Christian Welzel. 2005. *Modernization, Cultural Change, and Democracy: The Human Development Sequence*. New York: Cambridge University Press; Russell J. Dalton. 2004. *Democratic Challenges, Democratic Choices: The Erosion of Political Support in Advanced Industrial Democracies*. New York: Oxford University Press.

31. Robert D. Putnam. 2000. *Bowling Alone: The Collapse and Revival of American Community*. New York: Simon and Schuster.

32. Mattei Dogan, Ed. 2005. *Political Mistrust and the Discrediting of Politicians*. Leiden: Brill.

33. Suzanne Garment. 1991. *Scandal: The Crisis of Mistrust in American Politics*. New York: Random House; Gary Orren. 1997. 'Fall from grace: The public's loss of faith in government.' In Joseph S. Nye, Jr., Philip D. Zelikow, and David C. King (Eds.). *Why People Don't Trust Government*. Chicago: University of Chicago Press.

34. For time-series analysis of American public opinion, however, see V. A. Chanley, T. J. Rudolph, and W. M. Rahn. 2000. 'The origins and consequences of public trust in government: A time series analysis.' *Public Opinion Quarterly* 64(3): 239–256. For cross-national analysis, see Christopher J. Anderson and Yuliya V. Tverdova. 2003. 'Corruption, political allegiances, and attitudes toward government in contemporary democracies.' *American Journal of Political Science* 47(1): 91–109; Alejandro Moreno. 2002. 'Corruption and democracy: A cultural assessment.' *Comparative Sociology* 1(3–4): 495–507.

35. Harold D. Clarke, Euel W. Elliott, William Mishler, Marianne C. Stewart, Paul F. Whiteley, and Gary Zuk. 1992. *Controversies in Political Economy*. Boulder, CO: Westview Press; Christopher J. Anderson. 1995. *Blaming the Government: Citizens and the Economy in Five European Democracies*. New York: M. E. Sharpe.

36. Tim Groeling and Matthew A. Baum. 2008. 'Crossing the water's edge: Elite rhetoric, media coverage, and the rally-round-the-flag phenomenon.' *Journal of Politics* 70(4): 1065–1085.

37. Kimberly Gross, Paul R. Brewer, and Sean Aday. 2001. 'Confidence in government and emotional responses to terrorism after September 11, 2001.' *American Politics*

Review 37(1): 107–128; V. A. Chaney. 2002. 'Trust in government in the aftermath of 9/11: Determinants and consequences.' *Political Psychology* 23(3): 469–483.

38. M. Grimes. 2006. 'Organizing consent: The role of procedural fairness in political trust and compliance.' *European Journal of Political Research* 45(2): 285–315; Charles F. Andrain and James T. Smith. 2006. *Political Democracy, Trust and Social Justice.* Boston: Northeastern University Press.

39. Colin Hay. 2007. *Why We Hate Politics.* Cambridge: Polity Press.

40. Russell J. Dalton. 2004. *Democratic Challenges, Democratic Choices: The Erosion of Political Support in Advanced Industrial Democracies.* New York: Oxford University Press.

41. Christopher J. Anderson. 1995. *Blaming the Government: Citizens and the Economy in Five European Democracies.* New York: M. E. Sharpe; Christopher J. Anderson and Christine A. Guillory. 1997. 'Political institutions and satisfaction with democracy.' *American Political Science Review* 91(1): 66–81; Christopher J. Anderson, Andre Blais, Shaun Bowler, Todd Donovan, and Ola Listhaug. 2005. *Losers' Consent: Elections and Democratic Legitimacy.* New York: Oxford University Press; Henar Criado and Francisco Herreros. 2007. 'Political support taking into account the institutional context.' *Comparative Political Studies* 40(2): 1511–1532; Kees Aarts and Jacques Thomassen. 2008. 'Satisfaction with democracy: Do institutions matter?' *Electoral Studies* 27(1): 5–18.

42. Gabriel A. Almond and Sidney Verba. 1963. *The Civic Culture.* Princeton, NJ: Princeton University Press.

43. See, for example, Colin Hay. 2007. *Why We Hate Politics.* Cambridge: Polity Press; Gerry Stoker. 2006. *Why Politics Matters: Making Democracy Work.* London: Palgrave/Macmillan.

44. Samuel Barnes and Max Kaase. 1979. *Political Action: Mass Participation in Five Western Democracies.* Beverly Hills, CA: Sage; Edward N. Muller, Thomas O. Jukam, and Mitchell A. Seligson. 1982. 'Diffuse political support and anti-system political behavior.' *American Journal of Political Science* 26(3): 240–264.

45. Pippa Norris. 2005. *Democratic Phoenix.* Cambridge: Cambridge University Press.

46. John A. Booth and Mitchell A. Seligson. 2009. *The Legitimacy Puzzle in Latin America: Political Support and Democracy in Eight Nations.* New York: Cambridge University Press.

47. John T. Scholz and Mark Lubell. 1998. 'Trust and taxpaying: Testing the heuristic approach to collective action.' *American Journal of Political Science* 49(3): 398–417.

48. Seymour Martin Lipset. 1983. *Political Man: The Social Bases of Politics.* 2nd ed. London: Heinemann, p. 64. The concept of legitimacy is also discussed in Stephen M. Weatherford. 1992. 'Measuring political legitimacy.' *American Political Science Review* 86: 149–66; Bruce Gilley. 2006. 'The meaning and measure of state legitimacy: Results for 72 countries.' *European Journal of Political Research* 45: 499–525.

49. Freedom House. 2009. *Freedom in the World 2009.* Washington, DC: Freedom House. www.freedomhouse.org. For a detailed discussion of trends and indicators, see Pippa Norris. 2008. *Driving Democracy: Do Power-Sharing Institutions Work?* Cambridge: Cambridge University Press, Ch. 3.

50. Arch Puddington. 2009. 'Freedom in the world 2009: Setbacks and resilience.' *Freedom in the World, 2009.* Washington, DC: Freedom House. http://www.freedomhouse.org/uploads/fiw09/FIW09_OverviewEssay_Final.pdf.

51. For a discussion about the conditions leading toward the derailment of democratic regimes, see M. Steven Fish and Jason Wittenberg. 2009. 'Failed democratization.' In Christian W. Haerpfer, Patrick Bernhagen, Ronald Inglehart, and Christian Welzel (Eds.). *Democratization*. Oxford: Oxford University Press. See also Ethan B. Kapstein and Nathan Converse. 2008. *The Fate of Young Democracies*. New York: Cambridge University Press; Ethan B. Kapstein and Nathan Converse. 2008. 'Why democracies fail.' *Journal of Democracy* 19(4): 57–68.

52. Freedom House. 2009. *Freedom in the World, 2009*. Washington, DC: Freedom House.

53. Thomas Carothers. 2006. 'The backlash against democracy promotion.' *Foreign Affairs* 85(2): 55–68; Scott N. Cole. 2007. 'Hugo Chavez and President Bush's credibility gap: The struggle against US democracy promotion.' *International Political Science Review* 28(4): 493–507.

54. Larry Diamond. 2008. *The Spirit of Democracy: The Struggle to Build Free Societies throughout the World*. New York: Times Books; Larry Diamond. 2008. 'The democratic rollback – The resurgence of the predatory state.' *Foreign Affairs* 87(2): 36–48; Arch Puddington. 2008. 'Freedom in retreat: Is the tide turning? Findings of Freedom in the World 2008.' Washington, DC: Freedom House. www.freedomhouse.org.

55. Samuel P. Huntington. 1991. *The Third Wave: Democratization in the Late Twentieth Century*. Norman: University of Oklahoma Press. See also Renske Doorenspleet. 2000. 'Reassessing the three waves of democratization.' *World Politics* 52: 384–406; Renske Doorenspleet. 2005. *Democratic Transitions: Exploring the Structural Sources during the Fourth Wave*. Boulder, CO: Lynne Rienner; Zachary Elkins and Beth Simmons. 2005. 'On waves, clusters, and diffusion: A conceptual framework.' *Annals of the American Academy of Political and Social Science* 598: 33–51.

Chapter 2. The Conceptual Framework

1. Russell Hardin, Ed. 2004. *Trust and Trustworthiness*. New York: Russell Sage Foundation.

2. David Easton. 1965. *A Framework for Political Analysis*. Englewood Cliffs, NJ: Prentice-Hall; David Easton. 1975. 'Reassessment of the concept of political support.' *British Journal of Political Science* 5(4): 435–457.

3. Stephen M. Weatherford. 1992. 'Measuring political legitimacy.' *American Political Science Review* 86: 149–166.

4. See, for instance, Gerry Stoker. 2006. *Why Politics Matters: Making Democracy Work*. London: Palgrave/Macmillan.

5. For details, see http://www.elections2009-results.eu/en/hist_turnout_eu_en.html.

6. For a discussion of the meaning of political trust, see Margaret Levi and Laura Stoker. 2000. 'Political trust and trustworthiness.' *Annual Review of Political Science* 3: 475–508.

7. David Easton. 1965. *A Framework for Political Analysis*. Englewood Cliffs, NJ: Prentice-Hall; David Easton. 1975. 'Reassessment of the concept of political support.' *British Journal of Political Science* 5(4): 435–457.

8. David Easton. 1975. 'Reassessment of the concept of political support.' *British Journal of Political Science* 5(4): 444.

9. Damarys Canache, Jeffrey J. Mondak, and Mitchell A. Seligson. 2001. 'Meaning and measurement in cross-national research on satisfaction with democracy.' *Public Opinion Quarterly* 65: 506–528.

10. Edward Muller and Rhomas Jukam. 1977. 'On the meaning of political support.' *American Political Science Review* 71: 1561–1595.

11. David Easton. 1965. *A Framework for Political Analysis*. Englewood Cliffs, NJ: Prentice-Hall.

12. See, for example, the Pew Research Center on People and the Press. 2008. 'Bush and Public Opinion Reviewing the Bush Years and the Public's Final Verdict.' December 18, 2008. http://people-press.org/report/478/bush-legacy-public-opinion.

13. See also Jack Citrin and Samantha Luks. 2001. 'Political trust revisited: Déjà vu all over again?' In John R. Hibbing and Elizabeth Theiss-Morse (Eds). *What Is It about Government That Americans Dislike?* Cambridge: Cambridge University Press.

14. There is an extensive theoretical literature on the concepts of nationalism and national identity. See, for example, Michael Ignatieff. 1993. *Blood and Belonging*. London: Chatto and Windus; Benedict Anderson. 1996. *Imagined Communities: Reflections on the Origin and Spread of Nationalism*. London: Verso; Michael Billig. 1995. *Banal Nationalism*. London: Sage; Earnest Gellner. 1983. *Nations and Nationalism*. Oxford: Blackwell.

15. Anthony D. Smith. 1991. *National Identity*. London: Penguin, Ch. 7.

16. Paul Collier and Nicholas Sambanis, Eds. 2005. *Understanding Civil War*. Washington, DC: World Bank; Michael W. Doyle and Nicholas Sambanis. 2006. *Making War and Building Peace*. Princeton: Princeton University Press.

17. Tim Groeling and Matthew A. Baum. 2008. 'Crossing the water's edge: Elite rhetoric, media coverage, and the rally-round-the-flag phenomenon.' *Journal of Politics* 70(4): 1065–1085.

18. For a discussion, see U. Beck. 2006. *The Cosmopolitan Vision*. Cambridge: Polity; U. Beck and N. Sznaider. 2006. 'Unpacking cosmopolitanism for the humanities and social sciences: A research agenda.' *British Journal of Sociology* 57(1): 1–23; U. Hannerz. 1990. 'Cosmopolitans and locals in world culture.' In Michael Featherstone (Ed.). *Global Culture: Nationalism, Globalization and Modernity*, London: Sage.

19. For a more detailed discussion of these ideas, see Pippa Norris and Ronald Inglehart. 2009. *Cosmopolitan Communications*. Cambridge: Cambridge University Press.

20. See Pippa Norris and Ronald Inglehart. 2009. *Cosmopolitan Communications*. Cambridge: Cambridge University Press.

21. Joseph A. Schumpeter. 1952. *Capitalism, Socialism and Democracy*. 4th ed. London: George Allen and Unwin.

22. Michael E. Alvarez, José Antonio Cheibub, Fernando Limongi, and Adam Przeworski. 1996. 'Classifying political regimes.' *Studies in International Comparative Development* 31: 3–36; Adam Przeworski, Michael E. Alvarez, José Antonio Cheibub, and Fernando Limongi. 2000. *Democracy and Development: Political Institutions and Well-Being in the World, 1950–1990*. New York: Cambridge University Press. For a defense of the minimalist approach, see Adam Przeworski. 1999. 'Minimalist conception of democracy: A defense.' In Ian Shapiro and Casiano Hacker-Cordon (Eds.). *Democracy's Value*. Cambridge: Cambridge University Press.

23. Robert A. Dahl. 1956. *A Preface to Democratic Theory*. Chicago: University of Chicago Press; Robert A. Dahl. 1971. *Polyarchy*. New Haven, CT: Yale University Press; Robert A. Dahl and Charles E. Lindblom. 1953. *Politics, Economics, and Welfare*. New York: HarperCollins; Robert A. Dahl. 1989. *Democracy and Its Critics*. New Haven, CT: Yale University Press, p. 221; Robert A. Dahl. 2005. 'What political institutions does large-scale democracy require?' *Political Science Quarterly* 120(2): 187–197.

24. Robert Dahl. 1989. *Democracy and Its Critics*. New Haven, CT: Yale University Press, p. 221

25. See Dieter Fuchs, Giovanna Guidorossi, and Palle Svensson. 1995. 'Support for the democratic system.' In Hans-Dieter Klingemann and Dieter Fuchs (Eds.). *Citizens and the State*. Oxford: Oxford University Press.

26. See, for example, Jacques Thomassen. 1995. 'Support for democratic values.' In Hans-Dieter Klingemann and Dieter Fuchs (Eds). *Citizens and the State*. Oxford: Oxford University Press; Marta Lagos. 2003. 'Support for and satisfaction with democracy.' *International Journal of Public Opinion Research* 15(4): 471–487; Larry Diamond and Marc F. Plattner. 2008. *How People View Democracy*. Baltimore: Johns Hopkins University Press.

27. For the analysis of this item, see Yun-han Chu, Michael Bratton, Marta Lagos, Sandeep Shastri and Mark Tessler. 2008. 'Public opinion and democratic legitimacy.' In Larry Diamond and Marc F. Plattner (Eds.). 2008. *How People View Democracy*. Baltimore: Johns Hopkins University Press.

28. Russell J. Dalton and Doh Chull Shin. 2006. 'Democratic aspirations and social modernization.' In Russell J. Dalton and Doh Chull Shin (Eds.). *Citizens, Democracy and Markets around the Pacific Rim*. Oxford: Oxford University Press.

29. See, for example, Alexander F. Wagner, Friedrich Schneider, and Martin Halla. 2009. 'The quality of institutions and satisfaction with democracy in Western Europe: A panel analysis.' *European Journal of Political Economy* 25(1): 30–41.

30. Jonas Linde and Joakim Ekman. 2003. 'Satisfaction with democracy: A note on a frequently used indicator in comparative politics.' *European Journal of Political Research* 42(3): 391–408.

31. Richard Rose, William Mishler, and Christian W. Haerpfer. 1998. *Democracy and Its Alternatives*. Baltimore: Johns Hopkins University Press; Christian W. Haerpfer. 2008. 'Support for democracy and autocracy in Russia and the Commonwealth of Independent States, 1992–2002.' *International Political Science Review* 29(4): 411–431.

32. Russell J. Dalton and Doh Chull Shin. 2006. 'Democratic aspirations and social modernization.' In Russell J. Dalton and Doh Chull Shin (Eds.). *Citizens, Democracy and Markets around the Pacific Rim*. Oxford: Oxford University Press.

33. Jonas Linde and Joakim Ekman. 2003. 'Satisfaction with democracy: A note on a frequently used indicator in comparative politics.' *European Journal of Political Research* 42(3): 391–408.

34. See Seymour Martin Lipset and William C. Schneider. 1983. *The Confidence Gap: Business, Labor, and Government in the Public Mind*. New York: Free Press; Ola Listhaug and Matti Wiberg. 1995. 'Confidence in political and private institutions.' In Hans-Dieter Klingemann and Dieter Fuchs (Eds.). *Citizens and the State*. Oxford: Oxford University Press.

35. The NORC GSS questions remain somewhat ambiguous to interpret. The items ask about 'the people running' these agencies, but this does not refer to any individual

incumbents by name or office (such as 'your congressional representative,' 'the chief justice,' 'your bank manager,' or 'your doctor'). Even the item concerning the executive branch is framed collectively, to include the White House, all departments, secretaries of state in cabinet, and federal bureaucrats, and it does not refer by name to individual presidents. As such, although the wording is imprecise, it seems most likely that people will usually respond with their general impressions of each institution, although these judgments may inevitably be colored by evaluations of specific incumbent officeholders.

36. See, for example, Lilliard E. Richardson, Jr., David J. Houston, and Chris Sissie Hadjiharalambous. 2001. 'Public confidence in the leaders of American governmental institutions.' In John R. Hibbing and Elizabeth Theiss-Morse. (Eds). *What Is It about Government That Americans Dislike?* Cambridge: Cambridge University Press; Russell J. Dalton. 2004. *Democratic Challenges, Democratic Choices: The Erosion of Political Support in Advanced Industrial Democracies.* New York: Oxford University Press, Figure 2.4.

37. Kenneth Newton and Pippa Norris. 2000. 'Confidence in public institutions: Faith, culture, or performance.' In S. J. Pharr and R. D. Putnam (Eds.). *Disaffected Democracies: What's Troubling the Trilateral Countries?* Princeton: Princeton University Press, pp. 52–73.

38. David Easton. 1975. 'Reassessment of the concept of political support.' *British Journal of Political Science* 5(4): 436.

39. Harold D. Clarke and Marianne Stewart. 1995. 'Economic evaluations, prime ministerial approval and governing party support: Rival models considered.' *British Journal of Political Science* 25(2):145–170.

40. For the comparison of these items used in other established democracies, see Russell J. Dalton. 2004. *Democratic Challenges, Democratic Choices: The Erosion of Political Support in Advanced Industrial Democracies.* New York: Oxford University Press, Table 2.2.

41. Following are the four standard ANES questions: RIGHT: *"How much of the time do you think you can trust the government in Washington to do what is right – just about always, most of the time or only some of the time?"*; WASTE: *"Do you think that people in the government waste a lot of money we pay in taxes, waste some of it, or don't waste very much of it?"*; INTERESTS: *"Would you say the government is pretty much run by a few big interests looking out for themselves or that it is run for the benefit of all the people?"*; CROOKED: *"Do you think that quite a few of the people running the government are (1958–1972: a little) crooked, not very many are, or do you think hardly any of them are crooked (1958–1972: at all)?"* It should be noted that it is unclear who is the object of these questions as 'the government,' when American decision making is divided horizontally among the executive, legislative, and judicial branches, as well as vertically among districts, states, and the federal levels.

42. Paul R. Abramson and Ada W. Finifter. 1981. 'On the meaning of political trust: New evidence from items introduced in 1978.' *American Journal of Political Science* 25(2): 297–307; Edward N. Muller and Thomas O. Jukam. 1977. 'On the meaning of political support.' *American Political Science Review* 71: 1561–1595.

43. Margaret Levi and Laura Stoker. 2000. 'Political trust and trustworthiness.' *Annual Review of Political Science* 3: 475–508.

44. Gabriel A. Almond and Sidney Verba. 1963. *The Civic Culture.* Princeton, NJ: Princeton University Press, p. 14.

45. Ronald Inglehart. 1997. *Modernization and Postmodernization: Cultural, Economic and Political Change in 43 Societies*. Princeton: Princeton University Press; Shalom Schwartz. 2007. 'Value orientations: Measurement, antecedents and consequences across nations.' In Roger Jowell, Caroline Roberts, Rory Fitzgerald, and Gillian Eva (Eds.). *Measuring Attitudes Cross-nationally: Lessons from the European Social Survey*. London: Sage.

46. Susan Banducci, T. Donovan, and Jeff A. Karp. 1999. 'Proportional representation and attitudes about politics: Results from New Zealand.' *Electoral Studies*, 18(4): 533–555; Susan Banducci and Jeff A. Karp. 1999. 'Perceptions of fairness and support for proportional representation.' *Political Behavior* 21(3): 217–238; Stuart Weir. 2005. 'Waiting for change: Public opinion and electoral reform. *Political Quarterly* 63(2): 197–219; John Curtice. 2004. 'Proportional representation in Scotland: Public reaction and voter behaviour.' *Representation*, 40: 329–341.

47. Harry Eckstein. 1961. *A Theory of Stable Democracy*. Princeton, NJ: Woodrow Wilson Center, Princeton University.

48. Richard Sinnott. 2000. 'Knowledge and the position of attitudes to a European foreign policy on the real-to-random continuum.' *International Journal of Public Opinion Research* 12(2): 113–137.

49. Philip Converse. 1970. 'Attitudes and non-attitudes.' In E. R. Tufte (Ed). *Quantitative Analysis of Social Problems*. New York: Addison-Wesley.

50. John Zaller. 1992. *The Nature and Origins of Mass Public Opinion*. Cambridge: Cambridge University Press.

51. David M. Farrell and Michael Gallagher. 2002. 'British voters and their criteria for evaluating electoral systems.' *British Journal of Politics and International Relations* 1(3): 293–316.

52. See, for example, Russell J. Dalton. 2004. *Democratic Challenges, Democratic Choices: The Erosion of Political Support in Advanced Industrial Democracies*. New York: Oxford University Press, Table 2.3.

53. The most comprehensive summaries of the comparative evidence in established democracies are available in Hermann Schmitt and Soren Holmberg. 1995. 'Political parties in decline?' In Hans-Dieter Klingemann and Dieter Fuchs (Eds.). *Citizens and the State*. Oxford: Oxford University Press; Russell J. Dalton and Martin P. Wattenberg. 2001. *Parties without Partisans: Political Change in Advanced Industrialized Democracies*. Oxford: Oxford University Press.

54. Peter Mair and Ingrid van Biezen. 2001. 'Party membership in twenty European democracies 1980–2000.' *Party Politics* 7(1): 5–22; Susan Scarrow. 2001. 'Parties without Members?' In Russell J. Dalton and Martin Wattenberg (Eds.). *Parties without Partisans*. New York: Oxford University Press.

55. Peter Mair. 2008. 'The challenge to party government.' *West European Politics* 31(1): 211–234.

56. Richard S. Katz and Peter Mair. 1995. 'Changing models of party organization and party democracy: The emergence of the cartel party.' *Party Politics* 1(1): 5–28; Richard S. Katz and Peter Mair. 1996. 'Cadre, Catch-all or Cartel? A Rejoinder.' *Party Politics* 2(4): 525–534.

57. Pierre Bourdieu. 1970. *Reproduction in Education, Culture and Society*. London: Sage; James S. Coleman. 1988. 'Social capital in the creation of human capital.' *American Journal of Sociology* 94: 95–120; James S. Coleman. 1990. *Foundations of Social Theory*. Cambridge: Belknap. For a discussion of the history of the concept, see Stephen Baron, John Field, and Tom Schuller (Eds). 2000. *Social Capital: Critical Perspectives*. Oxford: Oxford University Press.

58. Robert D. Putnam. 1993. *Making Democracy Work: Civic Traditions in Modern Italy*. Princeton, NJ: Princeton University Press; Robert D. Putnam. 1996. 'The strange disappearance of civic America.' *American Prospect*, 24 (Winter): 34–48; Robert D. Putnam. 2000. *Bowling Alone: The Collapse and Revival of American Community*. New York: Simon and Schuster; Robert D. Putnam (Ed.). 2004. *The Dynamics of Social Capital*. Oxford: Oxford University Press.

59. Kenneth Newton and Pippa Norris. 2000. 'Confidence in public institutions: Faith, culture, or performance.' In S. J. Pharr and R. D. Putnam (Eds.). *Disaffected Democracies: What's Troubling the Trilateral Countries?* Princeton: Princeton University Press, pp. 52–73; Kenneth Newton. 2006. 'Political support: Social capital, civil society and political and economic performance.' *Political Studies* 54(4): 846–864.

60. Sonja Zmerli and Ken Newton. 2008. 'Social trust and attitudes toward democracy.' *Public Opinion Quarterly* 72(4): 706–724.

61. See, for example, Gerry Stoker. 2006. *Why Politics Matters*. Basingstoke, Hampshire: Palgrave/Macmillan.

62. Mark Franklin. 2004. *Voter Turnout and the Dynamics of Electoral Competition in Established Democracies since 1945*. Cambridge: Cambridge University Press.

63. See Pippa Norris. 1999. 'Conclusions. The growth of critical citizens and its consequences.' In Pippa Norris (Ed.). *Critical Citizens: Global Support for Democratic Governance*. Oxford: Oxford University Press, Ch. 13; Russell J. Dalton. 2004. *Democratic Challenges, Democratic Choices: The Erosion of Political Support in Advanced Industrial Democracies*. New York: Oxford University Press, Ch. 8.

64. J. A. Goldstone. 2008. 'Pathways to state failure.' *Conflict Management and Peace Science* 25(4): 285–296.

65. W. W. Brinkerhoff. 2005. 'Rebuilding governance in failed states and post-conflict societies: Core concepts and cross-cutting themes.' *Public Administration and Development* 25: 3; M. Francois. 2006. 'Promoting stability and development in fragile and failed states.' *Development Policy Review* 24: 141.

Chapter 3. Evidence and Methods

1. See the Ipsos/MORI May 29–31, 2009 commissioned by the BBC. http://www .ipsos-mori.com/content/home-features/three-in-four-believe-britains-governance-needs-im.ashx.

2. Jan Delhey and Kenneth Newton. 2005. 'Predicting cross-national levels of social trust: Global pattern or Nordic exceptionalism?' *European Sociological Review* 21(4): 311–327. For a comparison of confidence in parliaments in EU member states, see Ola Listhaug and Matti Wiberg. 1995. 'Confidence in political and private institutions.' In Hans-Dieter Klingemann and Dieter Fuchs (Eds.). *Citizens and the State*. Oxford: Oxford University Press; Pedro G. Magalhaes. 2006. 'Confidence in parliaments: Performance, representation and accountability.' In Mariano Torcal and José R. Montero (Eds.). *Political Disaffection in Contemporary Democracies: Social Capital, Institutions, and Politics*. London: Routledge.

3. Full methodological details about the World Values Surveys, including the questionnaires, sampling procedures, fieldwork procedures, principal investigators, and organization can be found at http://wvs.isr.umich.edu/wvs-samp.html.

4. These countries are ranked as equally 'free' according to the 2008 Freedom House assessments of political rights and civil liberties. Freedom House. 2008. *Freedom in the World*. www.freedomhouse.org.

5. Colin Hay. 2007. *Why We Hate Politics*. Cambridge: Polity Press; Gerry Stoker. 2006. *Why Politics Matters: Making Democracy Work*. London: Palgrave/Macmillan.

6. Susan J. Tolchin. 1996. *The Angry American: How Voter Rage Is Changing the Nation*. Boulder, CO: Westview; E. J. Dionne, Jr., 1991. *Why Americans Hate Politics*. New York: Simon and Schuster.

7. Russell J. Dalton, 2004. *Democratic Challenges, Democratic Choices: The Erosion of Political Support in Advanced Industrial Democracies*. New York: Oxford University Press, p. 3.

8. Geraldo L. Munck and Jay Verkuilen. 2002. 'Conceptualizing and measuring democracy: Evaluating alternative indices.' *Comparative Political Studies* 35(1): 5–34.

9. Jonas Linde and Joakim Ekman. 2003. 'Satisfaction with democracy: A note on a frequently used indicator in comparative politics.' *European Journal of Political Research* 42(3): 391–408.

10. See, for example, Marc J. Hetherington and Thomas J. Rudolph. 2008. 'Priming, performance, and the dynamics of political trust.' *Journal of Politics* 70(2): 498–512.

11. Jack Citrin and Samantha Luks. 2001. 'Political trust revisited: Déjà vu all over again?' In John R. Hibbing and Elizabeth Theiss-Morse (Eds.). *What Is It about Government That Americans Dislike?* Cambridge: Cambridge University Press.

12. Hans-Dieter Klingemann. 1999. 'Mapping political support in the 1990s.' In Pippa Norris (Ed). 1999. *Critical Citizens: Global Support for Democratic Governance*. Oxford: Oxford University Press, Table 2.1; Russell J. Dalton, 2004. *Democratic Challenges, Democratic Choices: The Erosion of Political Support in Advanced Industrial Democracies*. New York: Oxford University Press, Table 3.1.

13. Ariel C. Armony and Hector E. Schamis. 2005. 'Babel in democratization studies.' *Journal of Democracy* 16(4): 113–128.

14. Larry Diamond. 1996. *Developing Democracy: Toward Consolidation*. Baltimore: Johns Hopkins University Press; Robert J. Barro. 1999. 'Determinants of democracy.' *Journal of Political Economy* 107(6): 158–183; Ronald Inglehart and Christopher Welzel. 2005. *Modernization, Cultural Change, and Democracy: The Human Development Sequence*. New York: Cambridge University Press.

15. David Collier and Robert Adcock. 1999. 'Democracy and dichotomies: A pragmatic approach to choices about concepts.' *Annual Review of Political Science* 1: 537–565.

16. Arend Lijphart. 1999. *Patterns of Democracy: Government Forms and Performance in Thirty-six Countries*. New Haven: Yale University Press.

17. Robert A. Dahl. 1956. *A Preface to Democratic Theory*. Chicago: University of Chicago Press; Robert A. Dahl. 1971. *Polyarchy*. New Haven, CT: Yale University Press.

18. Freedom House. 2007. *Freedom in the World 2006*. Washington, DC: Freedom House. www.freedomhouse.org.

19. Fareed Zakaria. 1997. 'The rise of illiberal democracy.' *Foreign Affairs* 76(6): 22–41; Larry Diamond. 2002. 'Thinking about hybrid regimes.' *Journal of Democracy* 13(2): 21–35; Steven Levitsky and Lucan A. Way. 2002. 'The rise of competitive authoritarianism.' *Journal of Democracy* 13(2): 51–65; Lucan A. Way and Steven Levitsky. 2006. 'The dynamics of autocratic coercion after the Cold War.' *Communist and Post-Communist Studies* 39(3): 387–410.

20. See Geraldo L. Munck and Jay Verkuilen. 2002. 'Conceptualizing and measuring democracy: Evaluating alternative indices.' *Comparative Political Studies* 35(1): 5–34; Pippa Norris. 2008. *Driving Democracy*. New York: Cambridge University Press, Ch. 3.

21. Monty Marshall and Keith Jaggers. 2003. *Polity IV Project: Political Regime Characteristics and Transitions, 1800–2003*. http://www.cidcm.umd.edu/inscr/polity/; Monty Marshall, Ted Robert Gurr, Christian Davenport, and Keith Jaggers. 2002. 'Polity IV, 1800–1999: Comments on Munck and Verkuilen.' *Comparative Political Studies* 35(1): 40–45.

22. UNDP. 2007. *Governance Indicators: A Users' Guide*. 2nd Edition. Oslo: UNDP. http://www.undp.org/oslocentre/flagship/governance_indicators_project.html; see also the University of Goteborg's Quality of Governance dataset. http://www.qog.pol.gu.se/.

23. http://www.prsgroup.com/.

24. Daniel Kaufmann, Aart Kraay, and M. Mastruzzi. May 2003. Governance Matters III: Governance Indicators 1996–2002. Washington, DC: World Bank, Policy Research Working Paper; Daniel Kaufmann, Aart Kraay, and Massimo Mastruzzi. 2007. Governance Matters VI: Aggregate and Individual Governance Indicators, 1996–2006. Washington, DC: World Bank, Policy Research Working Paper; Daniel Kaufmann, Aart Kraay, and Massimo Mastruzzi. 2007. 'Growth and governance: A rejoinder. *Journal of Politics* 69(2): 570–572. For a critical discussion, see Merilee S. Grindle, 2004. 'Good enough governance: Poverty reduction and reform in developing countries.' *Governance* 17(4): 525–548; Ved P. Nanda. 2006. 'The good governance concept revisited.' *Annals American Association of the Political and Social Sciences* 603: 263–283; Merilee S. Grindle. 2007. 'Good enough governance revisited.' *Development Policy Review* 25(5): 553–574.

25. CIRI. Human Rights Data Project. http://ciri.binghamton.edu/.

26. For a collection of these resources, see Pippa Norris. 2008. *Democracy Cross-national Data* and *Democracy Time-Series Data*. Both available at www.pippa norris.com.

27. See the Quality of Governance dataset available at the University of Goteborg. http://www.qog.pol.gu.se/.

28. Media Tenor uses professionally trained analysts, not software solutions, for the entire process of media content analysis. Analysts identify and categorize each report, sentence by sentence and issue by issue, according to a set of more than 700 defined criteria. Each report's content is then appropriately coded and entered into a globally linked database. Analyst remuneration is based on the results of intercoder reliability, validity, and sample check tests. For more details about the methodology and data, see http://www.mediatenor.com/.

29. For a discussion of the advantages of mixed research designs, see Henry Brady and David Collier. 2004. *Rethinking social inquiry: Diverse tools, shared standards.* New York: Rowman and Littlefield.

30. Robert Bickel. 2007. *Multilevel Analysis for Applied Research: It's Just Regression!* New York: Guilford Press.

31. James A. Stimson. 1985. 'Regression in time and space: A statistical essay.' *American Journal of Political Science* 29: 914–947; Cheng M. Hsiao. 1986. *Analysis of Panel Data*. Cambridge: Cambridge University Press; Sven E. Wilson and David M. Butler. 2007. 'A lot more to do: The sensitivity of time-series cross-section analyses to simple alternative specifications.' *Political Analysis* 15(2): 101–123.

32. Nathaniel Beck and Jonathan Katz. 1995. 'What to do (and not to do) with time-series cross-section data.' *American Political Science Review* 89: 634–647; Nathaniel Beck and Jonathan Katz. 1996. 'Nuisance vs. substance: Specifying and estimating time-series cross-sectional models.' In J. Freeman (Ed.). *Political Analysis*. Ann Arbor: University of Michigan Press.

33. See Alexander L. George and Andrew Bennett. 2004. *Case Studies and Theory Development*. Cambridge, MA: MIT Press.

34. For a discussion of the potential problem of selection bias in comparative politics, see Barbara Geddes. 2003. *Paradigms and Sand Castles: Theory Building and Research Design in Comparative Politics*. Ann Arbor: University of Michigan Press, Ch. 3; David Collier, James Mahoney, and Jason Seawright. 2004. 'Claiming too much: Warnings about selection bias.' In Henry E. Brady and David Collier (Eds.). *Rethinking Social Inquiry: Diverse Tools, Shared Standards*. Lanham, MD: Rowman and Littlefield.

Chapter 4. Trends in the United States and Western Europe

1. Huge national variations and periodic fluctuations are also noted by others when comparing trust in national parliaments; see Bernhard Wessels. 2009. 'Trust in political institutions.' In Jacques Thomassen (Ed.). *The Legitimacy of the European Union after Enlargement*. Oxford: Oxford University Press.

2. See, for example, the claims in Gerry Stoker. 2006. *Why Politics Matters: Making Democracy Work*. London: Palgrave/Macmillan, Ch. 2.

3. See Stephen Earl Bennett. 2001. 'Were the halcyon days really golden?' John R. Hibbing and Elizabeth Theiss-Morse (Eds.). *What Is It about Government That Americans Dislike?* Cambridge: Cambridge University Press.

4. Samuel P. Huntington. 1991. *The Third Wave: Democratization in the Late Twentieth Century*. Norman: University of Oklahoma Press.

5. For the intellectual history of the origins of the civic culture study, see Gabriel Almond. 1996. 'The civic culture: Prehistory, retrospect, and prospect' (http://repositories.cdlib.org/csd/96-01) and Gerardo L. Munck and Richard Snyder. 2007. *Passion, Craft, and Method in Comparative Politics*. Baltimore: Johns Hopkins University Press.

6. Gabriel A. Almond and Sidney Verba. 1963. *The Civic Culture*. Princeton, NJ: Princeton University Press, p. 314.

7. Gabriel A. Almond and Sidney Verba. 1963. *The Civic Culture*. Princeton, NJ: Princeton University Press, p. 308.

8. Samuel Barnes and Max Kaase. 1979. Political Action: Mass Participation in Five Western Democracies. Beverly Hills, CA: Sage.

9. Michel Crozier, Samuel P. Huntington, and Joji Watanuki. 1975. *The Crisis of Democracy: Report on the Governability of Democracies to the Trilateral Commission*. New York: New York University Press. See also Samuel P. Huntington. 1981. *American Politics: The Promise of Disharmony*. Cambridge, MA: Harvard University Press.

10. Seymour Martin Lipset and William C. Schneider. 1983. *The Confidence Gap: Business, Labor, and Government in the Public Mind*. New York: Free Press, p. 6. See also Joseph S. Nye, Philip D. Zelikow, and David C. King, Eds. 1997. *Why People Don't Trust Government*. Cambridge, MA: Harvard University Press.

11. See, in particular, Ola Listhaug and Matti Wiberg. 1995. 'Confidence in political and private institutions.' In Hans-Dieter Klingemann and Dieter Fuchs (Eds.). *Citizens and the State*. Oxford: Oxford University Press; Ola Listhaug. 1995. 'The dynamics of trust in politicians.' In Hans-Dieter Klingemann and Dieter Fuchs (Eds.). *Citizens and the State*. Oxford: Oxford University Press.

12. Susan J. Pharr and Robert D. Putnam, Eds. 2000. *Disaffected Democracies: What's Troubling the Trilateral Countries?* Princeton, NJ: Princeton University Press; Mattei Dogan, Ed. 2005. *Political Mistrust and the Discrediting of Politicians*. The Netherlands: Brill; Gerry Stoker. 2006. *Why Politics Matters: Making Democracy Work*. London: Palgrave/Macmillan; Mariano Torcal and José R. Montero, Eds. 2006. *Political Disaffection in Contemporary Democracies: Social Capital, Institutions, and Politics*. London: Routledge; Colin Hay. 2007. *Why We Hate Politics*. Cambridge: Polity Press.

13. Russell J. Dalton. 1999. 'Political support in advanced industrialized democracies.' In Pippa Norris (Ed.). *Critical Citizens: Global Support for Democratic Governance*. New York: Oxford University Press. See also Russell J. Dalton and Martin P. Wattenberg, Eds. 2002. *Parties without Partisans: Political Change in Advanced Industrial Democracies*. Oxford: Oxford University Press; Russell J. Dalton. 2004. *Democratic Challenges, Democratic Choices: The Erosion of Political Support in Advanced Industrial Democracies*. New York: Oxford University Press.

14. Michael Kenny. 2009. 'Taking the temperature of the British political elite 3: When grubby is the order of the day...' *Parliamentary Affairs* 62(3): 503–513.

15. Seymour Martin Lipset. 1996. *American Exceptionalism: A Double-Edged Sword*. New York: W. W. Norton.

16. See, for example, World Public Opinion. 2008. *World Public Opinion on Governance and Democracy*. Program on International Policy Attitudes at the University of Maryland. www.WorldPublicOpinion.org.

17. Russell Hardin. 2006. *Trust*. Cambridge: Polity Press.

18. Jack Citrin. 1974. 'Comment: The political relevance of trust in government.' *American Political Science Review* 68: 973–988; Jack Citrin and Donald Philip Green. 1986. 'Presidential leadership and the resurgence of trust in government.' *British Journal of Political Science* 16: 431–453.

19. Arthur H. Miller. 1974. 'Political issues and trust in government, 1964–1970.' *American Political Science Review* 68: 951–972; Arthur H. Miller. 1974. 'Rejoinder to "Comment" by Jack Citrin: Political discontent or ritualism?' *American Political Science Review* 68: 989–1001; Arthur H. Miller and Stephen A. Borrelli. 1991. 'Confidence in government during the 1980s.' *American Politics Quarterly* 19: 147–173.

20. Marc J. Hetherington. 2005. *Why Trust Matters*. Princeton, NJ: Princeton University Press, p. 15.

21. Paul R. Abramson and Ada W. Finifter. 1981. 'On the meaning of political trust: New evidence from items introduced in 1978.' *American Journal of Political Science* 25(2): 297–307.

22. See the ANES Guide to Public Opinion and Electoral Behavior. http://www.election studies.org/nesguide/graphs/g5a_1_2.htm.

23. Jack Citrin and Donald Green. 1986. 'Presidential leadership and trust in government.' *British Journal of Political Science* 16: 431–453. See also Virginia A. Chanley, Thomas J. Rudolph, and Wendy M. Rahn. 2001. 'Public trust in government in the Reagan years and beyond.' In John R. Hibbing and Elizabeth Theiss-Morse

(Eds.) 2001. *What Is It about Government That Americans Dislike?* Cambridge: Cambridge University Press.

24. Marc J. Hetherington. 2005. *Why Trust Matters.* Princeton, NJ: Princeton University Press.

25. The New York Times/CBS News surveys have carried items comparable to the ANES measures for trust in the federal government from February 1976 to February 2010. In this series, the proportion expressing trust in the federal government 'always' or 'most of the time' was 28% in the poll prior to 9/11; the proportion peaked at 55% following the events of 9/11, before falling back further to 19% by February 2010. See http://www.nytimes.com/2010/02/12/us/politics/12poll .html?hp. For Gallup series, 'Trust in Government,' see www.gallup.com.

26. Ola Listhaug. 1995. 'The dynamics of trust in politicians.' In Hans-Dieter Klingemann and Dieter Fuchs (Eds.). *Citizens and the State.* Oxford: Oxford University Press.

27. Russell J. Dalton. 2004. Democratic Challenges, Democratic Choices: The Erosion of Political Support in Advanced Industrial Democracies. New York: Oxford University Press, pp. 29–31.

28. For details, see the Gallup poll: http://www.gallup.com/poll/124787/Decade-Review-Four-Key-Trends.aspx.

29. John R. Hibbing and Elizabeth Theiss-Morse. 1995. *Congress as Public Enemy.* New York: Cambridge University Press.

30. Steven Van de Walle, Steven Van Roosbroek, and Geert Bouckaert. 2008. 'Trust in the public sector: Is there any evidence for a long-term decline?' *International Review of Administrative Sciences* 74(1): 47–64.

31. Gabriel A. Almond and Sidney Verba. 1963. *The Civic Culture.* Princeton, NJ: Princeton University Press.

32. Russell J. Dalton. 2004. Democratic Challenges, Democratic Choices: The Erosion of Political Support in Advanced Industrial Democracies. New York: Oxford University Press.

33. Richard S. Katz et al. 1992. 'The membership of political parties in European democracies, 1960–1990.' *European Journal of Political Research* 22: 329–345; Susan Scarrow. 2000. 'Parties without members? Party organization in a changing electoral environment.' In R. J. Dalton and M. P. Wattenberg (Eds.). *Parties without Partisans: Political Change in Advanced Industrial Democracies.* Oxford: Oxford University Press; Peter Mair and Ingrid van Biezen. 2001. 'Party membership in twenty European democracies 1980–2000.' *Party Politics* 7(1): 5–22; Ingrid van Biezen, Peter Mair, and Thomas Poguntke. 2009. 'Going, Going, . . . Gone? Party Membership in the 21st Century.' Paper presented at the Joint Workshops at the European Consortium for Political Research, Lisbon.

34. Russell J. Dalton. 2004. Democratic Challenges, Democratic Choices: The Erosion of Political Support in Advanced Industrial Democracies. New York: Oxford University Press, p. 32.

35. J. Maesschalck and S. Van de Walle. 2006. 'Policy failure and corruption in Belgium: Is federalism to blame?' *West European Politics* 29(5): 999–1017.

36. See John Curtice and Roger Jowell. 1995. 'The skeptical electorate.' In Roger Jowell et al. (Eds.). *British Social Attitudes: The 12th Report.* Aldershot: Ashgate, pp. 140–172; John Curtice and Roger Jowell. 1997. 'Trust in the political system.' In Roger Jowell et al. (Eds.). *British Social Attitudes: The 14th Report.* Aldershot: Ashgate.

37. See the Committee on Standards in Public Life. http://www.public-standards.gov.uk/.
38. For some of the many previous studies using this measure, see Christopher J. Anderson and Christine A. Guillory. 1997. 'Political institutions and satisfaction with democracy.' *American Political Science Review* 91(1): 66–81; Marta Lagos. 2003. 'Support for and satisfaction with democracy.' *International Journal of Public Opinion Research* 15(4): 471–487; André Blais and F. Gelineau. 2007. 'Winning, losing and satisfaction with democracy.' *Political Studies* 55: 425–441; Kees Aarts and Jacques Thomassen. 2008. 'Satisfaction with democracy: Do institutions matter?' *Electoral Studies* 27(1): 5-18; Alexander F. Wagner, Friedrich Schneider, and Martin Halla. 2009. 'The quality of institutions and satisfaction with democracy in Western Europe: A panel analysis.' *European Journal of Political Economy* 25 (1): 30–41.
39. For a debate concerning the meaning, see D. Canache, J. J. Mondak, and Mitch A. Seligson. 2001. 'Meaning and measurement in cross-national research on satisfaction with democracy.' *Public Opinion Quarterly* 65: 506–528; Jonas Linde and Joakim Ekman. 2003. 'Satisfaction with democracy: A note on a frequently used indicator in comparative politics.' *European Journal of Political Research* 42(3): 391–408.
40. Jonas Linde and Joakim Ekman. 2003. 'Satisfaction with democracy: A note on a frequently used indicator in comparative politics.' *European Journal of Political Research* 42(3): 391–408.
41. For a discussion about the Italian case, see Paolo Segatti. 'Italy, forty years of political disaffection: A longitudinal exploration.' In Mariano Torcal and José R. Montero (Eds). 2006. *Political Disaffection in Contemporary Democracies: Social Capital, Institutions, and Politics*. London: Routledge.
42. Sophie Duchesne and Andrè-Paul Frognier. 1995. 'Is there a European identity?' In Oskar Niedermayer and Richard Sinnott (Eds.). *Public Opinion and Internationalized Governance*. Oxford: Oxford University Press; Angelika Scheuer. 1999. 'A political community?' In Hermann Schmitt and Jacques Thomassen (Ed.). *Political Representation and Legitimacy in the European Union*. Oxford: Oxford University Press; T. Risse. 2001. 'A European identity? Europeanization and the evolution of nation-state identities.' In M. G. Cowles, J. Caporaso, and T. Risse (Eds.). *Transforming Europe*. Ithaca, NY: Cornell University Press. See also B. Nelson, D. Roberts, and W. Veit, Eds. *The Idea of Europe: Problems of National and Transnational Identity*. Oxford: Berg; Lauren M. McLaren. 2005. *Identity, Interests and Attitudes to European Integration*. London: Palgrave Macmillan.
43. Susan Pharr and Robert Putnam, Eds. 2000. *Disaffected Democracies: What's Troubling the Trilateral Countries?* Princeton, NJ: Princeton University Press; Mariano Torcal and José R. Montero. 2006. *Political Disaffection in Contemporary Democracies: Social Capital, Institutions, and Politics*. London: Routledge; Mattei Dogan, Ed. 2005. *Political Mistrust and the Discrediting of Politicians*. The Netherlands: Brill.
44. David Held, Anthony McGrew, David Goldblatt, and Jonathan Perraton. 1999. *Global Transformations: Politics, Economics, and Culture*. Stanford, CA: Stanford University Press, Ch. 7.
45. See also Pippa Norris and Ronald Inglehart. 2009. *Cosmopolitan Communications*. New York: Cambridge University Press.

46. Margaret Levi and Laura Stoker. 2000. 'Political trust and trustworthiness.' *Annual Review of Political Science* 3: 475–508.

Chapter 5. Comparing Political Support around the World

 1. Similar conclusions are reached by Berhard Wessels. 2009. 'Trust in political institutions.' In Jacques Thomassen (Ed.). *The Legitimacy of the European Union after Enlargement*. Oxford: Oxford University Press.
 2. Marc J. Hetherington. 2005. *Why Trust Matters*. Princeton, NJ: Princeton University Press.
 3. Bruce Cain, Russell J. Dalton, and Susan Scarrow, Eds. *Democracy Transformed? The Expansion of Political Access in Advanced Industrialized Democracies*. Oxford: Oxford University Press.
 4. See, for example, Council of Europe. Forum for the Future of Democracy. http://www.coe.int/t/dgap/democracy/Default_en.asp.
 5. Gabriel A. Almond and Sidney Verba. 1963. *The Civic Culture*. Princeton: Princeton University Press, p. 308.
 6. Sidney Tarrow. 1989. *Democracy and Disorder: Protest and Politics in Italy, 1965–1975*. New York: Oxford University Press; Leonardo Morlino and Marco Tarchi. 1996. 'The dissatisfied society: The roots of political change in Italy.' *European Journal of Political Research* 30(1): 41–63; Doug McAdams, Charles Tilly, and Sidney Tarrow. 2001. *Dynamics of Contention*. New York: Cambridge University Press; Martin J. Bull and James L. Newell. 2006. *Italian Politics*. Cambridge: Polity Press.
 7. Samuel P. Huntington. 1991. *The Third Wave: Democratization in the Late Twentieth Century*. Norman: University of Oklahoma Press. See also Renske Doorenspleet. 2000. 'Reassessing the three waves of democratization.' *World Politics* 52: 384–406; Renske Doorenspleet. 2005. *Democratic Transitions: Exploring the Structural Sources during the Fourth Wave*. Boulder, CO: Lynne Rienner.
 8. For a discussion about the causes of derailment of potential democracies, see M. Steven Fish and Jason Wittenberg. 'Failed democratization.' In Christian W. Haerpfer, Patrick Bernhagen, Ronald Inglehart, and Christian Welzel (Eds.). 2009. *Democratization*. Oxford: Oxford University Press. See also Ethan B. Kapstein and Nathan Converse. 2008. *The Fate of Young Democracies*. New York: Cambridge University Press; Ethan B. Kapstein and Nathan Converse. 2008. 'Why democracies fail.' *Journal of Democracy* 19(4): 57–68.
 9. Zachary Elkins, Tom Ginsburg, and James Melton. 2009. *The Endurance of National Constitutions*. New York: Cambridge University Press.
10. Robert Bates. 2009. *When Things Fell Apart: State Failure in Late-Century Africa*. New York: Cambridge University Press.
11. Arch Puddington. 2010. 'Freedom in the world 2010: Erosion of freedom intensifies.' Freedom House. *Freedom in the World 2010*. www.freedomhouse.org.
12. Hans-Dieter Klingemann. 1999. 'Mapping political support in the 1990s.' In Pippa Norris (Ed.). 1999. *Critical Citizens: Global Support for Democratic Governance*. Oxford: Oxford University Press.
13. Unfortunately, similar evidence is unavailable to compare approval of specific incumbent officeholders, such as the popularity of particular party leaders or presidents.

14. Anthony Heath, Steve Fisher, and S. Smith. 2005. 'The globalization of public opinion research.' *Annual Review of Political Science* 8: 297–333.

15. It should be noted that social surveys face serious challenges when conducted in repressive states, which lack rights to freedom of expression. Under these conditions, citizens may be fearful of voicing explicit criticisms of official government agencies, exercising processes of self-censorship in their responses to survey interviewers. This should be borne in mind when interpreting the survey data, although it remains difficult to test any effects of self-censorship from available empirical evidence. On the other hand, citizens in autocracies such as China, Vietnam, and Iran expressed widespread approval of democratic values (see Table 5.3), suggesting that they did not feel any need to suppress the expression of these political attitudes.

16. Russell J. Dalton, 2004. *Democratic Challenges, Democratic Choices: The Erosion of Political Support in Advanced Industrial Democracies.* New York: Oxford University Press.

17. Christopher J. Anderson and Christine A. Guillory. 1997. 'Political institutions and satisfaction with democracy.' *American Political Science Review* 91(1): 66–81; Neil Nevitte and Mebs Kanji. 2002. 'Authority orientations and political support: A cross-national analysis of satisfaction with governments and democracy.' *Comparative Sociology* 1(3–4): 387–412; Christopher J. Anderson, Andre Blais, Shaun Bowler, Todd Donovan, and Ola Listhaug. 2005. *Losers' Consent: Elections and Democratic Legitimacy.* New York: Oxford University Press; Alexander F. Wagner, Friedrich Schneider, and Martin Halla. 2009. 'The quality of institutions and satisfaction with democracy in Western Europe: A panel analysis.' *European Journal of Political Economy* 25(1): 30–41; Kees Aarts and Jacques Thomassen. 2008. 'Satisfaction with democracy: Do institutions matter?' *Electoral Studies* 27(1): 5–18.

18. For a debate concerning the meaning, see D. Canache, J. J. Mondak, and Mitch A. Seligson. 2001. 'Meaning and measurement in cross-national research on satisfaction with democracy.' *Public Opinion Quarterly* 65: 506–528; Jonas Linde and Joakim Ekman. 2003. 'Satisfaction with democracy: A note on a frequently used indicator in comparative politics.' *European Journal of Political Research* 42(3): 391–408.

19. Jonas Linde and Joakim Ekman. 2003. 'Satisfaction with democracy: A note on a frequently used indicator in comparative politics.' *European Journal of Political Research* 42(3): 391–408.

20. Naoimi Chazan. 1988. "Democracy and democratic rule in Ghana." In Larry Diamond, Juan Linz and Seymour Martin Lipset (Eds.). *Democracy in Developing Countries: Africa.* Boulder, CO: Lynne Rienner; Joseph Aye. 2000. *Deepening Democracy in Ghana.* Accra: Freedom Publications.

21. William Mishler and Richard Rose. 1995. 'Trajectories of fear and hope: Support for democracy in post-communist Europe.' *Comparative Political Studies* 28: 553–581; Richard Rose and William Mishler. 1996. 'Testing the Churchill hypothesis: Popular support for democracy and its alternatives.' *Journal of Public Policy* 16: 29–58; Richard Rose, William Mishler, and Christian Haerpfer. 1998. *Democracy and Its Alternatives in Post-Communist Europe: Testing the Churchill Hypothesis.* Cambridge: Polity Press; Roderic Camp (Ed.). 2001. *Citizen Views of Democracy in Latin America.* Pittsburgh: University of Pittsburgh Press; Michael Bratton and

Robert Mattes. 2001. 'Support for democracy in Africa: Intrinsic or instrumental.' *British Journal of Political Science* 31(3): 447–474; Michael Bratton, Robert Mattes, and E. Gyimah-Boadi. 2004. *Public Opinion, Democracy, and Market.* Cambridge: Cambridge University Press; Russell J. Dalton and Doh Chull Shin, Eds. 2006. *Citizens, Democracy and Markets around the Pacific Rim.* Oxford: Oxford University Press; Larry Diamond and Marc F. Plattner. 2008. *How People View Democracy.* Baltimore: Johns Hopkins University Press; Yun-han Chu, Larry Diamond, Andrew J. Nathan, and Doh Chull Shin, Eds. 2008. *How East Asians View Democracy.* New York: Columbia University Press.

22. Andreas Schedler and Rudolpho Sarsfield. 2007. 'Democrats with adjectives: Linking direct and indirect measures of democratic support.' *European Journal of Political Research* 46(5): 637–659.

23. Ronald Inglehart. 2003. 'How solid is mass support for democracy: And how do we measure it?' *PS: Political Science and Politics* 36: 51–57; Larry Diamond and Marc F. Plattner (Eds.). 2008. *How People View Democracy.* Baltimore: Johns Hopkins University Press.

24. Donald Emmerson. 1995. 'Singapore and the "Asian Values" debate.' *Journal of Democracy* 6(4): 95–105.

25. Z. Wang. 2005. 'Before the emergence of critical citizens: Economic development and political trust in China.' *International Review of Sociology* 15(1): 155–171.

26. Russell Dalton and Doh Chull Shin, Eds. 2006. *Citizens, Democracy and Markets around the Pacific Rim.* Oxford: Oxford University Press; Yun-han Chu, Larry Diamond, Andrew J. Nathan, and Doh Chull Shin, Eds. 2008. *How East Asians View Democracy.* New York: Columbia University Press.

27. Larry Diamond. 2008. 'Introduction.' In *How People View Democracy.* Larry Diamond and Marc F. Plattner (Eds.). Baltimore: Johns Hopkins University Press, p. xi.

28. Mark Tessler and E. Gao. 2005. 'Gauging Arab support for democracy.' *Journal of Democracy* 16(3): 83–97; Mark Tessler. 2002. 'Do Islamic orientations influence attitudes toward democracy in the Arab world? Evidence from Egypt, Jordan, Morocco, and Algeria.' *International Journal of Comparative Sociology* 43(3–5): 229–249; Amaney Jamal and Mark Tessler. 2008. 'The Arab aspiration for democracy.' In Larry Diamond and Marc F. Plattner (Eds.). *How People View Democracy.* Baltimore: Johns Hopkins University Press, Table 1.

29. Larry Diamond and Marc F. Plattner, Eds. 2008. 'Introduction.' In *How People View Democracy.* Baltimore: Johns Hopkins University Press.

30. Larry Diamond and Marc F. Plattner, Eds. 2008. In *How People View Democracy.* Baltimore: Johns Hopkins University Press.

31. Francis Fukuyama. 1992. *The End of History and the Last Man.* New York: Free Press.

32. Andreas Schedler and Rudolpho Sarsfield. 2007. 'Democrats with adjectives: Linking direct and indirect measures of democratic support.' *European Journal of Political Research* 46(5): 637–659.

33. William Mishler and Richard Rose. 1995. 'Trajectories of fear and hope: Support for democracy in post-communist Europe.' *Comparative Political Studies* 28: 553–581; William Mishler and Richard Rose. 2002. 'Learning and re-learning regime support: The dynamics of post-communist regimes.' *European Journal of Political Research* 41: 5. Richard Rose, William Mishler, and Christian Haerpfer. 1998.

Democracy and Its Alternatives in Post-Communist Europe: Testing the Churchill Hypothesis. Cambridge: Polity Press.

34. Rokeach, Milton. 1973. *The Nature of Human Values*. New York: Free Press.
35. Michael Ignatieff. 1993. *Blood and Belonging*. London: Chatto and Windus; Benedict Anderson. 1996. *Imagined Communities: Reflections on the Origin and Spread of Nationalism*. London: Verso; Michael Billig. 1995. *Banal Nationalism*. London: Sage; Earnest Gellner. 1983. *Nations and Nationalism*. Oxford: Blackwell.
36. For a detailed discussion, see Pippa Norris and Ronald Inglehart. 2009. *Cosmopolitan Communications*. Cambridge: Cambridge University Press, Ch. 6.
37. For a detailed discussion, see Pippa Norris and Ronald Inglehart. 2009. *Cosmopolitan Communications*. Cambridge: Cambridge University Press, Ch. 6.

Chapter 6. Trends in Democratic Deficits

1. Susan Pharr and Robert Putnam, Eds. 2000. *Disaffected Democracies: What's Troubling the Trilateral Countries?* Princeton: Princeton University Press; Mariano Torcal and José R. Montero. 2006. *Political Disaffection in Contemporary Democracies: Social Capital, Institutions, and Politics*. London: Routledge; Richard I. Hofferbert and Hans-Dieter Klingemann. 2001. 'Democracy and its discontents in post-wall Germany.' *International Political Science Review* 22(4): 363–378.
2. John R. Hibbing and Elizabeth Theiss-Morse. 1995. *Congress as Public Enemy*. New York: Cambridge University Press.
3. See also Steven Van de Walle, Steven Van Roosbroek, and Geert Bouckaert. 2008. 'Trust in the public sector: Is there any evidence for a long-term decline?' *International Review of Administrative Sciences* 74(1): 47–64.
4. Similar regression analysis models were run to monitor trends in confidence 1981–2007 in the judiciary, civil service, and police, but none proved significant.
5. Sophie Duchesne and Andrè-Paul Frognier. 1995. 'Is there a European identity?' In Oskar Niedermayer and Richard Sinnott (Eds.). *Public Opinion and Internationalized Governance*. Oxford: Oxford University Press; Angelika Scheuer. 1999. 'A political community?' In Hermann Schmitt and Jacques Thomassen (Eds.). *Political Representation and Legitimacy in the European Union*. Oxford: Oxford University Press; T. Risse. 2001. 'A European identity? Europeanization and the evolution of nation-state identities.' In M. G. Cowles, J. Caporaso, and T. Risse (Eds.).*Transforming Europe*. Ithaca, NY: Cornell University Press. See also B. Nelson, D. Roberts, and W. Veit, Eds. *The Idea of Europe: Problems of National and Transnational Identity*. Oxford: Berg; Lauren M. McLaren. 2005. *Identity, Interests and Attitudes to European Integration*. London: Palgrave Macmillan.
6. Roderic Camp, Ed. 2001. *Citizen Views of Democracy in Latin America*. Pittsburgh: University of Pittsburgh Press; Marta Lagos. 2003. 'Support for and satisfaction with democracy.' *International Journal of Public Opinion Research* 15(4): 471–487.
7. See, for example, Min-Hua Huang, Yu-tzung Chang, and Yun-han Chu. 2008. 'Identifying sources of democratic legitimacy: A multilevel analysis.' *Electoral Studies* 27(1): 45–62. See also, however, Richard I. Hofferbert and Hans-Dieter Klingemann. 2001. 'Democracy and its discontents in post-wall Germany.' *International Political Science Review* 22(4): 363–378.
8. See also Russell J. Dalton and Doh Chull Shin, Eds. 2006. *Citizens, Democracy and Markets around the Pacific Rim*. Oxford: Oxford University Press; Z. Wang. 2005.

'Before the emergence of critical citizens: Economic development and political trust in China.' *International Review of Sociology* 15(1): 155–171; Tianjian Shi. 'China: Democratic values supporting an authoritarian system.' In Yun-han Chu, Larry Diamond, Andrew J. Nathan, and Doh Chull Shin (Eds.). 2008. *How East Asians View Democracy*. New York: Columbia University Press.

9. Louis Edward Inglehart. 1998. *Press and Speech Freedoms in the World, from Antiquity until 1998: A Chronology*. Westport, CT: Greenwood Press; Leonard R. Sussman. 2001. *Press Freedom in Our Genes*. Reston, VA: World Press Freedom Committee; Alasdair Roberts. 2006. *Blacked Out: Government Secrecy in the Information Age*. New York: Cambridge University Press.

10. Pippa Norris and Ronald Inglehart. 2010. 'Limits on press freedom and regime support.' In *Public Sentinel: News Media and Governance Reform*. Washington, DC: World Bank; J. J. Kennedy. 2009. 'Maintaining popular support for the Chinese Communist Party: The influence of education and the state-controlled media.' *Political Studies* 57(3): 517–536.

11. World Bank. World Development Indicators. http://data.worldbank.org/indicator.

12. Z. Wang. 2005. 'Before the emergence of critical citizens: Economic development and political trust in China.' *International Review of Sociology* 15(1): 155–171

13. Tianjian Shi. 2008. 'China: Democratic values supporting an authoritarian system.' In Yun-han Chu, Larry Diamond, Andrew J. Nathan, and Doh Chull Shin (Eds.). *How East Asians View Democracy*. New York: Columbia University Press.

Chapter 7. Rising Aspirations?

1. For an overview, see Filippo Sabbetti. 2007. 'Democracy and civic culture.' In Carles Boix and Susan C. Stokes (Eds.). *The Oxford Handbook of Comparative Politics*. New York: Oxford University Press.

2. The primary publications are Ronald Inglehart. 1977. *The Silent Revolution: Changing Values and Political Styles among Western Publics*. Princeton, NJ: Princeton University Press; Ronald Inglehart. 1990. *Culture Shift in Advanced Industrial Society*. Princeton, NJ: Princeton University Press; Ronald Inglehart. 1997. *Modernization and Postmodernization: Cultural, Economic and Political Change in 43 Societies*. Princeton, NJ: Princeton University Press; Ronald Inglehart and Christian Welzel. 2003. 'Political culture and democracy: Analyzing cross-level linkages.' *Comparative Politics* 36(1): 61–70; Ronald Inglehart and Christian Welzel. 2005. *Modernization, Cultural Change, and Democracy: The Human Development Sequence*. New York: Cambridge University Press; Christian W. Haerpfer, Patrick Bernhagen, Ronald Inglehart, and Christian Welzel, Eds. 2009. *Democratization*. Oxford: Oxford University Press.

3. Ronald Inglehart. 2003. 'How solid is mass support for democracy: And how can we measure it?' *PS: Political Science and Politics* 36(1): 51–57.

4. See the discussion in Jeffrey Berry. 1984. *The Interest Group Society*. Boston: Little, Brown; Jack L. Walker. 1991. *Mobilizing Interest Groups in America*: Ann Arbor: University of Michigan Press.

5. Pierre Bourdieu. 1970. *Reproduction in Education, Culture and Society*. London: Sage; James S. Coleman. 1988. 'Social capital in the creation of human capital.' *American Journal of Sociology* 94: 95–120; James S. Coleman. 1990. *Foundations of Social Theory*. Cambridge, MA: Belknap. For a discussion of the history of the concept, see also the introduction in Stephen Baron, John Field, and Tom Schuller, Eds. 2000. *Social Capital: Critical Perspectives*. Oxford: Oxford University Press.

6. The primary works are Robert D. Putnam. 1993. *Making Democracy Work: Civic Traditions in Modern Italy*. Princeton, NJ: Princeton University Press; Robert D. Putnam. 2000. *Bowling Alone: The Collapse and Revival of American Community*. New York: Simon and Schuster; Susan Pharr and Robert Putnam, Eds. 2000. *Disaffected Democracies: What's Troubling the Trilateral Countries?* Princeton, NJ: Princeton University Press; Robert D. Putnam, Ed. 2006. *The Dynamics of Social Capital*. Oxford: Oxford University Press.

7. Ethan B. Kapstein and Nathan Converse. 2008. 'Why democracies fail.' *Journal of Democracy* 19(4): 57–68.

8. Daniel Lerner. 1958. *The Passing of Traditional Society: Modernizing the Middle East*. New York: Free Press; Seymour Martin Lipset. 1959. 'Some social requisites of democracy: Economic development and political legitimacy.' *American Political Science Review* 53: 69–105; Seymour Martin Lipset. 1960. *Political Man: The Social Basis of Politics*. New York: Doubleday; Walt W. Rostow. 1952. *The Process of Economic Growth*. New York: W. W. Norton; Walt W. Rostow. 1960. *The Stages of Economic Growth*. Cambridge: Cambridge University Press; Karl W. Deutsch. 1964. 'Social mobilization and political development.' *American Political Science Review* 55: 493–514; Daniel Bell. 1999. *The Coming of Post-Industrial Society: A Venture in Social Forecasting*. New York: Basic Books; Seymour Martin Lipset, Kyoung-Ryung Seong, and John Charles Torres. 1993. 'A comparative analysis of the social requisites of democracy.' *International Social Science Journal* 45(2): 154–175.

9. Daniel Bell. 1999. *The Coming of Post-Industrial Society: A Venture in Social Forecasting*. New York: Basic Books. (1st edition 1973)

10. Pippa Norris. 2010. 'The globalization of comparative public opinion research.' In Neil Robinson and Todd Landman (Eds.). *The Sage Handbook of Comparative Politics*. London: Sage.

11. For the recent work on the links between democracy and culture, see Ronald Inglehart and Christian Welzel. 2003. 'Political culture and democracy: Analyzing cross-level linkages.' *Comparative Politics* 36(1): 61–70; Ronald Inglehart and Christian Welzel. 2005. *Modernization, Cultural Change, and Democracy: The Human Development Sequence*. New York: Cambridge University Press; Christian W. Haerpfer, Patrick Bernhagen, Ronald Inglehart, and Christian Welzel, Eds. 2009. *Democratization*. Oxford: Oxford University Press.

12. Ronald Inglehart. 1997. *Modernization and Postmodernization: Cultural, Economic and Political Change in 43 Societies*. Princeton, NJ: Princeton University Press.

13. Ronald Inglehart. 1977. *The Silent Revolution: Changing Values and Political Styles among Western Publics*. Princeton, NJ: Princeton University Press.

14. Ronald Inglehart and Christian Welzel. 2005. *Modernization, Cultural Change, and Democracy: The Human Development Sequence*. New York: Cambridge University Press, p. 52.

15. Christian Welzel. 2007. 'Are levels of democracy affected by mass attitudes? Testing attainment and sustainment effects on democracy.' *International Political Science Review* 28(4): 397–424; Christian Welzel and Ronald Inglehart. 2008. 'The role of ordinary people in democratization.' *Journal of Democracy* 19(1): 126–140; Ronald Inglehart and Christian Welzel. 2009. 'How development leads to democracy: What we know about modernization.' *Foreign Affairs* 88(2): 33–37.

16. Ronald Inglehart and Christian Welzel. 2005. *Modernization, Cultural Change, and Democracy: The Human Development Sequence*. New York: Cambridge

University Press, p. 56. See also, however, Jan Teorell and Axel Hadenius. 2006. 'Democracy without democratic values: A rejoinder to Welzel and Inglehart.' *Studies in Comparative International Development* 41(3): 95–111; Christian Welzel and Ronald Inglehart. 2006. 'Emancipative values and democracy: Response to Hadenius and Teorell.' *Studies in Comparative International Development* 41(3): 74–94; Christian Welzel. 2007. 'Are levels of democracy affected by mass attitudes? Testing attainment and sustainment effects on democracy.' *International Political Science Review* 28(4): 397–424.

17. Ronald Inglehart and Christian Welzel. 2005. *Modernization, Cultural Change, and Democracy: The Human Development Sequence.* New York: Cambridge University Press; Christian W. Haerpfer, Patrick Bernhagen, Ronald Inglehart, and Christian Welzel, Eds. 2009. *Democratization.* Oxford: Oxford University Press.

18. Christopher J. Anderson and Christine A. Guillory. 1997. 'Political institutions and satisfaction with democracy.' *American Political Science Review* 91(1): 66–81.

19. Richard Rose, William Mishler, and Christian Haerpfer. 1998. *Democracy and Its Alternatives in Post-Communist Europe: Testing the Churchill Hypothesis.* Cambridge: Polity Press.

20. Stephen W. Raudenbush and Anthony S. Bryk. 2002. *Hierarchical Linear Models.* 2nd ed. Thousand Oaks, CA: Sage; Andrew Gelman and Jennifer Hill. 2007. *Data Analysis Using Regression and Multilevel/Hierarchical Models.* New York: Cambridge University Press; Robert Bickel. 2007. *Multilevel Analysis for Applied Research: It's Just Regression!* New York: Guilford Press.

21. Damarys Canache, Jeffrey J. Mondak, and Mitchell A. Seligson. 2001. 'Meaning and measurement in cross-national research on satisfaction with democracy.' *Public Opinion Quarterly* 65: 506–528; Ronald Inglehart and Christian Welzel. 2003. 'Political culture and democracy: Analyzing cross-level linkages.' *Comparative Politics* 36(1): 61–70; Christian Welzel. 2007. 'Are levels of democracy affected by mass attitudes? Testing attainment and sustainment effects on democracy.' *International Political Science Review* 28(4): 397–424.

22. See Jason M. Wells and Jonathan Krieckhaus. 2006. 'Does national context influence democratic satisfaction? A multi-level analysis.' *Political Research Quarterly* 59(4): 569–578.

23. Further information on the construction and ranking of the UNDP Human Development Index is available from http://hdr.undp.org/en/statistics/.

24. Larry Diamond and Marc F. Plattner. 2008. *How People View Democracy.* Baltimore: Johns Hopkins University Press.

25. Russell J. Dalton. 1984. 'Cognitive mobilization and partisan dealignment in advanced industrial democracies.' *Journal of Politics* 46: 264–284; Russell J. Dalton. 2004. *Democratic Challenges, Democratic Choices: The Erosion of Political Support in Advanced Industrial Democracies.* New York: Oxford University Press; Russell J. Dalton. 2007. *Citizen Politics: Public Opinion and Political Parties in Advanced Western Democracies.* Washington, DC: CQ Press; Russell J. Dalton. 2009. *The Good Citizen: How a Younger Generation Is Reshaping American Politics.* Rev. ed. Washington, DC: CQ Press.

26. Norman Nie, J. Junn, and K. Stehlik-Barry. 1996. *Education and Democratic Citizenship in America.* Chicago: University of Chicago Press.

27. Eamonn Callan. 1997. *Creating Citizens: Political Education and Liberal Democracy.* New York: Oxford University Press; James D. Chesney and Otto Feinstein.

1997. *Building Civic Literacy and Citizen Power*. Upper Saddle River, NJ: Prentice-Hall; Henry Milner. 2002. *Civic Literacy: How Informed Citizens Make Democracy Work*. Hanover: University Press of New England; Stephen Elkin and Karol Edward Soltan. 1999. *Citizen Competence and Democratic Institutions*. University Park: Pennsylvania State University Press; Judith Torney-Purta, John Schwillle, and Jo-Ann Amadeo. 1999. *Civic Education across Countries: Twenty-four National Case Studies*. In *The IEA Civic Education Project*. Amsterdam: IEA; Judith Torney-Purta, Ranier Lehmann, Hans Oswald, and Wilfram Schulz. 2001. *Citizenship and Education in Twenty-Eight Countries: Civic Knowledge and Engagement at Age Fourteen*. Amsterdam: IEA.

28. Sidney Verba and Norman Nie. 1972. *Participation in America: Political Democracy and Social Equality*. New York: Harper and Row; Sidney Verba, Norman Nie, and Jae-on Kim. 1978. *Participation and Political Equality: A Seven-Nation Comparison*. New York: Cambridge University Press; Sidney Verba, Kay Schlozman, and Henry Brady. 1995. *Voice and Equality: Civic Volunteerism in American Politics*. Cambridge: Harvard University Press.

29. Dieter Fuchs, Giovanna Guidorossi, and Palle Svensson. 1995. 'Support for the democratic system.' In Hans-Dieter Klingemann and Dieter Fuchs (Eds.). *Citizens and the State*. Oxford: Oxford University Press.

30. Ola Listhaug and Matti Wiberg. 1995. 'Confidence in political and private institutions.' In Hans-Dieter Klingemann and Dieter Fuchs (Eds.). *Citizens and the State*. Oxford: Oxford University Press.

31. Henry Milner. 2002. *Civic Literacy: How Informed Citizens Make Democracy Work*. Hanover: University Press of New England.

32. For empirical studies of the socialization process, see J. Kelley and N. D. DeGraaf. 1997. 'National context, parental socialization, and religious belief: Results from 15 nations.' *American Sociological Review* 62(4): 639–659; S. M. Myers. 1996. 'An interactive model of religiosity inheritance: The importance of family context.' *American Sociological Review* 61(5): 858–866.

33. See, for example, David Easton and Jack Dennis. 1969. *Children in the Political System: Origins of Political Legitimacy*. New York: McGraw-Hill; R. Hess and Judith Torney. 1967. *The Development of Political Attitudes in Children*. Chicago: Aldine Press; Fred I. Greenstein. 1970. *Children and Politics*. Rev. ed. New Haven, CT: Yale University Press; M. Kent Jennings and Richard Niemi. 1974. *The Political Character of Adolescence*. Princeton, NJ: Princeton University Press; Roberta Sigel and Marilyn Hoskin. 1981. *The Political Involvement of Adolescents*. New Brunswick, NJ: Rutgers University Press; S. Dash and Richard Niemi. 1992. 'Democratic attitudes in multicultural settings: Across national assessment of political socialization.' *Youth and Society* 23: 313–334; M. Kent Jennings, Laura Stoker, and Jake Bowers. 2009. 'Politics across generations: Family transmission reexamined.' *Journal of Politics* 71(3): 782–799.

34. Donald Sears and C. L. Funk. 1999. 'Evidence of the long-term persistence of adults' political predispositions.' *Journal of Politics* 61: 1–28.

35. Russell J. Dalton. 2004. *Democratic Challenges, Democratic Choices: The Erosion of Political Support in Advanced Industrial Democracies*. New York: Oxford University Press, Ch. 4.

36. Ronald Inglehart. 1999. 'Post-modernization erodes respect for authority, but increases support for democracy.' In Pippa Norris (Ed.). *Critical Citizens: Global Support for Democratic Government*. Oxford: Oxford University Press.

37. For a review of the literature, see Kenneth Newton. 2007. 'Social and political trust.' In Russell J. Dalton and Hans-Dieter Klingemann (Eds.). *The Oxford Handbook of Political Behavior*. Oxford: Oxford University Press.

38. Robert D. Putnam. 1993. *Making Democracy Work: Civic Traditions in Modern Italy*. Princeton, NJ: Princeton University Press; Robert D. Putnam. 1996. 'The strange disappearance of civic America.' *American Prospect* 24 (Winter): 34–48; Robert D. Putnam. 2000. *Bowling Alone: The Collapse and Revival of American Community*. New York: Simon and Schuster. More recent comparative research is presented in Susan Pharr and Robert Putnam, Eds. 2000. *Disaffected Democracies: What's Troubling the Trilateral Countries?* Princeton, NJ: Princeton University Press; Robert D. Putnam, Ed. 2006. *The Dynamics of Social Capital*. Oxford: Oxford University Press.

39. Robert D. Putnam. 2000. *Bowling Alone: The Collapse and Revival of American Community*. New York: Simon and Schuster.

40. The comparative literature is too large to summarize here but this includes, inter alia, Michael Foley and Bob Edwards. 1998. 'Beyond Tocqueville: Civil society and social capital in comparative perspective.' *American Behavioral Scientist* 42(1): 5–20; Jan Willem van Deth, Ed. 1999. *Social Capital and European Democracy*. New York: Routledge; Peter Hall. 1999. 'Social capital in Britain.' *British Journal of Political Science* 29: 417–461; Partha Dasgupta and Ismail Serageldin, Eds. 2000. *Social Capital: A Multifaceted Perspective*. Washington, DC: World Bank; Robert D. Putnam, Ed. 2002. *Democracy in Flux*. Oxford: Oxford University Press; Pamela Paxton. 2002. 'Social capital and democracy: An interdependent relationship.' *American Sociological Review* 67(2): 254–277; Marc Hooghe and Dietlind Stolle, Eds. 2003. *Generating Social Capital: Civil Society and Institutions in Comparative Perspective*. New York: Palgrave Macmillan; János Kornai, Bo Rothstein, and Susan Rose-Ackerman, Eds. 2004. *Creating Social Trust in Post-Socialist Transitions*. New York: Palgrave Macmillan; Pippa Norris. 2004. *Democratic Phoenix*. Cambridge: Cambridge University Press, Ch. 8; Charles F. Andrain and James T. Smith. 2006. *Political Democracy, Trust and Social Justice: A Comparative Overview*. Boston: Northeastern University Press, Ch. 3.

41. Kenneth Newton and Pippa Norris. 2000. 'Confidence in public institutions: Faith, culture or performance?' In Susan Pharr and Robert Putnam (Eds.). 2000. *Disaffected Democracies: What's Troubling the Trilateral Countries?* Princeton, NJ: Princeton University Press. See also Kenneth Newton, 1999. 'Social and political trust.' In Pippa Norris (Ed.). *Critical Citizens: Global Support for Democratic Government*. Oxford: Oxford University Press; Kenneth Newton. 1997. 'Social capital and democracy.' *American Behavioral Scientist* 40(5): 575–586; Kenneth Newton. 2006. 'Political support: Social capital, civil society and political and economic performance.' *Political Studies* 54(4): 846–864; Kenneth Newton. 2007. 'Social and political trust.' In Russell J. Dalton and Hans-Dieter Klingemann (Eds.). *The Oxford Handbook of Political Behavior*. Oxford: Oxford University Press.

42. Sonja Zmerli and Kenneth Newton. 2008. 'Social trust and attitudes toward democracy.' *Public Opinion Quarterly* 72(4): 706–724.

43. Robert Putnam. 1993. *Making Democracy Work: Civic Traditions in Modern Italy*. Princeton, NJ: Princeton University Press, pp. 89–90.

44. Susan Pharr and Robert Putnam, Eds. 2000. *Disaffected Democracies: What's Troubling the Trilateral Countries?* Princeton, NJ: Princeton University Press.

45. Diego Gambetta, Ed. 1988. *Trust: Making and Breaking Cooperative Relations.* Oxford: Blackwell; R. W. Jackman and Arthur Miller. 1998. 'Social capital and politics.' *Annual Review of Political Science* 1: 47–73; Edward N. Muller and Mitchell A. Seligson. 1994. 'Civic culture and democracy: The question of causal relationships.' *American Political Science Review* 88(3): 635–652; Pamela Paxton. 2002. 'Social capital and democracy: An interdependent relationship.' *American Sociological Review* 67(2): 254–277.

46. Bo Rothstein. 2005. *Social Traps and the Problem of Trust.* New York: Cambridge University Press.

47. Sonja Zmerli and Kenneth Newton. 2008. 'Social trust and attitudes toward democracy.' *Public Opinion Quarterly* 72(4): 706–724.

48. For the analysis of this measure using previous waves of the World Values Survey, see also Pippa Norris. 2002. *Democratic Phoenix.* Cambridge: Cambridge University Press, Ch. 8.

49. Robert D. Putnam. 1994. *Making Democracy Work.* Princeton, NJ: Princeton University Press.

50. Robert D. Putnam. 2000. *Bowling Alone: The Collapse and Revival of American Community.* New York: Simon and Schuster.

51. Jan Willhem van Deth, M. Maraffi, Kenneth Newton, and Paul F. Whitely, Eds. 1999. *Social Capital and European Democracy.* London, Routledge; Pamela Paxton. 2002. 'Social capital and democracy: An interdependent relationship.' *American Sociological Review* 67(2): 254–277; Eric Uslaner. 2003. 'Trust, democracy and governance: Can government policies influence generalized trust?' In Marc Hooghe and Dietlind Stolle (Eds.). *Generating Social Capital: Civil Society and Institutions in Comparative Perspective.* New York: Palgrave Macmillan; Staffan Kumlin and Bo Rothstein. 2005. 'Making and breaking social capital: The impact of welfare state institutions.' *Comparative Political Studies* 38(4): 339–365; Bo Rothstein. 2005. *Social Traps and the Problem of Trust.* New York: Cambridge University Press; W. Van Oorschot, W. Arts, and L. Halman. 2005. 'Welfare state effects on social capital and informal solidarity in the European Union: Evidence from the 1999/2000 European Values Study.' *Policy and Politics* 33(1): 33–54.

Chapter 8. Democratic Knowledge

1. See Larry Diamond and Marc F. Plattner, Eds. *How People View Democracy.* Baltimore: Johns Hopkins University Press.

2. Robert Rohrschneider. 1996. 'Institutional learning versus value diffusion: The evolution of democratic values among parliamentarians in Eastern and Western Germany.' *Journal of Politics* 58: 442–466; Robert Rohrschneider. 1998. *Learning Democracy: Democratic and Economic Values in Unified Germany.* Oxford: Oxford University Press; Richard Rose, William Mishler, and Christian Haerpfer. 1998. *Democracy and Its Alternatives.* Cambridge: Polity Press; William Mishler and Richard Rose. 2002. 'Learning and re-learning regime support: The dynamics of post-communist regimes.' *European Journal of Political Research* 41: 5; Robert Mattes and Michael Bratton. 2007. 'Learning about democracy in Africa: Awareness, performance and experience.' *American Journal of Political Science* 51(1): 192–217.

3. David O. Sears. 1975. 'Political socialization.' In *Handbook of Political Science.* Vol. 2, Fred I. Greenstein and Nelson W. Polsby (Eds.). Reading: Addison-Wesley; James G. Gimpel, J. Celeste Lay, and Jason E. Schuknecht. 2003. *Cultivating*

Democracy: Civic Environments and Political Socialization in America. Washington, DC: Brookings Institution Press; Joan E. Grusec and Paul D. Hastings, Eds. 2006. *Handbook of Socialization: Theory and Research.* New York: Guilford Press; Edward S. Greenberg, Ed. 2009. *Political Socialization.* Chicago: Aldine Transaction.

4. M. Kent Jennings. 1996. 'Political knowledge over time and across generations.' *Public Opinion Quarterly* 60(2): 228–252; M. Kent Jennings, Laura Stoker, and J. Bowers. 2009. 'Politics across generations: Family transmission reexamined.' *Journal of Politics* 71(3): 782–799.

5. Pippa Norris and Ronald Inglehart. 2009. *Cosmopolitan Communications.* New York: Cambridge University Press, Ch. 9.

6. Pippa Norris. 2000. *A Virtuous Circle.* New York: Cambridge University Press.

7. Pippa Norris and Ronald Inglehart. 2009. *Cosmopolitan Communications.* New York: Cambridge University Press, Ch. 9.

8. W. P. Eveland and D. A. Scheufele. 2000. 'Connecting news media use with gaps in knowledge and participation.' *Political Communication* 17(3): 215–237; Pippa Norris and Christina Holtz-Bacha. 2001. 'To entertain, inform and educate: Still the role of public television in the 1990s?' *Political Communications* 18(2); Yoori Hwang and S. H. Jeong. 2009. 'Revisiting the knowledge gap hypothesis: A meta-analysis of thirty-five years of research.' *Journalism and Mass Communication Quarterly* 86(3): 513–532.

9. Philip Converse. 1964. 'The nature of belief systems in mass publics.' In David E. Apter (Ed.). *Ideology and Discontent.* New York: Free Press.

10. John Zaller. 1992. *The Nature and Origins of Mass Opinion.* New York: Cambridge University Press, Ch. 2.

11. See Willem E. Saris and Paul M. Sniderman (Eds.). 2004. *Studies in Public Opinion: Attitudes, Nonattitudes, Measurement Error, and Change.* Princeton, NJ: Princeton University Press.

12. John Zaller. 1993. *The Nature of Mass Public Opinion.* Cambridge: Cambridge University Press.

13. Andreas Schedler and Rudolpho Sarsfield. 2007. 'Democrats with adjectives: Linking direct and indirect measures of democratic support.' *European Journal of Political Research* 46(5): 637–659.

14. Bryan Caplan. 2007. *The Myth of the Rational Voter.* Princeton, NJ: Princeton University Press.

15. Michael Delli-Carpini and Scott Keeter. 1997. *What Americans Know about Politics and Why It Matters.* New Haven, CT: Yale University Press, Ch.2.

16. Ronald Inglehart and Christian Welzel. 2003. 'Political culture and democracy: Analyzing cross-level linkages.' *Comparative Politics* 36(1): 61–70; Ronald Inglehart. 2003. 'How solid is mass support for democracy: And how do we measure it?' *PS: Political Science and Politics* 36: 51–57; Christian Welzel. 2007. 'Are levels of democracy affected by mass attitudes? Testing attainment and sustainment effects on democracy.' *International Political Science Review* 28(4): 397–424; Christian Welzel and Ronald Inglehart. 2008. 'The role of ordinary people in democratization.' In Larry Diamond and Marc F. Plattner (Eds). *How People View Democracy.* Baltimore: Johns Hopkins University Press.

17. For a critique and response, however, see Axel Hadenius and Jan Teorell. 2005. 'Cultural and economic prerequisites of democracy: Reassessing recent evidence.' *Studies in Comparative International Development* 39(4): 87–106; Christian

Welzel and Ronald Inglehart. 2006. 'Emancipative values and democracy: Response to Hadenius and Teorell.' *Studies in Comparative International Development* 41(3): 74–94; Jan Teorell and Axel Hadenius. 2006. 'Democracy without democratic values: A rejoinder to Welzel and Inglehart.' *Studies in Comparative International Development* 41(3): 95–111.

18. Ronald Inglehart. 2003. 'How solid is mass support for democracy: And how do we measure it?' *PS: Political Science and Politics* 36: 51–57.

19. See Freedom House. 2009. *Freedom around the World.* http://www.freedom house.org/template.cfm?page=410&year=2008.

20. Amnesty International. June 20, 2009. 'Arrests and deaths continue in Iran as authorities tighten grip.' http://www.amnesty.org/en/news-and-updates/news/ arrests-deaths-continue-iran-authorities-tighten-grip-20090722.

21. Pippa Norris. 2008. *Driving Democracy: Do Power-Sharing Institutions Work?* Cambridge: Cambridge University Press.

22. David Held. 2006. *Models of Democracy.* 3rd ed. Palo Alto, CA: Stanford University Press.

23. Pippa Norris. 2008. *Driving Democracy: Do Power-sharing Institutions Work?* Cambridge: Cambridge University Press.

24. David Collier and Steven Levitsky. 1997. 'Democracy with adjectives.' *World Politics* 49: 430–451; Andreas Schedler and Rudolpho Sarsfield. 2007. 'Democrats with adjectives: Linking direct and indirect measures of democratic support.' *European Journal of Political Research* 46(5): 637–659.

25. John Keane. 2009. *The Life and Death of Democracy.* New York: W. W. Norton.

26. Geraldo L. Munck. 2009. *Measuring Democracy.* Baltimore: Johns Hopkins University Press.

27. Well-known examples of influential myths include American polls showing that in July 2006, a majority of Republicans continued to believe that before the Iraq war, Saddam Hussein had weapons of mass destruction or a major program for developing them, a perception bolstered by the rhetoric of the Bush administration, despite the report from UN inspectors discounting such claims. World Public Opinion. 2006. 'Iraq: The Separate Realities of Republicans and Democrats.' http://www.worldpublicopinion.org/pipa/articles/brunitedstatescanadara/186.php? lb=brusc&pnt=186&nid=&id=. Similarly, despite overwhelming evidence that President Obama was born in Hawaii, following discussion on the conservative talk show radio circuit, U.S. polls in July 2009 reported that less than a majority of Republicans believed that President Obama was a natural-born citizen. Research 2000/Daily Kos poll July 31, 2009. http://www.dailykos.com/storyonly/ 2009/7/31/760087/-Birthers-are-mostly-Republican-and-Southern.

28. Tianjian Shi. 'China: Democratic values supporting an authoritarian system.' In Yun-han Chu, Larry Diamond, Andrew J. Nathan, and Doh Chull Shin (Eds.). 2008. *How East Asians View Democracy.* New York: Columbia University Press.

29. Frederic G. Schaffer. 1998. *Democracy in Translation: Understanding Politics in an Unfamiliar Culture.* Ithaca, NY: Cornell University Press.

30. Tian Jian Shi. 2000. 'Cultural values and democracy in the People's Republic of China.' *China Quarterly* 162: 540–559; Tianjian Shi. 2008. 'China: Democratic values supporting an authoritarian system.' In Yun-han Chu, Larry Diamond, Andrew J. Nathan, and Doh Chull Shin (Eds.). *How East Asians View Democracy.* New York: Columbia University Press; Tian Jian Shi. 2009. 'Talking Past Each

Other? Different Understandings of Democracy and Their Consequences.' Paper presented at the IPSA 21st World Congress, Santiago.

31. Richard I. Hofferbert and Hans-Dieter Klingemann. 2001. 'Democracy and its discontents in post-wall Germany.' *International Political Science Review* 22(4): 363–378. See also Dieter Fuchs. 1999. 'The democratic culture of Unified Germany.' In Pippa Norris (Ed.). *Critical Citizens: Global Support for Democratic Governance*. Oxford: Oxford University Press.

32. This problem is often encountered when ideas such as the left-right continuum or the liberal-conservative scale are interpreted quite differently in different societies; for example, 'liberal' in the United States is usually understood as social liberalism located on the 'left' of the political spectrum, while 'liberal' in Europe is commonly regarded as 'economic' or 'free market' liberalism located on the center-right. See, for example, Jan van Deth, Ed. 1998. *Comparative Politics: The Problem of Equivalence*. London: Routledge; Willem E. Sarids and Irmtraud Gallhofer. 2007. 'Can questions travel successfully?' In Roger Jowell, Caroline Roberts, Rory Fitzgerald, and Gillian Eva (Eds.). *Measuring Attitudes Cross-nationally: Lessons from the European Social Survey*. London: Sage.

33. Russell J. Dalton, Doh C. Shin, and Willy Jou. 2008. 'How people understand democracy.' In Larry Diamond and Marc F. Plattner (Eds.). 2008. *How People View Democracy*. Baltimore: Johns Hopkins University Press.

34. Gary King, Christopher J. L. Murray, Joshua A. Salomon, and Ajay Tandon. 2004. 'Enhancing the validity and cross-cultural comparability of survey research.' *American Political Science Review* 98(1): 191–207. See also http://gking.harvard.edu/vign/; Michael Bratton. 2009. 'Anchoring the "D" Word in Comparative Survey Research.' Paper presented at the Conference on Democracy Audits and Governmental Indicators, University of California, Berkeley, October 30–31, 2009.

35. Michael Bratton and Robert Mattes. 2001. 'Support for democracy in Africa: Intrinsic or instrumental.' *British Journal of Political Science* 31(3): 447–474.

36. Alejandro Moreno. 2001. 'Democracy and mass belief systems in Latin America.' In Roderic Ai Camp (Ed.). *Citizen Views of Democracy in Latin America*. Pittsburgh: University of Pittsburgh Press.

37. Michael Bratton and Robert Mattes. 2001. 'Support for democracy in Africa: Intrinsic or instrumental.' *British Journal of Political Science* 31(3): 447–474.

38. For some of the extensive literature debating these claims, see D. S. Brown. 1999. 'Reading, writing, and regime type: Democracy's impact on primary school enrollment.' *Political Research Quarterly* 52(4): 681–707; D. S. Brown. 1999. 'Democracy and social spending in Latin America, 1980–92.' *American Political Science Review* 93: 779; Adam Przeworski, Michael E. Alvarez, Jose Antonio Cheibub, and Fernando Limongi. 2000. *Democracy and Development: Political Institutions and Well-Being in the World, 1950–1990*. New York: Cambridge University Press; Morton Halperin, Joseph T. Siegle, and Michael Weinstein. 2005. *The Democracy Advantage*. New York: Routledge; Casey B. Mulligan, R. Gil, and X. Sala-a-martin. 2004. 'Do democracies have different public policies than non-democracies?' *Journal of Economic Perspectives* 18(1): 51–74; Michael Ross. 2006. 'Is democracy good for the poor?' *American Journal of Political Science* 50(4): 860–874.

39. Michael X. Delli Carpini and Scott Keeter. 1993. 'Measuring political knowledge: Putting 1st things 1st.' *American Journal of Political Science* 37(4): 1179–1206;

Michael X. Delli Carpini and Scott Keeter. 1996. *What Americans Know about Politics and Why It Matters*. New Haven, CT: Yale University Press.

40. John Zaller. 1993. *The Nature and Origins of Mass Opinion*. New York: Cambridge University Press; Doris Graber. 2001. *Processing Politics. Learning from Television in the Internet Age*. Chicago: University of Chicago Press.

41. Arthur Lupia. 1994. 'Shortcuts versus encyclopedias: Information and voting-behavior in California insurance reform elections.' *American Political Science Review* 88(1): 63–76. Arthur Lupia and Mathew D. McCubbins. 1998. *The Democratic Dilemma*. Cambridge: Cambridge University Press.

42. Robert A. Dahl. 1971. *Polyarchy: Participation and Opposition*. New Haven: Yale University Press.

43. Robert A. Dahl. 1971. *Polyarchy: Participation and Opposition*. New Haven: Yale University Press.

44. Lawrence LeDuc. 2003. *The Politics of Direct Democracy: Referendums in Global Perspective*. Peterborough, ON: Broadview Press.

45. Robert A. Dahl. 1971. *Polyarchy: Participation and Opposition*. New Haven: Yale University Press.

46. For more details, see Pippa Norris and Ronald Inglehart. 2009. *Cosmopolitan Communications*. New York: Cambridge University Press, Ch. 5.

47. For instance, the Pew Research Center regularly monitors public awareness of many issues in American politics, reporting that even after a year-long debate about health care reform, in January 2010 only one-third of Americans were aware of Senate legislative rules or party voting on this issue. The Pew Research Center, January 2010. 'Public Knowledge: Senate Legislative Process a Mystery to Many.' http://pewresearch.org/pubs/1478/political-iq-quiz-knowledge-filibuster-debt-colbert-steele.

48. Lucan Way. 2005. 'Authoritarian State Building and the Sources of Regime Competitiveness in the Fourth Wave: The Cases of Belarus, Moldova, Russia, and Ukraine.' *World Politics* 57(2): 231–261.

Chapter 9. Negative News

1. Michael Robinson. 1976. 'Public affairs television and the growth of political malaise: The case of "the selling of the president."' *American Political Science Review* 70(3): 409–432; Thomas E. Patterson. 1993. *Out of Order*. New York: Alfred A. Knopf; Patricia Moy and Mochael Pfau. 2000. *With Malice Toward All? The Media and Public Confidence in Democratic Institutions*. Westport, CT: Praeger; Thomas E. Patterson. 2002. *The Vanishing Voter*. New York: Alfred A. Knopf.

2. Suzanne Garment. 1991. *Scandal: The Crisis of Mistrust in American Politics*. New York: Random House; Gary Orren. 1997. 'Fall from grace: The public's loss of faith in government.' In Joseph S. Nye, Jr., Philip D. Zelikow, and David C. King (Eds.). *Why People Don't Trust Government*. Chicago: University of Chicago Press; Mark Grossman. 2003. *Political Corruption in America: An Encyclopedia of Scandals, Power, and Greed*. 2nd ed. New York: ABC-Clio.

3. Kim Fridkin Kahn and P. J. Kenney. 1999. 'Do negative campaigns mobilize or suppress turnout? Clarifying the relationship between negativity and participation.' *American Political Science Review* 93: 877; Kim Fridkin Kahn and P. J.

Kenney. 2008. 'The dimensions of negative messages.' *American Politics Research* 36(5): 694–723.

4. Richard R. Lau and I. B. Rovner. 2009. 'Negative campaigning.' *Annual Review of Political Science* 12: 285–306; Nicholas A. Valentino. 2001. 'A spiral of cynicism for some: The contingent effects of campaign news frames on participation and confidence in government.' *Political Communication* 18: 347; James M. Avery. 2009. 'Videomalaise or virtuous circle? The influence of the news media on political trust.' *International Journal of Press-Politics* 14(4): 410–433.

5. John Zaller. 1998. 'Monica Lewinsky's contribution to political science.' *PS: Political Science and Politics* 31(2): 182; D. J. Smyth and S. W. Taylor. 2003. 'Presidential popularity: What matters most, macroeconomics or scandals?' *Applied Economics Letters* 10(9): 585–588; D. V. Shah, M. D. Watts, and D. Domke, et al. 2002. 'News framing and cueing of issue regimes: Explaining Clinton's public approval in spite of scandal.' *Public Opinion Quarterly* 66(3): 339–370.

6. Joseph N. Cappella and Kathleen H. Jamieson. 1997. *Spiral of Cynicism*. New York: Oxford University Press; Pippa Norris. 2000. *A Virtuous Circle: Political Communications in Post-Industrial Democracies*. New York: Cambridge University Press; J. Kleinnijenhuis, A. M. J. van Hoof, and D. Oegema. 2006. 'Negative news and the sleeper effect of distrust.' *Harvard International Journal of Press-Politics* 11(2): 86–104; Marc J. Hetherington and Thomas J. Rudolph. 2008. 'Priming, performance and the dynamics of political trust.' *Journal of Politics* 70(2): 498–512.

7. Kurt Lang and Gladys Lang. 1966. 'The mass media and voting.' In Bernard Berelson and M. Janowitz (Eds.). *Reader in Public Opinion and Communication*. New York: Free Press. According to the Langs: "*Television's style in chronicling political events can affect the fundamental orientation of the voter towards his government. . . . The media, we contend, can stir up in individuals defensive reactions by their emphasis on crisis and conflict in lieu of clarifying normal decision-making processes.*"

8. Michael Robinson. 1976. 'Public affairs television and the growth of political malaise: The case of "the selling of the president."' *American Political Science Review* 70(3): 409–432, 425.

9. Thomas E. Patterson. 1993. *Out of Order*. New York: Alfred A. Knopf; Thomas E. Patterson. 2002. *The Vanishing Voter*. New York: Alfred A. Knopf.

10. Joseph N. Cappella and Kathleen H. Jamieson. 1997. *Spiral of Cynicism*. New York: Oxford University Press.

11. Robert Putnam. 1995. 'Tuning in, tuning out: The strange disappearance of social capital in America.' *PS: Political Science and Politics* 28 (December): 664–683.

12. D. R. Fan, R. O. Wyatt, and K. Keltner. 2001. 'The suicidal messenger: How press reporting affects public confidence in the press, the military, and organized religion.' *Communication Research* 28(6): 826–852.

13. Claes H. de Vreese and M. Elenbaas. 2008. 'Media in the game of politics: Effects of strategic meta-coverage on political cynicism.' *International Journal of Press-Politics* 13 (3): 285–309.

14. Hans Mathias Kepplinger. 2000. 'The declining image of the German political elite.' *Harvard International Journal of Press-Politics* 5(4): 71–80.

15. Susan J. Pharr. 2000. 'Official misconduct and public distrust: Japan and the trilateral democracies.' In Susan J. Pharr and Robert D. Putnam (Eds.). *Disaffected*

Democracies: What's Troubling the Trilateral Countries? Princeton, NJ: Princeton University Press.

16. Pippa Norris. 2000. *A Virtuous Circle.* New York: Cambridge University Press.

17. Pippa Norris. 2000. *A Virtuous Circle.* New York: Cambridge University Press.

18. See Kenneth Newton. 1997. 'Politics and the news media: Mobilisation or video-malaise?' In Roger Jowell, John Curtice, Alison Park, Katarina Thomson, and Lindsay Brook (Eds.). *British Social Attitudes: The 14th Report.* Aldershot: Ashgate; Claes H. de Vreese. 2005. 'The spiral of cynicism reconsidered.' *European Journal of Communication* 20(3): 283–301; P. S. Martin. 2008. 'The mass media as sentinel: Why bad news about issues is good news for participation.' *Political Communication* 25(2): 180–193.

19. See, for example, Diana C. Mutz and Byron Reeves. 2005. 'The new video-malaise: Effects of television incivility on political trust.' *American Political Science Review* 99: 1–15; James M. Avery. 2009. 'Videomalaise or virtuous circle? The influence of the news media on political trust.' *International Journal of Press-Politics* 14(4): 410–433.

20. Patricia Moy and Mochael Pfau. 2000. *With Malice Toward All? The Media and Public Confidence in Democratic Institutions.* Westport, CT: Praeger.

21. James Lull and Stephen Hinerman, Eds. 1997. *Media Scandals.* Cambridge: Polity Press; John Garrard and James L. Newell, Eds. 2006. *Scandals in Past and Contemporary Politics.* Manchester: University of Manchester Press.

22. Michael Schudson. 1992. *Watergate in American Memory: How We Remember, Forget and Reconstruct the Past.* New York: Basic Books; John B. Thompson. 2000. *Political Scandal: Power and Visibility in the Media Age.* Cambridge: Polity.

23. Tobias Jones. 2005. *The Dark Heart of Italy.* New York: North Point Press.

24. Michael Kenny. 2009. 'Taking the temperature of the British political elite 3: When grubby is the order of the day.' *Parliamentary Affairs* 62(4): 663–672.

25. Silvio Waisbord. 2000. *Watchdog Journalism in South America: News, Accountability, and Democracy.* New York: Columbia University Press; Charles H. Blake and Stephen D. Morris, Eds. 2009. *Corruption and Democracy in Latin America.* Pitt Latin American Studies. Pittsburgh: University of Pittsburgh Press.

26. Susan Rose-Ackerman. 1999. *Corruption and Government: Causes, Consequences and Reform.* Cambridge: Cambridge University Press; Alan Doig. 2000. *Corruption and Democratization.* London: Frank Cass; Arnold Heidenheimer, Ed. 2002. *Political Corruption: Concepts and Contexts.* New Brunswick: Transaction Publishers; Michael Johnston. 2006. *Syndromes of Corruption: Wealth, Power, and Democracy.* New York: Cambridge University Press; Daniel Treisman. 2007. 'What have we learned about the causes of corruption from ten years of cross-national empirical research?' *Annual Review of Political Science* 10: 211–244.

27. See, for example, Wolfgang Donsbach. 1995. 'Lapdogs, watchdogs and junkyard dogs.' *Media Studies Journal* 9(4): 17–30; Bart Cammaerts and Nico Carpentier, Eds. 2007. *Reclaiming the Media: Communication Rights and Democratic Media Roles.* London: Intellect.

28. B. Fjaestad and P. G. Holmlov. 1976. 'The journalist's view.' *Journal of Communication.* 2: 108–114; J. W. L. Johnstone, E. J. Slawski, and W. W. Bowman. 1976. *The News People.* Urbana: University of Illinois Press; David Weaver and C. G. Wilhoit. 1986. *The American Journalist.* Bloomington: University of Indiana Press; Renate Köcher. 1986. 'Bloodhounds or missionaries: Role definitions of German and British journalists.' *European Journal of Communication* 1(1): 43–64.

29. M. J. Yusha'u. 2009. 'Investigative journalism and scandal reporting in the Nigerian press.' *Ecquid Novi-African Journalism Studies* 30(2): 155–174.

30. Mattei Dogan, Ed. 2005. *Political Mistrust and the Discrediting of Politicians.* Leiden: Brill. See also Sighard Neckel. 2005. 'Political scandals.' In Mattei Dogan (Ed.). *Political Mistrust and the Discrediting of Politicians.* Leiden: Brill.

31. James Lull and Stephen Hinerman, Eds. 1997. *Media Scandals.* Cambridge: Polity Press.

32. M. L. Smith, A. E. Rengifo, and B. K. Vollman. 2008. 'Trajectories of abuse and disclosure: Child sexual abuse by Catholic priests.' *Criminal Justice and Behavior* 35(5): 570–582.

33. V. A. Chanley, T. J. Rudolph, and W. M. Rahn, 2000. 'The origins and consequences of public trust in government: A time series analysis.' *Public Opinion Quarterly* 64(3): 239–256. See also Alejandro Moreno. 2002. 'Corruption and democracy: A cultural assessment.' *Comparative Sociology* 1(3–4): 495–507.

34. Paul Gronke and John Brehm. 2002. 'History, heterogeneity, and presidential approval: A modified ARCH approach.' *Electoral Studies* 21(3): 425–452; John Zaller. 1998. 'Monica Lewinsky's contribution to political science.' *PS: Political Science and Politics* 31(2): 182; D. J. Smyth and S. W. Taylor. 2003. 'Presidential popularity: What matters most, macroeconomics or scandals?' *Applied Economics Letters* 10(9): 585–588; D. V. Shah, M. D. Watts, and D. Domke et al. 2002. 'News framing and cueing of issue regimes: Explaining Clinton's public approval in spite of scandal.' *Public Opinion Quarterly* 66(3): 339–370.

35. Christopher J. Anderson and Yuliya V. Tverdova. 2003. 'Corruption, political allegiances, and attitudes toward government in contemporary democracies.' *American Journal of Political Science* 47(1): 91–109

36. Charles F. Andrain and James T. Smith. 2006. *Political Democracy, Trust and Social Justice.* Boston: Northeastern University Press, pp. 56–57; Aymo Brunetti and Beatrice Weder. 2003. 'A free press is bad news for corruption.' *Journal of Public Economics* 87(7–8): 1801–1824.

37. Jason M. Wells and Jonathan Krieckhaus. 2006. 'Does national context influence democratic satisfaction? A multi-level analysis.' *Political Research Quarterly* 59(4): 569–578.

38. See, for example, Sheila Coronel. 2010. 'Corruption and the watchdog role of the news media.' In Pippa Norris (Ed.). *Public Sentinel: News Media and the Governance Agenda.* Washington, DC: World Bank; Howard Tumbler and Silvio Waisbord. 2004. 'Political scandals and media across democracies.' *American Behavioral Scientist* 47: 7.

39. For a chronology of these events, see Mark Grossman. 2008. *Political Corruption in America: An Encyclopedia of Scandals, Power, and Greed.* 3rd ed. Grey House Publishing, http://en.wikipedia.org/wiki/Political_scandals_of_the_United_States; http://en.wikipedia.org/wiki/Political_scandals_in_the_United_Kingdom.

40. For full methodological details, see http://www.mediatenor.com/.

41. Details of the survey methodology and British results from Ipsos MORI are available at http://www.ipsos-mori.com.

42. Nathaniel Beck and Jonathan Katz. 1995. 'What to do (and not to do) with time-series cross-section data.' *American Political Science Review* 89: 634–647.

43. The Gallup Organization. http://www.gallup.com/. For details of trends and the updated series of comparable survey results from a number of major U.S. polling organizations, see http://www.PollingReport.com.

Chapter 10. Failing Performance?

1. David Easton and Jack Dennis. 1969. *Children in the Political System: Origins of Political Legitimacy*. New York: McGraw-Hill.
2. Russell Hardin. 1996. 'Trustworthiness.' *Ethics* 107: 26–42; Russell Hardin. 1999. 'Do we want trust in government?' In Mark E. Warren (Ed.). *Democracy and Trust*. Cambridge: Cambridge University Press, pp. 22–41; Russell Hardin, Ed. 2004. *Trust and Trustworthiness*. New York: Russell Sage Foundation; Russell Hardin. 2006. *Trust*. Cambridge: Polity.
3. Russell Hardin. 2006. *Trust*. Cambridge: Polity, p. 17.
4. Charles F. Andrain and James T. Smith. 2006. *Political Democracy, Trust and Social Justice: A Comparative Overview*. Boston: Northeastern University Press; Min-Hua Huang, Yu-tzung Chang, and Yun-han Chu. 2008. 'Identifying sources of democratic legitimacy: A multilevel analysis.' *Electoral Studies* 27(1): 45–62.
5. Freedom House. 2009. *Freedom in the World 2009*. Washington, DC: Freedom House. www.freedomhouse.org.
6. Thomas Carothers. 2002. 'The end of the transition paradigm.' *Journal of Democracy* 13: 5–21; Fareed Zakaria. 1997. 'The rise of illiberal democracy.' *Foreign Affairs* 76(6): 22–41; Larry Diamond. 2002. 'Thinking about hybrid regimes.' *Journal of Democracy* 13(2): 21–35; Steven Levitsky and Lucan A. Way. 2002. 'The rise of competitive authoritarianism.' *Journal of Democracy* 13(2): 51–65; Lucan A. Way and Steven Levitsky. 2006. 'The dynamics of autocratic coercion after the cold war.' *Communist and Post-Communist Studies* 39(3): 387–410.
7. Michael Bratton and Robert Mattes. 2001. 'Support for democracy in Africa: Intrinsic or instrumental.' *British Journal of Political Science* 31(3): 447–474.
8. Geoffrey Evans and Stephen Whitefield. 1995. 'The politics and economics of democratic commitment: Support for democracy in transition societies.' *British Journal of Political Science* 25(4): 485–513; Stephen Whitefield and Geoffrey Evans. 1999. 'Political culture versus rational choice: Explaining responses to transition in the Czech Republic and Slovakia.' *British Journal of Political Science* 29(1): 129–154.
9. Alexander F. Wagner, Friedrich Schneider, and Martin Halla. 2009. 'The quality of institutions and satisfaction with democracy in Western Europe: A panel analysis.' *European Journal of Political Economy* 25(1): 30–41.
10. Min-Hua Huang, Yu-tzung Chang, and Yun-han Chu. 2008. 'Identifying sources of democratic legitimacy: A multilevel analysis.' *Electoral Studies* 27(1): 45–62. See also B. G. Bishin, R. R. Barr, and M. J. Lebo. 2006. 'The impact of economic versus institutional factors in elite evaluation of presidential progress toward democracy in Latin America.' *Comparative Political Studies* 39 (10): 1194–1219.
11. John R. Hibbing and Elizabeth Theiss-Morse. 1995. *Congress as Public Enemy*. New York: Cambridge University Press; John R. Hibbing and Elizabeth Theiss-Morse. 2002. *Stealth Democracy: Americans' Beliefs about How Government Should Work*. New York: Cambridge University Press.
12. Tian Jian Shi. 2000. 'Cultural values and democracy in the People's Republic of China.' *China Quarterly* 162: 540–559. Tian Jian Shi. 2001. 'Cultural values and political trust: A comparison of the People's Republic of China and Taiwan.' *Comparative Politics* 33(4): 401–415.
13. See, for example, Kenneth Newton and Pippa Norris. 2000. 'Confidence in public institutions: Faith, culture, or performance.' In Susan J. Pharr and Robert D.

Putnam (Eds.). *Disaffected Democracies: What's Troubling the Trilateral Countries?* Princeton: Princeton University Press, pp. 52–73; Alexander F. Wagner, Friedrich Schneider, and Martin Halla. 2009. 'The quality of institutions and satisfaction with democracy in Western Europe: A panel analysis.' *European Journal of Political Economy* 25(1): 30–41.

14. Pippa Norris. 2010. 'Measuring democratic governance.' In Mark Bevir (Ed.). *The Sage Handbook of Governance*. London: Sage. The University of Goteborg's Quality of Governance Institute has developed a dedicated Web site and an integrated dataset collecting these indicators. See http://www.qog.pol.gu.se/. See also UNDP. 2007. *Governance Indicators: A Users' Guide*. 2nd ed. Oslo: UNDP.

15. UNDP. 2007. *Governance Indicators: A Users' Guide*. 2nd ed. Oslo: UNDP. http://www.undp.org/oslocentre/flagship/governance_indicators_project.html; see also the University of Goteborg's Quality of Governance dataset http://www.qog.pol.gu.se/.

16. See Freedom in the World. 'Methodology.' http://www.freedomhouse.org/template.cfm?page=351&ana_page=341&year=2008; Reporters without Borders. http://www.rsf.org/en-classement69–2007.html.

17. The University of Goteborg's Quality of Governance dataset. http://www.qog.pol.gu.se/.

18. For details, see Pippa Norris. 2008. *Driving Democracy: Do Power-Sharing Institutions Work?* New York: Cambridge University Press, Ch. 3.

19. Kees Aarts and Jacques Thomassen. 2008. 'Satisfaction with democracy: Do institutions matter?' *Electoral Studies* 27(1): 5–18.

20. World Bank. 2007. 'Strengthening World Bank Group Engagement on Governance and Anticorruption.' http://www.worldbank.org/html/extdr/comments/governancefeedback/.

21. See, for example, Alexander F. Wagner, Friedrich Schneider, and Martin Halla. 2009. 'The quality of institutions and satisfaction with democracy in Western Europe: A panel analysis.' *European Journal of Political Economy* 25(1): 30–41.

22. Derick W. Brinkerhoff and Arthur A. Goldsmith. 2005. 'Institutional dualism and international development: A revisionist interpretation of good governance.' *Administration and Society* 37(2): 199–225.

23. Merilee Grindle. 2004. 'Good enough governance: Poverty reduction and reform in developing countries.' *Governance* 17(4): 525–548.

24. David L. Cingranelli and David L. Richards. 2004. *The Cingranelli-Richards (CIRI) Human Rights Database Coder Manual*. http://ciri.binghamton.edu/.

25. For more details, see UNDP. Human Development Report. http://hdr.undp.org/en/media/HDR_20072008_Tech_Note_1.pdf.

26. Alexander F. Wagner, Friedrich Schneider, and Martin Halla. 2009. 'The quality of institutions and satisfaction with democracy in Western Europe: A panel analysis.' *European Journal of Political Economy* 25(1): 30–41.

27. Michael Lewis Beck. 1988. *Economics and Elections: The Major Western Democracies*. Ann Arbor: University of Michigan Press; Harold D. Clarke, Euel W. Elliott, William Mishler, Marianne C. Stewart, Paul F. Whiteley, and Gary Zuk. 1992. *Controversies in Political Economy*. Boulder, CO: Westview Press.

28. Stephen M. Weatherford. 1987. 'How does government performance influence political support?' *Political Behavior* 9: 5–28; Steven E. Finke, Edward N. Muller, and Mitchell A. Seligson. 1987. 'Economic crisis, incumbent performance and regime support.' *British Journal of Political Science* 19: 329–351; Harold D. Clarke,

Nitish Dutt, and Allan Kornberg. 1993. 'The political economy of attitudes toward polity and society in Western European democracies.' *Journal of Politics* 55(4): 998–1021; Christopher J. Anderson. 1995. *Blaming the Government: Citizens and the Economy in Five European Democracies.* New York: M. E. Sharpe; Ian McAllister. 1999. 'The economic performance of governments.' In Pippa Norris (Ed.). *Critical Citizens: Global Support for Democratic Governance.* New York: Oxford University Press.

29. For a detailed account of the links between public preferences and policy responsiveness, see Stuart N. Soroka and Christopher Wlezien. 2010. *Degrees of Democracy: Politics, Public Opinion and Policy.* New York: Cambridge University Press.

30. Colin Hay. 2007. *Why We Hate Politics.* Cambridge: Polity.

31. Russell J. Dalton. 2004. *Democratic Challenges, Democratic Choices: The Erosion of Political Support in Advanced Industrial Democracies.* New York: Oxford University Press.

32. See Steven E. Finke, Edward N. Muller, and Mitchell A. Seligson. 1987. 'Economic crisis, incumbent performance and regime support.' *British Journal of Political Science* 19: 329–351; Stephen M. Weatherford. 1987. 'How does government performance influence political support?' *Political Behavior* 9: 5–28; Kenneth Newton. 2006. 'Political support: Social capital, civil society and political and economic performance.' *Political Studies* 54(4): 846–864.

33. Harold D. Clarke, N. Dutt, and Alan Kornberg. 1993. 'The political-economy of attitudes toward polity and society in Western-European democracies.' *Journal of Politics* 55(4): 998–1021.

34. Ian McAllister. 1999. 'The economic performance of governments.' In Pippa Norris (Ed.). *Critical Citizens: Global Support for Democratic Governance.* New York: Oxford University Press.

35. Robert Z. Lawrence. 1997. 'Is it really the economy, stupid?' In Joseph Nye, Philip D. Zelikow, and David C. King (Eds.). *Why People Don't Trust Government.* Cambridge: Harvard University Press.

36. Charles F. Andrain and James T. Smith. 2006. *Political Democracy, Trust and Social Justice.* Boston: Northeastern University Press.

37. Derek Bok. 1997. 'Measuring the performance of government.' In Joseph Nye, Philip D. Zelikow and David C. King (Eds.). *Why People Don't Trust Government.* Cambridge: Harvard University Press; Edeltraud Roller. 2005. *The Performance of Democracies: Political Institutions and Public Policy.* Oxford: Oxford University Press.

38. Susan J. Pharr. 2000. 'Official misconduct and public distrust: Japan and the trilateral democracies.' In Susan J. Pharr and Robert D. Putnam (Eds.). *Disaffected Democracies: What's Troubling the Trilateral Countries?* Princeton, NJ: Princeton University Press; Leonardo Morlino and Marco Tarchi. 1996. 'The dissatisfied society: The roots of political change in Italy.' *European Journal of Political Research* 30(1): 41–63.

39. Robert Lawrence. 1997. 'Is it really the economy, stupid?' In Joseph S. Nye, Philip D. Zelikow, and David C. King (Eds.). *Why People Don't Trust Government.* Cambridge: Harvard University Press.

40. Edeltraud Roller. 2005. *The Performance of Democracies: Political Institutions and Public Policy.* Oxford: Oxford University Press.

41. See, for example, Gøsta Esping-Andersen. 1990. *The Three Worlds of Welfare Capitalism.* Cambridge: Cambridge University Press; Francis G. Castles, Ed. 1998.

Comparative Public Policy: Patterns of Post-War Transformation. Cheltenham: Edward Elgar; Edeltraud Roller. 2005. *The Performance of Democracies: Political Institutions and Public Policy*. Oxford: Oxford University Press; Jessica R. Adolino and Charles H. Blake. 2001. *Comparing Public Policies: Issues and Choices in Six Industrialized Countries*. Washington, DC: CQ Press.

42. See, for example, the literature review in E. Diener, E. M. Suh, R. E. Lucas, and H. L. Smith. 1999. 'Subjective well-being: Three decades of progress.' *Psychological Bulletin* 125(2): 276–302.

43. John F. Helliwell. 2003. 'How's life? Combining individual and national variables to explain subjective well-being.' *Economic Modelling* 20(2): 331–360; Ronald Inglehart, Roberto Foa, Christopher Peterson, and Christian Welzel. 2008. 'Development, freedom, and rising happiness: A global perspective (1981–2007).' *Perspectives on Psychological Science* 3(4): 264–285; Richard Eckersley. 2009. 'Population measures of subjective wellbeing: How useful are they?' *Social Indicators Research* 94(1): 1–12.

44. D. Kahneman, E. Diener, and N. Schwarz, Eds. 1999. *Well-being: The Foundations of Hedonic Psychology*. New York: Russell Sage Foundation.

45. The Pew Center on the People and the Press. 'What Americans Know 1989–2007.' people-press.org/reports/pdf/319.pdf.

46. John F. Helliwell. 2003. 'How's life? Combining individual and national variables to explain subjective well-being.' *Economic Modelling* 20(2): 331–360.

47. Christopher J. Anderson, Andre Blais, Shaun Bowler, Todd Donovan, and Ola Listhaug. 2005. *Losers' Consent: Elections and Democratic Legitimacy*. New York: Oxford University Press.

48. For a review of the extensive literature, see Rudy B. Andweg. 2000. 'Consociational democracy.' *Annual Review of Politics* 3: 509–536. For the development of alternative versions of this concept, see Gerhard Lehmbruch. 1967. *Proporzdemokratie. Politisches System und politische Kultur in der Schweiz und Osterreich*. Tubingen: Mohr; Jurg Steiner. 1974. *Amicable Agreement versus Majority Rule: Conflict Resolution in Switzerland*. Chapel Hill: University of North Carolina Press; Hans Daalder. 1974. 'The consociational democracy theme.' *World Politics* 26: 604–621; Kenneth McRae, Ed. 1974. *Consociational Democracy: Conflict Accommodation in Segmented Societies*. Toronto: McClelland and Stewart; Klaus Armingeon. 2002. 'The effects of negotiation democracy: A comparative analysis.' *European Journal of Political Research* 41: 81; Arend Lijphart. 2002. 'Negotiation democracy versus consensus democracy: Parallel conclusions and recommendations.' *European Journal of Political Research* 41(1): 107–113.

49. Pippa Norris. 2008. *Driving Democracy: Do Power-Sharing Institutions Work?* New York: Cambridge University Press.

50. Christopher J. Anderson. 1995. *Blaming the Government: Citizens and the Economy in Five European Democracies*. New York: M. E. Sharpe; Christopher J. Anderson and Christine A. Guillory. 1997. 'Political Institutions and Satisfaction with Democracy.' *American Political Science Review* 91(1): 66–81; Christopher J. Anderson, Andre Blais, Shaun Bowler, Todd Donovan, and Ola Listhaug. 2005. *Losers' Consent: Elections and Democratic Legitimacy*. New York: Oxford University Press.

51. Pippa Norris. 2008. *Driving Democracy: Do Power-Sharing Institutions Work?* New York: Cambridge University Press.

52. David Easton. 1975. 'A reassessment of the concept of political support.' *British Journal of Political Science,* 5: 435–457.

Chapter 11. The Consequences for Citizenship, Governance, and Democratization

1. Francis Fukuyama. 1989. 'The end of history?' *National Interest* (Summer); Francis Fukuyama. 1992. *The End of History and the Last Man.* New York: Free Press.
2. Arch Puddington. 2009. 'Freedom in the world 2009: Setbacks and resilience.' *Freedom in the World, 2009.* Washington, DC: Freedom House.
3. Larry Diamond. 2008. *The Spirit of Democracy: The Struggle to Build Free Societies throughout the World.* New York: Times Books.
4. Samuel P. Huntington. 1991. *The Third Wave: Democratization in the Late Twentieth Century.* Norman: University of Oklahoma Press.
5. Ethan B. Kapstein and Nathan Converse. 2008. *The Fate of Young Democracies.* New York: Cambridge University Press.
6. On the fall in turnout in post-industrial societies, see Mark Gray and Miki Caul. 2000. 'Declining voter turnout in advanced industrial democracies, 1950 to 1997.' *Comparative Political Studies* 33(9): 1091–1122.
7. On trends in party membership, see Peter Mair. 2001. 'Party membership in twenty European democracies 1980–2000.' *Party Politics* 7(1): 5–22; Susan Scarrow. 2001. 'Parties without members?' In Russell J. Dalton and Martin Wattenberg (Eds.). *Parties without Partisans.* New York: Oxford University Press.
8. For a summary of the partisan dealignment theory and evidence, see Russell J. Dalton and Martin Wattenberg, Eds. 2001. *Parties without Partisans.* New York: Oxford University Press.
9. C. Kerr. 1983. *The Future of Industrial Societies: Convergence or Continuing Diversity?* Cambridge, MA: Harvard University Press; L. Griffin, H. McCammon, and C. Bosko. 1990. 'The unmaking of a movement? The crisis of U.S. trade unions in comparative perspective.' In M. Hallinan, D. Klein, and J. Glass (Eds.). *Changes in Societal Institutions.* New York: Plenum. For the alternative view, however, that institutional arrangements affect levels of union density, see Bernhard Ebbinghaus and Jelle Visser. 1999. 'When institutions matter: Union growth and decline in Western Europe, 1950–1995.' *European Sociological Review* 15(2): 135–158; and also S. Blashke. 2000. 'Union density and European integration: Diverging convergence.' *European Journal of Industrial Relations* 6(2): 217–236.
10. Steve Bruce. 1996. *Religion in the Modern World: From Cathedrals to Cults.* Oxford: Oxford University Press; Sheena Ashford and Noel Timms. 1992. *What Europe Thinks: A Study of Western European Values.* Aldershot: Dartmouth; Wolfgang Jagodzinski and Karel Dobbelaere. 1995. 'Secularization and church religiosity.' In Jan W. van Deth and Elinor Scarbrough (Eds.). *The Impact of Values.* Oxford: Oxford University Press; L. Voye. 1999. 'Secularization in a context of advanced modernity.' *Sociology of Religion* 60(3): 275–288; Pippa Norris and Ronald Inglehart. 2004. *Sacred and Secular.* New York: Cambridge University Press. For the counter-argument, however, see Peter L. Berger, Ed. 1999. *The Desecularization of the World.* Washington, DC: Ethics and Public Policy Center; Rodney Stark. 1999. 'Secularization, RIP.' *Sociology of Religion* 60(3): 249–273.
11. For a discussion about the evidence for the diversity and complexity of trends in social capital across many post-industrial societies, see Robert Putnam, Ed. 2004.

The Dynamics of Social Capital. Oxford: Oxford University Press; Jan Willem van Deth, Ed. 1997. *Private Groups and Public Life: Social Participation, Voluntary Associations and Political Involvement in Representative Democracies.* London: Routledge; J. E. Curtis, E. G. Grabb, and D. E. Baer. 1992. 'Voluntary association membership in 15 countries – a comparative analysis.' *American Sociological Review* 57(2): 139–152; Laura Morales. 2009. *Joining Political Organizations: Institutions, Mobilization and Participation in Western Democracies.* Essex: ECPR Monographs.

12. Robert Putnam. 2000. *Bowling Alone.* New York: Simon and Schuster, p. 46.

13. See Eurobarometer 2008. http://ec.europa.eu/public_opinion.

14. See Sidney Verba and Norman Nie. 1972. *Participation in America: Political Democracy and Social Equality.* New York: Harper and Row; Sidney Verba, Norman Nie, and Jae-on Kim. 1978. *Participation and Political Equality: A Seven-Nation Comparison.* New York: Cambridge University Press; Sidney Verba, Kay Schlozman, and Henry E. Brady. 1995. *Voice and Equality: Civic Voluntarism in American Politics.* Cambridge: Harvard University Press; Pippa Norris. 1999. *Democratic Phoenix.* New York: Cambridge University Press.

15. Russell J. Dalton. 2004. *Democratic Challenges, Democratic Choices.* Oxford: Oxford University Press, p. 176.

16. Ted Robert Gurr. 1970. *Why Men Rebel.* Princeton, NJ: Princeton University Press.

17. Michel Crozier, Samuel P. Huntington, and Joji Watanuki. 1975. *The Crisis of Democracy: Report on the Governability of Democracies to the Trilateral Commission.* New York: New York University Press. See also Samuel P. Huntington. 1975. 'The democratic distemper.' *Public Interest* 41: 9–38.

18. Adam Roberts and Timothy Garton Ash. 2009. *Civil Resistance and Power Politics: The Experience of Non-violent Action from Gandhi to the Present.* Oxford: Oxford University Press. See also Daniel Drache. 2008. *Defiant Publics: The Unprecedented Reach of the Global Citizen.* Cambridge: Polity; Christian W. Haerpfer. 2008. 'Support for democracy and autocracy in Russia and the Commonwealth of Independent States, 1992–2002.' *International Political Science Review* 29(4): 411–431.

19. Pippa Norris, Stefaan Walgrave, and Peter Van Aelst. 2004. 'Who demonstrates? Anti-state rebels, conventional participants, or everyone?' *Comparative Politics* 37(2): 189–206.

20. Russell J. Dalton. 2004. *Democratic Challenges, Democratic Choices.* Oxford: Oxford University Press, p. 177.

21. Barbara G. Farah, Samuel H. Barnes, and Felix Heunis. 1979. 'Political dissatisfaction.' In Samuel H. Barnes and Max Kaase (Eds.). *Political Action: Mass Participation in Five Western Democracies.* Beverly Hills, CA: Sage.

22. Jacques Thomassen. 1990. 'Economic crisis, dissatisfaction and protest.' In M. Kent Jennings, Jan van Deth, et al. (Eds.). *Continuities in Political Action.* New York: Walter de Gruyter. See also R. Koopman. 1996. 'New social movements and changes in political participation in Western Europe.' *West European Politics* 19(1): 28–50.

23. Peter van Aelst, Stefaan Walgrave, and Kristof Decoster. 1999. 'Politiek wantrouwen en protest. Over het democratisch kapitaal van Belgische betogers.' *Tijdschrift voor Sociologie* 20: 441–470; Pippa Norris, Stefaan Walgrave, and Peter Van Aelst. 2004. 'Who demonstrates? Anti-state rebels, conventional participants,

or everyone?' *Comparative Politics* 37(2): 189–206; Pippa Norris, Stefaan Walgrave, and Peter van Aelst. 2006. 'Does protest signify disaffection? Demonstrators in a postindustrial democracy.' In Mariano Torcal and Jose Ramón Montero (Eds.). *Political Disaffection in Contemporary Democracies: Social Capital, Institutions and Politics*. London: Routledge, pp. 279–307.

24. John A. Booth and Mitchell A. Seligson. 2009. *The Legitimacy Puzzle in Latin America: Political Support and Democracy in Eight Nations*. New York: Cambridge University Press.

25. Pippa Norris, Stefaan Walgrave, and Peter Van Aelst. 2004. 'Who demonstrates? Anti-state rebels, conventional participants, or everyone?' *Comparative Politics* 37(2): 189–206.

26. Russell J. Dalton. 2004. *Democratic Challenges, Democratic Choices*. Oxford: Oxford University Press, p. 177.

27. David Easton. 1965. *A Framework for Political Analysis*. Englewood Cliffs, NJ: Prentice-Hall.

28. Pippa Norris. 1999. 'The growth of critical citizens and its consequences.' In Pippa Norris (Ed.). *Critical Citizens: Global Support for Democratic Governance*. New York: Oxford University Press; John T. Scholz and Mark Lubell. 1998. 'Trust and taxpaying: Testing the heuristic approach to collective action.' *American Journal of Political Science* 42: 398–417.

29. Russell J. Dalton. 2004. *Democratic Challenges, Democratic Choices*. Oxford: Oxford University Press, pp. 169–171.

30. Christopher J. Anderson and Yuliya V. Tverdova. 2003. 'Corruption, political allegiances, and attitudes toward government in contemporary democracies.' *American Journal of Political Science* 47(1): 91–109.

31. Tom R. Tyler. 1990. *Why People Obey the Law*. New Haven: Yale University Press; Brigitte Geissel. 2008. 'Do critical citizens foster better governance? A comparative study.' *West European Politics* 31(5): 855–873.

32. For a discussion, see Barbara Geddes. 1999. 'What do we know about democratization after twenty years?' *Annual Review of Political Science* 2: 115–144; Pippa Norris. 2008. *Driving Democracy*. Cambridge: Cambridge University Press.

33. Seymour Martin Lipset. 1959. 'Some social requisites of democracy: Economic development and political legitimacy.' *American Political Science Review* 53: 69–105.

34. Daron Acemoglu and J. A. Robinson. 2006. *Economic Origins of Dictatorship and Democracy*. New York: Cambridge University Press.

35. Arend Lijphart. 1969. 'Consociational democracy.' *World Politics* 21: 207–225; Arend Lijphart. 1975. *The Politics of Accommodation: Pluralism and Democracy in the Netherlands*. Berkeley: University of California Press; Arend Lijphart. 1999. *Patterns of Democracy: Government Forms and Performance in 36 Countries*. New Haven: Yale University Press; Arend Lijphart. 2008. *Thinking about Democracy: Power Sharing and Majority Rule in Theory and Practice*. New York: Routledge.

36. See Thomas Carothers. 1999. *Aiding Democracy Abroad*. Washington, DC: Carnegie Endowment for International Peace; J. Peter Burnell, Ed. 2000. *Democracy Assistance: International Co-Operation for Democratization*. London: Frank Cass; Jon C. Pevehouse. 2004. *Democracy from Above: Regional Organizations and Democratization*. New York: Cambridge University Press.

37. For the early classics, see Harry Eckstein. 1961. *A Theory of Stable Democracy*. Princeton, NJ: Woodrow Wilson Center, Princeton University; Gabriel A. Almond

and Sidney Verba. 1963. *The Civic Culture.* Princeton, NJ: Princeton University Press; Lucian Pye and Sidney Verba, Eds. 1965. *Political Culture and Political Development.* Princeton, NJ: Princeton University Press.

38. For the contemporary revival of cultural accounts of democratization, see, for example, Ronald Inglehart and Christian Welzel. 2005. *Modernization, Cultural Change, and Democracy: The Human Development Sequence.* New York: Cambridge University Press; Russell J. Dalton and Doh Chull Shin, Eds. 2006. *Citizens, Democracy and Markets around the Pacific Rim.* Oxford: Oxford University Press; Christian Welzel. 2007. 'Are levels of democracy affected by mass attitudes? Testing attainment and sustainment effects on democracy.' *International Political Science Review* 28(4): 397–424.

39. Harry Eckstein. 1961. *A Theory of Stable Democracy.* Princeton, NJ: Woodrow Wilson Center, Princeton University.

40. Nancy G. Bermeo. 2003. *Ordinary People in Extraordinary Times: The Citizenry and the Breakdown of Democracy.* Princeton, NJ: Princeton University Press.

41. Gabriel A. Almond and Sidney Verba. 1963. *The Civic Culture.* Princeton, NJ: Princeton University Press; Lucian Pye and Sidney Verba, Eds. 1965. *Political Culture and Political Development.* Princeton, NJ: Princeton University Press.

42. Harry Eckstein. 1961. *A Theory of Stable Democracy.* Princeton, NJ: Woodrow Wilson Center, Princeton University.

43. Seymour Martin Lipset. 1983. *Political Man: The Social Bases of Politics.* 2nd ed. London: Heinemann, p. 64. The concept of legitimacy is also discussed in Stephen M. Weatherford. 1992. 'Measuring political legitimacy.' *American Political Science Review* 86: 149–166; Bruce Gilley. 2006. 'The meaning and measure of state legitimacy: Results for 72 countries.' *European Journal of Political Research* 45: 499–525.

44. Garth S. Jowett and Victoria O'Donnell. 2006. *Propaganda and Persuasion.* 4th ed. Thousand Oaks, CA: Sage.

45. Nancy G. Bermeo. 2003. *Ordinary People in Extraordinary Times: The Citizenry and the Breakdown of Democracy.* Princeton, NJ: Princeton University Press. See also Richard Rose. 2008. *Understanding Post-communist Transformation: A Bottom Up Approach.* New York: Routledge.

46. Edward Mansfield and Jack Snyder. 2007. *Electing to Fight: Why Emerging Democracies Go to War.* Cambridge, MA: MIT Press.

47. John A. Booth and Mitchell A. Seligson. 2009. *The Legitimacy Puzzle in Latin America: Political Support and Democracy in Eight Nations.* New York: Cambridge University Press, Ch. 1.

48. Phillip Converse. 1964. 'The nature of belief systems in mass publics.' In David E. Apter (Ed.). *Ideology and Discontent.* New York: Free Press. See also Herbert McClosky and Laid Brill. 1983. *Dimensions of Tolerance: What Americans Believe about Civil Liberties.* New York: Russell Sage Foundation; Herbert McClosky and John Zaller. 1994. *The American Ethos: Public Attitudes towards Capitalism and Democracy.* Cambridge: Harvard University Press.

49. Herbert Hyman and Paul Sheatsley. 1954. 'The current status of American public opinion.' In Daniel Katz, Dorwin Cartwright, Samuel Eldersveld, and Alfred McClung Lee (Eds.). *Public Opinion and Propaganda.* New York: Holt, Rinehart and Winston.

50. Ronald Inglehart and Christian Welzel. 2005. *Modernization, Cultural Change, and Democracy: The Human Development Sequence.* New York: Cambridge University Press, pp. 182–183.

51. Joseph A. Schumpeter. 1950. *Capitalism, Socialism and Democracy.* 3rd ed. New York: Harper and Row.
52. Michael Alvarez, José Antonio Cheibub, Fernando Limongi, and Adam Przeworski. 1996. 'Classifying political regimes.' *Studies in International Comparative Development* 31: 3–36; Adam Przeworski, Michael E. Alvarez, Jose Antonio Cheibub, and Fernando Limongi. 2000. *Democracy and Development: Political Institutions and Well-Being in the World, 1950–1990.* New York: Cambridge University Press; Jose Cheibub and Jennifer Gandhi. 2005. 'A six-fold measure of democracies and dictatorships.' Unpublished paper. For a discussion of the virtues of adopting a minimalist conceptualization and measure, see Adam Przeworski. 1999. 'Minimalist conception of democracy: A defense.' In Ian Shapiro and Casiano Hacker-Cordon (Eds.). *Democracy's Value.* Cambridge: Cambridge University Press.
53. Zachary Elkins, Tom Gindburg, and James Melton. 2009. *The Endurance of National Constitutions.* New York: Cambridge University Press.
54. Seymour Martin Lipset. 1959. 'Some social requisites of democracy: Economic development and political legitimacy.' *American Political Science Review* 53: 69–105.
55. Marc J. Hetherington. 2004. *Why Trust Matters: Declining Political Trust and the Demise of American Liberalism.* Princeton, NJ: Princeton University Press; T. J. Rudolph and J. Evans. 2005. 'Political trust, ideology, and public support for government spending.' *American Journal of Political Science* 49(3): 660–671.
56. Pippa Norris. Forthcoming. 'Cultural explanations of electoral reform: A policy cycle model.' *West European Politics.*
57. Christian Welzel. 2007. 'Are levels of democracy affected by mass attitudes? Testing attainment and sustainment effects on democracy.' *International Political Science Review* 28(4): 397–424.

Chapter 12. Conclusions and Implications

1. Pippa Norris, Ed. 1999. *Critical Citizens: Global Support for Democratic Governance.* New York: Oxford University Press.
2. Gabriel A. Almond and Sidney Verba. 1963. *The Civic Culture.* Princeton, NJ: Princeton University Press; Lucian Pye and Sidney Verba, Eds. 1965. *Political Culture and Political Development.* Princeton, NJ: Princeton University Press.
3. Michel Crozier, Samuel P. Huntington, and Joji Watanuki. 1975. *The Crisis of Democracy: Report on the Governability of Democracies to the Trilateral Commission.* New York: New York University Press. See also Samuel P. Huntington. 1981. *American Politics: The Promise of Disharmony.* Cambridge: Harvard University Press.
4. For a discussion, see Pippa Norris. 2007. 'Political activism: New challenges, new opportunities.' In Carles Boix and Susan Stokes (Eds.). *The Oxford Handbook of Comparative Politics.* Oxford: Oxford University Press, pp. 628–652; Pippa Norris. 2009. 'Political activism.' In Paul Heywood (Ed.). *Developments in European Politics.* London: Palgrave Macmillan.
5. For the comparative literature, see Susan Pharr and Robert Putnam, Eds. 2000. *Disaffected Democracies: What's Troubling the Trilateral Countries?* Princeton, NJ: Princeton University Press; Russell J. Dalton. 2004. *Democratic Challenges, Democratic Choices: The Erosion of Political Support in Advanced Industrial Democracies.* New York: Oxford University Press; Mattei Dogan, Ed. 2005. *Political Mistrust and the Discrediting of Politicians.* The Netherlands: Brill; Mariano

Torcal and José R. Montero. 2006. *Political Disaffection in Contemporary Democracies: Social Capital, Institutions, and Politics.* London: Routledge. For the U.S. literature, see Joseph S. Nye, Philip D. Zelikow, and David C. King, Eds. 1997. *Why People Don't Trust Government.* Cambridge, MA: Harvard University Press; Robert D. Putnam. 2000. *Bowling Alone: The Collapse and Revival of American Community.* New York: Simon and Schuster; John R. Hibbing and Elizabeth Theiss-Morse, Eds. 2001. *What Is It about Government That Americans Dislike?* Cambridge: Cambridge University Press; Peter Wood. 2004. *A Bee in the Mouth: Anger in America Now.* New York: Encounter Books.

6. Russell J. Dalton. 2004. *Democratic Challenges, Democratic Choices: The Erosion of Political Support in Advanced Industrial Democracies.* New York: Oxford University Press, p. 191.

7. See, for example, the New York Times/CBS Poll February 2010. http://www.nytimes.com/2010/02/12/us/politics/12poll.html?ref=politics.

8. Gerry Stoker. 2006. *Why Politics Matters: Making Democracy Work.* London: Palgrave/Macmillan; Colin Hay. 2007. *Why We Hate Politics.* Cambridge: Polity Press; Michael Kenny. 2009. 'Taking the Temperature of the British Political Elite 3: When Grubby Is the Order of the Day.' *Parliamentary Affairs* 62(4): 663–672.

9. Hans Mathias Kepplinger. 2000. 'The declining image of the German political elite.' *Harvard International Journal of Press-Politics* 5(4): 71–80; Susan J. Pharr. 2000. 'Official misconduct and public distrust: Japan and the Trilateral democracies.' In Susan J. Pharr and Robert D. Putnam (Eds.). *Disaffected Democracies: What's Troubling the Trilateral Countries?* Princeton, NJ: Princeton University Press.

10. For reviews of some of these initiatives, see Bruce Cain, Russell J. Dalton, and Susan Scarrow, Eds. 2003. *Democracy Transformed? The Expansion of Political Access in Advanced Industrialized Democracies.* Oxford: Oxford University Press; Boaventura de Sousa Santos, Ed. 2007. *Democratizing Democracy: Beyond the Liberal Democratic Cannon.* London: Verso; Graham Smith. 2009. *Democratic Innovations: Designing Institutions for Citizen Participation.* New York: Cambridge University Press; Joan DeBardeleben and Jon H. Pammett, Eds. 2009. *Activating the Citizen: Dilemmas of Participation in Europe and Canada.* New York: Palgrave/Macmillan.

11. Christopher Hood and David Heald, Eds. 2006. *Transparency: The Key to Better Governance.* Oxford: Oxford University Press; Kristin M. Lord. 2007. *The Perils and Promise of Global Transparency: Why the Information Revolution May Not Lead to Security, Democracy, or Peace.* New York: SUNY Press; Ann Florini. 2007. *The Right to Know: Transparency for an Open World.* New York: Columbia University Press; John Keane. 2009. *The Life and Death of Democracy.* New York: W. W. Norton.

12. Michael Gallagher and Paul Mitchell, Eds. *The Politics of Electoral Systems.* Oxford: Oxford University Press; Joseph M. Colomer, Ed. 2004. *Handbook of Electoral System Choice.* New York: Palgrave Macmillan; Zachary Elkins, Tom Ginsburg, and James Melton. 2009. *The Endurance of National Constitutions.* New York: Cambridge University Press.

13. Larry Diamond. 2008. *The Spirit of Democracy: The Struggle to Build Free Societies Throughout the World.* New York: Times Books; Larry Diamond. 2008. 'The democratic rollback: The resurgence of the predatory state.' *Foreign Affairs* 87(2): 36–48.

14. Arch Puddington. 2009. 'Freedom in the world 2009: Setbacks and resilience.' *Freedom in the World, 2009*. Washington, DC: Freedom House.

15. Roderic Camp, Ed. 2001. *Citizen Views of Democracy in Latin America*. Pittsburgh: University of Pittsburgh Press; Marta Lagos. 2003. 'Support for and satisfaction with democracy.' *International Journal of Public Opinion Research* 15(4): 471–487; Marta Lagos. 2003. 'Public Opinion.' In Jorge I. Dominguez and Michael Shifter (Eds.). *Constructing Democratic Governance in Latin America*. Baltimore, MD: Johns Hopkins University Press; Rodolfo Sarsfield and F. Echegaray. 2006. 'Opening the black box: How satisfaction with democracy and its perceived efficacy affect regime preference in Latin America.' *International Journal of Public Opinion Research* 18(2): 153–173.

16. C. Graham and A. Sukhtankar. 2004. 'Does economic crisis reduce support for markets and democracy in Latin America? Some evidence from surveys of public opinion and well being.' *Journal of Latin American Studies* 36(2): 349–377; F. Panizza. 2005. 'Unarmed utopia revisited: The resurgence of left-of-centre politics in Latin America.' *Political Studies* 53(4): 716–734.

17. Robert Rotberg, Ed. 2007. *Worst of the Worst: Dealing with Repressive and Rogue Nations*. Washington, DC: Brookings Institution Press; Arch Puddington. 2010. 'Freedom in the world 2010: Erosion of freedom intensifies.' Freedom House. *Freedom in the World 2010*. www.freedomhouse.org.

18. Robert E. Bates. 2009. *When Things Fall Apart: State Failure in Late-century Africa*. Cambridge: Cambridge University Press.

19. Michael Bratton and Nicholas Van De Walle. 1997. *Democratic Experiments in Africa*. New York: Cambridge University Press.

20. Marina Ottoway and Thomas Caothers, Eds. 2005. *Uncharted Journey: Promoting Democracy in the Middle East*. Washington, DC: Carnegie; Marina Ottoway and Julia Choucair-Vizoso, Eds. 2008. *Beyond the Façade: Political Reform in the Arab World*. Washington, DC: Carnegie.

21. K. Dalacoura. 2005. 'US democracy promotion in the Arab Middle East since 11 September 2001: A critique.' *International Affairs* 81(5): 963–970; Thomas Carothers. 2006. 'The backlash against democracy promotion.' *Foreign Affairs* 85(2): 55–68.

22. Michael McFaul. 2005. 'Transitions from postcommunism.' *Journal of Democracy* 16: 5–19; Gerhard Simon. 2006. 'An orange-tinged revolution – The Ukrainian path to democracy.' *Russian Politics and Law* 44(2): 5–27; P. D'Anieri. 2005. 'What has changed in Ukrainian politics? Assessing the implications of the Orange Revolution.' *Problems of Post-Communism* 52(5): 82–91; Robert K. Christensen, Edward R. Rakhimkulov, and Charles R. Wise. 2005. 'The Ukrainian Orange Revolution brought more than a new president: What kind of democracy will the institutional changes bring?' *Communist and Post-Communist Studies* 38(2): 207–230; Charles Fairbanks, Jr. 2007. 'Revolution reconsidered.' *Journal of Democracy* 18(1): 42–56.

23. Adam Roberts and Timothy Garton Ash. 2009. *Civil Resistance and Power Politics: The Experience of Non-violent Action from Gandhi to the Present*. Oxford: Oxford University Press.

24. Thomas Carothers. 2009. 'Democracy Promotion under Obama: Finding a Way Forward.' *Carnegie Foundation Policy Brief* 77 (February 2009). http://www.carnegieendowment.org/files/democracy_promotion_obama.pdf.

25. Harry Eckstein. 1961. *A Theory of Stable Democracy*. Princeton, NJ: Woodrow Wilson Center, Princeton University.

26. Pippa Norris. 2008. *Driving Democracy*. New York: Cambridge University Press.
27. Stephen M. Weatherford. 1992. 'Measuring political legitimacy.' *American Political Science Review* 86: 149–166.
28. The World Bank. 2009. 'Swimming against the tide: How developing countries are coping with the global crisis.' Background Paper prepared by World Bank Staff for the G20 Finance Ministers and Central Bank Governors Meeting, Horsham, United Kingdom on March 13–14, 2009.
29. United Nations. 2008. *The Millennium Development Goals Report 2008*. New York: United Nations; Paul Collier. 2007. *The Bottom Billion*. New York/Oxford: Oxford University Press.
30. Michael Doyle and Nicholas Sambanis. 2006. *Making War and Building Peace*. Princeton, NJ: Princeton University Press.
31. Similar conclusions were reached in the review of the literature by Margaret Levi and Laura Stoker. 2000. 'Political trust and trustworthiness.' *Annual Review of Political Science* 3: 475–508.
32. Ronald Inglehart and Christian Welzel. 2005. *Modernization, Cultural Change, and Democracy: The Human Development Sequence*. New York: Cambridge University Press; Robert D. Putnam. 2000. *Bowling Alone: The Collapse and Revival of American Community*. New York: Simon and Schuster; Russell J. Dalton. 2004. *Democratic Challenges, Democratic Choices: The Erosion of Political Support in Advanced Industrial Democracies*. New York: Oxford University Press.
33. Russell J. Dalton. 2004. *Democratic Challenges, Democratic Choices: The Erosion of Political Support in Advanced Industrial Democracies*. New York: Oxford University Press.
34. Mark E. Warren, Ed. 1999. *Democracy and Trust*. New York: Cambridge University Press; Russell Hardin, Ed. 2004. *Trust and Trustworthiness*. New York: Russell Sage Foundation.

Technical Appendix C. Methods

1. Robert Bickel. 2007. *Multilevel Analysis for Applied Research: It's Just Regression!* New York: Guilford Press.
2. Stephen W. Raudenbush and Anthony S. Bryk. 2002. *Hierarchical Linear Models*. 2nd ed. Thousand Oaks, CA: Sage; Andrew Gelman and Jennifer Hill. 2007. *Data Analysis Using Regression and Multilevel/Hierarchical Models*. New York: Cambridge University Press.

Selected Bibliography

Aarts, Kees. 1995. 'Intermediate organizations and interest representation.' In *Citizens and the State*, ed. Hans-Dieter Klingemann. Oxford: Oxford University Press.

Aarts, Kees and Jacques Thomassen. 2008. 'Satisfaction with democracy: Do institutions matter?' *Electoral Studies* 27(1): 5–18.

Abramson, Paul R. 1983. *Political Attitudes in America: Formation and Change*. San Francisco: W. H. Freeman.

Abramson, Paul R. and Ada W. Finifter. 1981. 'On the meaning of political trust: New evidence from items introduced in 1978.' *American Journal of Political Science* 25(2): 297–307.

Abramson, Paul R. and Ronald Inglehart. 1995. *Value Change in Global Perspective*. Ann Arbor: University of Michigan Press.

Almond, Gabriel A. 1980. 'The intellectual history of the civic culture concept.' In *The Civic Culture Revisited*, ed. Gabriel A. Almond and Sidney Verba. Boston: Little, Brown, pp. 1–36.

Almond, Gabriel A. 1983. 'Communism and political culture theory.' *Comparative Politics* 15: 127–138.

Almond, Gabriel A. 1993. 'Forward: The return to political culture.' In *Political Culture and Democracy in Developing Countries*, ed. Larry Diamond. Boulder, CO: Lynne Rienner, pp. ix–xii.

Almond, Gabriel A. and G. Bingham Powell. 1978. *Comparative Politics: System, Process, and Policy*. Boston: Little, Brown.

Almond, Gabriel A. and Sidney Verba. 1963. *The Civic Culture: Political Attitudes and Democracy in Five Nations*. Princeton: Princeton University Press.

Anderson, Christopher J. 1995. *Blaming the Government: Citizens and the Economy in Five European Democracies*. New York: M. E. Sharpe.

Anderson, Christopher J. 1998. 'Parties, party systems, and satisfaction with democratic performance in the new Europe.' *Political Studies* 46: 572–588.

Anderson, Christopher J., Andre Blais, Shaun Bowler, Todd Donovan, and Ola Listhaug. 2005. *Losers' Consent: Elections and Democratic Legitimacy*. New York: Oxford University Press.

Anderson, Christopher J. and Christine A. Guillory. 1997. 'Political institutions and satisfaction with democracy.' *American Political Science Review* 91(1): 66–81.

Anderson, Christopher J. and Andrew J. Lotempio. 2002. 'Winning, losing and political trust in America.' *British Journal of Political Science* 32(2): 335–351.

Anderson, Christopher J. and Yuliya V. Tverdova. 2003. 'Corruption, political allegiances, and attitudes toward government in contemporary democracies.' *American Journal of Political Science* 47(1): 91–109.

Anderson, Christopher J. and Y. V. Tverdova. 2001. 'Winners, losers, and attitudes about government in contemporary democracies.' *International Political Science Review* 22: 321–338.

Andrain, Charles F. and James T. Smith. 2006. *Political Democracy, Trust and Social Justice: A Comparative Overview*. Boston: Northeastern University Press.

Avery, James M. 2009. 'Videomalaise or virtuous circle? The influence of the news media on political trust.' *International Journal of Press-Politics* 14(4): 410–433.

Banducci, Susan A. and Jeff A. Karp. 2003. 'How elections change the way citizens view the political system: Campaigns, media effects and electoral outcomes in comparative perspective.' *British Journal of Political Science* 33(3): 443–467.

Barber, Benjamin. 1984. *Strong Democracy*. Berkeley: University of California Press.

Barnes, Samuel and Max Kaase. 1979. *Political Action: Mass Participation in Five Western Democracies*. Beverly Hills: Sage.

Basanez, Miguel, Ronald Inglehart, and Alejandro Moreno. 1998. *Human Values and Beliefs: A Cross Cultural Sourcebook*. Ann Arbor: University of Michigan Press.

Beetham, David. 1994. *Defining and Measuring Democracy*. London: Sage.

Bellah, Robert, Richard Madsen, William M. Sullivan, Ann Swindler, and Steven M. Tipton. 1985. *Habits of the Heart: Individualism and Commitment in American Life*. Berkeley: University of California Press.

Bennett, Stephen Earl. 2001. 'Were the halcyon days really golden? An analysis of Americans' attitudes about the political System, 1945–1965.' In *What Is It about Government That Americans Dislike?* ed. John R. Hibbing and Elizabeth Theiss-Morse. Cambridge: Cambridge University Press, pp. 47–58.

Bermeo, Nancy G. 2003. *Ordinary People in Extraordinary Times: The Citizenry and the Breakdown of Democracy*. Princeton, NJ: Princeton University Press.

Bianco, William T. 1994. *Trust: Representatives and Constituents*. Ann Arbor: University of Michigan Press.

Biezen, Ingrid van, Peter Mair, and Thomas Poguntke. 2009. 'Going, Going, . . . Gone? Party Membership in the 21st Century.' Paper presented at the Joint Workshops at the European Consortium for Political Research, Lisbon.

Birch, Anthony H. 1984. 'Overload, ungovernability and delegitimation: The theories and the British case.' *British Journal of Political Science* 14: 135–60.

Bishin, B. G., R. R. Barr, and M. J. Lebo. 2006. 'The impact of economic versus institutional factors in elite evaluation of presidential progress toward democracy in Latin America.' *Comparative Political Studies* 39(10): 1194–1219.

Blais, André and F. Gelineau. 2007. 'Winning, losing and satisfaction with democracy.' *Political Studies* 55: 425–441.

Blendon, Robert, John M. Benson, Richard Morin, Drew E. Altman, Mollyann Brodie, Mario Brossard, and Matt James. 1997. 'Changing attitudes in America.' In *Why People Don't Trust Government*, ed. Joseph Nye, Philip Zelikow, and David King. Cambridge: Harvard University Press.

Bobbio, Norberto. 1987. *The Future of Democracy: A Defence of the Rules of the Game*. Minneapolis: University of Minnesota Press.

Bok, Derek. 1997. 'Measuring the performance of government.' In *Why People Don't Trust Government*, ed. Joseph Nye, Philip D. Zelikow, and David C. King. Cambridge: Harvard University Press.

Bollen, Kenneth. 1993. 'Liberal democracy: Validity and method factors in cross-national measures.' *American Sociological Review* 54: 612–621.

Booth, John A. and Mitchell A. Seligson. 1994. 'Paths to democracy and the political culture of Costa Rica, Mexico and Nicaragua.' In *Political Culture and Democracy in Developing Countries*, ed. Larry Diamond. Boulder, CO: Lynne Rienner.

Booth, John A. and Mitchell A. Seligson. 2009. *The Legitimacy Puzzle in Latin America: Political Support and Democracy in Eight Nations*. New York: Cambridge University Press.

Bourdieu, Pierre. 1970. *Reproduction in Education, Culture and Society*. London: Sage.

Bovens, Mark and Anchrit Wille. 2008. 'Deciphering the Dutch drop: Ten explanations for decreasing political trust in the Netherlands.' *International Review of Administrative Sciences* 74: 283–305.

Bowler, Shaun and Todd Donovan. 2002. 'Democracy, institutions and attitudes about citizen influence on government.' *British Journal of Political Science* 32: 371–390.

Braithwaite, Valerie and Margaret Levi (Eds.). 2003. *Trust and Governance*. New York: Russell Sage Foundation.

Bratton, Michael and Robert Mattes. 2001. 'Support for democracy in Africa: Intrinsic or instrumental?' *British Journal of Political Science* 31(3): 447–474.

Bratton, Michael, Robert Mattes, and E. Gyimah-Boadi. 2004. *Public Opinion, Democracy, and Market Reform in Africa*. Cambridge: Cambridge University Press.

Bratton, Michael and Nicholas Van De Walle. 1997. *Democratic Experiments in Africa*. New York: Cambridge University Press.

Brehm, John and Wendy Rahn. 1997. 'Individual-level evidence for the causes and consequences of social capital.' *American Journal of Political Science* 41(3): 999–1023.

Cain, Bruce, Russell J. Dalton, and Susan Scarrow (Eds.). 2003. *Democracy Transformed? The Expansion of Political Access in Advanced Industrialized Democracies*. Oxford: Oxford University Press.

Camp, Roderic (Ed.). 2001. *Citizen Views of Democracy in Latin America*. Pittsburgh: University of Pittsburgh Press.

Canache, Damarys, Jeffrey J. Mondak, and Mitchell A. Seligson. 2001. 'Meaning and measurement in cross-national research on satisfaction with democracy.' *Public Opinion Quarterly* 65: 506–528.

Cappella, Joseph N., and Kathleen H. Jamieson. 1997. *Spiral of Cynicism*. New York: Oxford University Press.

Carothers, Thomas. 2009. 'Democracy promotion under Obama: Finding a way forward.' *Carnegie Foundation Policy Brief* 77 (February).

Catterberg, Gabriela and Alejandro Moreno. 2006. 'The individual bases of political trust: Trends in new and established democracies.' *International Journal of Public Opinion Research* 18(1): 31–48.

Chaney, Virginia A. 2002. 'Trust in government in the aftermath of 9/11: Determinants and consequences.' *Political Psychology* 23(3): 469–483.

Chaney, Virgina A., Thomas J. Rudolph, and Wendy M. Rahn. 2000. 'The origins and consequences of public trust in government: A time series analysis.' *Public Opinion Quarterly* 64: 239–256.

Chong, Dennis, Herbert McClosky, and John Zaller. 1983. 'Patterns of support for democratic and capitalist values in the United States.' *British Journal of Political Science* 13(4): 401–440.

Chu, Yun-han, Larry Diamond, Andrew J. Nathan, and Doh Chull Shin (Eds.). 2008. *How East Asians View Democracy*. New York: Columbia University Press.

Churchill, Winston. 1947. House of Commons. *Hansard*, 11 November, col. 206.

Citrin, Jack. 1974. 'Comment: The political relevance of trust in government.' *American Political Science Review* 68: 973–988.

Citrin, Jack and Donald Green. 1986. 'Presidential leadership and trust in government.' *British Journal of Political Science* 16: 431–453.

Citrin, Jack and Samantha Luks. 2001. 'Political trust revisited: Déjà vu all over again?' In *What Is It about Government That Americans Dislike?* ed. John R. Hibbing and Elizabeth Theiss-Morse. Cambridge: Cambridge University Press, pp. 9–27.

Clarke, Harold D., Nitish Dutt, and Allan Kornberg. 1993. 'The political economy of attitudes toward polity and society in Western European democracies.' *Journal of Politics* 55(4): 998–1021.

Clarke, Harold D., Euel W. Elliott, William Mishler, Marianne C. Stewart, Paul F. Whiteley, and Gary Zuk. 1992. *Controversies in Political Economy*. Boulder, CO: Westview Press.

Clarke, Harold D. and Allan Kornberg. 1989. 'Public reactions to economic performance and political support in contemporary liberal democracies.' In *Economic Decline and Political Change: Canada, Great Britain, the United States*, ed. Harold Clarke et al. Pittsburgh: University of Pittsburgh Press.

Clarke, Harold D. and Marianne Stewart. 1995. 'Economic evaluations, prime ministerial approval and governing party support: Rival models considered.' *British Journal of Political Science* 25(2): 145–170.

Coleman, James S. 1988. 'Social capital in the creation of human capital.' *American Journal of Sociology* 94: 95–120.

Coleman, James S. 1990. *Foundations of Social Theory*. Cambridge: Belknap.

Conover, Pamela Johnston, Stanley Feldman, and Kathleen Knight. 1986. 'Judging inflation and unemployment: The origins of retrospective evaluations.' *Journal of Politics* 48: 565–588.

Conradt, David P. 1980. 'The changing German political culture.' In *The Civic Culture Revisited*, ed. Gabriel A. Almond and Sidney Verba. Boston: Little, Brown.

Conradt, David P. 1991. 'From output orientation to regime support: Changing German political culture.' In *Social and Political Structures in West Germany: From Authoritarianism to Postindustrial Democracy*, ed. Ursula Hoffmann-Lange. Boulder, CO: Westview Press, pp. 127–142.

Converse, Phillip E. 1964. 'The nature of belief systems in mass publics.' In *Ideology and Discontent*, ed. David E. Apter. New York: Free Press.

Cook, Timothy E. and Paul Gronke. 2005. 'The skeptical American: Revisiting the meanings of trust in government and confidence in institutions.' *Journal of Politics* 67: 784–803.

Coppedge, Michael and Wolfgang Reinicke. 1990. 'Measuring polyarchy.' *Studies in Comparative International Development*, 25: 51–72.

Cox, Gary W. 1997. *Making Votes Count*. New York: Cambridge University Press.

Craig, Stephen C. 1993. *The Malevolent Leaders: Popular Discontent in America*. Boulder, CO: Westview Press.

Craig, Stephen C. 1996. *Broken Contracts: Changing Relationships between Americans and Their Government.* Boulder, CO: Westview Press.

Craig, Stephen C. and Michael A. Maggiotto. 1981. 'Political discontent and political action.' *Journal of Politics* 43: 514–522.

Criado, Henar and Francisco Herreros. 2007. 'Political support taking into account the institutional context.' *Comparative Political Studies* 40(2): 1511–1532.

Crozier, Michel, Samuel P. Huntington, and Joji Watanuki. 1975. *The Crisis of Democracy: Report on the Governability of Democracies to the Trilateral Commission.* New York: New York University Press.

Curtice, John and Roger Jowell. 1995. 'The skeptical electorate.' In *British Social Attitudes: The 12th Report,* ed. Roger Jowell et al. Aldershot: Ashgate, pp. 140–172.

Curtice, John and Roger Jowell. 1997. 'Trust in the political system.' In *British Social Attitudes: The 14th Report,* ed. Roger Jowell et al. Aldershot: Ashgate.

Dahl, Robert A. 1971. *Polyarchy: Participation and Opposition.* New Haven: Yale University Press.

Dahl, Robert A. 1989. *Democracy and Its Critics.* New Haven: Yale University Press.

Dalton, Russell J. 1994. 'Communists and democrats: Democratic attitudes in the two Germanies.' *British Journal of Political Science* 24: 469–493.

Dalton, Russell J. 2004. *Democratic Challenges, Democratic Choices: The Erosion of Political Support in Advanced Industrial Democracies.* New York: Oxford University Press.

Dalton, Russell J. 2007. *Citizen Politics: Public Opinion and Political Parties in Advanced Western Democracies.* Washington, DC: CQ Press.

Dalton, Russell J. and Doh Chull Shin (Eds.). 2006. *Citizens, Democracy and Markets around the Pacific Rim.* Oxford: Oxford University Press.

Dalton, Russell J., Scott C. Flanagan, Paul A. Beck, and James E. Alt. 1984. *Electoral Change in Advanced Industrial Democracies: Realignment or Dealignment?* Princeton: Princeton University Press.

Dalton, Russell J. and Manfred Kuechler (Eds.). 1990. *Challenging the Political Order: New Social and Political Movements in Western Democracies.* New York: Oxford University Press.

Dalton, Russell J. and Martin P. Wattenberg (Eds.). 2002. *Parties without Partisans: Political Change in Advanced Industrial Democracies.* Oxford: Oxford University Press.

Davids, Y. D. and A. Hadland. 2008. 'Satisfaction with the way democracy is working in Post-Apartheid South Africa.' *Politikon* 35(3): 277–291.

de Tocqueville, Alexis. 1956. *Democracy in America.* New York: Anchor Books.

de Vreese, Claes H. 2005. 'The spiral of cynicism reconsidered.' *European Journal of Communication* 20(3): 283–301.

Delhey, Jan and Kenneth Newton. 2005. 'Predicting cross-national levels of social trust: Global pattern or Nordic exceptionalism?' *European Sociological Review* 21(4): 311–327.

Delli-Carpini, Michael, and Scott Keeter. 1997. *What Americans Know about Politics and Why It Matters.* New Haven, CT: Yale University Press.

Deth, Jan van, Jose R. Montero, and Anders Westholm (Eds.). 2006. *Citizenship and Involvement in European Democracies: A Comparative Perspective.* London: Routledge.

Diamond, Larry. 1994. *Political Culture and Democracy in Developing Countries.* Boulder, CO: Lynne Rienner.

Diamond, Larry. 1996. 'Is the third wave over?' *Journal of Democracy* 7(3): 20–27.

Diamond, Larry. 2002. 'Thinking about hybrid regimes.' *Journal of Democracy* 13(2): 21–35.

Diamond, Larry. 2008. *The Spirit of Democracy: The Struggle to Build Free Societies throughout the World*. New York: Times Books.

Diamond, Larry J., Juan J. Linz, and Seymour M. Lipset. 1995. *Politics in Developing Countries: Comparing Experiences with Democracy*. 2nd ed. Boulder, CO: Lynne Rienner.

Diamond, Larry and Marc F. Plattner. 2008. *How People View Democracy*. Baltimore: Johns Hopkins University Press.

Diamond, Larry J., Marc F. Plattner, and Yun-han T. H. Chu. 1997. *Consolidating the Third Wave Democracies*. Baltimore: Johns Hopkins University Press.

Dionne, E. J., Jr. 1991. *Why Americans Hate Politics*. New York: Simon and Schuster.

Dogan, Mattei (Ed.). 2005. *Political Mistrust and the Discrediting of Politicians*. The Netherlands: Brill.

Downs, Anthony. 1957. *An Economic Theory of Democracy*. New York: Harper and Row.

Drache, Daniel. 2008. *Defiant Publics: The Unprecedented Reach of the Global Citizen*. Cambridge: Polity.

Duch, Raymond M. 1993. 'Tolerating economic reform: Popular support for transition to a free market in the former Soviet Union.' *American Political Science Review* 87(3): 590–608.

Duverger, Maurice. 1969. *Partis Politiques*. 3rd ed. Translated by Barbara and Robert North. London: Methuen.

Easton, David. 1965. *A Framework for Political Analysis*. Englewood Cliffs, NJ: Prentice-Hall.

Easton, David. 1965. *A Systems Analysis of Political Life*. New York: Wiley.

Easton, David. 1975. 'A reassessment of the concept of political support.' *British Journal of Political Science*, 5: 435–457.

Easton, David and Jack Dennis. 1969. *Children in the Political System: Origins of Political Legitimacy*. New York: McGraw-Hill.

Eckersley, Richard. 2009. 'Population measures of subjective wellbeing: How useful are they?' *Social Indicators Research* 94(1): 1–12.

Eckstein, Harry. 1961. *A Theory of Stable Democracy*. Princeton, NJ: Woodrow Wilson Center, Princeton University.

Eckstein, Harry. 1988. 'A culturalist theory of political change.' *American Political Science Review* 82: 789–804.

Elazar, Daniel J. 1997. 'Contrasting unitary and federal systems.' *International Political Science Review* 18(3): 237–251.

Elkins, Zachary, Tom Ginsburg, and James Melton. 2009. *The Endurance of National Constitutions*. New York: Cambridge University Press.

Emmerson, Donald. 1995. 'Singapore and the "Asian Values" Debate.' *Journal of Democracy* 6(4): 95–105.

Ester, Peter, Loek Halman, and Ruud deMoor. 1993. *The Individualizing Society*. Tilburg: Tilburg University Press.

Evans, Geoffrey and Stephen Whitefield. 1995. 'The politics and economics of democratic commitment: Support for democracy in transition societies.' *British Journal of Political Science* 25(4): 485–513.

Fallows, James. 1996. *Breaking the News: How the Media Undermine American Democracy*. New York: Pantheon.

Farah, Barbara G., Samuel H. Barnes, and Felix Heunis. 1979. 'Political dissatisfaction.' In *Political Action: Mass Participation in Five Western Democracies*, ed. Samuel H. Barnes and Max Kaase. Beverly Hills, CA: Sage.

Finifter, Ada W. 1970. 'Dimensions of political alienation.' *American Political Science Review* 64(2): 389–410.

Finke, Steven E., Edward N. Muller, and Mitchell A. Seligson. 1987. 'Economic crisis, incumbent performance and regime support.' *British Journal of Political Science* 19: 329–351.

Foley, Michael W. and Robert Edwards. 1997. 'Escape from politics? Social theory and the social capital debate.' *American Behavioral Scientist* 40(5): 550–561.

Fox Piven, Frances and Richard Cloward. 1988. *Why Americans Don't Vote*. New York: Pantheon.

Franklin, Mark, Tom Mackie, and Henry Valen. 1992. *Electoral Change: Responses to Evolving Social and Attitudinal Structures in Western Countries*. New York: Cambridge University Press.

Freedom House. 2009. *Freedom in the World: The Annual Survey of Political Rights and Civil Liberties*. New York: Freedom House.

Fuchs, Dieter. 1993. 'Trends of political support in the Federal Republic of Germany.' In *Political Culture in Germany*, ed. Dirk Berg-Schlosser and Ralf Rytlewski. London: Macmillan, pp. 232–268.

Fuchs, Dieter. 1999. 'The democratic culture of unified Germany.' In *Critical Citizens: Global Support for Democratic Governance*, ed. Pippa Norris. Oxford: Oxford University Press.

Fuchs, Dieter, Giovanna Guidorossi, and Palle Svensson. 1995. 'Support for the democratic system.' In *Citizens and the State*, ed. Hans-Dieter Klingemann and Dieter Fuchs. Oxford: Oxford University Press.

Fuchs, Dieter and Hans-Dieter Klingemann. 1995. 'Citizens and the state: A relationship transformed.' In *Citizens and the State*, ed. Hans-Dieter Klingemann and Dieter Fuchs. Oxford: Oxford University Press.

Fuchs, Dieter and Edeltraud Roller. 1998. 'Cultural conditions of the transformation to liberal democracies in Central and Eastern Europe.' In *Post-Communist Publics*, ed. Laszlo Bruzst, János Simon, and Samuel H. Barnes. Budapest: Ungarische Akademie der Wissenschaften.

Fukuyama, Francis. 1991. *The End of History and the Last Man*. New York: Free Press.

Fukuyama, Francis. 1995. *Trust: The Social Virtues and the Creation of Prosperity*. New York: Free Press.

Gamson, William. 1968. *Power and Discontent*. Homewood: Dorsey Press.

Garment, Suzanne. 1991. *Scandal: The Crisis of Mistrust in American Politics*. New York: Random House.

Geissel, Brigitte. 2008. 'Do critical citizens foster better governance? A comparative study.' *West European Politics* 31(5): 855–873.

Geissel, Brigette. 2008. 'Reflections and findings on the critical citizen: Civic education – What for?' *European Journal of Political Research* 47(1): 34–63.

Gibson, James L., Raymond M. Duch, and Kent L. Tedin. 1992. 'Democratic values and the transformation of the Soviet Union.' *Journal of Politics* 54(2): 329–371.

Gilley, Bruce. 2006. 'The meaning and measure of state legitimacy: Results for 72 countries.' *European Journal of Political Research* 45: 499–525.

Grimes, M. 2006. 'Organizing consent: The role of procedural fairness in political trust and compliance.' *European Journal of Political Research* 45(2): 285–315.

Groeling, Tim and Matthew A. Baum. 2008. 'Crossing the water's edge: Elite rhetoric, media coverage, and the rally-round-the-flag phenomenon.' *Journal of Politics* 70(4): 1065–1085.

Gross, Kimberly, Paul R. Brewer, and Sean Aday. 2001. 'Confidence in government and emotional responses to terrorism after September 11, 2001.' *American Politics Review* 37(1): 107–128.

Gunther, Richard, P. Nikiforos Diamandouros, and Hans-Jürgen Puhle (Eds.). 1995. *The Politics of Democratic Consolidation: Southern Europe in Comparative Perspective*. Baltimore: Johns Hopkins University Press.

Gurr, Ted. 1971. *Why Men Rebel*. Princeton: Princeton University Press.

Hadenius, Axel. 1994. 'The duration of democracy.' In *Defining and Measuring Democracy*, ed. David Beetham. London: Sage.

Hadenius, Axel (Ed.). 1997. *Democracy's Victory and Crisis*. Cambridge: Cambridge University Press.

Hadenius, Axel and Jan Teorell. 2005. 'Cultural and economic prerequisites of democracy: Reassessing recent evidence.' *Studies in Comparative International Development* 39(4): 87–106.

Haerpfer, Christian W. 2008. 'Support for democracy and autocracy in Russia and the Commonwealth of Independent States, 1992–2002.' *International Political Science Review* 29(4): 411–431.

Haerpfer, Christian W., Patrick Bernhagen, Ronald F. Inglehart, and Christian Welzel. 2009. *Democratization*. Oxford: Oxford University Press.

Haller M., and R. Ressler. 2006. 'National and European identity: A study of their meanings and interrelationships.' *Revue Francaise de Sociologie* 47(4): 817–+.

Hardin, Russell. 1996. 'Trustworthiness.' *Ethics* 107: 26–42.

Hardin, Russell. 1999. 'Do we want trust in government?' In *Democracy and Trust*, ed. Mark E. Warren. Cambridge: Cambridge University Press, pp. 22–41.

Hardin, Russell (Ed.). 2004. *Trust and Trustworthiness*. New York: Russell Sage Foundation.

Hardin, Russell. 2006. *Trust*. Cambridge: Polity.

Harmel, Robert and John D. Robertson. 1986. 'Government stability and regime support: A cross-national analysis.' *Journal of Politics* 48: 1029–1040.

Hart, Roderick. 1994. *Seducing America*. New York: Oxford University Press.

Hay, Colin. 2007. *Why We Hate Politics*. Cambridge: Polity Press.

Hayward, Jack. 1995. *The Crisis of Representation in Europe*. London: Frank Cass.

Held, David. 1987. *Models of Democracy*. Stanford: Stanford University Press.

Hetherington, Marc J. 1998. 'The political relevance of political trust.' *American Political Science Review* 92(4): 791–808.

Hetherington, Marc J. 2005. *Why Trust Matters*. Princeton, NJ: Princeton University Press.

Hetherington, Marc J. and Thomas J. Rudolph. 2008. 'Priming, performance and the dynamics of political trust.' *Journal of Politics* 70(2): 498–512.

Hibbing, John R. and Elizabeth Theiss-Morse. 1995. *Congress as Public Enemy*. New York: Cambridge University Press.

Hibbing, John R., and Elizabeth Theiss-Morse (Eds.). 2001. *What Is It about Government That Americans Dislike?* Cambridge: Cambridge University Press.

Hibbing, John R. and Elizabeth Theiss-Morse. 2002. *Stealth Democracy: Americans' Beliefs about How Government Should Work*. New York: Cambridge University Press.

Hirschman, Albert O. 1970. *Exit, Voice and Loyalty*. Cambridge: Harvard University Press.

Hofferbert, Richard I. and Hans-Dieter Klingemann. 2001. 'Democracy and its discontents in post-wall Germany.' *International Political Science Review* 22(4): 363–378.

Huang, Min-Hua, Yu-tzung Chang, and Yun-han Chu. 2008. 'Identifying sources of democratic legitimacy: A multilevel analysis.' *Electoral Studies* 27(1): 45–62.

Huntington, Samuel P. 1975. 'The democratic distemper.' *Public Interest* 41: 9–38.

Huntington, Samuel. 1981. *American Politics: The Promise of Disharmony*. Cambridge: Harvard University Press.

Huntington, Samuel P. 1991. *The Third Wave: Democratization in the Late Twentieth Century*. Norman: University of Oklahoma Press.

IDEA. 1997. *The International IDEA Handbook of Electoral System Design*. Stockholm: International Institute for Democracy and Electoral Assistance.

IDEA. 2002. *Voter Turnout since 1945: A Global Report*. Stockholm: International Institute for Democracy and Electoral Assistance.

Inglehart, Ronald. 1977. *The Silent Revolution: Changing Values and Political Styles among Western Publics*. Princeton: Princeton University Press.

Inglehart, Ronald. 1990. *Culture Shift in Advanced Industrial Society*. Princeton: Princeton University Press.

Inglehart, Ronald. 1997. 'The erosion of institutional authority and post-materialist values.' In *Why Americans Mistrust Government*, ed. Joseph S. Nye, Philip D. Zelikow, and David C. King. Cambridge: Harvard University Press.

Inglehart, Ronald. 1997. *Modernization and Postmodernization: Cultural, Economic and Political Change in 43 Societies*. Princeton: Princeton University Press.

Inglehart, Ronald. 2003. 'How solid is mass support for democracy: And how do we measure it?' *PS: Political Science and Politics* 36(1): 51–57.

Inglehart, Ronald and Paul Abramson. 1994. 'Economic security and value change.' *American Political Science Review* 88: 336–354.

Inglehart, Ronald and Gabriela Catterberg. 2002. 'Trends in political action: The developmental trend and the post-honeymoon decline.' *International Journal of Comparative Sociology* 43(3–5): 300–316.

Inglehart Ronald, Roberto Foa, Christopher Peterson, and Christian Welzel. 2008. 'Development, freedom, and rising happiness: A global perspective (1981–2007).' *Perspectives on Psychological Science* 3(4): 264–285.

Inglehart, Ronald and Christian Welzel. 2003. 'Political culture and democracy: Analyzing cross-level linkages.' *Comparative Politics* 36(1): 61–79.

Inglehart, Ronald and Christian Welzel. 2005. *Modernization, cultural change, and democracy: The human development sequence*. New York: Cambridge University Press.

Inglehart, Ronald and Christian Welzel. 2009. 'How development leads to democracy: What we know about modernization.' *Foreign Affairs* 88(2): 33–+.

Iyengar, Shanto. 1991. *Is Anyone Responsible? How Television Frames Political Issues*. Chicago: University of Chicago Press.

Jackman, R. W. and Arthur Miller. 1998. 'Social capital and politics.' *Annual Review of Political Science* 1: 47–73.

Jamal, Amaney and Mark Tessler. 2008. 'The Arab aspiration for democracy.' In *How People View Democracy*, ed. Larry Diamond and Marc F. Plattner. Baltimore: Johns Hopkins University Press.

Jennings, M. Kent. 1991. 'Thinking about social injustice.' *Political Psychology* 12: 187–204.

Jennings, M. Kent and Jan van Deth. 1989. *Continuities in Political Action*. Berlin: deGruyter.

Jowell, Roger and Richard Topf. 1988. 'Trust in the establishment.' In *British Social Attitudes: The 5th Report*, ed. R. Jowell, S. Witherspoon, and L. Brook. Brookfield: Gower.

Kaase, Max and Kenneth Newton (Eds.). 1995. *Beliefs in Government*. New York: Oxford University Press.

Kaina, Viktoria. 2008. 'Declining trust in elites and why we should worry about it – With empirical evidence from Germany.' *Government and Opposition* 43(3): 405–423.

Katz, Richard S. and Peter Mair. 1994. *How Parties Organize: Change and Adaptation in Party Organizations in Western Democracies*. Thousand Oaks: Sage.

Kepplinger, Hans Mathias. 2000. 'The declining image of the German political elite.' *Harvard International Journal of Press-Politics* 5(4): 71–80.

Kinder, Donald and D. Roderick Kiewiet. 1979. 'Economic discontent and political behavior: The role of personal grievances and collective economic judgments in congressional voting.' *American Journal of Political Science* 23: 281–325.

Kinder, Donald and D. Roderick Kiewiet. 1981. 'Socio-tropic politics: The American case.' *British Journal of Political Science* 11: 129–161.

Kinder, Donald and W. R. Mebane. 1983. 'Politics and economics in everyday life.' In *The Political Process and Economic Change*, ed. K. B. Monroe. New York: Agathon Press.

King, Anthony. 1975. 'Overload: Problems of governing in the 1970s.' *Political Studies* 23: 284–296.

King, David C. 1997. 'The polarization of American political parties and mistrust of government.' In *Why Americans Mistrust Government*, ed. Joseph S. Nye, Philip D. Zelikow, and David C. King. Cambridge: Harvard University Press.

Kitschelt, Herbert. 1994. *The Transformation of European Social Democracy*. Cambridge: Cambridge University Press.

Klingemann, Hans-Dieter. 1999. 'Mapping political support in the 1990s.' In *Critical Citizens: Global Support for Democratic Governance*, ed. Pippa Norris. Oxford: Oxford University Press.

Klingemann, Hans-Dieter and Dieter Fuchs (Eds.). 1995. *Citizens and the State*. Oxford: Oxford University Press.

Klingemann, Hans-Dieter, Dieter Fuchs, and Jan Zielonka (Eds.). 2006. *Democracy and Political Culture in Eastern Europe*. London: Routledge.

Klingemann, Hans-Dieter and Richard I. Hofferbert. 1994. 'Germany: A new "wall in the mind"?' *Journal of Democracy* 5: 30–44.

Koechler, Hans. 1987. *The Crisis of Representative Democracy*. New York: P. Lang.

Kohli, Atul. 1990. *Democracy and Discontent: India's Growing Crisis of Governability*. New York: Cambridge University Press.

Kornberg, Allan and Harold D. Clarke. 1992. *Citizens and Community: Political Support in a Representative Democracy*. Cambridge: Cambridge University Press.

Kuechler, Manfred. 1991. 'The dynamics of mass political support in Western Europe.' In *Eurobarometer*, ed. Karlheinz Reif and Ronald Inglehart. London: Macmillan.

Kumlin, S. and Bo Rothstein. 2005. 'Making and breaking social capital: The impact of welfare state institutions.' *Comparative Political Studies* 38: 339–365.

Laakso, Markuu and Rein Taagepera. 1979. '"Effective" number of parties: A measure with application to West Europe.' *Comparative Political Studies* 12: 3–27.

Ladd, Everett C. 1996. 'The dates just don't show erosion of America's social capital.' *Public Perspective* 7(4).

Lagos, Marta. 2003. 'Support for and satisfaction with democracy.' *International Journal of Public Opinion Research* 15(4): 471–487.

Lane, Jan-Erik, David McKay, and Kenneth Newton (Eds.). 1997. *Political Data Handbook*. 2nd ed. Oxford: Oxford University Press.

Lawrence, R. Z. 1997. 'Is it really the economy, stupid?' In *Why People Don't Trust Government*, ed. Joseph S. Nye, Philip D. Zelikow, and David C. King. Cambridge: Harvard University Press.

LeDuc, Lawrence, Richard G. Niemi, and Pippa Norris. 2010. 'Building and sustaining democracy.' In *Comparing Democracies 3*, ed. Lawrence LeDuc, Richard G. Niemi, and Pippa Norris. London: Sage, Ch. 1.

LeDuc, Lawrence, Richard G. Niemi, and Pippa Norris. 2010. *Comparing Democracies 3: Elections and Voting in Global Perspectives*. Thousand Oaks: Sage Publications.

Levi, Margaret and Laura Stoker. 2000. 'Political trust and trustworthiness.' *Annual Review of Political Science* 3: 475–508.

Levitsky, Steven and Lucan A. Way. 2002. 'The rise of competitive authoritarianism.' *Journal of Democracy* 13(2): 51–65.

Lewis-Beck, Michael. 1988. *Economics and Elections: The Major Western Democracies*. Ann Arbor: University of Michigan Press.

Lijphart, Arend. 1977. *Democracy in Plural Societies: A Comparative Exploration*. New Haven: Yale University Press.

Lijphart, Arend. 1984. *Democracies: Patterns of Majoritarian and Consensus Government in Twenty-One Countries*. New Haven: Yale University Press.

Lijphart, Arend (Ed.). 1992. *Parliamentary versus Presidential Government*. Oxford: Oxford University Press.

Lijphart, Arend. 1994. 'Democracies: Forms, performance and constitutional engineering.' *European Journal of Political Research* 25: 1–17.

Lijphart, Arend. 1994. *Electoral Systems and Party Systems: A Study of Twenty-Seven Democracies, 1945–1990*. New York: Oxford University Press.

Lijphart, Arend. 1999. *Patterns of Democracy: Government Forms and Performance in Thirty-six Countries*. New Haven: Yale University Press.

Lijphart, Arend and Bernard Grofman. 1984. *Choosing an Electoral System: Issues and Alternatives*. New York: Praeger.

Lijphart, Arend and Carlos H. Waisman. 1996. *Institutional Design in New Democracies: Eastern Europe and Latin America*. Boulder: Westview Press.

Linde, Jonas and Joakim Ekman. 2003. 'Satisfaction with democracy: A note on a frequently used indicator in comparative politics.' *European Journal of Political Research* 42(3): 391–408.

Linz, Juan J. 1990. 'The perils of presidentialism.' *Journal of Democracy* 1(1).

Linz, Juan J. and Alfred C. Stepan. 1978. *The Breakdown of Democratic Regimes*. Baltimore: Johns Hopkins University Press.

Linz, Juan J. and Alfred C. Stepan. 1996. *Problems of Democratic Transition and Consolidation: Southern Europe, South America and Post-Communist Europe*. Baltimore: Johns Hopkins University Press.

Lipset, Seymour M. 1959. 'Some social requisites of democracy, economic development and political legitimacy.' *American Political Science Review* 53: 69–105.

Lipset, Seymour M. 1981. *Political Man*. Baltimore: Johns Hopkins University Press.

Lipset, Seymour M. 1990. *Continental Divide: The Values and Institutions of the United States and Canada*. New York: Routledge.

Lipset, Seymour M. 1993. 'A comparative analysis of the social requisites of democracy.' *International Social Science Journal* 136(2): 155–175.

Lipset, Seymour M. 1994. 'The social requisites of democracy revisited.' *American Sociological Review* 59: 1–22.

Lipset, Seymour M. 1996. *American Exceptionalism: A Double Edged Sword*. New York: W. W. Norton.

Lipset, Seymour M. and Stein Rokkan (Eds.). 1967. *Party Systems and Voter Alignments*. New York: Free Press.

Lipset, Seymour M. and William C. Schneider. 1983. *The Confidence Gap: Business, Labor, and Government in the Public Mind*. New York: Free Press.

Lipset, Seymour M. and William C. Schneider. 1987. *The Confidence Gap: Business, Labor, and Government in the Public Mind*. Rev. 2nd ed. Baltimore: Johns Hopkins University Press.

Listhaug, Ola. 1995. 'The dynamics of trust in politicians.' In *Citizens and the State*, ed. Hans-Dieter Klingemann and Dieter Fuchs. Oxford: Oxford University Press.

Listhaug, Ola, Bernt Aarndal, and Ingunn Opheim Ellis. 2009. 'Institutional variation and political support.' In *The Comparative Study of Electoral Systems*, ed. Hans-Dieter Klingemann. Oxford: Oxford University Press.

Listhaug, Ola and Matti Wiberg. 1995. 'Confidence in political and private institutions.' In *Citizens and the State*, ed. Hans-Dieter Klingemann and Dieter Fuchs. Oxford: Oxford University Press.

Lockerbie, B. 1993. 'Economic dissatisfaction and political alienation in Western Europe.' *European Journal of Political Research* 23: 281–293.

Lull, James and Stephen Hinerman (Eds.). 1997. *Media Scandals*. Cambridge: Polity Press.

MacKuen, Michael B., Robert S. Erickson, and James A. Stimson. 1992. 'Peasants or bankers? The American electorate and the U.S. economy.' *American Political Science Review* 86: 597–611.

Maesschalck, J. and Steven Van de Walle. 2006. 'Policy failure and corruption in Belgium: Is federalism to blame?' *West European Politics* 29(5): 999–1017.

Magalhaes, Pedro G. 2006. 'Confidence in parliaments: Performance, representation and accountability.' In *Political Disaffection in Contemporary Democracies: Social Capital, Institutions, and Politics*, ed. Mariano Torcal and José R. Montero. London: Routledge.

Mair, Peter. 1997. *Party System Change*. Oxford: Oxford University Press.

Mair, Peter. 2009. *Ruling the Void: The Hollowing of Western Democracy*. London: Verso.

Mair, Peter and Ingrid van Biezen. 2001. 'Party membership in twenty European democracies 1980–2000.' *Party Politics* 7(1): 5–22.

Mattes, Robert and Michael Bratton. 2007. 'Learning about democracy in Africa: Awareness, performance and experience.' *American Journal of Political Science* 51(1): 192–217.

McAdam, Doug, John D. McCarthy, and Mayer N. Zald. 1996. *Comparative Perspectives on Social Movements*. Cambridge: Cambridge University Press.

McAllister, Ian. 1999. 'The economic performance of governments.' In *Critical Citizens: Global Support for Democratic Governance*, ed. Pippa Norris. New York: Oxford University Press.

McClosky, Herbert and Alida Brill. 1983. *Dimensions of Tolerance: What Americans Believe about Civil Liberties.* New York: Russell Sage Foundation.

McClosky, Herbert and John Zaller. 1984. *The American Ethos: Public Attitudes toward Capitalism and Democracy.* Cambridge: Harvard University Press.

McGregor, James P. 1991. 'Value structures in a developed socialist system: The case of Czechoslovakia.' *Comparative Politics* 23: 181–199.

McQuaid, Kim. 1989. *The Anxious Years: America in the Vietnam-Watergate Era.* New York: Basic Books.

McRae, Kenneth D. 1997. 'Contrasting styles of democratic decision-making: Adversarial versus consensual politics.' *International Political Science Review* 18(3).

Meyer, K., D. Tope, and A. M. Price. 2008. 'Religion and support for democracy: A cross-national examination.' *Sociological Spectrum* 28(5): 625–653.

Miller, Arthur H. 1974. 'Political issues and trust in government, 1964–1970.' *American Political Science Review* 68: 951–972.

Miller, Arthur H. 1974. 'Rejoinder to "Comment" by Jack Citrin: Political discontent or ritualism?' *American Political Science Review* 68: 989–1001.

Miller, Arthur H. and Stephen A. Borrelli. 1991. 'Confidence in government during the 1980s.' *American Politics Quarterly* 19(2): 147–173.

Miller, Arthur H., Vicki L. Hesli, and William M. Reisinger. 1996. 'Understanding political change in post-Soviet societies.' *American Political Science Review* 90(1): 153–166.

Miller, Arthur H., Vicki L. Hesli, and William M. Reisinger. 1997. 'Conceptions of democracy among mass and elite in post-Soviet societies.' *British Journal of Political Science* 27(2): 157–190.

Miller, Arthur H. and Ola Listhaug. 1990. 'Political parties and confidence in government: A comparison of Norway, Sweden and the United States.' *British Journal of Political Science* 29: 357–386.

Miller, Stephen D. and David O. Sears. 1985. 'Stability and change in social tolerance: A test of the persistence hypothesis.' *American Journal of Political Science* 30: 214–236.

Miller, William L., Stephen White, and Paul Heywood. 1998. *Values and Political Change in Postcommunist Europe.* New York: St. Martin's Press.

Milner, Henry. 2002. *Civic literacy: How informed citizens make democracy work.* Hanover: University Press of New England.

Mishler, William. 2001. 'What are the origins of political trust? Testing institutional and cultural theories in post-communist societies.' *Comparative Political Studies* 34: 30.

Mishler, William and Richard Rose. 2002. 'Learning and re-learning regime support: The dynamics of post-communist regimes.' *European Journal of Political Research* 41: 5.

Mishler, William and Richard Rose. 1994. 'Support for parliaments and regimes in the transition toward democracy.' *Legislative Studies Quarterly* 19: 5–32.

Mishler, William and Richard Rose. 1995. 'Trajectories of fear and hope: Support for democracy in post-communist Europe.' *Comparative Political Studies* 28: 553–581.

Mishler, William and Richard Rose. 1995. 'Trust, distrust and skepticism: Popular evaluations of civil and political institutions in post-communist societies.' *Journal of Politics* 59(2): 418–451.

Misztal, Barbara A. 1996. *Trust in Modern Societies.* Oxford: Blackwell.

Moehler, Devra C. 2009. 'Critical citizens and submissive subjects: Election losers and winners in Africa.' *British Journal of Political Science* 39: 345–366.

Monroe, James A. 1990. *The Democratic Wish*. New York: Basic Books.

Monroe, Kristen. 1984. *Presidential Popularity and the Economy*. New York: Praeger.

Montero, José R., S. Zmerli, and Kenneth Newton. 2008. 'Social trust, political confidence, and satisfaction with democracy.' *Revista Espanola De Investigaciones Sociologicas*, 122: 11–54.

Moreno, Alejandro. 2002. 'Corruption and democracy: A cultural assessment.' *Comparative Sociology* 1 (3–4): 495–507.

Morlino, Leonardo and Jose R. Montero. 1995. 'Legitimacy and democracy in Southern Europe.' In *The Politics of Democratic Consolidation: Southern Europe in Comparative Perspective*, ed. R. Gunter, N. Diamandorous, and Hans-Jurgen Puhle. Baltimore: Johns Hopkins University Press.

Morlino, Leonardo and Marco Tarchi. 1996. 'The dissatisfied society: The roots of political change in Italy.' *European Journal of Political Research* 30(1): 41–63.

Muller, Edward N. 1977. 'Behavioral correlates of political support.' *American Political Science Review* 71(2): 454–467.

Muller, Edward N. 1979. *Aggressive Political Participation*. Princeton: Princeton University Press.

Muller, Edward N. and Thomas O. Jukam. 1977. 'On the meaning of political support.' *American Political Science Review* 71: 1561–1595.

Muller, Edward N., Thomas O. Jukam, and Mitchell A. Seligson. 1982. 'Diffuse political support and anti-system political behavior.' *American Journal of Political Science* 26(3): 240–264.

Muller, Edward N. and Mitchell A. Seligson. 1994. 'Civic culture and democracy: The question of causal relationships.' *American Political Science Review* 88(3): 635–652.

Muller, Edward N. and Carol J. Williams. 1980. 'Dynamics of political support-alienation.' *Comparative Political Studies* 13(1): 33–59.

Nelson, Michael. 1995. 'Why Americans hate politics and politicians.' *PS: Political Science and Politics* 28: 72–77.

Nevitte, Neil and Mebs Kanji. 2002. 'Authority orientations and political support: A cross-national analysis of satisfaction with governments and democracy.' *Comparative Sociology* 1(3–4): 387–412.

Newton, Kenneth. 1997. 'Politics and the news media: Mobilization or videomalaise?' In *British Social Attitudes: The 14th Report*, ed. Roger Jowell et al. Aldershot: Ashgate, Vol. 14.

Newton, Kenneth. 1997. 'Social capital and democracy.' *American Behavioral Scientist* 40(5): 575–586.

Newton, Kenneth. 2006. 'Political support: Social capital, civil society and political and economic performance.' *Political Studies* 54(4): 846–864.

Newton, Kenneth. 2007. 'Social and political trust.' In *The Oxford Handbook of Political Behavior*, ed. Russell J. Dalton and Hans-Dieter Klingemann. Oxford: Oxford University Press.

Newton, Kenneth and Pippa Norris. 2000. 'Confidence in public institutions: Faith, culture, or performance.' In *Disaffected Democracies: What's Troubling the Trilateral Countries?* ed. Susan J. Pharr and Robert D. Putnam. Princeton: Princeton University Press, pp. 52–73.

Norpoth, Helmut. 1992. *Confidence Regained: Economics, Mrs. Thatcher, and the British Voter*. Ann Arbor: University of Michigan Press.

Norris, Pippa. 1995. 'The politics of electoral reform.' *International Political Science Review* 16(1): 1–14.

Norris, Pippa. 1996. 'Does television erode social capital? A reply to Putnam.' *PS: Political Science and Politics* 29: 474–480.

Norris, Pippa. 1997. 'Choosing electoral systems: Proportional, majoritarian and mixed systems.' *International Political Science Review* 18(3).

Norris, Pippa (Ed.). 1999. *Critical Citizens: Global Support for Democratic Governance*. Oxford: Oxford University Press.

Norris, Pippa. 2000. *A Virtuous Circle: Political Communications in Post-Industrial Democracies*. New York: Cambridge University Press.

Norris, Pippa. 2001. *Digital Divide: Civic Engagement, Information Poverty and the Internet Worldwide*. New York: Cambridge University Press.

Norris, Pippa. 2002. *Democratic Phoenix*. Cambridge: Cambridge University Press.

Norris, Pippa. 2004. 'Global political communication.' In *Comparing Political Communication: Theories, Cases and Challenges*, ed. Frank Esser and Barbara Pfetsch. Cambridge: Cambridge University Press, pp. 115–150.

Norris, Pippa. 2007. 'Political activism: New challenges, new opportunities.' *The Oxford Handbook of Comparative Politics*, ed. Carles Boix and Susan Stokes. Oxford: Oxford University Press, pp. 628–652.

Norris, Pippa. 2008. *Driving Democracy: Do Power-Sharing Institutions Work?* Cambridge: Cambridge University Press.

Norris, Pippa. 2009. 'Confidence in the United Nations: Cosmopolitan and nationalistic attitudes.' In *The Global System, Democracy and Values*, ed. Yilmaz Esmer and Thorleif Pettersson. Uppsala: Uppsala University Press.

Norris, Pippa. 2010. 'The globalization of comparative public opinion research.' In *The Sage Handbook of Comparative Politics*, ed. Neil Robinson and Todd Landman. London: Sage.

Norris, Pippa. 2010. 'Political activism.' *Developments in European Politics*, ed. Paul Heywood. London: Palgrave Macmillan.

Norris, Pippa and Ronald Inglehart. 2009. *Cosmopolitan Communications*. Cambridge: Cambridge University Press.

Nozick, Robert. 1974. *Anarchy, State, and Utopia*. New York: Basic Books.

Nye, Joseph S., Philip D. Zelikow, and David C. King (Eds.). 1997. *Why People Don't Trust Government*. Cambridge, MA: Harvard University Press.

O'Donnell, Guillermo. 1994. 'Delegative democracy.' *Journal of Democracy* 5(1): 55–69.

O'Donnell, Guillermo, Philippe Schmitter, and Lawrence Whitehead. 1986. *Transitions from Authoritarian Rule*. Baltimore: Johns Hopkins University Press.

Olson, Mancur, Jr. 1965. *The Logic of Collective Action*. Cambridge, MA: Harvard University Press.

Parker, Suzanne L. and Glenn R. Parker. 1993. 'Why do we trust our congressmen?' *Journal of Politics* 55(2): 442–453.

Parry, Geraint. 1976. 'Trust, distrust and consensus.' *British Journal of Political Science* 6: 129–142

Parry, Geraint, George Moyser, and Neil Day. 1992. *Political Participation and Democracy in Britain*. Cambridge: Cambridge University Press.

Parsons, Talcott. 1951. *The Social System*. London: Routledge and Kegan Paul.

Parsons, Talcott. 1969. *Politics and Social Structure*. New York: Free Press.

Patterson, Samuel C. and Gregory A. Caldeira. 1990. 'Standing up for Congress: Variations in public esteem since the 1960s.' *Legislative Studies Quarterly* 15(1): 25–47.

Patterson, Thomas E. 1993. *Out of Order*. New York: Alfred A. Knopf.

Patterson, Thomas E. 2002. *The Vanishing Voter*. New York: Alfred A. Knopf.

Pattie, Charles, Patrick Seyd, and Paul Whiteley. 2004. *Citizenship in Britain: Values, Participation and Democracy*. Cambridge: Cambridge University Press.

Paxton, Pamela. 2002. 'Social capital and democracy: An interdependent relationship.' *American Sociological Review* 67(2): 254–277.

Peffley, Mark. 1984. 'The voter as juror: Attributing responsibility for economic conditions.' *Political Behavior* 6: 275–294.

Pempel, T. J. 1990. *Uncommon Democracies: The One Party Dominant Regimes*. Ithaca, NY: Cornell University Press.

Pharr, Susan J. and Robert D. Putnam (Eds.). 2000. *Disaffected Democracies: What's Troubling the Trilateral Countries?* Princeton, NJ: Princeton University Press.

Pharr, Susan J., Robert D. Putnam, and Russell J. Dalton. 2000. 'A quarter century of declining confidence.' *Journal of Democracy* 11(2): 5–25.

Powell, G. Bingham, Jr. 1982. *Contemporary Democracies*. Cambridge: Harvard University Press.

Powell, G. Bingham, Jr. 1989. 'Constitutional design and citizen electoral control.' *Journal of Theoretical Politics* 1(2): 107–130.

Przeworski, Adam. 1991. *Democracy and the Market: Political and Economic Reform in Eastern Europe and Latin America*. Cambridge: Cambridge University Press.

Przeworski, Adam and Henry Teune. 1970. *The Logic of Comparative Social Inquiry*. New York: Wiley.

Puddington, Arch. 2010. 'Freedom in the World 2010: Erosion of Freedom Intensifies.' Freedom House. *Freedom in the World 2010*. www.freedomhouse.org.

Putnam, Robert D. 1994. *Making Democracy Work*. Princeton, NJ: Princeton University Press.

Putnam, Robert D. 1995. 'Bowling alone: America's declining social capital.' *Journal of Democracy* 6: 65–78.

Putnam, Robert D. 1995. 'Tuning in, tuning out: The strange disappearance of social capital in America.' *PS: Political Science and Politics* 28(4): 664–683.

Putnam, Robert D. 1996. 'The strange disappearance of civic America.' *American Prospect* 24.

Putnam, Robert D. 2000. *Bowling Alone: The Collapse and Revival of American Community*. New York: Simon and Schuster.

Putnam, Robert D. (Ed.). 2004. *Democracies in Flux: The Evolution of Social Capital in Contemporary Society*. Oxford: Oxford University Press.

Pye, Lucian W. 1985. *Asian Power and Politics*. Cambridge, MA: Harvard University Press.

Pye, Lucian W. and Sidney Verba (Eds.). 1965. *Political Culture and Political Development*. Princeton, NJ: Princeton University Press.

Raboy, Marc and Bernard Dagenais. 1992. *Media, Crisis and Democracy: Mass Communications and the Disruption of Social Order*. London: Sage.

Rae, Douglas W. 1971. *The Political Consequences of Electoral Laws*. Rev. ed. New Haven: Yale University Press.

Ragin, Charles. 1987. *The Comparative Method*. Berkeley: University of California Press.

Robinson, Michael. 1976. 'Public affairs television and the growth of political malaise: The case of the selling of the Pentagon.' *American Political Science Review* 70: 409–432.

Rogowski, Ronald. 1974. *Rational Legitimacy: A Theory of Political Support.* Princeton, NJ: Princeton University Press.

Rohrschneider, Robert. 1994. 'Report from the laboratory: The influence of institutions on political elites' democratic values in Germany.' *American Political Science Review* 88: 927–941.

Rohrschneider, Robert. 1996. 'Institutional learning versus value diffusion: The evolution of democratic values among parliamentarians in Eastern and Western Germany.' *Journal of Politics* 58: 442–466.

Rohrschneider, Robert. 1998. *Learning Democracy: Democratic and Economic Values in Unified Germany.* Oxford: Oxford University Press.

Rokeach, Milton. 1973. *The Nature of Human Values.* New York: Free Press.

Roller, Edeltraud. 2005. *The Performance of Democracies: Political Institutions and Public Policy.* Oxford: Oxford University Press.

Rose, Richard. 1984. *Do Parties Make a Difference?* 2nd ed. London: Macmillan.

Rose, Richard and William Mishler. 1994. 'Mass reaction to regime change in Eastern Europe: Polarization or leaders and laggards?' *British Journal of Political Science* 24: 159–182.

Rose, Richard and William Mishler. 1996. 'Testing the Churchill hypothesis: Popular support for democracy and its alternatives.' *Journal of Public Policy* 16: 29–58.

Rose, Richard, William Mishler, and Christian Haerpfer. 1998. *Democracy and Its Alternatives in Post-Communist Europe: Testing the Churchill Hypothesis.* Cambridge: Polity Press.

Rosenstone, Steven J. and John M. Hansen. 1993. *Mobilization, Participation, and Democracy in America.* New York: Macmillan.

Rothstein, Bo. 2005. *Social Traps and the Problem of Trust.* New York: Cambridge University Press.

Rudolph, T. J. and J. Evans. 2005. 'Political trust, ideology, and public support for government spending.' *American Journal of Political Science* 49(3): 660–671.

Rustow, Dankwart A. 1970. 'Transitions to democracy.' *Comparative Politics* 2: 337–363.

Sabato, Larry. 1991. *Feeding Frenzy: How Attack Journalism Has Transformed American Politics.* New York: Free Press.

Samuelson, Robert J. 1995. *The Good Life and Its Discontents.* New York: Random House.

Sarsfield, R. and F. Echegaray. 2006. 'Opening the black box: How satisfaction with democracy and its perceived efficacy affect regime preference in Latin America.' *International Journal of Public Opinion Research* 18: 153–173.

Sartori, Giovanni. 1976. *Parties and Party Systems: A Framework for Analysis.* New York: Cambridge University Press.

Sartori, Giovanni. 1987. *The Theory of Democracy Revisited.* Chatham, NJ: Chatham House.

Sartori, Giovanni. 1994. *Comparative Constitutional Engineering.* London: Macmillan.

Saward, Michael. 1994. 'Democratic theory and indices of democratization.' In *Defining and Measuring Democracy*, ed. David Beetham. London: Sage, pp. 6–24.

Schaffer, Frederic G. 1998. *Democracy in Translation: Understanding Politics in an Unfamiliar Culture.* Ithaca, NY: Cornell University Press.

Schedler, Andreas and Rudolpho Sarsfield. 2007. 'Democrats with adjectives: Linking direct and indirect measures of democratic support.' *European Journal of Political Research* 46(5): 637–659.

Schmitt, Herman and Sören Holmberg. 1995. 'Political Parties in Decline?' In *Citizens and the State*, ed. Hans-Dieter Klingemann and Dieter Fuchs. Oxford: Oxford University Press.

Schumpeter, Joseph A. 1952. *Capitalism, Socialism and Democracy*. 4th ed. London: George Allen and Unwin.

Sears, David O. 1975. 'Political socialization.' In *Handbook of Political Science*, vol. 2, ed. Fred I. Greenstein and Nelson W. Polsby. Reading: Addison-Wesley.

Segatti, Paolo. 'Italy, forty years of political disaffection: A longitudinal exploration.' In *Political Disaffection in Contemporary Democracies: Social Capital, Institutions, and Politics*, ed. Mariano Torcal and José R. Montero. London: Routledge.

Shaw, Greg M. and Stephanie L. Reinhart. 2001. 'Trends: Devolution and confidence in government.' *Public Opinion Quarterly* 65: 369–388.

Shi, Tian Jian. 2000. 'Cultural values and democracy in the People's Republic of China.' *China Quarterly* 162: 540–559.

Shi, Tian Jian. 2001. 'Cultural values and political trust: A comparison of the People's Republic of China and Taiwan.' *Comparative Politics* 33(4): 401–+.

Shi, Tian Jian. 2009. 'Talking Past Each Other? Different Understandings of Democracy and Their Consequences.' Paper presented at the IPSA 21st World Congress, Santiago.

Smith, Amy E. 2009. 'Legitimate grievances: Preferences for democracy, system support, and political participation in Bolivia.' *Latin American Research Review* 44(3): 102–126.

Starr, Harvey. 1991. 'Democratic dominoes: Diffusion approaches to the spread of democracy in the international system.' *Journal of Conflict Resolution* 35: 356–381.

Stoker, Gerry. 2006. *Why Politics Matters: Making Democracy Work*. London: Palgrave/Macmillan.

Sundquist, James L. 1980. 'The crisis of competence in our national government.' *Political Science Quarterly* 95: 183–208.

Sztompka, Piotr. 1996. 'Trust and emerging democracy.' *International Sociology* 11(I): 37–62.

Taagepera, Rein and Matthew S. Shugart. 1989. *Seats and Votes: The Effects and Determinants of Electoral Systems*. New Haven: Yale University Press.

Tarrow, Sidney. 1996. 'Making social science work across space and time: A critical reflection on Robert Putnam's *Making Democracy Work*.' *American Political Science Review* 90: 389–397.

Teixeira, Ruy A. 1992. *The Disappearing American Voter*. Washington, DC: Brookings Institution.

Teorell, Jan and Axel Hadenius. 2006. 'Democracy without democratic values: A rejoinder to Welzel and Inglehart.' *Studies in Comparative International Development* 41(3): 95–111.

Tessler, Mark. 2002. 'Do Islamic orientations influence attitudes toward democracy in the Arab world? Evidence from Egypt, Jordan, Morocco, and Algeria.' *International Journal of Comparative Sociology* 43(3–5): 229–249.

Tessler, Mark. 2002. 'Islam and democracy in the Middle East: The impact of religious orientations on attitudes toward democracy in four Arab countries.' *Comparative Politics* 34: 337.

Tessler, Mark and E. Gao. 2005. 'Gauging Arab support for democracy.' *Journal of Democracy* 16(3): 83–97.

Thomassen, Jacques. 1990. 'Economic crisis, dissatisfaction and protest.' In *Continuitites in Political Action*, ed. M. Kent Jennings, Jan van Deth, et al. New York: Walter de Gruyter.

Thomassen, Jacques. 1995. 'Support for democratic values.' In *Citizens and the State*, ed. Hans-Dieter Klingemann and Dieter Fuchs. Oxford: Oxford University Press.

Thomassen, Jacques (Ed.). 2009. *The Legitimacy of the European Union after Enlargement*. Oxford: Oxford University Press.

Thomassen, Jacques and Henk Van DerKonk. 2009. 'Effectiveness and political support in old and new democracies.' In *The Comparative Study of Electoral Systems*, ed. Hans-Dieter Klingemann. Oxford: Oxford University Press.

Thompson, Mark. 2001. 'Whatever happened to "Asian Values"?' *Journal of Democracy* 12: 154–165.

Tolbert, C. J. and K. Mossberger. 2006. 'The effects of e-government on trust and confidence in government.' *Public Administration Review* 66(3): 354–369.

Tolchin, Susan J. 1996. *The Angry American: How Voter Rage Is Changing the Nation*. Boulder, CO: Westview Press.

Topf, Richard. 1989. 'Political change and political culture in Britain: 1959–87.' In *Contemporary Political Culture*, ed. J. Gibbins. London: Sage.

Topf, Richard. 1995. 'Beyond electoral participation.' In *Citizens and the State*, ed. Hans-Dieter Klingemann and Dieter Fuchs. Oxford: Oxford University Press.

Topf, Richard, Peter Mohler, and Anthony Heath. 1989. 'Pride in one's country: Britain and West Germany.' In *British Social Attitudes: Special International Report*, ed. R. Jowell, S. Witherspoon, and L. Brook. Brookfield, VT: Gower.

Torcal, Mariano and José R. Montero (Eds.). 2006. *Political Disaffection in Contemporary Democracies: Social Capital, Institutions, and Politics*. London: Routledge.

Transparency International. 2008. *Transparency International Publishes 2008 Corruption Perception Index*. Berlin: Transparency International.

Tyler, Tom R., Kenneth Rasinski, and Kathleen McGraw. 1985. 'The influence of perceived injustice upon support for the president, political authorities, and government institutions.' *Journal of Applied Social Psychology* 15: 700–725.

Ulbig, S. G. 2002. 'Policies, procedures, and people: Sources of support for government?' *Social Science Quarterly* 83(3): 789–809.

Valentino, Nicholas A. 2001. 'A spiral of cynicism for some: The contingent effects of campaign news frames on participation and confidence in government.' *Political Communication* 18: 347.

Verba, Sidney. 1965. 'Conclusion: Comparative political culture.' In *Political Culture and Political Development*, ed. Lucian W. Pye and Sidney Verba. Princeton: Princeton University Press, pp. 512–560.

Verba, Sidney and Norman Nie. 1972. *Participation in America: Political Democracy and Social Equality*. New York: Harper and Row.

Verba, Sidney, Norman Nie, and Jae-on Kim. 1978. *Participation and Political Equality: A Seven-Nation Comparison*. New York: Cambridge University Press.

Verba, Sidney, Kay Schlozman, and Henry Brady. 1995. *Voice and Equality: Civic Volunteerism in American Politics*. Cambridge: Harvard University Press.

Wagner, Alexander F., Friedrich Schneider, and Martin Halla. 2009. 'The quality of institutions and satisfaction with democracy in Western Europe: A panel analysis.' *European Journal of Political Economy* 25(1): 30–41.

Waldron-Moore, P. 1999. 'Eastern Europe at the crossroads of democratic transition – Evaluating support for democratic institutions, satisfaction with democratic government, and consolidation of democratic regimes.' *Comparative Political Studies* 32(1): 32–62.

Walle, Steven Van de, Steven Van Roosbroek, and Geert Bouckaert. 2008. 'Trust in the public sector: Is there any evidence for a long-term decline?' *International Review of Administrative Sciences* 74(1): 47–64.

Wang, Z. 2005. 'Before the emergence of critical citizens: Economic development and political trust in China.' *International Review of Sociology* 15(1): 155–171.

Warren, Mark E. (Ed.). 1999. *Democracy and Trust.* New York: Cambridge University Press.

Wattenberg, Martin P. 1991. *The Rise of Candidate Centered Politics.* Cambridge: Harvard University Press.

Wattenberg, Martin P. 2002. *Where Have All the Voters Gone?* Cambridge, MA: Harvard University Press.

Way, Lucan A. and Steven Levitsky. 2006. 'The dynamics of autocratic coercion after the Cold War.' *Communist and Post-Communist Studies* 39(3): 387–410.

Weatherford, Stephen M. 1984. 'Economic "stagflation" and public support for the political system.' *British Journal of Political Science* 14: 187–205.

Weatherford, Stephen M. 1987. 'How does government performance influence political support?' *Political Behavior* 9: 5–28.

Weatherford, Stephen M. 1991. 'Mapping the ties that bind: Legitimacy, representation and alienation.' *Western Political Quarterly* 44: 251–276.

Weatherford, Stephen M. 1992. 'Measuring political legitimacy.' *American Political Science Review* 86: 149–166.

Weaver, R. K., and Bert A. Rockman (Eds.). 1993. *Do Institutions Matter?* Washington, DC: Brookings Institution.

Weil, Frederick D. 1987. 'Cohort regimes, and the legitimation of democracy: West Germany since 1945.' *American Sociological Review* 52: 308–324.

Weil, Frederick D. 1989. 'The sources and structure of legitimation in Western democracies. A consolidated model tested with time-series data in six countries since World War II.' *American Sociological Review* 54: 682–706.

Weil, Frederick D. 1993. 'The development of democratic attitudes in Eastern and Western Germany in a comparative perspective.' In *Research on Democracy and Society. Vol. 1, Democratization in Eastern and Western Europe*, ed. Frederick D. Weil. Greenwich, CT: JAI Press, pp. 195–225.

Weisberg, Jacob. 1996. *In Defence of Government: The Fall and Rise of Public Trust.* New York: Scribner.

Wells, Jason M. and Jonathan Krieckhaus. 2006. 'Does national context influence democratic satisfaction? A multi-level analysis.' *Political Research Quarterly* 59(4): 569–578.

Welzel, Christian. 2007. 'Are levels of democracy affected by mass attitudes? Testing attainment and sustainment effects on democracy.' *International Political Science Review* 28(4): 397–424.

Welzel, Christian and Ronald Inglehart. 2006. 'Emancipative values and democracy: Response to Hadenius and Teorell.' *Studies in Comparative International Development* 41(3): 74–94.

Welzel, Christian and Ronald Inglehart. 2008. 'The role of ordinary people in democratization.' In *How People View Democracy*, ed. Larry Diamond and Marc F. Plattner. Baltimore: Johns Hopkins University Press.

Welzel, Christian and Ronald Inglehart. 2008. 'The role of ordinary people in democratization.' *Journal of Democracy* 19(1): 126–140.

Wessels, Bernhard. 2009. 'Trust in political institutions.' In *The Legitimacy of the European Union after Enlargement*, ed. Jacques Thomassen. Oxford: Oxford University Press.

White, Stephen, Richard Rose, and Ian McAllister. 1997. *How Russia Votes*. Chatham, NJ: Chatham House.

Widfeldt, Anders. 1995. 'Party membership and party representativeness.' In *Citizens and the State*, ed. Hans-Dieter Klingemann and Dieter Fuchs. Oxford: Oxford University Press.

Williams, Bernard. 1988. 'Formal structures and social reality.' In *Trust: Making and Breaking Co-operative Relation*, ed. Diego Gambetta. Oxford: Blackwell.

Wright, James D. 1976. *The Dissent of the Governed*. New York: Academic Press.

Zakaria, Fareed. 1997. 'The rise of illiberal democracy.' *Foreign Affairs* 76(6): 22–41.

Zmerli, Sonja and Kenneth Newton. 2008. 'Social trust and attitudes toward democracy.' *Public Opinion Quarterly* 72(4): 706–724.

Zmerli, Sonja, Kenneth Newton, and Jose Ramon Montero. 2006. 'Trust in people, confidence in institutions, and satisfaction with democracy.' In *Citizenship and Involvement in European Democracies: A Comparative Perspective*, ed. Jan van Deth, Jose Ramon Montero, and Anders Westholm. London: Routledge.

Zukin, Cliff, Scott Keeter, Molly Andolina, Krista Jenkins, and Michael X. Delli Carpini. 2006. *A New Engagement? Political Participation, Civic Life, and the Changing American Citizen*. New York: Oxford University Press.

Index